The Future of Money:

A new way to create wealth, work, and a wiser world

The Future of Money:

A new way to create wealth, work, and a wiser world

Bernard Lietaer

CENTURY · LONDON

Bernard Lietaer has asserted his rights under the Copyright, Designs and Patents Act, 1988, to be identified as the author of this work.

First published in 2001 by Century,
The Random House Group Limited,
20 Vauxhall Bridge Road, London SW1V 2SA

Random House Australia (Pty) Limited
20 Alfred Street, Milsons Point,
Sydney, New South Wales 2061, Australia

Random House New Zealand Limited
18 Poland Road, Glenfield,
Auckland 10, New Zealand

Random House (Pty) Limited
Endulini, 5a Jubilee Road, Parktown 2193, South Africa

The Random House Group Limited Reg. No. 954009

Papers used by Random House
are natural, recyclable products made from wood grown in
sustainable forests. The manufacturing processes conform to
the environmental regulations of the country of origin.

ISBN 0 7126 8399 2

Companies, institutions and other organizations wishing to make
bulk purchases of books published by Random House should
contact their local bookstore or Random House direct:
Special Sales Director
Random House, 20 Vauxhall Bridge Road, London SW1V 2SA
Tel 020 7840 8470   Fax 020 7828 6681

www.randomhouse.co.uk

Typeset by MATS, Southend-on-Sea, Essex
Printed and bound in the United Kingdom by
Biddles Ltd, Guildford and King's Lynn

For your children.
For the children's children,
and the trees.

Contents

About the Author

Bernard Lietaer had thirty years of professional experiences which tend to mutually exclude each other, such as central banker and general manager of currency funds; senior consultant to both multinational corporations and developing countries; university professor and top executive of electronic payment systems.

As a senior central bank executive in Belgium he was closely involved in the design and implementation of the ECU, the convergence mechanism which led to the European single currency. He was subsequently identified by *Business Week* as the world's top currency trader, while General Manager of the most successful off-shore currency fund (1987-91). He was a professional consultant for over a dozen years to multinational corporations on four continents; and moved to the other end of the spectrum by advising developing countries in Latin America on how to optimize hard currency earnings. He was a Professor of International Finance; and also President of the most comprehensive and cost-effective electronic payment system in the world.

During the course of his career, he has anticipated major monetary changes. His first book prepared the tools to manage currencies in floating exhanges[1], which occurred two years later. Another of his books was the first to announce the Latin American debt crisis of the 1980s[2].

He wrote *The Future of Money* while a Fellow at the Center for Sustainable Resources at the University of California at Berkeley and Visiting Professor at Sonoma State University, California. This book is unique in that it integrates the author's varied professional perspectives into a coherent view on money.

The Future of Money and its sequel *The Mystery of Money* are the basis of an international television series currently in production.

More information and direct contact for answers to your questions are available in an on-line 'Money Conference' on www.futuremoney.net and on www.transaction.net/money/

[1]*Financial Management of Foreign Exhange: An Operational Technique to Reduce Risks* (Cambridge, Mass.: MIT Press, 1970)

[2]*Europe+Latin America+the Multinationals: a Positive Sum Game for the Exhange of Raw Materials and Technology* (London: Saxon House, 1979)

Preface

Deep in our hearts, we all want to leave a better world for our children and we cherish the hope that we may experience this for ourselves in our own lifetime.

However, there is growing concern that many of the challenges we now face are unrelenting and more and more people question our ability to address them effectively. Indeed, despite some breakthroughs and the valiant efforts in the public and private sectors, the challenges to our planet and society are growing both in scope and severity with each passing decade.

In this new Millennium, we are being challenged by four megatrends that are converging upon us over the next twenty years, namely:

- Climate change and loss of bio-diversity;
- An unprecedented growth in the number of elderly (the 'Age Wave');
- Monetary Instability;
- and an Information Revolution.

(The evidence for each one of these megatrends and for the collective breakdowns they will provoke are described in Chapter 1.)

Why is this? Why have our efforts, the countless billions of pounds and dollars spent all over the world, the many treaties enacted and initiatives taken, not stopped the destruction of our environment, nor effectively addressed a myriad of social issues? Is it possible that our attentions and efforts are misdirected?

Or are the challenges and issues facing our world today being fuelled by an even deeper systematic problem?

The short answer to this last question is yes.

The Future of Money is a compendium report about solutions already implemented by thousands of people around the world, who have had the courage to first identify, then directly address the underlying mechanism of their problems. Their initiatives to date are small-scale, but I see them as seedlings which – if allowed to grow – have the potential to provide effective and permanent solutions by which conditions for mankind and other living systems may improve – dramatically – within our own lifetimes.

The underlying mechanisms referred to here turn out to be specific features of our money system. Money or lack thereof, is a fundamental component of our lives. It is not, however, just the lack of money that is precipitating present trends or preventing us from addressing current challenges. Rather, it is the limited functionality of our money and monetary system that is a major force behind our present disorders. Many of the problems we face, and the solutions we seek, reside within the architecture of our current monetary system and in our understanding of, and our agreements around, money.

Fish to do not comprehend the nature of the water in which they live. Similarly, people have trouble understanding the nature of money. We allocate a great portion of our physical, emotional, and mental energy to getting, keeping, and spending money – but how many of us really know what money is or where it comes from?

In pre-Victorian England the world was oblivious of pollution, greenhouse effects and overpopulation. Nationalism, competition, endless growth and colonization were encouraged. These values are what shaped the monetary and banking systems we inherited.

However, is this what best serves our world today? I submit that those aspects of our monetary system that met the objectives of another time and age are now inadequate for the challenges facing us during an Information Age. This is particularly true in light of the fact that working solutions are already underway, with thousands of communities around the world taking their own money initiatives.

They are creating new wealth, while solving social problems without taxation or regulation. They are empowering self-organizing communities, while increasing overall economic and social stability. Finally, they enable the creation of very necessary social capital without attaching the established capital formation process.

Many attempts at money reform have failed in the past, because they were trying to attach or radically change the official money system itself. There are three reasons why I believe the current, on-going monetary initiatives have a better chance of success than ever before:

- First and foremost, these money innovations are not attacking the official money system. What they do instead is complement the conventional money system, providing new tools that can operate in parallel with it, without replacing it. That is why I call them '*complementary* currencies', and not, 'alternative' ones.
- The second reason is that they have already proven to be capable of addressing breakdowns of a new nature to which no solutions have

been forthcoming within the conventional money paradigm.

- Finally, the availability of information technologies necessary to implement new money systems has become universal enough that a democratization of money innovations has become reality.

My career has taken me to the four corners of the earth, where I have witnessed extremely different worlds ranging from dire poverty and hunger to opulence and extravagance. Writing this book has, therefore, not been a cool, abstract intellectual exercise. Rather, it is an exploration into a deeper meaning of money.

Money not only permeates every facet of our lives, but is also hot-wired to our sensibilities. Thus I too have run through a whole gamut of emotions, playing and working with money both on a personal and professional level. While I have learned to deal with money from a professional, hyper-rational distance, I have also personally experienced extraordinary highs along with moments of bitter humiliation and bewilderment. The low of my currency trading days was when I became caught in the ebb-tide of George Soros' cornering of the Pound Sterling in the early 1990s. This instantaneously shattered my professional reputation as the 'world's top currency trader'. I lost the illusion of my own Midas touch, and most of my own money as well.

Perhaps the most salient outcome of my experiences with money has been a broader, more grounded view of its worth to us as human beings and its potential pitfalls. Money not only has the potential to contribute to global abundance, sustainability, and peace of mind if used wisely; but when restricted in its flow it also has the ability to engender unfathomable suffering and hardship. It is from this multi-ocular perspective that I am synthesizing here what I have learned so far about this mysterious thing called money.

This is not a book on economics or economic theory. I am not an economist. My expertise lies in international finance and money systems. This is why I have adopted here a whole systems approach to money. Whole systems takes into account a broader, more comprehensive arena than economics does; it integrates not only economic interactions but also their most important side-effects. This includes specifically in our case the effects of different money systems on the quality of human interactions, on society at large, and on ecological systems. In essence, money is a lifeblood flowing through ourselves, our society, our global human community, and should be acknowledged and treated consciously.

Part One of *The Future of Money* elucidates the mysteries of the current official currency system. Part Two widens the view to encompass and feature newly emerging money systems. Therefore, this book deals with money in the world outside of us, describing how different money systems shape society.

The forthcoming *Mystery of Money*, *Beyond Greed and Scarcity* completes our examination of money by delving into the world residing inside our own heads. It thereby steps up the scope of our money landscape one last notch by exploring the world of the collective psychology of money and of the emotions triggered by different money systems.

> **Sidebars**
>
> Short vignettes or intriguing anecdotes illustrating a point will be enclosed in sidebars like this. They can be skipped without impeding the overall comprehension of the main text. But you may miss a few laughs and surprises in the process.

Stories

There will also be stories that take many forms, from totally real to quite imaginary. Although they make a point where they appear, they can also stand alone.

Invitation

Finally, I would like to thank everyone from almost every country in the world, who has contributed, knowingly and unknowingly, to my grand tour of duty in money systems. Each of you has made an invaluable contribution to this chronicle of new ways of looking at money. Thank you from the bottom of my heart.

And, if we are meeting for the first time here or we are old friends or passing acquaintances, I now invite you to turn the page and explore the choices that await us all as we prepare for, and trust in, a deeper grounding to our common wealth.

Part One

Part One: What *Is* Money?

- ■ *'Economics is about money, and that's why it is good.'*

  WOODY ALLEN

  And money is about . . . what?

- ■ *'Money ranks as one of the primary materials with which mankind builds the architecture of civilization.'*

  LEWIS LAPHAM[1]

- ■ *'We invented money and we use it, yet we cannot . . . understand its laws or control its actions. It has a life of its own.'*

  LIONEL TRILLING[2]

When we think about money, we tend to take for granted its basic characteristics, which have remained unchanged for centuries. We are not likely to visit the hidden assumptions embedded in our familiar money system, and we are even less likely to re-examine them in search of solutions.

Part One brings our hidden assumptions about money to the surface. In doing so, it also brings to light new potentials for our interactions with money. It is not about how to make, invest or spend money. There are already plenty of books about all of that. It is about the concept of money, and how different money systems shape different societies.

You will learn why fundamental changes in our money system have become *inevitable*. While these changes may seem *frightening* in their scale, they also hold the promise of *unprecedented opportunity*.

The Information Age promises to change fundamentally within decades our entire economy and payment habits. Whether gradual or cataclysmic, significant worldwide changes are under way in the realm of money. The well-known contemporary management expert Peter Drucker claims: 'Every few hundred years in Western history there occurs a sharp transformation. Within a few short decades, society – its world view, its basic values, its social and political structures, its arts, its key institutions – rearranges itself, and the people born then cannot even imagine a world in which their grandparents lived and into which their own parents were born. We are currently living through such a transformation.'[3]

When no safety net has been prepared, experiencing such an unparalleled shift can be very frightening. Just ask any one of the one billion Latin Americans, Asians or Eastern Europeans who are still reeling from their own personal encounter with the cataclysmic monetary changes that occurred as a direct consequence of a radical shift in power from their governments to international financial markets. James Carville, who directed Bill Clinton's campaign in 1992, remarked: 'I used to think that if there was reincarnation, I wanted to come back as the President, or the Pope. But now I want to be the financial market: you can intimidate *anybody*.'

Nevertheless, this transition offers us also an *unprecedented opportunity*. When money changes, a lot more changes. Almost everything can become possible. With such a fundamental shift will come the opportunity for innovation far beyond what previous generations could even imagine.

■ Synthesis of Part One

Money matters. The way money is created and administered in a given society makes a deep impression on values and relationships within that society. More specifically, the *type* of currency used in a society encourages – or discourages – specific emotions and behaviour patterns.

Our prevailing system is an unconscious product of the modern Industrial Age world view, and it remains the most powerful and persistent designer and enforcer of the values and dominant emotions of that age. For instance, all our national currencies make it easier to interact economically with our fellow citizens than with 'foreigners', and therefore encourages national consciousness. Similarly, these currencies were designed to foster competition among their users, rather than cooperation. Money is also the hidden engine of the perpetual growth treadmill that has become the hallmark of industrial societies. Finally, the current system encourages individual accumulation, and ruthlessly punishes those who don't follow that injunction.

However, after centuries of an almost complete hegemony of our 'normal' national currencies (US$, pound, yen, Deutschemark, etc.) as the exclusive means of economic exchanges, the past decade has seen a reappearance of various forms of private currencies.

For starters, up to one quarter of global trade is now done using barter: i.e. using no currency at all, national or other. Pepsi Cola, for example, ships its profits from Russia in the form of vodka, which it then sells in the US and Europe for cash. The French have built nuclear power stations in the Middle East against payments in oil. In addition, new forms of corporate *scrip* are taking hold, such as the various frequent-flyer systems, wherein points or 'miles' can increasingly be earned with, and used for, services other than airline tickets (e.g., taxis, hotels, long-distance telephone, etc.). These are currencies in the making for the 'international travelling élite'. Further below the radar beams of officialdom is the remarkable and explosive growth of grass-roots complementary currencies of various kinds. As of January 2000, over 2,500 local currency systems are operational in more than a dozen different countries, including 400 in the UK alone.

What does all this mean?

■ Chapter by chapter outline

Chapter 1 identifies four megatrends currently at work, which will force a fundamental change of our money system over the next two decades. It also shows how this change can be used as an opportunity to solve problems which appear hopeless if we remain stuck in the existing money paradigm.

Money has always appeared mysterious. For thousands of years the mystery of money was religious in nature. Today, money remains shrouded just as effectively by academic jargon and esoteric equations. This is why in Chapter 2 we elucidate the mystery surrounding it. We must also understand the main characteristics of our current money system, and why it has been so naturally adopted worldwide during the Industrial Age.

Today's fastest growing economy in the world is the cyber economy. Already in 1996, 20 million Netizens made at least one purchase on the Net, resulting in $36 billion in sales. Estimates for the year 2000 reach $200 billion. Until recently, almost all payments on the Net have been done by credit card. Credit card bills are normally paid by cheque, outside the Net. Hundreds of projects are under way to entirely computerize the traditional national currencies, as well as the newer forms of private currencies. In Chapter 3, we will show how this can and will transform our societies – to a greater extent than even those introducing the changes may realize.

By exploring contrasting scenarios, in Chapter 4 we will clarify how changes in our current money system could pull our societies in very different directions. Each scenario will depict a world where a different kind of currency has prevailed, and what impact this would have over a period of twenty years.

Before anything else, we need to establish the basics. A Primer is available at the end of this book. It clarifies the roles of the key players in today's monetary game, the recent developments in the global foreign exchange markets, and their impact on your life. If you are very familiar with these topics, skip the Primer, and go straight to Chapter 1. But if you feel you need a refresher course, or if these domains are new to you, the Primer will bring you painlessly up to speed on how our conventional money is created, who controls it, and how the money world really works. It synthesizes a library of intimidating tomes in a form inviting for the layperson.

Money – The Root of All Possibilities

■ *'Money is like an iron ring we put through our nose.*
It is now leading us wherever it wants.
We just forgot that we are the ones who designed it.'

MARK KINNEY

■ *'The future is not some place we are going to, but one we are creating.*
The paths are not to be found, but made, and the activity of making them
changes both the maker and the destination.'

JOHN SCHAAR

■ *'The modern crises are, in fact, man-made*
and differ from many of their predecessors in that they can be dealt with.'

SECOND REPORT TO THE CLUB OF ROME[4]

■ The Time-Compacting Machine

Once upon a time, the very inventive inhabitants of an extraordinarily lush and beautiful planet created, much to their surprise, a gigantic machine. Most surprising to them was the discovery that this machine compacted time. Because of this remarkable feature, their colossal invention actually forced them to become aware of some incompatibilities that lay precariously between their most cherished, well-established habits and their own survival.

One day, these people realized that four powerful megatrends were converging like giant pistons towards the same place and time. Perhaps because they had each been generated by the very inventive people themselves, these four megatrends were hard for the people to see, and harder still for them to address. The Time-Compacting Machine created by these ingenious, yet sadly shortsighted, people is represented in Figure 1.1. If you look closely, you may find that these people, their planet and their Time-Compacting Machine are very familiar.

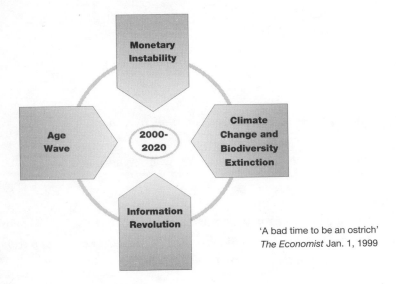

'A bad time to be an ostrich'
The Economist Jan. 1, 1999

Figure 1.1 The Time-Compacting Machine

This extraordinary Time-Compacting Machine consists of four giant megatrend pistons moving at varying speeds towards the same destination. Imagine that two pistons are like icebergs – an *Age Wave* and *Global Climate Change and Species Extinction* – both moving at a glacier-like pace, but with inexorable inertia, towards the same place and time. The other two giant pistons – *Monetary Instability* on one side and the *Information Revolution* on the other – are moving faster and more erratically, like ships – *Titanics* – and are also heading towards the same place and time.

All four of these megatrends will be briefly described. Each issue will be synthesized into a single, hard 'money question', a substantial question to which some kind of response will occur – either by default or by design – within the next decade. The rest of this book will reveal how these 'money questions' can be turned around into a surprising opportunity to make Sustainable Abundance a reality.

The first step is to recognize that this is 'a bad time to be an ostrich', according to an editorial in *The Economist* on January 1, 1999. An ostrich may experience some short-term psychological comfort, but vital parts of its anatomy are at high risk. In short, the time has come to pull our heads out of the sand. We start with the Age Wave – the slowest of these megatrends, but also the one that is most inexorably certain.

■ 1. Age Wave

For 99% of the existence of our species, life expectancy has been estimated at about 18 years. Over the past century, particularly the past few decades, the combined impact of dramatic advances in hygiene, nutrition, lifestyle and medicine has had a cumulative effect on the number of years that people can expect to live. In the developed world, life expectancy has now risen to 80 years for women, and to 76 years for men. One remarkable consequence is that *two out of three of all human beings who have ever reached the age of 65 are alive today*. The age of 65 was initially chosen by Bismarck as an official 'retirement age'[5] during the 19th century, when the life expectancy in Germany was 48 years. Very few people were expected to reach that hallowed age, and our entire social contract of jobs and pension systems was geared to take care of those few people.

Over the next few decades, a demographic transformation that is totally predictable will take place – all the people involved are accounted for today. In the developed world, about one person in seven is now over 65 years of age. Compare that with only one in 11 people back in 1960. Within two decades, one out of every five people will reach that canonical age; and by 2030 almost one out of every four! (Figure 1.2).

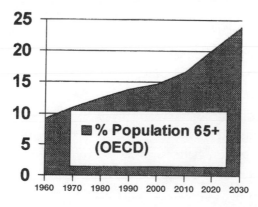

Figure 1.2 The Grey Wave: Percentage of total population aged 65 or over (OECD)[6]

This unprecedented 'Age Wave' will transform the economics and politics of the world. One expert's opinion is that 'Global ageing will become not just the transcendent economic issue of the 21st century, but the transcendent political issue as well. It will dominate and haunt the public-policy agendas of the developed countries and force renegotiations of their social contracts.'[7] There are no historical precedents for handling the issues this Age Wave is raising around the world.

Global ageing: some facts and figures[8]

- In Florida today, almost one in five people (18.5%) are 65 years or older. It represents a model of the future everywhere. This 'Florida benchmark' will be reached for the following countries as a whole in the years indicated:
Italy 2003
Japan 2005
Germany 2006
UK 2016
France 2016
Canada 2021
USA 2023
- This ageing process is not only an issue in developed countries. In fact, in developing countries, the ageing process is starting somewhat later, but will unfold faster than in the developed areas. For instance, in France it took one century for the elderly to grow from 7 to 14% of the population. For South Korea, Taiwan, Singapore and China this is projected to happen in a time span of only 25 years.
- The United Nations forecasts that by 2050, the number of people aged 65 to 84 worldwide will grow from 400 million to 1.3 billion (a three-fold increase). The number of people aged 85 and older will grow from 26 million to 175 million (a six-fold increase). Finally, centenarians (100 and over) will grow from 135,000 to 2.2 million (a sixteen-fold increase).

This global greying trend does offer a few positive effects. For instance, you are more likely than anybody in previous generations to join this unprecedented population of the elderly. One could even hope that, with such a high percentage of mature people, the incoming Knowledge Society might evolve into an era that deserves to be called a Wisdom Age. Time will tell.

More sobering issues, however, will need to be addressed during the current transition period. For example, unfunded pension liabilities are a serious problem. These are benefits already earned by today's workers, but for which no reserves exist because the funds have been paid out as benefits to the currently retired population. These unfunded liabilities have now accumulated to *$35 trillion* in the OECD countries alone[9] (this is more than four years of the entire Gross National Product of the US economy). Adding in healthcare to the cost would more than double that figure. And even these staggering numbers do not take into account the future growth in the number of the elderly reflected in Figure 1.2.

■ The following hard 'money question' synthesizes the socio-economic dilemma that this Age Wave presents: ***How will society provide the elderly with the money to match their longevity?***

■ 2. Information revolution

Two hundred years ago, Benjamin Franklin claimed that if everyone were to work productively, the working day would need be only five hours. Sixty years ago, Bertrand Russell, the English philosopher, and Lewis Mumford, an American authority on culture, both estimated that a 20-hour working week should be enough time to produce all the necessary goods and services in our society. For the past 30 years, many economists have forecast reduced working weeks or retirement at age 38. *The New York Times* predicted on October 19, 1967 that 'By the year 2000, people will work no more than four days a week and less than eight hours a day. With legal holidays and long vacations, this could result in annual working period of 147 days and 218 days off.'

In contrast with all these predictions, what has actually been happening is a fierce, global struggle for jobs. At least 700 million able and willing people are chronically unemployed or under-employed worldwide. Unemployment used to be primarily a Third World problem, but has now spread to 'developed' countries as well. Europe is experiencing its worst job crisis since the 1930s; Japan its worst employment crunch ever. In the US, the same scramble for jobs has resulted in a worsening of working conditions, rather than straightforward unemployment. While American labour productivity has grown by 30% between 1973 and 1993, pay has dropped by about 20% in real terms over the same time period. At the same time, average working hours increased by 15% and white-collar workaholism has become a tacit requirement to keep your job. According to psychologist Barbara Killinger, 'Workaholism has become the major source of marital breakdown.'[10] The United Nations International Labor Organization labels job stress 'a global phenomenon'.[11]

The harsh reality is that the post-industrial global economy does not need – and therefore cannot and will not provide – jobs for the six billion people on the planet today, not to speak of the eight billion forecast for 2019. Jobless growth for major corporations worldwide is not a forecast, but an established trend. The extent to which the writing is on the wall can be comprehended from statistics quoted by William Greider:[12] the world's 500 largest corporations have managed to increase their production and sales by 700% over the past 20 years, while at the same time *reducing* their total workforce.

Economists will correctly argue that productivity improvements in one sector tend to create jobs in other sectors, and that therefore 'in the long run' technological change doesn't matter. However, nobody can claim that technological shifts are not generating massive *displacements* of jobs, fundamental changes of the qualifications required to perform a function. If the changes are rapid – as is the case with Information Technology – such job displacements are just as destructive as permanent job losses. How many steelworkers can realistically expect to be retrained as computer pro-grammers or corporate lawyers, however strong the demand is in these sectors? William Bridges, an expert on the future of employment, has concluded that 'within a generation, our scramble for jobs will look like a fight over deck chairs on the *Titanic*'.[13]

To add insult to injury, the only societies in the world today that work fewer than four hours a day are the surviving 'primitive' hunter-gatherer tribes, living roughly as they have done over the past 20,000 years. Similarly, the common agricultural labourer in 10th to 13th century mediaeval Europe spent less than half of his waking hours at work.[14] Are we going wrong somewhere?

Wassily Leontieff, Nobel Prize-winning economist, has summarized the overall process as follows: 'The role of humans as the most important factor of production is bound to diminish in the same way that the role of horses in agricultural production was first diminished and then eliminated by the introduction of tractors.'[15] We could let the horses peacefully die out, but what do we do with people?

■ The 'money question' here is: ***How can we provide a living to additional billions of people when our technologies make jobless growth a clear possibility?***

■ 3. Climate change and biodiversity extinction

Consider the following facts:

■ The year 1998 has been declared by the UN Insurance Initiative (convened by insurance and reinsurance companies from around the world) as the worst year *ever* for natural disasters. The year 1999 may even top that! The frequency of major natural disasters is now *treble* what it was in the 1960s. The insurance losses due to storms, floods, droughts and fires for 1998 alone are higher than what was paid out for the entire decade of the 1980s according to Munich Re, the world's largest reinsurance company. Eighty-five per cent of all insurance payments worldwide now go towards compensating for natural disasters. A combination of deforestation and climate change is blamed for these problems.[16] Of course, all this measures only the minority of the assets in the world which are actually insured in the first place. Another measure of Nature's increased violence is that four times more people now die in natural disasters than in all war and civil disturbances combined.

Climate change: some findings

- Engineers designing storm sewers, bridges and culverts used to plan for 'hundred-year storms'. Thomas Karl, of the National Oceanic and Atmospheric Administration says 'There isn't really a hundred-year event anymore. We seem to be getting these storms of the century every couple of years'. Some storms of 97-98, like hurricane Mitch, have qualified as a 'five-hundred year storm'.

- Charles Keeling of the Scripps Institution of Oceanography has shown that spring starts about a week earlier globally and that temperature swings are growing stronger (*Nature* July 1996).The years 1990, 1995 and 1997 included the warmest days in the Northern Hemisphere in the past 500 years (*Nature* April 22, 1998). Furthermore, there is more and more evidence that permanent climate change is possible in remarkably short time periods, in the time lapse of decades instead of centuries, as was thought until now.

- The freezing level of the atmosphere – the height at which the air temperature reaches freezing – has been gaining altitude since 1970 at the rate of nearly five metres per year. Tropical glaciers are melting at what the Ohio State researchers term 'striking rates'. 'The Lewis glacier on Mount Kenya has lost 40% of its mass, in the Ruwenzori all the glaciers are in massive retreat. Everything in Patagonia is retreating. . . . We've seen that plants are moving up the mountain. . . . I frankly don't know what additional evidence you need,' claims Ellen Mosley Thompson of the Ohio University Team.

- The European research satellites ERS-1 and ERS-2 have shown that the West Atlantic Ice sheet in Antarctica is receding at the rate of more than one kilometre (6/10th of a mile) per year. Barclay Kamb, a noted glaciologist at Caltech, comments 'I was rather skeptical of this idea of Antarctic Ice Sheet disintegration. . . . But now, the evidence for rapid ice changes is good enough that the worst-case scenarios are worth worrying about. . . . If the ice sheet disintegrated, sea levels would rise by about five metres (20 feet).' This would drown many coastlines around the world, transform most harbour cities into swamps, and make many islands in the Pacific uninhabitable.[17] On April 17, 1998, US government scientists reported that a 75-square-mile chunk of the Larsen ice shelf (eastern side of the Antarctica's ice sheet) had broken loose and blamed the break-up on global climate change. 'This may be the beginning of the end of the Larsen ice shelf' said US National Snow and Ice Data Center researcher Ted Scambos.

> ■ The Canadian ice-breaker *Des Groseillers* has been frozen in place in the Arctic as an Ice-Station since September 1997 for project SHEBA, the most comprehensive attempt at establishing a heat budget for the Arctic Ocean. 'The final results are not yet in, but SHEBA has already determined one worrying fact: the sea ice is thinner and less stable than usual, and the icecap is receding rapidly.'[18]
>
> ■ About half of the planet's population lives in the 'coastal areas' which would be directly affected by changes in the sea level.[19]

■ Substantial changes in weather patterns have been observed everywhere (see sidebar).

■ In 1998, the American Museum of Natural History made a survey among professional biologists (*not* ecologists), the majority of whom work for large corporations. A striking 69% of them have concluded that we are living now through the 'sixth extinction'. This species extinction seems to be happening more rapidly and affecting a wider range of biodiversity than any of the previous five. This is even faster than the last extinction, over 60 million years ago, when an asteroid may have wiped out the dinosaurs. The claim is that we are in the process of losing between 30% and 70% of the planet's biodiversity within a time span of only 20 to 30 years. The other difference from all previous extinction is that this one is due to the actions of one species – our own – which also claims to be the only one endowed with intelligence and consciousness.

■ The following public *Warning to Humanity* was unanimously agreed by 1,600 scientists, including a majority of living Nobel Prize winners in the sciences: 'A great change in stewardship of the Earth and the life on it is required, if vast human misery is to be avoided and our global home on this planet is not be irretrievably mutilated. . . . If not checked, many of our current practices may so put at serious risk the future that we wish for human society and the plant and animal kingdoms, and may so alter the living world, that it will be unable to sustain life in the manner that we know. Fundamental changes are urgent if we are to avoid the collision our present course will bring about.'[20]

■ In a separate initiative, a global meeting of 2,800 economists, including Nobel Prize winners James Tobin and John Harsanyi, unanimously agreed on the following opinion: 'Global climate change is a *real and pressing danger*', carrying with it significant environmental, economic, social and geopolitical risks.[21]

All these exhortations invariably seem to hit a brick wall wherever serious financial interests are involved. Financial markets focus on the next quarter's results, and even if a particular CEO were to advocate longer-term priorities at the expense of immediate results, he or she would be ruthlessly punished or even removed from office. Only when we have resolved the next 'money question' will there be any real chance to address the climate change and the biodiversity extinction problems in a timely and systematic way.

- So our bottom-line question here is: *How can we resolve the conflict between short-term financial interests and long-term sustainability?*

■ 4. Monetary instability

Michel Camdessus, the first to be elected three times as managing director of the International Monetary Fund (IMF), went on record as describing the Mexican crisis of December 1994 as 'the first financial crisis of the 21st century'. A total economic meltdown was avoided only because the US cobbled together a last-minute emergency package on an unprecedented scale – $50 billion. However, after the Mexican crash, even M. Camdessus did not expect the scale and speed of the South-east Asian crisis of 1997, which dwarfed the Mexican episode and necessitated emergency packages that made the Mexican bail-out look puny. This was followed by the Russian crash of 1998 and by the Brazilian crisis in early 1999. Unless precautions are taken, there is at least a 50-50 chance that the next five to ten years will see a dollar crisis that would amount to a global money meltdown. Currently, the monetary crisis has spread to three continents. Mr Robert Rubin, the then US Secretary of Treasury, adds: 'The number of countries experiencing difficulties at once is something we have never seen before.'

Paul Krugman, 'the most acclaimed economist of his generation',[22] somberly concludes in 'Return of Depression Economics' in *Foreign Affairs:* 'As little as two years ago, I and most of my colleagues were quite confident that although the world would continue to suffer economic difficulties, those problems would not bear much resemblance to the crisis of the 1930s. ... The truth is that the world economy poses more dangers than we had imagined. Problems we thought we knew how to cure have once again become intractable, like temporarily suppressed bacteria that eventually evolve a resistance to antibiotics. . . . There is, in short, a definite whiff of the 1930s in the air.'[23]

In the Primer you will learn why these repeated crashes are not random accidents, but signs of systemic dislocations of the official monetary system. This implies that no country should consider itself immune from such problems: not China, not the UK, not even all of Europe, nor the US.

■ The last money question is straightforward: ***How can we prepare for the possibility of a monetary crisis?***

■ Money at the core of the Time-Compacting Machine

The extraordinary convergence of these four megatrends over the next two decades shows why Peter Russell was right in predicting that 'over the next 20 years, as much change will happen in the world as has occurred over the past 200 years'.[24] I would add that, in order to deal with the challenges just described, we are going *to have to change as much in our consciousness about money over the next 20 years as we have over the past 5,000 years.*

Figure 1.3 summarizes the four money questions of the Time-Compacting Machine. Whether we like it or not, there will be some kind of answer for each one of these questions. Together, they indicate that something fundamental will have to change in our current way of dealing with money.

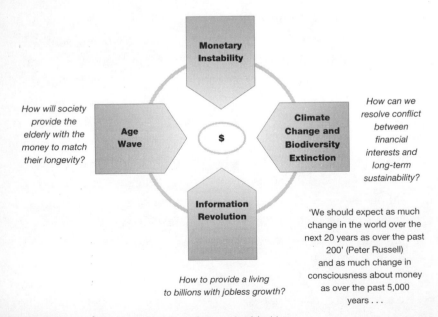

How will society provide the elderly with the money to match their longevity?

How can we resolve conflict between financial interests and long-term sustainability?

How to provide a living to billions with jobless growth?

'We should expect as much change in the world over the next 20 years as over the past 200' (Peter Russell) and as much change in consciousness about money as over the past 5,000 years . . .

Figure 1.3 Money at the Core of the Time-Compacting Machine

Today's interpretation of money needs to be questioned if we are to address these issues. Remaining locked within the prevailing money paradigm amounts to collectively doing what the cartoonist Cardon depicts so soberly.

Cardon Cartoon 'Remaining locked in the prevailing interpretation of money . . .'

■ What is Sustainable Abundance?

However, another outcome is also available – one that would lead to 'Sustainable Abundance'. Sustainable Abundance provides humanity with the ability to flourish and grow materially, emotionally and spiritually without squandering resources from the future. A synonym could be *wise growth*. It is characteristic of a community, society, country or global system that gives people the opportunity to express their highest creative calling, without diminishing the prospects for coming generations to enjoy the same or a better way of life. It is about having our material needs met so that we can explore our highest potentiality as human beings.

With such a fundamental commitment, it would be considered our birthright to have a fair chance to develop our true potential – unhampered by a lack of money. Sustainable Abundance addresses issues ranging from grinding poverty in the Third World to the bleakness of community decay in the industrialized areas, from ecological breakdown to the wasting of a child's mind due to lack of educational opportunity.

Sustainable Abundance is *not* about taking away from the haves to distribute to the have nots. On the contrary, it is about giving everybody a fair chance of *creating new wealth*. By learning the principles of Sustainable Abundance, you can become a part of this quiet but momentous evolution.

> 'In times of extraordinary change,
>
> it is no failure to fall short of realizing all that we might dream –
>
> the failure is to fall short of dreaming all that we might realize.'[25]

While Sustainable Abundance may seem like a dream, it has now become a realistic possibility. All the necessary seedlings have sprouted and are beginning to take root. The story of these seedlings, the various innovations now occurring within money systems, will be told here. You will also discover why this avenue of change is becoming more plausible as we move through the current information revolution from an Industrial Age economy towards the incoming values of an Age of Knowledge.

Sustainable Abundance may sound to some like an oxymoron, a contradiction in terms. 'Greens' support sustainability, but are sometimes suspicious of abundance. Business will be in favour of abundance, but may question the emphasis on sustainability. These apparent contradictions will be resolved once the possibilities of new currency systems are fully understood.

The following core thesis forms the foundation of this book. *We are now engaged in a structural shift of the world system, and this shift offers an unprecedented opportunity to give birth to Sustainable Abundance.*

Structural change has been formally defined as follows. 'In systems terms changing structure means changing the *information links in a system*: the content and timeliness of the data that the actors in the system have to work with, and the goals, incentives, costs and feedbacks that motivate or constrain behavior.'[26]

What is remarkable is that – even after identifying the key role of information systems in structural change – the most important of our economic information systems, our money system, has been ignored as a key leverage point for inducing the necessary and desirable changes. This is the void that this book intends to fill.

Money as an Information System

Money is our *oldest* information system – even 'writing was invented in Mesopotamia as a method of book-keeping'.[27] The earliest texts available, from 3200 BC in Uruk, are records of various financial transactions, including secured and unsecured lending and 'foreign exchange' transactions.

Money is our *most pervasive* information system, as it percolates through billions of daily exchanges in all strata of society.

Today, money has become a truly *global* information system – now that trillions of dollars are moving at the speed of light in a totally integrated, round-the-clock, computerized foreign exchange market.

Money has also become our most *universal* information system, now that even 'communist' China has decided to rely primarily on private monetary incentives to motivate its vast population.

In short, our contemporary global money system plays a role similar to the *autonomous nervous system* of the human body because it is essential to the functioning of the whole, but has remained until now mostly unconscious, beyond the control of an individual's will-power. In this metaphor, our objective here is to bring *conscious awareness and choice* to the implications of using different money systems.

The fact that changes in money systems are increasingly possible during an information revolution should come as no surprise. Money is modern society's central information system, akin to the nervous system in our own bodies (see sidebar). Mutations in a nervous system are relatively rare but rather important events in the biological evolution of a species. Similarly, a change in the nature of our money system has the potential to facilitate a fundamental shift in our societies.

It is also important to understand that Sustainable Abundance is not a state, but a process.[28]

To participate in this process, we will need to:

- Understand the premises upon which our existing money system is based;
- Become aware of the existence of other money systems that can perform functions which conventional national currencies have proved ill-equipped to fulfil;
- Based upon this understanding, make informed choices about which currencies to use for what types of transactions – choices that are compatible with the type of relationship, reciprocal or competitive – that we want to establish with our counterpart in any given exchange.

You will see that conventional national currencies and monetary systems are programmed to produce competition and to remain scarce. With a choice of currencies available, it will make sense to continue using conventional currencies to do business, to purchase a car or petrol, and to pay your telephone bill. However, you may want to consider using a cooperation-inducing currency to interact with your neighbours, take care of the elderly, or broaden the learning horizons of your children. One can see these two types of currencies as *complementary* to each other, to be used in parallel. It will even often make sense to use them in mixed payments (part conventional national currency, part complementary currency).

A remarkable variety of non-conventional currencies have already been spawned by current information technologies. Some have become familiar, like the Frequent-Flyer Miles. Initially, they were a simple marketing gimmick to build customer loyalty. However, as they have become increasingly redeemable in a variety of services besides airline tickets – such as long-distance phone calls, taxi services, hotels, even magazines – they have developed into a 'corporate scrip', a private currency issued by airlines. Just as significantly, non-conventional currencies include local community currencies – still considered as marginal curiosities by most people (e.g. LETS currencies, Time Dollars, Ithaca HOURS, etc.). They also include the Japanese 'Caring Relationship Tickets' designed specifically for elderly care, and a Brazilian garbage recycling currency. All these non-traditional currencies are prototypes of the emerging money revolution.

The future of money therefore lies not only with the further computerization of our conventional currencies – such as dollars, euros or yen – via smart cards and other new information technologies. Such changes will happen. But these same information technologies also make it possible for new non-conventional complementary currencies to enter the mainstream and provide new tools for addressing some of our most pressing challenges, both locally and globally.

However, Sustainable Abundance is only one of the possible outcomes from the current transition period. It is a development that is neither automatic nor preordained. It would require a shift in our perception of our relationship to money, the first in centuries.

Please note that none of the approaches proposed here is a permanent solution. Instead, they are transition tools, useful for perhaps the next ten to 20 years, as we move from the Industrial Age to a Knowledge Age. We are living through an interval, a supremely uncomfortable time, when we are realizing, along with philosopher Thomas Berry, that 'we are in between stories. The Old Story is not functioning properly any more, and we have not learned the New Story.' This book focuses on what we can do in this interval 'between stories'.

■ What prevents Sustainable Abundance?

The first hindrance to Sustainable Abundance is that *we are largely ignorant about our money system*, about the way money is created and managed in our societies. Even professional financial managers rarely understand how specific behaviour patterns are programmed into our transactions by the type of money we use. We all live deeply enmeshed in a planetary money machine, most cogs of which we are unable to perceive, let alone understand or manage. Yet the prevailing money system prescribes all of our economics, and much of our current social behaviour and political climate. Our lack of awareness also explains some strange facts. For instance, we have the capacity to produce enough food for everyone on this planet and there is ample work as well, but obtaining the money to pay for it all is another matter. This means that the key to Sustainable Abundance lies within the money system itself, the very system about which, ironically, we have remained largely unaware – until now.

The second hindrance to Sustainable Abundance is the inertia of tradition and its related vested interests. However, this way of exerting power is now slipping away for the simple reason that as information technologies spread, so does control over currency creation and the related monetary interactions.

It is essential to understand that *the money system is currently undergoing irreversible changes – with profound implications*. As the Time-Compacting Machine illustrates, using the existing money system to control society's economic well-being has become counterproductive. Over the last decade, we have seen the official global money system take on unparalleled power, beyond the control of any authority, national or international. The global monetary crises, that periodically make media headlines, expose the cracks in the old money system. The changes go beyond the introduction of the single European currency (the euro), smart cards, the explosion of e-commerce or even a reform of the international monetary institutions. With the growing impact of the information revolution, and with repeated shocks to the *status quo*, symptoms of a much deeper mutation are becoming visible.

One implication of the above is that we see changes in *who* is issuing money – not only traditional national banking systems, but private corporations and local communities as well. There are also changes in the *conditions* for issuing currency, such as the advent of interest-free money. Choosing to use different types of currencies can result in different social behaviours – some money systems foster cooperation while others encourage competition. By becoming aware of the various money systems and their effects, we can choose among these currencies when making different kinds of financial transactions. *Thus our ability to make knowledgeable choices allows us to imagine, devise and support different futures.*

With some understanding of the concepts behind Sustainable

Abundance, we can now address what it means in practice. The four vignettes that follow provide insights into what Sustainable Abundance might look like in daily life for different parts of society around the world.

■ Four seasons in 2020

All four cameos are set in the year 2020. Each relates to one of the 'mega-trends' in the Time-Compacting Machine, and illustrates how it is possible, using an existing complementary money system, to reconfigure an oncoming crisis into an opportunity for creating Sustainable Abundance. The vignettes provide a foretaste of what Sustainable Abundance might look and feel like in 2020. Some of them may appear almost magical at first. Nevertheless, as the science fiction writer Arthur C. Clarke points out: 'magic is any sufficiently developed technology'. What is behind each of these stories is technology – related to money. Each vignette illustrates the result of a money innovation that has been successfully implemented, and is an ongoing project currently somewhere in the world. Following each vignette is a first look at where to find an early prototype, today, that demonstrates the realism and plausibility of these stories.

The supporting evidence for the soundness of these new money technologies, and the possibilities that emerge from them, is the focus of the remainder of this book.

■ Spring

Mr Yamada's retirement plan

Tomorrow is Mr Yamada's 109th birthday – an important day. Everything has been carefully prepared for the feast. Mr Yamada has manicured the Japanese tea garden through which the guests will enter. His eyesight is too weak for a driving licence, but still good enough for him to enjoy the Zen-like peace of his bushes and rocks, and to notice the first buds of spring breaking through on his dwarf cherry tree.

In a few moments, one of his neighbours, a student at the nearby university, will come to bring him his evening meal and help him in the all-important daily bath ritual. He has enjoyed the dignity of independent living for all these years, and his wisdom and life experience are respected by his family and neighbours.

'Good evening, Yamada-san,' says the student. 'I have brought your favourite fish stew, *Yosenabe*, as you like it.' Mr Yamada smiles back.

Life can be beautiful at 109, even on the meagre pension of a long-retired bank clerk.

Japan has one of the fastest-ageing populations of the developed world. Already today, some 1.8 million elderly or handicapped Japanese need daily care. By the year 2005, the population over 65 years of age will reach 18.5% of the total.

On his retirement, Mr Tsutomu Hotta, a highly respected former Attorney General and Minister of Justice, decided to do something about this problem. He created a private organization called the Sawayaka Welfare Institute in 1995, that has been implementing a special currency called *Hureai Kippu* (literally 'Caring Relationship Tickets'). The unit of account is an hour of service. Different kinds of services have different valuations (e.g. shopping or food preparation for an elderly person is valued at a lower hourly rate than body care for them). About 100 different non profit organizations agreed to use the same standard unit. The people providing the services can accumulate the credits in a 'healthcare time savings account' on which they may draw when they need credits for themselves, for example if they are ill. These credits *complement* the normal healthcare insurance programme payable in yen, the Japanese national currency. In addition, many prefer to transfer part or all of their *Hureai Kippu* credits to their parents who may live in another part of the country. Two private electronic clearing houses have sprung up to perform such transfers on a regional level. The Japanese government is currently evaluating the possibility of creating an official national clearing house to make such transfers available for all types of healthcare time credits everywhere in the country.

One particularly important finding has emerged. Because they have experienced a higher quality of care in their relationships with care-givers, the elderly tend to prefer the services provided by people paid in *Hureai Kippu* over those paid in yen. To the student in our vignette, Mr Yamada is a sort of surrogate for his own elderly father, who lives in another part of the country and to whom he sends part of his time credits.

As of 1999, this is all happening as a complement to the National Health Insurance Plan, which covers the necessary professional health services payable in yen. For instance, if Mr Yamada needed regular kidney dialysis or a professional chiropractic session, this would be covered by Health

Insurance in yen. Mr Hotta foresees that 'about one third to half of the conventional monetary functions will be picked up by these new currencies. As a result, the severity of any recession and unemployment will be significantly reduced.'[29]

In an independent development, a health insurance company in New York state known as Elderplan, has been accepting since 1987 up to one quarter of its healthcare insurance premiums in Time Dollars, the brainchild of Edgar Cahn, a well-known lawyer and professor in Washington DC. Elderplan also operates a 'Care Bank' where participants have already earned 97,623 hours of services up to June 1999. It started as a home repair service that fixed potential problems before they caused accidents. The Care Bank has as its motto: A broken towel bar is a broken hip waiting to happen.[30] Here again, the users report that they enjoy the quality in human relations made possible by this approach. During the year 2000, the Elderplan system is spreading beyond Brooklyn to Queens, Staten Island and Manhattan.

The *Hureai Kippu*, Elderplan, and several other community-enhancing currencies will be described in more detail in Chapter 6.

■ Summer

A World in balance

It's 1 p.m. For Anna, head of customer service in the largest telecommunications company based in Munich, the day is over. Using the high-speed underground, she returns to her other community, the village nestled in the foothills of the Alps, 15 minutes away.

She really enjoys her job, but she can't wait to get back to her studio and continue her work with stained glass. She has just started her most ambitious project to date – a large stained-glass window depicting seminal events in her little town's history. At her village's next arts festival, which lasts two weeks during the summer, she will donate the window to the Permanent Learning Centre.

All of Anna's company colleagues have a similar lifestyle. Wolfgang in Finance is into African dance and has formed his own dance troupe; Birgit in MIS, whose passion is wood carving, is considering making the special wooden frames for Anna's window; Reiner in Human Resources restores old lutes and other musical instruments.

Because complementary currency systems support both types of activities, everybody in Anna's village has the choice to have a dual career. Some people choose full-time work in a traditional corporate job. Some concentrate their energy on their artistic interests, earning mostly community currencies. Many combine the two because greater choice is available, and because life is simply more livable in a 'World in Balance'.

With the growth in productivity that has resulted from the Information Revolution, Juliet Schor, associate professor of Economics at Harvard University, asserts that 'We actually could have chosen a four-hour day. Or a working year of six months. Or every worker in the US could now be taking every other year off from work – with pay.'

German sociologist Ulrich Becker similarly claims that 'There is a life beyond the alternatives of unemployment and stress at work . . . It must be possible for every human being autonomously to shape his or her life and create a balance between family, paid employment, leisure and political commitment.'[31]

So why don't we achieve this?

The closest prototypes that we can find in the new millennium for a 'World in Balance' is occurring in Bali and some other traditional societies. People visiting Bali are astonished by the unusually vibrant and artistic quality of daily life. Almost every man is an accomplished artist; every woman a graceful dancer; all find ways to be creative. Every village has 50 or more festival holidays throughout the year, with elaborate ephemeral artful expressions.[32] Houses have elegant carvings, landscapes are exquisite.

What is so different about Bali and the Balinese? What if the world, our cities, our lives, became more like those of Bali? Many tourists visiting Bali are not aware that the Balinese consider the performances they see as 'practice sessions'. The 'real performances' happen in the temple or for temple-organized activities. The Balinese dedicate between 30% and 40% of their working hours to the temple, which organizes the cooperative, caring, artistic, and religious activities. These are what I later define as the 'Cooperative' dimension of life. Most Balinese adults also have a professional job where they spend the other two-thirds of their working hours – in what I call the 'Competitive' economy, the only one we know in the West.

'Temple time' is part of a long tradition of a 'gift economy' in Bali. In the Western world, during the current transition period from the Post-Industrial Age, we may not be ready for a pure gift economy. Nevertheless, it is possible for our future to include a 'Cooperative' dimension in everyday life.

What if we needed only a transition tool, a process through which we can rebuild community and our trust in a gift economy?

Communities around the world have already created and implemented several types of complementary currencies that are compatible with, even result in, a gift economy. Called 'mutual credit' currencies, they can always be created in amounts that are sufficient, rather than scarce. In contrast with competition-programmed national currencies, they are not scarcity based. They are created *by the participants at the moment of their transaction*. For instance, if you perform a service of one hour for me, you get a credit of one hour and I get a debit for the same amount. A simple barter would occur if I did something in exchange for you that is also valued at one hour. But using the mutual credit currency, you can purchase fresh eggs at the market, and I can cancel my debit with someone else. That means that we have created a true currency – one that is not artificially scarce. *Whenever we agree on a transaction, we can always create the money.*

One of the first scarcities to address is job scarcity. There are now 2,500 complementary currency systems operational in the world today, most of which have sprung up to generate local *work* in high unemployment areas. More than 400 communities in the UK have started their own electronic complementary currency system called the Local Exchange Trading System (LETS). Similarly, in Germany they are called *Tauschring*, in France *Grains de Sel*, and several hundred such grass-roots projects are now operational in these countries as well. In the US, 39 communities have followed Ithaca, NY, in creating their own paper currency, redeemable only within the community. All of these systems will be explained in detail later.

These initiatives are often treated as marginal curiosities by mainstream media and academic circles. However, in New Zealand, Australia, Scotland and 30 different US states, regional governments have been funding the start-up of such systems because they have proved effective in solving local employment problems. The European Union is funding pilot complementary currency programmes in four deliberately very different settings and technologies: two in the countryside of Ireland and Scotland, and two in the major cities of Madrid and Amsterdam. In New Zealand, the central bank has discovered that complementary currencies actually *help* to control the overall inflation in the national currency. More about this will be described in Chapters 5 and 8.

We can each only imagine what we would create if 40% of our working hours were available for 'temple time', whatever form that might take. Using this approach, would it not be possible for the Information Revolution to evolve into an authentic Age of Knowledge? What would each of us like to learn? What improvements would you like to make in your life?

Imagine what you could create on your own or with others.

■ Autumn

A Bechtel Corporation board meeting in 2020

The following text is an extract from the minutes of the annual board meeting of Bechtel Corporation, the largest construction and civil engineering company in the world.

'The board considered the two main investment projects on today's agenda:

■ A 300-year nature restoration project of the Southern Himalayan watershed
■ A 500-year reforestation project of the sub-Sahara desert

The board decided unanimously to implement the 500-year sub-Sahara project, given that the Internal Rate of Return on this project is clearly superior. The chairman added that the contribution of this project to overall global climate stability has been an additional incentive for his own vote for this project.'

Most business decisions today are made with horizons of less than five years, if not from one quarter to the next. Even the 'long bond', the longest-term conservative investment available today in dollars, has a maximum horizon of 30 years. Under contemporary financial criteria, a decision like the one above is unthinkable.

A pragmatic currency system will be presented later that would make decisions of this kind not only possible, but completely logical. Under such a money system, long-term concerns would be the norm, the *spontaneous* response. These concerns would be not only compatible with financial self-interest, but driven by it. No regulations or artificial tax incentives would be required to motivate corporations and individuals to think and act with the proverbial 'seventh generation' in mind.

There have been at least two civilizations which had embedded in their monetary systems a key feature that made it 'profitable' for people to make investments for the very long term. These two historical precedents are Pharaonic Egypt and the 'Age of the Cathedrals' (the 'Central Middle Ages' of 10-13th century Western Europe). In both cases, this same feature, known as demurrage (a form of negative interest which discourages hoarding in the form of currency), was operational for centuries. The record shows that people spontaneously created buildings and artforms that were designed to last for ever. You can still visit them today. This key mechanism behind such a money system can be replicated and efficiently adapted for the 21st century. Chapter 8 describes in detail how this is possible.

Of our bounty of 20th century creations, which ones will our descendants be able to visit in the year 3000?

If such a long-term oriented money system were operational today, what would be the 'cathedrals of the 21st century'?

What would you imagine them to be? They don't have to be temples or buildings.

■ Winter

Your grandniece's trip to China

Your grandniece is passionate about early Chinese calligraphy and poetry. She has decided to improve her fluency in Mandarin Chinese by going for a six-month residency in China starting next year.

Here is her budget for this endeavour.

- Airline travel: paid in frequent-flyer miles that both she and her parents have accumulated.
- Local expenses: she has been saving her 'Caring Relationship Tickets' over the past few years by taking care of two elderly neighbours in the university town where she studies. She will simply transfer her credits over the Net to be exchanged for the local currency of the Chinese university town where she plans to live.
- As your Christmas gift, you have decided to add £500 in conventional national currency for incidental expenses that she may have along the way, and as a safety net for any unexpected emergency needs.

Having the option of using sufficiency-based currencies for part of our needs can make a big difference. A complementary currency clearing house could be operating globally on the Net even today. Its purpose would be to enable those participating in any type of complementary currency (LETS,

Time Dollars, *Hureai Kippu*, etc.) to trade with each other over the Net, each using their own currency. Even the idea of your grandniece using complementary currencies as an exchange system during her trip is not new. The Global Eco-village Network (GEN), an association of eco-villages founded in 1994, recommends such joint projects and exchanges between the different participating communities.[33]

Complementary currency systems and private payment systems can provide a useful *safety net* under the official monetary system. A spare tyre may seem rather redundant – until you have a puncture on the motorway. In the monetary domain, the privately run 'Golden Crown' payment system is used by a group of Russian corporations to barter among themselves. This is a real-life demonstration of just how useful a 'spare tyre' can be when the national currency gets into serious trouble.[34] The same life-saving importance was demonstrated at the grass-roots level with the availability of local currencies after the crash of the baht in Thailand during 1997-98, and the ongoing *Redes de Trueque* (literally 'barter networks') active in Argentina for years. Grass-roots currencies are explored in Chapters 5 to 7.

■ Creating Sustainable Abundance with complementary currencies

Without throwing away the positive contributions of the existing system, we can add new possibilities. It is often said that all crises contain hidden opportunities. The Chinese ideogram for 'crisis' even contains explicitly the root 'opportunity'. The opportunity that will be described in the pages following may seem as extraordinary as the crisis itself. You will discover how it is possible to turn the Time-Compacting Machine into a Sustainable Abundance Machine. This can be accomplished by revisiting the prevailing interpretation of money, by understanding how money actually operates, and by acting upon that knowledge.

The core thesis of this book can now be restated more pointedly as follows: *proven money innovations can solve the four 'money questions', summarized in Figure 1.3, and engender Sustainable Abundance within one generation.* The key is to introduce – in parallel with the existing money system – *complementary currencies* that have *already proved* that they can contribute to solving these uncompromisingly tough questions.

A complementary currency refers to an agreement among a group of people and/or corporations to accept a non-traditional currency as a medium of exchange. They are called complementary because their intent is *not* to replace the conventional national currency but to perform social functions that the official currency was not designed to fulfil.

Together, the exchanges facilitated by the conventional national currency economies *and* the complementary currencies form what I will define as the Integral Economy. The Integral Economy includes the processes studied by traditional economic theory, and goes beyond it. For instance, it includes transactions in the 2,500 complementary currency systems already operational today in local communities in a dozen countries around the world.

Such are the money innovations that were the basis for the Four Seasons vignettes of 2020.

We can now begin to see how the Time-Compacting Machine could be transformed into a Sustainable Abundance Machine. Figure 1.4 shows how the four cameo stories fit into this process.

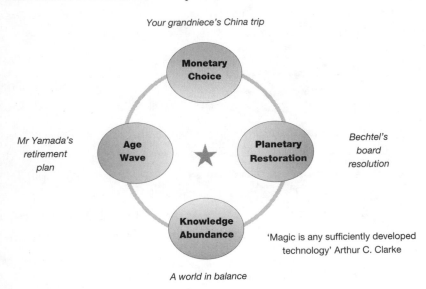

Figure 1.4 Mapping the Four Seasons vignettes to transform the Time-Compacting Machine into a Sustainable Abundance Machine

This book provides detailed evidence that such a mutation is a realistic possibility.

■ A road map to your money, your future

The first necessary step is to demystify today's conventional national and international money system and identify the changes that are looming in that system. This is the purpose of the balance of Part One, What *is* Money? It lifts the veil around money to familiarize us with its nature, and with the creation and operation of conventional national currencies. In addition, the new money frontier – the 'cybersphere' – is explored, in which many of the currency innovations are brewing. An enquiry is then launched into different possible futures for our money system and how they would reshape society. This last step uses scenarios that depict different worlds in the year 2020.

With an understanding of all this, it will become possible for you to perceive what is unique about the money innovations going on in the world, which is the subject of Part Two: Choosing Your Future of Money. This describes the extensive choice in non-conventional currencies operational today. You will learn how different objectives can be supported   or hindered – by a currency. Specifically, the creation of work opportunities, the revival of neighbourhoods, and the re-aligning of long-term sustainability with current financial interests, can all be achieved by using particular currencies designed for such ends.

But let us begin at the beginning, by exploring some deceptively 'obvious' features of today, conventional money.

CHAPTER 2

Today's Money

■ *'The study of money, above all fields in economics,*
is the one in which complexity is used to disguise truth, or evade truth,
not to reveal it.'

JOHN KENNETH GALBRAITH[35]

■ *'The thing that separates man from animals is money.'*

GERTRUDE STEIN, 1936

■ *'The only thing money cannot buy is meaning.'*

JACOB NEEDLEMAN[36]

'Mum, could I have some money to buy some sweets?' For most of us, our first experience of money is as a necessary object in the ritual of getting the things we want from shops. We accept it with the pragmatism of an innocent child, unaware of the mystery behind the transaction.

As we mature, we become conversant in many adult mysteries. We learn where babies come from, and participate in that process. We learn that all living things eventually die, and witness the death of a relative, friend, or perhaps a pet. We learn how our government works, and who makes the rules by which we are required to live.

And yet one of the central mysteries of our lives as social beings – money – remains completely obscure to virtually everyone. Most people probably suspect that the answer to the nature of money comes from the study of economics or monetary theory, and we all know these fields are boring – full of equations and devoid of emotional juice.

Ironically, money itself is a very emotionally juicy topic. Throwing money on the ground in a public place gets as much attention as taking off our clothes. Those who work in financial markets recognize that strong emotions rule most money issues: emotions that are ubiquitous, violent, volatile and overwhelmingly powerful. Strangely, neither economics nor monetary theories consider the emotional nature of money. In fact, in order to study money 'scientifically', they deliberately suppress its basically emotional nature. What is going on here?

The creation of money is largely invisible to the untrained eye, and seems almost miraculous. Most people, when they find out where money really comes from, are as disbelieving as some children when they first find out where babies come from. 'How could this possibly be true?' they wonder.

Economics textbooks deal with the question of what money *does*, but not with what money *is*. By asking the deceptively simple question 'What *is* money?' we are put in touch with money's age-old magic. This chapter will clarify the mystery by showing that money is not a thing, but an agreement – usually an unconscious one.

In contemporary society, we not only agree to participate in the existing money system – unconsciously – but we also bestow extraordinary power on that system. Here the nature of that power will be explored, as well as the four key features of modern money that we usually take for granted. For instance, national currencies make economic interaction with our fellow citizens more desirable than with 'foreigners', thereby cultivating national consciousness. Less obvious is the mechanism of the interest, which will be shown to foster competition among users of the currency.

■ A 'simple' question

The best-known economist of the 20th century, John Maynard Keynes, *must* have understood money. He was, after all, the chairman of the team who designed our current monetary system, known as the Bretton Woods Agreement. Marcel Labordère, a French financial journalist, postulated in a letter to Keynes: 'It is self-evident that man will never be able to know what money is no more than he will be able to know what God is in the spiritual world. Money is not the infinite, but the indefinite, an astounding complex of all sorts of psychological as well as material reactions.'[37]

Keynes's answer to Labordère was not preserved, but we can deduce his opinion on the topic from his quip: 'I know of only three people who really understand money. A professor at another university; one of my students; and a rather junior clerk at the Bank of England.' A prudent man, he didn't name them. What Keynes is saying is that you can go right to the top of the hierarchy of experts and still not find an answer to the deceptively simple question, 'What *is* money?'

■ Where is the money mystery coming from?

The representative of the Clinton administration to the IMF offered this revealing definition: 'Money is magic. Central bankers are magicians. Like all magicians, they don't like to show their tricks.' Was she referring to the real magic or simple parlour tricks? The answer is both. Magic and mystery have surrounded the money process during its entire evolution. There are two main reasons why money appears so mysterious:

■ Its history
■ The need to perpetuate the confidence game.

■ The history of money

Keynes pointed out that 'Money, like certain other elements in civilizations, is a far more ancient institution than we were taught to believe. Its origins are lost in the mists when the ice was melting, and may well stretch into the intervals in human history of the inter-glacial periods, when the weather was delightful and the mind free to be fertile with new ideas – in the islands of the Hesperides or Atlantis or some Eden of Central Asia.'[38]

While the exact origins of money are unknown, all its earlier forms were deeply related to the mysteries of the sacred, and its first role was as a symbol. A symbol is 'something which represents something else which is immaterial or abstract', according to the *Oxford English Dictionary*, which goes on to point out that all early symbols were related to religious concepts.

The mystery of the shekel

The Sumerians called their first coin the *'shekel'* because *'She'* meant *wheat*. *'Kel'* was a measurement similar to a bushel. Hence, this coin was a symbol of a value of one bushel of wheat. (The word 'shekel' survives in modern Hebrew as Israel's monetary unit.)

The original purpose of the shekel was for payment for sacred sexual intercourse at the temple of Inanna/Ishtar, the goddess of life, death and fertility. This temple, as well as being a ritual centre, was the storage place for the reserves of wheat that supported the priestesses, and also the community, in lean times.

So farmers fulfilled their religious obligations to society and the goddess by bringing their contribution of wheat to the temple and receiving in exchange this shekel coin, entitling them to visit the priestesses at festival time.

Two thousand years later, after the patriarchal system had changed the meaning and nature of these rituals, the Bible would describe these priestesses as 'temple prostitutes'. However, all this must be understood in its own cultural context. The 'sacred prostitutes' were representatives of the goddess, and intercourse with them was intercourse with the goddess of fertility herself, nothing to take lightly. At that time, fertility was truly a matter of life and death. If the crops failed, there was no alternative, and everyone starved or at least went hungry until next year. And, of course, completing the magic ritual properly insured the fertility in crops, animals, and children that were the requisites for future prosperity.

The reason why money, sex and death all became powerful taboos in the West relates to the fact that all three are attributes of the ancient Great Mother archetype, as illustrated by the shekel associations. The full implications for the collective psychology of this connection are explored elsewhere.[39]

On a large alabaster vase dating from 3100-2900 BC, a naked man brings a large basket filled with food to Inanna. The goddess is shown standing in front of a twin-doorpost entrance, symbolizing her temple. An ancient repair with copper rivets is visible above the head of the goddess, indicating that the vase was treasured at the time.
Alabaster vase, Uruk (Level III) h. 3 ft. Iraq Museum. Photograph Hirmer Verlag, Munich

One of the oldest coins is a Sumerian bronze piece dating back to about 3200 BC. On one side of the coin is a representation of a sheaf of wheat, and on the other is a representation of Inanna (the Ishtar of the Babylonians), the

Goddess of life, death, and fertility. It was called a 'shekel', and it was a sacred symbol embodying the mysteries of life's fertility (see sidebar). The shekel is by no means atypical. Throughout history, virtually every society has conferred some mysterious sacred qualities on its currency.

More than 2,500 years after the Sumerian shekel, the first Greek coins were actually tokens given to citizens as proof of payment of their dues. These tokens could be redeemed for participation in the annual *hecatomb* or sacred meal to be shared with the deities.

The Arab scholar Ibn Khaldun claimed that 'God created the two precious metals, gold and silver, to serve as a measure of all commodities . . .' Without further need for intervention by any religious institution, gold and silver remained symbolically associated respectively with the sun and moon. For centuries, their prices stabilized mysteriously in a fixed ratio of 1/13.5, astrologically determined to reflect the heavenly cycles. These two metals remained divinely ordained currencies after the astrological justification was long forgotten. There are many people who, to this day, claim that 'real' money would be a return to the gold standard. Some even keep invoking its biblical origins.[40]

There is some irony in the fact that the almighty dollar is no exception to this mystical phenomenon. Issued by a country with a scrupulous separation between Church and State since its founding, where school prayers can still stir a heated debate, the most ordinary one-dollar bill has as motto, 'In God we Trust'. That same bill is illustrated with both sides of the Great Seal of the United States. That seal has been described by Joseph Campbell as extraordinarily laden with esoteric symbols (see sidebar).

It can be fascinating to discover the next supporting mystique. Liberia, for instance, issued its legal tender coinage with the portraits of Captain James T. Kirk and Captain Jean-Luc Picard of the starship Enterprise, paying royalties to Viacom, owner of the Star Trek trademarks, in the process.[41] Until recently, it was the fashion to design banks to look like temples, complete with reverence lingering inside them. Even the first Internet bank, the First Security National Bank, with only an Internet address and no physical customer branch, felt the need to bow to custom by using a Greek Revival bank building as its first Webpage symbol.

Central bankers, in particular, still shroud their doings in priestly mystery. A hearing of the Chairman of the Federal Reserve in Congress has just as much ritual and studied ambiguities as the oracles of the priests of Apollo in Delphi in Ancient Greece. Two quotations illustrate this perfectly.

The esoteric dimension of the one-dollar bill
(Synthesis of a Joseph Campbell conference)

I invite you to look closely at the familiar one-dollar bill. The most interesting side is not where George Washington is engraved, but the one where the Great Seal of the United States is represented.

On the left, the obverse (normally hidden) side of the Great Seal provides an image of the Founding Fathers' interpretation of the Source of Manifestation. It has the truncated pyramid crowned by the Delta of Light with the all-seeing eye of God. It represents spiritual power commanding the foundation of matter. The eye depicts the 'opening of the eye' of Yahweh or of Brahma by which He created the physical world. This alludes to the eye that manifested the first world – we would say the Big Bang in our contemporary scientific language. The Latin text *Annuit Coeptis* translates as *'It supports our endeavour'*. It is interesting that the Latin here is gender-neutral, and therefore, does not necessarily imply a 'masculine' God. The other text, *Novus Ordo Seclorum*, means *'The New Order of the Centuries'*.

The other side of the seal (the officially visible one) represents the Source of Action, symbolized by the Eagle – symbol of Zeus, the only bird that could look into the sun. This eagle holds 13 arrows (symbol of power) in its left claw, and an olive branch (symbol of peace) in its right claw.

The number 13 – the number of transformation – represents at the exoteric level the number of initial founding states. However, here it also has to be taken in its esoteric meaning, given the extraordinary lengths to which this number is repeated in the figure. The number 13 is referred to no less than seven times! These are: the number of rows of stones in the pyramid, the number of stars, the number of leaves on the olive branch, the number of arrows in the claw, the number of letters in '*annuit coeptis'*, and the number of letters in the rest of the figure (including the Roman letters of the date) which amount to 26 (or 2x13).

Achieving the right number of letters has required introducing an orthographic 'mistake' in the Latin text (*seclorum* instead of the normal *seculorum*). The disposition of the 13 stars above the eagle forms a 'Seal of Solomon' (also called the 'Star of David') and is intended to give us some further clues. That six-pointed star is indeed one of the richest cabalistic and alchemical symbols. Do we need to go further to prove the point that, even in today's totally secular world, the currency bill most circulated globally is instilled with substantial 'mysterious sacred qualities'?

The first is my favourite Alan Greenspan witticism: 'If you have understood me, then I must *not* have made myself clear.' The other comes from William Greider in his well-named best-selling book on the Federal Reserve, *Secrets of the Temple:* 'Like the temple, the Fed did not answer to the people, it spoke for them. Its decrees were cast in a mysterious language people could not understand, but its voice, they knew, was powerful and important.'[42]

However, there is more to the mystery of money than just a reflection of the well-established conservatism of the financial world.

■ The needs of the confidence game

If a friend were to offer you a choice between a £20 note and a piece of paper on which was written, 'I promise to pay £20 to the bearer of this note', which would you prefer? You may know your friend as a sterling and trustworthy person. But if you try to exchange the little chit at the hardware shop for a new garden hose, the assistants won't take it. Even if they also know your friend, they will be concerned about the shop's ability to pay its suppliers with the note. So, naturally, you would prefer the £20 note, because lifelong experience has taught you that the £20 note will be accepted by everyone as worth £20. You have a deeply held belief – and here is the key – *not* that the £20 note is valuable, but that everyone else will accept it as valuable. It doesn't really matter what *you* think about your money, you still know that you can spend it. You believe that everyone else believes that the money is valuable. What we are talking about here is *a belief about a belief.*

Matters of belief and social convention can be powerful and practically indestructible. History abounds in examples of people who have chosen torture and death rather than change their beliefs. We also recognize that someone can choose to continue believing something, even when faced with ample evidence to the contrary. So belief has a formidable presence in the human psyche.

A belief about a belief, however, is a different animal altogether. It is a fragile and ephemeral thing. Perhaps nothing can shake my belief, but my belief about your belief can be eviscerated by a rumour, a mere hunch, a feeling. Moreover, a chain of belief about a belief is only as strong as its weakest link. If I think that someone on the other side of the world has stopped believing in the Mexican peso, the Thai baht, or the Russian rouble, then I have to fear that his neighbours may stop believing. As a result the whole house of cards may fall down, as it did for Mexico in

December 1994, for Thailand in late 1997, or for Russia in August 1998.

In brief, the game of money, exactly like the Ancient Greek oracles, is a confidence game. Whenever the emperor has no clothes (i.e. whenever a 'crisis of confidence' looms), those in the know hope that no guileless child will make an improper remark. Under such circumstances, a façade of regal confidence, mystery, decorum, and ritual serves to ensure that a long and fragile chain of beliefs will hold.

■ Why money is not a thing

We should now dissipate a key illusion in the magic about money: money is not a thing.

From the smallest to the biggest

Not only did money vary in the nature of the objects used as its symbol, but also in its size. The smallest coins were probably the small denominations of coins from Lydia, the place which Herodotus credited for having invented 'modern' coinage around 687 BC. Their smallest denomination was struck in 0.006 ounces (one-fifteenth of the weight of a modern US penny) in electrum, a naturally occurring alloy of gold and silver.

The record for the heaviest currency is unquestionably the Yap island's money, in the Caroline Islands of the West Pacific. They are gigantic six-feet wide round slices of a special limestone, cut from a rock on islands 400 miles away. They are a 'macho' currency, used ceremonially by men, without moving them from the place were they rest. Yap women used more practical money in the form of strings of mussels.

Inhabitants of the Yap islanders with some of their 'small change'. Yap 'coins' are indeed often much bigger than human size, some of them reaching up to four meters in diameter.

For most of history, money has definitely appeared to be a thing, in fact, an incredible variety of things (see sidebar). Without even mentioning the most recently prevailing forms of money, such as paper, gold, silver or bronze, Glyn Davies created a full money alphabet with a small selection of objects that served as symbolic of value: amber, beads, cowries, drums, eggs, feathers, gongs, hoes, ivory, jade, kettles, leather, mats, nails, oxen, pigs, quartz, rice, salt, thimbles, umiaks, wampums, yarns and zappozats, which are decorated axes.[43]

Interestingly, a simple thought experiment can separate the aura of money from any or all these things. Let us assume that you are stranded alone on a deserted island. If, when you were left stranded, you had a *thing* in your pocket – say a knife – that knife will still be useful as a knife on your island.

Now, you may take with you a million dollars in money in this fantasy, and you may have it in any form you like: cash, a cashier's cheque, credit cards, gold bars, Swiss francs, even any of the forms of the above money alphabet that strike your fancy. Whatever form you choose, on your island that money changes into paper, plastic, metal or whatever else, but it has ceased to be money.

Events in recent decades have further made evident the non-material nature of money. In 1971, the United States ceased to define the value of the dollar in terms of gold. Since that time, the dollar has represented a promise from the US government to redeem the dollar with – another dollar. At least when the dollar was backed with gold, we could more easily believe it had some objective value. With the demise of the dollar-gold equivalency, such self-deception has become more difficult.

For another analogy of money and magic – no magician's routine is complete without a disappearing act. Money has been performing this feat in a rather spectacular way. Once upon a time, when money was mostly gold and silver coins, banks started issuing pieces of paper that stated where the metal was kept. The sentence 'I will pay the bearer the sum of one Pound Sterling' which adornes the Pound bill is still a reminder of the weight and silver content of the metal currency. The next step in the disappearing act is already well under way. The vast majority of our paper money has further dematerialized into binary bits in computers belonging to our bankers, brokers, or other financial institutions, and there is serious talk that all of it may soon join the virtual world. Should we wait until the last paper bill has disappeared into a cyber-purse to wake up to the true non-material nature of money?

■ A working definition of money

Our working definition of money can now be very straightforward:

Money is an agreement, within a community, to use something as a means of payment.

Each one of these terms is essential in this definition. Seen as an *agreement*, money has much in common with other social contracts, such as political parties, nationality or marriage. These constructs are real, even if they exist only in people's minds. The money agreement can be attained formally or informally, freely or coerced, consciously or unconsciously. Later in this chapter, you will learn about the terms of our contemporary money agreement.

Money as an agreement is always valid only within a given *community*. Some currencies are operational only among a small group of friends (like tokens used in card games), for certain time periods (like the cigarette medium of exchange among frontline soldiers during World War II), or among the citizens of one particular nation (like most 'normal' national currencies today). Such a community can be the entire global community (as is the case of the US dollar by treaty, as long as it is accepted as reserve currency), or a geographically disparate group (such as Internet participants).

Finally, the key function that transforms the chosen object into a currency is its role *as means of payment*. Notice that the words 'means of payment' are used instead of the more traditional 'medium of exchange' (see sidebar). The nuance is useful to be able to include transactions which have ritual or customary purposes, instead of just commercial exchanges. After all, it is only in Western culture that total priority has been given to commercial exchanges, neglecting the other purposes for payments.

Means of payment vs. medium of exchange

Jonathan Williams, curator of the Department of Coins and Medals in the British Museum, makes the point 'it is arguable that Western culture and its money systems, far from being "normal", are actually an historical anomaly in their fixation on the commercial. If this is right, it would be an even greater mistake for Westerners to interpret other monetary systems as a more primitive version of their own.'

He gives the example of the use of cloth currency among the Lele in Congo until the middle of the 20th century. Payments in specific cloths woven in raffia were supposed to be made to reinforce or heal social ties among the Lele, for instance as payment for initiation fees into religious groups, marriage dues, rewards to wives for childbirths, compensation for fighting or wounds inflicted on others, or as tribute to chiefs. In addition, the same cloth currency could be used as payment for goods, but this medium of exchange function was considered marginal compared to the other social uses.[44]

There are also other functions that today's money tends to perform, such as unit of account, store of value, tool for speculation, and so on.[45] However, for the purposes of this book these functions are comparatively secondary, considering that there have been perfectly effective currencies that did not perform some or all of these other roles.

In summary, the 'magic' of money is bestowed on some 'thing' as soon as a community agrees on using it as a means of payment.

■ The origin of money's power

Besides magic, we also endow money with power. As Marcel Proust observed, 'Material objects have in themselves no power, but, since it is our practice to bestow power upon them...'[46] James Buchan eloquently described our rationale for doing so: 'The difference between a word and a piece of money is that money has always and will always symbolize different things to different people: a banknote may describe to one person a drink in a pub, a fairground ride to another, to a third a diamond ring, an act of charity to a fourth, relief from prosecution to a fifth and, to a sixth, simply the sensation of comfort or security. *For money is frozen desire* . . . . That process of wish and imagination, launched or completed a million times every second, is the engine of our civilization . . . For the objects of human desire are limitless, or rather limited only by the imagination, which amounts to the same thing.'[47]

■ Money shifts and power shifts

Money is, therefore, much more than a technical issue. Whenever a currency is accepted within a community, it makes an implicit statement about power in that community. So when priests or priestesses were in power, temples issued money. When kings dominated, Aristotle attributed to them personally the 'Sovereign right to issue currency'. In the Industrial Age nation-states became the paragon of power, so national currencies automatically became dominant.

Now that power is starting to shift away from the nation-states, it should not come as a surprise that new non-national currencies are emerging. Some people still assume that there is only one kind of money possible in the modern world – the familiar national currency, in the form of bills and coins.

The first magician's trick concerning money is to make us believe that we need the magician's help to create money. This is definitely not the case, unless we choose to take sleight of hand for reality. Different kinds of money have co-existed in the past, and do so now as well.

Frequent-flyer miles or Internet money are just early examples of corporate scrip that we should expect during an Information Age. Other examples will be given in the next chapter.

Before we explore these new, less familiar currencies, we need a firm basis from which to compare them with the key characteristics common to all our familiar national currencies and the social effects they tend to generate.

■ Today's money

All money systems serve to facilitate exchanges among people. Whenever a specific financial system is designed, the remarkable motivating power of money is invariably used to load the system with a host of other objectives – sometimes conscious, often unconscious – from the prestige of the gods or the ruler, to collective socio-economic motivations.

The main characteristics of today's system were pieced together in pre-Victorian England, just in time to trigger the Industrial Revolution. Its legacy – the money system that prevails today – looks as if its designers had asked: how can we create a money system that reinforces our nation-state, and concentrates resources to enable systematic and competitive heavy industrial development?

Even if its designers never asked such a question, the system has proved remarkably successful in meeting these objectives. Every country in the world, regardless of its level of development or its political orientation, has bought into this pre-Victorian construct. Even Communist countries have reproduced all its key features, except that banks became state-owned rather than private, which in practice did not prove beneficial.

■ Four key design features

All Industrial Age currencies have four key characteristics in common, which gradually came to be considered as self-evident for the first time in England between the 17th and early 18th centuries. It's not as if some conspiratorial group of Englishmen gathered in a dark, smoked-filled room to dream up the current money system. What happened instead was a slow and gradual evolution of payment and banking habits. This was accompanied by dramatic changes in personal insights and collective crises – such as the need to finance wars, or the political reactions to the South Sea Bubble of the 1720s. Such a combination of more or less conscious choices by the many and the few shaped a money system remarkably in tune with the pre-Victorian English *Zeitgeist*,[48] the priorities and mindset of an island country poised to carve out its empire in the world.

Many aspects of the modern money system can be traced back to the customs of medieval goldsmith money lending, or to Renaissance banks from Tuscany and Lombardy. But several of these hallowed traditions were dropped and replaced with brand new ones whenever they did not fit with the *Zeitgeist* of pre-Victorian England. For instance, charging interest on money – which had been prohibited on both moral and legal grounds for more than 20 centuries – suddenly became a normal and accepted practice.

While payment and banking technologies (i.e., *how* we do things) have continued to dramatically change and improve, the fundamental objectives pursued by the system (i.e., *why* we do them) seem not to have been seriously revisited since Victorian England. From the perspective of the objectives pursued by the money system, we are still living with what propelled us so effectively into and through the Industrial Revolution.

Four key features still characterize our 'normal' money systems and remain basically unquestioned: Money is typically geographically attached to a (1) nation-state. It is (2) 'fiat' money, i.e. created out of nothing, by (3) bank debt, against payment of (4) interest.

Perhaps this sounds obvious, even trivial, but the full implications of each one of these features are much less clear. When we question these assumptions, we can sometimes discover a wealth of new insights. Let us take a brief look at each one of them.

National currencies

We now have trouble imagining any currency other than those issued by a given country, or in the case of the euro, a group of countries. However, it is useful to remember that the concept of a nation-state itself is only a couple of centuries old.[49] Therefore, the vast majority of historical currencies were, in fact, private issues made by the sovereign or some other local authority.

However, if you want to create a national consciousness, the creation of a national currency is one of the more powerful tools available. It makes evident in everyday life the boundaries that are otherwise visible only in an atlas. In a recent example, during the break-up of the Soviet Union, one of the first acts of the newly independent republics was to issue their own currencies. 'A common currency translates into a common information system, so that its inputs and outputs can be measured and compared across the parts.'[50] Sharing a common currency creates an invisible, yet very effective, bond between all sectors of a society, and draws an information boundary between 'us' and 'them'. Similarly, the euro – the single currency that, as of January 1999, officially replaced national currencies in 11 European countries – has as one of its goals the creation of a more unified European consciousness.

The ubiquity of national currencies should not make us forget that during the few recent centuries when national currencies were issued, there was always another transnational currency available for global trade, namely gold. The only exception to this rule has been in the past twenty-five years or so, when one particular national currency – the US dollar – has become the global currency. This arrangement has serious negative consequences for all participants, including the US.

Lastly, emerging global non-geographic communities, such as the Internet, foretell significant changes in the transnational currency realm, which will be addressed later (Chapters 3 and 7).

'Fiat' money

The simple question 'Where does money come from?' propels us back into the world of magic. Not only does money perform the act of disappearing and reappearing, it is also, quite literally, created out of nothing. To understand this process fully, we need to look beyond appearances. At first sight, national currencies appear to be created on the printing presses of central banks or, in the case of the US, the Department of the Treasury. But this is not where money is created. The rabbit that appears to come out of the magician's hat is not really coming from the hat, either. If we want to know where the rabbit comes from, we need to track its path through the magician's sleeve.

If you want £100 in cash, what do you do? You go to your bank teller and ask for £100. He or she (or now with ATMs, 'it') will look up your account balance. If there is more than £100 in your account, that amount will be debited and you will be given the cash. If your balance is not large enough, you will get an apologetic smile or some other message, but not the money.

Your money is really what is in your account, because the familiar physical notes will be given to you on demand as long as there is a positive balance on your account. Similarly, the central bank will deliver to your bank as many notes as it wants, but it will debit the bank's account for the corresponding amount.

So how does the money appear in your bank account? Most of the time, it is there because you deposited your paycheque or some other form of income. But where does your employer get this money? To play on Truman's famous line: Where does each buck ultimately start?

Bank Debt

The origin of money as explained in the Primer may be surprising to some (see pages 304-306). Every dollar, pound, euro or any other national currency in circulation started as a bank loan. For instance, when you qualify for a £100,000 mortgage to buy a house, the bank enters a credit into your account and literally creates the £100,000 out of nothing. That is the moment when money is really born. Of course, these bank loans are typically secured by an asset such as a house, a car, a corporate guarantee, etc. Once you have the credit, you can draw the cheque to pay the seller of the house, who in turn deposits it in his bank account, and the money starts flowing infinitely through the system until someone reimburses a loan, at which point the money is destroyed, disappearing back into the void where it originated (see sidebar).

The void at the centre

The American author Ayn Rand asks the question: 'So you think that money is the root of all evil. Have you ever asked what is the root of all money?'

One of the main differences between Eastern and Western philosophies is that in the East the void is explicitly placed at the origin of everything, while in the West there is always a God, a *Logos* (word), a *Monad* (the One), some originating and organizing principle.

In fact, in the West the void has been hidden at the centre of our money system. Is this one of the reasons for its mesmerizing power?

This is why paper money is really 'the part of the national debt on which no interest is paid', as summarized by the Radcliffe Commission.[51] This simple process of creating money is dubbed with the appropriately fancy technical Latin name *fiat* money. *Fiat Lux* were the first words that God pronounced, according to Genesis: 'Let light be.' The next sentence is, 'And light was, and He saw it was good.' We are dealing with the truly godlike function of creating something out of nothing (*ex nihilo*) by the power of the word.

Little wonder that you may feel intimidated by your banker the next time you respectfully ask for a loan! Just as the magician needs a handkerchief to wave above the hat before the rabbit can appear, the banker has an additional veil. In the process of creating money, your attention will be drawn towards the boring technical aspects, such as mechanisms to foster competition among banks for deposits, reserve requirements, and the role of the central bank in fine-tuning the valves of the system.[52] While these technical features all have a perfectly valid purpose (so does the handkerchief), they all simply regulate how much fiat money each bank can create (the number of rabbits that can be pulled out of which hat).

What is particularly inventive about this scheme, that goes back to pre-Victorian England, is its ability to enable societies to solve the apparent contradiction between two objectives: creating and reinforcing the nation-state, while, at the same time, relying on private initiatives and competition among them. Specifically, it provides a smooth way to privatize the creation of the national currency (theoretically, a public function) as a privilege of the overall banking system, while still maintaining a competitive pressure between banks to obtain deposits from clients.

There is also one very important built-in aspect of bank-debt 'fiat' money systems. Jackson and McConnell have summarized it in a few words: 'Debt-money derives its value from its scarcity relative to its usefulness.'[53] In other words, for a bank-debt-based fiat currency system to function at all, scarcity has to be artificially and systematically introduced and maintained. This is one of the reasons why today's currency system is not self-regulating, but requires the active role of central banks to maintain that scarcity. One can even say that central banks compete with each other to keep their currency internationally scarce. This serves to maintain their relative value and scarcity as well.

We will see later that there also exist other types of currencies called 'mutual credit systems', which are more self-regulating than national currencies, and the value of which is maintained by the backing of goods and services they represent within the communities that accept them. These currencies can afford to be available in sufficiency, as opposed to requiring artificial scarcity.[54]

Usury and religions

Technically in Judaism, usury was only prohibited among Jews. 'Unto thy brother thou shalt not lend upon usury, that the Lord thy God may bless thee in all that thou settest thine hands to.' (Deuteronomy 23:20). This enabled Jews to lend with interest to non-Jews. This practice became one of the reasons for their unpopularity in the Middle Ages. Islam is more encompassing in its condemnation: 'What ye put out at usury to increase it with the substance of others, shall have no increase from God.' (Koran Sura 30:38). Given that the modern world evolution occurred mostly under Christian influence, it is this religion's change of direction over time that is really most relevant for our purposes. The historical importance of usury in the teachings of the Christian church can only be compared with today's emphasis on sexual sins and abortion. It was definitely one of the most persistent dogmas of the church. One of the earliest church fathers, Clement of Alexandria, specified, 'the law prohibits a brother from taking usury; designating as a brother not only him who is born of these same parents, but also one of the same race and sentiments . . . Do not regard this command as marked by philanthropy.'

The litany of councils specifically condemning this practice as one of the most despicable sins is really impressive: the Council of Elvira (AD 305-306), Arles (314), Nice (325), Cartage (348), Taragona (516), Aix-la-Chapelle (789), Paris (829), Tours (1153), the Lateran Council (1179), Lyons (1274), Vienna (1311). This last one was even more sweeping than the previous ones; any ruler who would not criminally punish anybody committing usury in his realm would be excommunicated (even if the ruler himself did not do it!). Since the practice was often concealed beneath various devices, money lenders were compelled to show their accounts to the ecclesiastical authorities. The fifth Lateran Council (1512-1517) reiterated the definition of the sin of usury as 'receiving any interest on money' once again.

Henry VIII legalized interest for the first time in the Western World in 1545, after he had broken ranks with the Pope. The first time that the original doctrine was questioned within the Catholic church itself was in 1822. A woman from Lyons, France, had received interest on money and was refused absolution unless she returned the ill-gotten gains. Bishop Rhedon requested a clarification from Rome, which responded, 'Let the petitioner be informed that a reply will be given her question when the proper time comes; . . . meanwhile she may receive sacramental absolution, if she is fully prepared to submit to the instructions of the Holy See.' A forthcoming resolution was promised again in 1830, and from the Office of Propaganda in 1873. This promised clarification never came. The sin of usury was never officially repealed, but was simply forgotten. The Canon Law of 1917 (Canon #1543), still operational today, makes it obligatory for bishops to invest, 'As the administrators are bound to fulfil their office with the solicitude of a good father of a family, they shall invest the surplus revenue of the church to the benefit of the church.' The issue of interest is not mentioned. Later still, usury is redefined as the charging of *excessive* interest.

Estelle and Mario Carota, two Mexican Catholics, in the hope of providing relief to Latin American countries when they were reeling under the debt crisis of the 1980s, made a formal request in 1985 to the Vatican to clarify its position on usury. They were informed by no less an authority than the Office of the Congregation for the Doctrine of the Faith, headed by Cardinal Ratzinger, that there had never been a new definition of the doctrine of usury, that there has never been any change. Their attempts at finding an expert opinion among the Jesuits, Augustinians, Dominicans, Salvatorians, and even professors of moral theology in Third World seminaries teaching theology of economic justice failed to turn up anybody who remembered the forgotten Doctrine of Usury.

This medieval painting gives a graphic idea of the extraordinary emphasis that used to be placed on condemning interest on money, something which has now become accepted as an 'obvious' feature of today's money.

The painting illustrates the traditional biblical Adam and Eve story with the snake coiled around the Tree of Knowledge. What is less usual is that the branches of the tree form the cardinal sins, represented as fearsome devils and commented by a Latin scroll describing each sin in lurid detail. What is most remarkable, however, is the text on the scroll commenting the tree trunk itself: the single word "Usuria" ("usury"). This graphically makes the point that usury was considered the most important sin of all . . . (Kreuzgang am Dom, 15th century, Brixen, Südtirol. Photo: S. Wessel).

Interest

The last obvious characteristic common to all official national currencies is interest. Here again, we believe that interest on money is somehow intrinsic to the process, forgetting that for most of history that was definitely not the case. In fact, all three 'religions of the Book' (Judaism, Christianity and Islam) emphatically outlawed usury, defined as *any* interest on money. Only Islamic religious leaders still remind anyone of this rule today. It is sometimes forgotten that the Catholic church, for instance, remained prominently in battle against the 'sin of usury' until the 19th century (see sidebar).

■ The effects of interest

The full implications of applying interest on the loans creating money are the least understood of the four characteristics. Nevertheless, the effects of interest on society are pervasive and powerful. They therefore warrant more detailed examination. The way interest is built into the money system has three consequences. These are:

1 Interest indirectly encourages systematic competition among the participants in the system.

2 Interest continually fuels the need for endless economic growth, even when actual standards of living remain stagnant.

3 Interest concentrates wealth by taxing the vast majority in favour of a small minority.

Each of these issues will be addressed in turn.

1 Encouraging Competition

The story from Australia (see box) illustrates the way interest is woven into our money fabric, and how it stimulates competition among the users of this currency.

The eleventh round

Once upon a time, in a small village in the Outback, people used barter for all their transactions. On every market day, people walked around with chickens, eggs, hams and breads, and engaged in prolonged negotiations among themselves to exchange what they needed. At key periods of the year, like harvests or whenever someone's barn needed big repairs after a storm, people recalled the tradition of helping each other out that they had brought from the old country. They knew that if they had a problem some day, others would aid them in return.

One market day, a stranger with shiny black shoes and an elegant white hat came by and observed the whole process with a sardonic smile. When he saw one farmer running around to corral the six chickens he wanted to exchange for a big ham, he could not refrain from laughing. 'Poor people,' he said, 'so primitive.' The farmer's wife overheard him and challenged the stranger, 'Do you think you can do a better job handling chickens?' 'Chickens, no,' responded the stranger. 'But there is a much better way to eliminate all that hassle.' 'Oh yes, how so?' asked the woman. 'See that tree there?' the stranger replied. 'Well, I will go wait there for one of you to bring me one large cowhide. Then have every family visit me. I'll explain the better way.'

And so it happened. He took the cowhide, and cut perfect leather rounds in it, and put an elaborate and graceful little stamp on each round. Then he gave to each family ten rounds, and explained that each represented the value of one chicken. 'Now you can trade and bargain with the rounds instead of the unwieldy chickens,' he explained.

It made sense. Everybody was impressed with the man with the shiny shoes and inspiring hat.

'Oh, by the way,' he added after every family had received their ten rounds, 'in a year's time, I will come back and sit under that same tree. I want you to each bring me back *11* rounds. That 11th round is a token of appreciation for the technological improvement I just made possible in your lives.' 'But where will the 11th round come from?' asked the farmer with the six chickens. 'You'll see,' said the man with a reassuring smile.

★★★

Assuming that the population and its annual production remain exactly the same during that next year, what do you think had to happen? Remember, that 11th round was never created. Therefore, bottom line, one of each 11 families will have to lose all its rounds, even if everybody managed their affairs well, in order to provide the 11th round to ten others.

So when a storm threatened the crop of one of the families, people became less generous with their time to help bring it in before disaster struck. While it was much more convenient to exchange the rounds instead of the chickens on market days, the new game also had the unintended side effect of actively discouraging the spontaneous cooperation that was traditional in the village. Instead, the new money game was generating a systemic undertow of competition among all the participants.

This is how today's money system pits the participants in the economy against each other. This story isolates the role of interest – the eleventh round – as part of the money creation process, and its impact on the participants.[55]

When the bank creates money by providing you with your £100,000 mortgage loan, it creates only the principal when it credits your account. However, it expects you to bring back £200,000 over the next twenty years or so. If you don't, you will lose your house. Your bank does not create the interest; it sends you out into the world to battle against everyone else to bring back the second £100,000. Because all the other banks do exactly the same thing, the system requires that some participants go bankrupt in order to provide you with this £100,000. To put it simply, when you pay back interest on your loan, you are using up someone else's principal.

In other words, the device used to create the scarcity indispensable for a bank-debt system to function involves having people compete for the money that has not been created, and penalizes them with bankruptcy whenever they do not succeed.

The interest rate decisions of central banks get our attention, and this is one of the reasons. The additional cost of increased interest results automatically in a proportional number of increased bankruptcies in the near future. This takes us back to the time when the high priests had to decide whether the gods would be satisfied with the sacrifice of only a goat – or require the sacrifice of the first-born son instead. Lower down on the totem pole, when your bank checks on your creditworthiness, it is really verifying whether you are capable of competing and winning against the other players, i.e., managing to wrestle out of them something that was never created.

In summary, the current monetary system obliges us to incur debt collectively, and to compete with others in the community, just to obtain the means to perform exchanges between us. No wonder 'it is a tough world out there', and that Darwin's observation of the 'survival of the fittest' was so readily accepted as self-evident truth by the 18th century English, as well as by any societies that have accepted, without question, the premises of the money system that they designed, such as we have today. Fortunately, we now have ample evidence that supports less harsh interpretations of the 'natural world' (see sidebar).

What is 'natural' – competition or cooperation?

Professor of bio-sociology Imanishi from Kyoto University has shown that the Darwinian vision of nature as a struggle for life has been completely blind to the many more frequent cases of co-evolution, symbiosis, joint development, and harmonious coexistence that prevail in all domains of evolution. Even our own bodies would not be able to survive long without the symbiotic collaboration of billions of micro-organisms in our digestive tract, for example.[56]

Evolutionary biologist Elisabet Sahtouris points out that predominantly competitive behaviour is a characteristic of a young species during its first forays in the world. In contrast, in mature systems like an old-growth forest, the competition for light, for instance, is balanced by intense cooperation among species. Species that do not learn to cooperate with the other species with which they are codependent invariably disappear.[57]

Our current money system is biased towards competition. Hence the need for complementary currency systems (described later) that would balance this bias by rewarding cooperation.

2   Need for endless growth

The main simplifying assumption of the 'eleventh round' is that everything remains the same until next year. In reality, we do not live in a world of zero growth of population, output or money supply. In the real world, there is typically some growth over time in all these variables, and the money system just preempts the first component of that growth to pay for the interest. Even in this respect, there are long-forgotten religious precedents for this process. The 'first fruit of the harvest' was ritually sacrificed as an offer to the gods in many ancient societies.

This dynamic also makes it much harder than in our Eleventh Round story to notice what is actually going on. Nevertheless, indefinitely compounded interest in the material world is a mathematical impossibility (see sidebar).

The 'Josefpfennig' or the impossible mathematics of compounded interest

Indefinitely compounded interest in the real world is a mathematical impossibility. For example, one pfennig invested by Josef at the birth of Christ at 4% compounded interest would have grown by the year 1749 to the value of one ball of gold of the weight of the earth. By 1990 it would have grown further to the value of 8,190 balls of gold of the weight of the earth. At 5%, by 1990 it would buy an incredible 134 billion balls of gold of the weight of planet earth![58]

In this dynamic view, the money system is like a treadmill that requires continuous economic growth, even if the real standard of living remains stagnant. The rate of interest fixes the average level of growth that is needed to remain at the same place. This need for perpetual growth is another fact of life that we tend to take for granted in modern societies, and that we usually do not associate with either interest or even our money system.

3   Concentration of wealth effect

A third systematic effect of interest on society is its continuous transfer of wealth from the vast majority to a small minority. The wealthiest people and organizations own most interest-bearing assets. They receive an uninterrupted rent from whoever needs to borrow in order to obtain the necessary medium of exchange. The best study on the transfer of wealth via interest from one social group to another was performed in Germany during the year 1982, when interest rates were at 5.5%.[59] All Germans were grouped in ten income categories of about 2.5 million households each. During that one year, transfers between these ten groups involved a gross total of DM 270 billion in interest payments received and paid. A stark way for presenting the process is to graph the net effect in the form of the net interest transfers (interest gained minus interest paid) for each of these 10 household categories (see Fig 2.1)

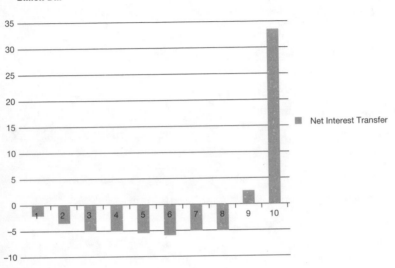

Billion DM

Net Interest Transfer

Figure 2.1 Net interest transferred (billion DM) for 10 groups of households of 2.5 million each (Germany – 1982)

The highest interest transfers occurred from the middle class (categories 3 to 8) which each transferred about DM 5 billion to the top 10% of the households (category 10). Even the lowest income households transferred DM 1.8 billion in interest per year to the highest group. The net effect is that the top 10% of households received a net transfer of DM 34.2 billion in interest from the rest of the society during that one year.

This graph clearly shows the systematic transfer of wealth from the bottom 80% of the population to the top 10%. This transfer was due exclusively to the monetary system in use, and is completely independent of the degree of cleverness or industriousness of the participants – the classic argument to justify large differences in income.

Financial wealth, by definition, is the accumulation of income over time. The final outcome is an accentuation of the imbalances in wealth distribution. For instance, 'the top 1% of Americans has now more personal wealth than the bottom 92% combined.'[60] This process of concentration keeps occurring on all levels. The assets of the tiny group of the top 500 families in the US rose from $2.5 to $5 trillion between 1983 and 1989.[61]

Globally, the world's 447 billionaires have agglomerated financial assets greater than the combined annual income of over half of the world's population.[62] The top three billionaires own now more wealth than the combined GDPs of 48 poorest countries in the world.[63]

Was it a concern for social justice and stability that previously motivated all three major religions – Judaism, Christianity, and Islam – unanimously to prohibit the practice of charging interest? It is intriguing that after interest became officially legal, almost all countries have felt the need to create income redistribution schemes to counteract at least part of this process. Some of them, such as the welfare system and progressive taxation, are increasingly being criticized for their ineffectiveness. Is this the fault of the overly efficient money system, or of the inefficient redistribution schemes? Or both?

■ What next?

The three side effects of interest – competition, the need for perpetual growth and wealth concentration – are the hidden engines that have propelled us into and through the Industrial Revolution. Both the best and the worst of what the Modern Age has achieved can, therefore, be indirectly attributed to these hidden effects of interest – the apparently banal feature of our officially prevailing money system.

There is a growing consensus that the Industrial Age is dying. We have begun navigating the uncharted waters of the Information Age. Curiously, unnoticed by mainstream media and academia, new monetary experiments have already started to thrive in a dozen countries around the world. My view is that these innovations offer realistic possibilities for gradually correcting the excesses and imbalances of the current system without revolutions or violence. Even more important, these new complementary currencies, operating in conjunction with the dominant national money system, create new wealth, both financial and social. It is no coincidence that these new currencies typically do not share any of the four obvious characteristics of the national currencies described above. For instance, they specifically do not involve interest.

It is worth remembering what John F. Kennedy remarked: 'Those who make peaceful revolution impossible will make violent revolution inevitable.'

CHAPTER 3

Cybersphere – The New Money Frontier

■ *'Money has evolved from shells to green paper to the artful arrangement of binary digits.'*

DEE HOCK, CHAIRMAN, VISA, 1968[64]

■ *'The real voyage of discovery consists not in seeking new landscapes, but in having new eyes.'*

MARCEL PROUST

■ *'Confusion is the word we invented to refer to an order we don't yet understand.'*

HENRY MILLER

In less than two decades, what Daniel Bell originally called the Post-Industrial Society is now commonly referred to as the Information, Knowledge or Communications Age. As information becomes our critical resource, there are sweeping implications not only for our economy, but also for the very fabric of our society.

We saw that our oldest information systems are money systems (chapter 1) – remember, even writing was initially invented to record financial transactions. So it is no surprise that money is again in the forefront in computerized cyberspace.

We can expect fundamental changes not only in payment systems for conventional currencies, but also the emergence of new *types* of money.

■ Post-Industrial Society=Knowledge Age

In the 1940s, IBM's first Chairman, Thomas Watson, predicted a world market for 'maybe five computers'. By 1975, about 50,000 were operating, and in 1997 more than 140 million.[65] By 1999, there are an additional 600 million computers-on-a-card currently in use worldwide,[66] as well as the innumerable 'invisible computers' that are built into routine appliances – a typical car today contains more computer-processing power than the first spacecraft that landed on the moon in 1969.

The reason for this explosive proliferation is simple: never before has the world seen such a dizzying drop in the price of an industrial product. We have become used to the idea that today's £1,000 laptop packs more power than the £10 million mainframe of 20 years ago. If car efficiency and costs had followed the same trend, you would now drive from Lisbon to Oslo and back to London via Athens on a fraction of a drop of petrol in a car costing less than £1.

When steam power was introduced, it was not much cheaper than water power, and it took from 1790 to 1850 for its real price to be cut in half.[67] Likewise, it took between 1890 and 1930 for the price of electricity to drop by just over half.[68] In contrast, the cost of computing power halves every 18 months. Named after the President of Intel, 'Moore's law' actually describes an even more impressive rate: every 18 months, computational speed doubles *and* the price drops by half.

Just one facet of it – the Internet – is the topic of an estimated 12,000 articles *per month* in the US press alone, and this does not even include what is written about the Internet on the Internet. Never before has any technological shift been heralded by such an information avalanche. George Gilder calls it 'the biggest technological juggernaut that ever rolled'. Bill Gates claims that 'the benefits and problems arising from the Internet Revolution will be much greater than those brought about by the PC revolution'. It is worth repeating that what drives the change are the gigantic falls in costs and speed not only in computer chips but also in communications in general (see sidebar).

Comparing communication costs

- Sending a 42-page document from New York to Tokyo normally takes five days by airmail and costs $7.40.
- You can get it there faster, but at a much higher cost: a courier delivers it in 24 hours for $26.25; or with a fax-machine in 31 minutes for $28.85.
- Compare all that with the e-mail alternative of two minutes and a cost of 9.5 cents. No wonder Internet traffic *doubles every 100 days*! If you read this text at the end

2000, during the time you finished reading this sentence, forty million e-mails would have been sent.

■ In 1980, telephone copper wires could carry one page of information per second. Today, one thin strand of optical fibre can transmit 90,000 volumes in one second. The drop in communication costs will further accelerate as the available bandwidth grows.

■ High-capacity, high-speed transmission networks are in the process of creating a 'Broadband Kingdom' where it will be cost-effective to leave the Internet 'always on' at work and/or home. Various technologies compete with fibre optics to create this world, including high-speed data delivery systems via television cable distribution, digital subscriber line technologies (DSL) which enable dramatic speed increases on traditional copper telephone wires, satellite operators, and wireless networks. All this competition means that the cost of data communications will continue to drop dramatically in the foreseeable future.[69]

Although scepticism is healthy when we are faced with so much hype, this Revolution could yet prove to be a real one.

Whole libraries are being written about the gee-whiz technologies involved. The focus here will be only on the meaning of this Information Revolution and the opportunity it represents for choosing our money systems in the near future.

To help us navigate this material, this chapter is organized under the following five headings:

- The nature of information
- Implications for the economy and society
- Implications for money
- Implications for banks and financial institutions
- Wisdom in the information age?

■ The nature of information

The power structure of every economic system has been designed to control some critical resource. Information, the raw material for creating knowledge, is the next likely candidate for that role. 'As far into the future as we can see, information will be playing the *prima donna* role in economic history that physical labour, stone, bronze, land, minerals, metals and energy once played.'[70]

As information becomes that key resource, its unique features will shape a very different society. For our purposes, Harlan Cleveland[71] and Howard Rheingold[72] have made the best inventories of those characteristics:[73, 74]

■ Information is shared, not exchanged. With any of the previous focus resources – from a flint spear-point to land, from a horse to a barrel of oil – if you acquired it from me, I lost it to you. After an exchange that involves information, both of us have it. In buying this book, for instance, or a magazine or permission to access a database, it may look as if a traditional exchange has occurred. However, what is bought, sold, and then owned, is the delivery mechanism, not the information. Even after it has been shared with the buyer, the message delivered is still retained by the seller. When you use software, you are not stopping millions of others from using it also, as was the case with the key resources of the past. As a consequence, information is what economists call a 'non-rival' product.

■ The most powerful catalyst of the transformation is not information but the communications revolution. Over the past decade, the total electronic communications worldwide have increased by a factor of four. However, during the *next* decade, we should expect another multiplication, this time by a factor of 45![75] Communicating information literally multiplies its power. Telecommunications has made information transportable. It travels through electronic networks at almost the speed of light and for a very low cost. The nature of information, therefore, is that it tends to leak. The more it leaks, the more of it we have, and the more of us have it. Government classifications, trade secrecy, intellectual property rights, and confidentiality are all attempts at artificially reducing this natural tendency to leak. Increasingly, these artificial attempts are failing because the actual information cannot be 'owned', but only the conduits of its delivery system. Although he admits to still searching for a patent lawyer willing to agree with him, Cleveland sees 'the expression "intellectual property" as an oxymoron, a contradiction in terms'.[76]

■ As a consequence of the two points above, information expands as it is used. Information spontaneously tends towards abundance, not scarcity. In one way, this is fast becoming a drawback: we all complain about information overload. What remains scarce and competitive is human attention, and our ability to understand, turn into knowledge, and use all the information available to us.

■ As an ideal possibility, conventional economic textbooks describe the theory of 'perfect competition'. This theory works from the assumption that all parties have all the information relevant to optimize a given purchase, that there are zero transaction costs and no barriers to entry for new suppliers. In 'real' world transactions, these conditions are rarely met. Interestingly, the cyber economy could become the first actual large-scale 'near-perfect market'. Information can definitely be more abundant and accessible to more people in cyberspace. The Net makes transaction costs lower than ever. And many of the usual barriers to entry, such as location, capital requirements, etc., are less applicable. Because comparison-shopping is so easy on the Net, it promises to be a fiercely price-sensitive market. Even so, the emerging market environment of the Information Age seems to conform perfectly to conventional economic theory.

■ In other important respects, information economics sets traditional economic theory completely on its head. One breakthrough is the realization that information and knowledge are the only factors of production not subject to the law of diminishing returns.[77] They enjoy a law of increasing returns.[78] In practice, this means that as information becomes more available, it also becomes more valuable. This has also been called the 'fax effect'. Imagine that you have bought the first fax machine ever produced. What is the value to you of that device? Practically nil, because there is no one else with whom to communicate at that point. However, every newly installed fax machine increases the value of your fax machine. This is an exact reversal of traditional economics, where scarcity determines value. For instance, gold or diamonds, land or any other traditional commodities are valuable because they are scarce.

■ Implications for the economy and society

What are the consequences of these characteristics for a society that uses information as its primary economic resource? First, such an economy is literally dematerializing. In 1996, Alan Greenspan noted: 'The US output today, if measured in tons, is the same as one hundred years ago, yet the GDP[79] has multiplied by a factor of twenty over that time.' The average weight of one real dollar's worth of US exports is now less than half of what it was in 1970. Even in 'manufactured' goods, 75% of the value now consists of the services embedded in it: research, design, sales, advertising, most of which could be 'delocated' anywhere in the world and transmitted via high-speed data lines. Along with the other factors, this dematerialization process makes it much harder for governments or regulatory agencies to measure, tax or regulate what is going on. For instance, the French government will find it more difficult to keep US media products out of France using import controls when these products can be channelled through satellite TV or the Internet. The switch to information-as-resource means that governments are less able to intervene in (or muck up, depending on your viewpoint) the high-speed train of social transformation that is headed our way.

■ The positive forces

Harlan Cleveland states most succinctly the positive implications:

'A society suddenly rich in information is not necessarily fairer or more exploitative, cleaner or dirtier, happier or unhappier than its industrial or agricultural predecessors. The quality, accuracy, relevance, and utility of information are not givens. They depend on who uses this new dominant resource, how astutely, for what purposes. What *is* different is that information is, in all sorts of ways, more *accessible* to more people than the world's key resources have ever been before. It was in the nature of *things* that the few had access to key resources and the many did not. The inherent characteristics of physical resources (natural and human-made) made possible the development of hierarchies of *power based on control* (of new weapons, of energy resources, of transport vehicles, of trade routes, of markets, and especially of knowledge); hierarchies of *influence based on secrecy;* hierarchies of *class based on ownership;* hierarchies of *privilege based on early access* to particular pieces of land or especially valuable resources; and hierarchies of *politics based on geography*.

' . . . Each of these five bases for hierarchy and discrimination is crumbling today because the old means of control are of dwindling efficacy. Secrets are harder and harder to keep, and ownership, early arrival, and geography are of declining significance in accessing, analysing and using knowledge and wisdom that are the really valuable legal tender of our time.

' . . . In the agricultural era, poverty and discrimination were explained and justified by the shortage of arable land. Women and strangers could hardly be expected to share in so scarce a resource. [. . .] In the industrial era, poverty was explained and justified by shortages of things: there just weren't enough minerals, food, fiber and manufactures to go around.

' . . . Theoretically at least, compared to things as resource, information-as-resource should encourage:

■ The spreading of benefits rather than the concentration of wealth (information can be more readily shared than petroleum, gold or even water)

■ The maximization of choice rather than the suppression of diversity (the informed are harder to regiment than the uninformed).'[80]

■ The negative forces

Paradoxically, the dynamics of information economics could also create an unprecedented concentration of power in the hands of a very few Information Age billionaires; business barons who bear scant resemblance to those who created wealth during the Industrial Age. Some people foresee the spread of a 'Winner-Takes-All' economic environment.[81] The trend towards increasingly exorbitant compensation for the very few at the top has been notorious. It started with movie stars, entertainment and sports heroes, and spread over the past decade to high-performance CEOs, traders, lawyers and doctors. Is this just a strange shift in societal values, or is this *also* a consequence of deep-seated forces in the information economy?

The 'network economist' Brian Arthur claims that positive marginal rates of return can propel some corporations into an almost impregnable monopoly. For instance, once a particular software moves towards becoming an industry standard, it will tend automatically to crowd out competitors until it captures 100% of the market. Microsoft's dominance in the PC software market is often cited as an example of this process in action. Are we inaugurating an era where *de facto* monopolies can emerge more easily than in the traditional Industrial economies? Have anti-trust laws designed for the Industrial Age become ineffective in cyberspace? Or are these compensation flare-ups and new types of monopolies just a last gasp of the transition from the Industrial Age? This is something like what happened to skilled weavers at the beginning of the industrialization process: their incomes soared after spinning was mechanized, only to crash when new machines replaced their own skills later on. This is what MIT economist Paul Krugman claims is going to happen. Take the case of high-priced actors: Mirage Entertainment Sciences describes itself as the first 'Posthuman Talent Agency'.[82] Its first 'synthetic image actor', a blonde and buxom beauty named Justine and produced on a CAD called Life F/x., is already available. 'We are even able to wrinkle the skin so it behaves like real tissue,' says Ivan Gulas, the Harvard clinical psychologist who is shaping the new actress for Hollywood's purposes. Today's actors may suddenly find themselves competing with Marilyn Monroe or Humphrey Bogart, or even a new 'ideal' synthesis of several of the best actors of all times. Similar early inroads being made in other high-paying jobs: robots that perform hip-replacement surgery; and expert systems that plan your will or prepare and file your tax returns. The first successful adaptive neuronet applications that replace currency or bond traders are being implemented because 'humans cannot keep up with the high speed of these information-dependent systems'.

In short, nobody should believe that he will remain forever immune to Information Age obsolescence. Everyone should be interested in a society that is viable for everybody. After all, we are only making the opening moves in the new global Information Age chess game, and nobody really knows how the game will unfold.

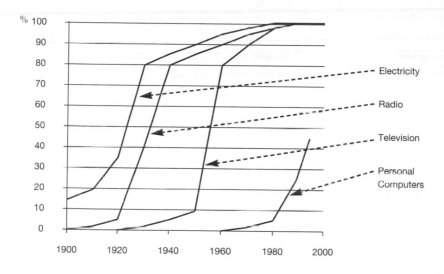

Figure 3.1 Curve of adoption of new technologies in the US (Source: IBM)

Given that these are still early days in this field, and that the implications of the Information Revolution entail two paradoxically opposing trends, what will be the final outcome? There is definitely room here to project any one of our favourite dreams and nightmares, and we will do some of that in the next chapter. Samuel Becket's teasing remark comes to mind: 'Everything will turn out all right – unless something foreseen happens.'

■ Distribution and retail

The Net is already completely altering the economics of the gigantic distribution and retail sector, by far the largest employer. In cyberspace, more and more people are comparison shopping and purchasing at wholesale prices, with no more effort than clicking a mouse. Instead of a retail economy with physical processes, we are already well on our way towards a wholesale economy with digital processes. In other words, the old way consisted of physically moving a product from manufacturer to wholesaler, and then to the retailer and finally to the consumer. In the new way, the middleman deals only with information, makes it available to the consumer in a palatable form, then communicates orders back to the manufacturer, who ships the merchandise directly to the consumer (the Cendant case study in Chapter 4 explains this process in detail). In such a switch, nothing remains the same. The prices charged to the consumer, for example, can be radically different.

■ Cheaper than wholesale?

The following example provides a taste of things to come.[83] You can buy the Virtual Vegas Turbo Blackjack computer game in a store for $29.95 or download it from the Net for $2.95 (one tenth of its 'normal' retail price). The CEO of Virtual Vegas, David Herschman, has figured out that, even with this drastic price reduction for the Net, he still makes more money on a Net sale than on a retail sale. Each $29.95 CD ROM version of the game has to pay for the retailers' and distributors' shares; for the production, packaging and shipping costs; for sales commissions and unpaid accounts. After all this, the income to Virtual Vegas is $4.50, out of which Herschman pays for his own staff and the infrastructure to manage distribution middlemen and production steps. In contrast, each $2.95 copy of the game paid for with CyberCoin and delivered over the Net costs him only 26 cents, yielding a $2.69 profit. At the Web price, many more copies will be sold. Herschman summarizes: 'The profit margin on the Web is huge. We make it once and . . . we could sell that from here to eternity.'

Nor is this the end of the cost compression game: Digital Equipment Corporation is launching its Millicent payment product to compete with CyberCoin, promising to reduce the costs of a Web transaction still further from 26 cents to the order of 0.1 cent (yes, one tenth of a cent!). Other companies such as Citibank, Verifone, and Microsoft are all known to be developing similar products, ensuring that these costs will remain *really* low.

"Can I call you back? I'm shopping."

New products?

Even so, it would be a mistake to look at the cyber economy as an unusually cost-effective new wholesale marketing outlet, or as a very special and fast growing export 'country' for existing products. It also promises to make possible totally different products. For instance, the new micro-payment technologies already offered by CyberCash make it economically interesting to 'unpack' products that we have always purchased as a unit. One could charge a very small fee for providing exactly what the consumer specifies. Instead of buying a whole cookery book, a magazine, a CD or even a newspaper, for a few cents, you could order only the sections, articles or songs that you really want.

The next Gutenberg revolution?

Purported to be the largest bookseller in the world, Amazon.com does not have a single bookshop. It started operations in 1994, and recorded sales of $16 million in 1996. In 1997, it sold $148 million worth of books, and in 1998, a staggering $460 million. Over two million titles are available at any time with the click of a mouse. Some people would like to extrapolate such dizzying trends for ever; as of November 1998, the Amazon.com stock market valuation was $6.3 billion. In 1998, the largest publisher the world, Bertelsmann of Germany, decided to acquire Barnes and Noble's Internet shop so it could partake directly in the electronic fray.

However, the real Internet book revolution is still invisible in the market place. Patents have been issued for a thin-leafed 'electronic book'. Such an 'e-book' looks like a normal book with a few hundred paper-thin pages, but each 'intelligent' page is controlled by its own computer chip and covered with millions of microscopic two-toned particles. The book's 'spine' hides the chips, power and connection plugs needed.[84] Unlike a computer screen, you can flip to any page back and forth, and remember where you were. It is totally flexible and infinitely reusable. This all-purpose e-book can be loaded with any content as needed, and the resolution is better than the text you are currently reading. Different formats are available: from newspaper to paperback-size, from child-proof to waterproof. You can throw your e-book in your backpack, read it on the bus or the beach – it is more rugged than the book you hold in your hand.

This is a second Gutenberg revolution in the making, where everybody can become an author and sell his or her book for the price of today's royalties. Bookshops could become mostly coffee shops, where one compares notes and tips about the most interesting websites that provide detailed ratings on the infinite supply of 'publications' available. For people who prefer good old traditional paper books, a printer-binder – located in the corner of the 'book shop', at the Post Office, or at a copy-centre – could even prepare such paper books to order. They could be hardcover or paperback, large or small print, with everything always 'in stock', exactly when the customer prefers it. The first 'print-on-demand' (POD) book was demonstrated at the 1998 'Chicago Book Expo'. The time from when the moment the book is ordered to when it is handed to the customer is less than five minutes, and it can be sold at the same price as a mass-produced book. During these five minutes, the book is downloaded, printed and bound, producing an exact clone of the normal edition.[85] Is this another nightmare or dream in the making? Another example of an industry (publishing) hit by the information revolution? Another sign that an age is dawning where we will breathe life into Cleveland's vision of increased choice and the democratic availability of information as the key resource?

Implications for money

An inscription in the lobby of New York's Library of Science, Industry and Business reads: 'Information about money has become almost as important as money itself.' The quote is from Walter Wriston, ex-Chairman of Citibank. He should know. Under his guidance and that of his successor, Citibank became the biggest investor of all banks in Information Technology ($1.75 billion in 1995).

Money made an early entry into the Information Age. Most financial transactions have been computerized for decades. Most of your own money is likely to reside in a bank or brokerage account, i.e. in a computer somewhere. The development of the cyber economy simply means that other aspects of economic activity are finally catching up with money in cyberspace.

■ Payment systems

In turn, the rise of commerce on the Net is sparking off a whole new wave of money applications. The expected bonanza is huge. By the end of 1997, 70% of the *Fortune* 1,000 corporations were ready to do business on the Net. The 1998 e-commerce Christmas season boom confirmed that the cyber economy has all the makings of the fastest-growing economy in the world.

Price Waterhouse estimates that by the year 2000, the number of Netizens will have soared to 168 million, and that they will buy some $175-200 billion of goods and services on the Net. Forrester Research's survey of business executives resulted in forecasts that the Internet trade among businesses alone will reach $300 billion by 2002. The market research company International Data estimates that the Internet economy – which includes on-line shopping, business-to-business purchasing and advertising – reached $200 billion in 1998, and will soar to $1 trillion by 2002. No wonder everybody is interested in creating cyber-payment services.

The implications of all this are hard to fathom. For some businesses, the Net has already become their biggest single distribution outlet. For example, Best Western's website generated 48,000 hotel nights for a value of $3.5 million in 1996. The website for Dell Computers registered a *daily* sales volume of over $1 million from 1997 onwards, with peaks of $6 million per day during the holiday seasons. Cisco's website cashes in on over $2.3 million on an average day. Such a website is a distributor's dream: a retail outlet with no rental costs, no employees, not even a light bulb is needed; the customers fill in their own orders and pre-payment slips; and orders roll in 24 hours a day, 365 days per year. In addition, corporations can skip all intermediaries and eliminate the cost of keeping inventories of finished products – they manufacture and ship directly to the specifications of the order placed on the Net.

The case of the retailer turning banker: the Tesco Clubcard

Tesco, one of the UK's largest retailers, introduced a remarkably successful loyalty programme that forced rival retailers to follow suit. The Tesco Clubcard is even credited with helping Tesco overtake rival Sainsbury as the UK's most successful retail chain.

Tesco Clubcard members earn one 'point' for every pound spent. These 'points' are consolidated in vouchers and product-specific coupons. In 1998, this helped Tesco increase customers by one third during the year. One in three UK households now are members and their *Clubcard* magazine is Europe's largest circulation customer magazine.

Since 1999, the scheme also provides a 'key' for each £25 transaction. With 100 keys, customers get a discount of up to three-quarters off the normal price on Clubcard deals.

Tesco Personal Finance is a key ingredient in this mix, directly competing with traditional banks by a better quality of customer service. Quarterly statements are sent out to 8.5 million members, including 100,000 different personalized variations. Tesco doesn't charge customers for withdrawing conventional money from the 350 ATMs which it operates around the UK. Every store also provides leaflets and a freephone service for other financial products such as interest-bearing saving accounts, loans, insurance, pensions and a Visa card.

A Clubcard Plus functions as an all-purpose banking service card in addition to a loyalty card, earning two Clubcard points for every pound spent, double the usual rate.

■ New money

The *real* revolution of possibilities unleashed by the Information Age will start to be seen when different *kinds* of currency follow the same electronic path that the national currencies are now blazing. The cybersphere is also the ideal new money frontier, the ideal space with ample opportunity for creativity around money to emerge. One example of such creativity was demonstrated in the UK by the Tesco Clubcard (see sidebar). But the blurring is even deeper than that. We already have airlines becoming retailers (e.g British Airways' Air Miles becoming redeemable for Sainsbury's retail vouchers) or getting involved in phone services (e.g. the new Lufthansa Senator cards are used not only to buy air tickets and keep track of frequent-flyer miles, but also for paying phone bills, car hire and other traveller's services). We have phone companies getting involved in retail payment systems (e.g. France Telecom's 1.2 million mobile phones are used to charge payments for goods and services; in another application one can buy a soft drink by dialling up its automat from a mobile phone). The Irish telecom operator makes more money from investing the 'float' – the unspent balances issued on phonecards – than they do from actual phone calls.[86] Cable TV becomes e-commerce networks (Canal Plus in France is providing this service now; and there will be 29 million set-top boxes operated by smart cards in Europe alone by 2003, ten times more than there will be shop terminals).[87] Zambian smart cards already have programmes for ten different types of currencies. All new PCs produced in the year 2000 have smart-card slots, and new smart cards use the same Multos platform so that you can download by telephone on it whenever you need it, for instance a Paris metro or a Eurostar application, a local library lending programme, launderette payments, healthcare insurance data or what is needed to change it into a phone card in Italy. In short, mobile phones, cable TV, computers, smart cards, complementary currencies and traditional payment systems are starting to converge and create a new money world in the process.[88]

Why should we expect that one of the most conspicuous legacies of the Industrial Age – our national currencies – would remain impervious to change? Even bankers, such as Citibank's CEO John Reed, agree that 'banking will become a bit of application software on an intelligent network'.[89] The 1998 merger between Citibank and Travelers Insurance proves that he means it. Similarly, the integration of frequent-flyer-miles incentives with traditional national currency-based credit cards shows the trend towards the future. In fact 40% of frequent-flyer miles are now not earned by flying; and two-thirds of British Airways' air miles are cashed in for something other than flights.

■ Implications for banks and financial services

From the 1980s onwards, banks found that they were forced to move into new arenas of businesses, performing totally different functions and facing different competitors. Instead of making money from the spread between customers' savings deposits and loans to businesses, banks are now in 'financial services'. Their biggest profit centres are likely to be credit cards, foreign exchange, derivative trading, securization, specialized insurance products or other exotic 'financial products' designed for sale to individuals and businesses.

As the Internet expands, it brings with it a second wave of computerization including Open Financial Services. 'Open Finance' is defined by Forrester

Research as 'emerging affluent consumers enjoying best-of-breed financial services combined with easy electronic movement of money. Open Finance means using technology to extend premium financial services that the wealthy enjoy to the mainstream investing public.'[90] This opens up a whole series of new issues for everybody, including tax authorities (see sidebar).

Taxation in cyberspace?

The US government Internet Tax Freedom Act of October 1998 has declared a three-year moratorium on taxation of all Internet transactions. But even after this moratorium lapses the questions arising from taxation in cyberspace promise to be far from trivial.

1   Whoever taxes cyberspace may lose the chance of leading in the world's new economy.
2   Who taxes an English customer who buys something on the Net from an Indian producer and pays for it, all under serious cryptographic protection? Just as critical, if one succeeds in taxing such transactions, how does one avoid double-taxation?
3   The issue of privacy and taxability are two sides of the same coin. A traceable transaction is easy to tax, but eliminates privacy; a transaction that respects privacy is difficult to tax. No easy compromise for this structural dilemma!
4   Furthermore, an estimated one sixth of all wealth in the world is now already in tax havens.[91] Open Finance will make such facilities available to much larger populations.

I claim that the ultimate answer will be to rethink the taxation game fundamentally. Industrial Age taxes were those on labour (which are counterproductive from an employment perspective), income, sales or value-added (the former intrusive from a privacy viewpoint, the latter socially regressive, and all increasingly hard to define and collect in cyberspace anyway).

Knowledge Age taxes will be those that are comparatively easier to identify and collect and which provide an additional social or sustainability incentive such as: pollution taxes, taxation on the use of land, energy or of non-renewable resources. Even from a theoretical economic viewpoint this approach makes more sense, given that these taxes would make explicit real costs which today's market system doesn't capture.

Such a systemic transfer of the taxation base has already started in some forward-thinking countries such as The Netherlands.

In Open Finance, the financial institutions that will be the winners are those that have positioned themselves to transfer *value* on the Net, instead of just national currencies. For example, the capacity to handle non-traditional currencies smoothly, as a complement in payment systems to the national currencies, will be a major plus. Payment systems that try to deal exclusively with national currencies will be at a structural disadvantage. For instance, how about sending an e-mail to your daughter stranded in a foreign country, with an attachment of some dollars *and* some frequent-flyer miles for her to buy an airline ticket home? How about paying for something on the Net with a mixture of dollars and corporate scrip or complementary currency?

Cendant[92] is already using mixed payments of dollars and its own 'netMarket Cash', like Tesco with its Clubcard credits.[93] Similarly, the first dual-currency smart cards for payments in a mix of dollars and complementary currency were being tested in Minneapolis in 1997 (as will be shown in Chapter 7). All this may sound strange to the habitual ways of thinking by today's established market leaders. But as Eric Hoffer put it: 'In times of change, those who are ready to learn will inherit the world, while those who believe they know will be marvelously prepared to deal with a world that has ceased to exist.'

Wisdom in the Information Age?

The coming of the Information Age does not just entail positive conse-quences. The one certainty it heralds is change. Resisting the change has proved to make the shift even more traumatic in the long run. The cost structure in favour of the Net is so overwhelming that the wave will be irresistible. It will also go global much faster than was the case of the Industrial Revolution.

It is important to remember that information-as-resource is only a raw material, the equivalent of a sack of coal during the early Industrial Age. It becomes truly useful only when it is transformed into knowledge and handled with wisdom. We therefore need to define the subtle but critical differences between the adjacent concepts of data, information, knowledge and wisdom.

A good starting point is T.S. Eliot's question:

'Where is the wisdom we have lost in knowledge?
Where is the knowledge we have lost in information?'

To which Harlan Cleveland adds: 'Where is the information we have lost in data?'[94]

Data are undigested observations without context. A list of phone numbers is an example of raw data.

Information is data organized, according to some system aimed at making it retrievable and hopefully useful to someone like you. An alphabetical listing in a phone book organizes the raw data of phone numbers in such a usable way.

Knowledge is information that has been internalized by you, integrated into everything else you know from experience and study, and that is therefore available to you as a basis for action in your life. You know that this particular phone number is your friend's number, and this links it with everything else you know about that friend. An increasingly important form of knowledge is learning how to find the information that is useful to you.

Wisdom adds depth, perspective and meaning to knowledge by integrating ways of knowing other than logic and analysis, such as intuition, or the intelligence and compassion from the heart. Wisdom is by definition multi-dimensional, crossing the boundaries between different fields and ways to knowledge. It is the ultimate synthesis which cannot be forced on or taught to someone else:

> 'We can be knowledgeable with other people's knowledge,
> but we cannot be wise with other's people wisdom.'
>
> (Michel de Montaigne 1533 – 1592).

In our Industrial Age coal metaphor, data is the coal vein still deep in the mine. Information is a sack of coal ready to use. Knowledge is the steel we make out of it. And wisdom is the bridge, and the new connections between people that it enables – which is the *real* purpose of the whole process.

If we are to realize the benefits of the Information Society, the transition will require both knowledge and wisdom. If we choose to have some degree of wisdom prevail, the Information Revolution could serve in the creation of Sustainable Abundance, rather than other possible scenarios depicted in the following chapter. This is why I also call Sustainable Abundance wise growth.

Some key points:

- Whether we like it or not, an information revolution is occurring now. Neo-Luddite attempts at stopping the process will prove even more futile during this transition than those of their predecessors during the Industrial Revolution.
- Information technology by itself is neither a magic bullet that will solve all our problems, nor a Frankenstein monster that will devour its creators. Potentially it is both, and now is the time to become vigilant and aware of the deeper underlying issues. That same technology is unleashing simultaneously two powerful opposing dynamics. One leads to Cleveland's 'fairness revolution' where information-as-resource becomes an opportunity to increase and spread wealth on an unprecedented scale. Another could lead to a 'Corporate Millennium' (next chapter) where 'information barons' play the role of the 'robber barons' of the early Industrial Age.

- What really matters is not the technology, but the way we use it. The whole money game is going to change. Additional choices beyond national currencies are both unavoidable and necessary. This process started before the new technologies were available, and such technologies have the capacity to amplify their spread and scale. For the first time in several centuries, new players are moving in to create totally new ways for defining money, creating it, and using it. This new money frontier provides unprecedented opportunities for rethinking the kind of money we want, and for incorporating features to help address issues our societies will be facing in the foreseeable future. For example, the possibilities that new money systems offer to address the unemployment problems likely to occur during the transition to the brave new information society should be of interest to many people. Similarly, elderly care, community and environmental restoration are goals to which a majority should be able to subscribe.

- Private corporate currencies are not a problem *per se*. After all, as outlined in the Primer and Chapter 2, our familiar 'national' currencies are bank-debt currencies, i.e. are in reality privately issued corporate currencies which have been homogenized on a national level. Potential problems may arise when currencies – private or public – become *de facto* or legally enforced monopolies, reducing people's choices, and leading to potential abuse of power by those who enjoy that monopoly.[95]

On the positive side, information-as-resource is giving more people than ever the opportunity to create their own currencies that can reflect their own values. The starting point is to be aware that choice in money systems exists, and that choice matters. Historically, most features within money systems have not been consciously designed. They just evolved and ended up reflecting whatever the power structure and the collective unconscious of the corresponding societies projected onto them. This time, we have the opportunity to do it differently. We know enough about money and the collective unconscious to open conversations about the available options. Conscious choice in money systems at all levels – global, national, corporate, grass-roots or individual – may well be the most powerful leverage point for determining whether or not the opportunities of the Information Age will produce Sustainable Abundance or some other outcome.

The consequences to society of the dominance of various types of currencies created by different actors are explored in the next chapter.

CHAPTER 4

Five Scenarios for the Future

■ *'Never has humanity combined so much power with so much disorder,*
  so much anxiety with so many playthings,
  so much knowledge with so much uncertainty.'

PAUL VALERY[96]

■ *'In writing scenarios, we spin myths – old and new –*
  that will be important in the future.'

PETER SCHWARTZ[97]

■ *'Humanity is entering a period of extreme alternatives.'*

BOTKIN, ELMANDJTA AND MALITZA[98]

This chapter explores future possibilities through scenarios, each of which is targeted for roughly one future generation, around the year 2020.

The 'Official Future' is a simple extrapolation of what has become familiar over the past couple of decades. You will see why such a scenario has zero probability of occurring. This is followed by four scenarios that are more plausible, each highlighting the implications for shaping our future societies of one of the changes currently possible in our money system. These scenarios are The Corporate Millennium, Careful Communities, Hell on Earth, and Sustainable Abundance. A cameo story captures the essence of the lifestyle for each scenario. Supporting evidence is provided to ground the plausibility of such an outcome, in graphic form whenever possible.

Finally, the four scenarios are placed in a broader perspective and the driving forces that have shaped them are identified.

■ Scenarios – windows on the future

Scenarios are tools that help us to think coherently through complex chains of events and relationships. They inform our decisions and choices today, aiming at creating a better future. They enable better-informed decisions that are robust against a wider range of future possibilities. Aristotle surmised a long time ago that if we know the future, we cannot change it; and if we can change it, we cannot know it. That is why scenarios are not simple extrapolations, forecasts or predictions.

One of the originators of scenario building, Napier Collyns, has called the process 'an imaginative leap into the future'. His colleague, Peter Schwartz, president of the Global Business Network, described them as 'tools for taking the long view; they're stories about how the world might turn out. [They are] stories about meaning. They explain why things might happen, and they give order and coherence to events. Stories are history's oldest way of organizing and communicating knowledge and one of the clearest channels into your mind's eye.'[99]

Such scenario building has three objectives:

1 To challenge habits in mindsets, mental models, images and beliefs. We all have our habitual ways of looking at the world, consistent with our attitudes and beliefs. Such mindsets can filter out useful insights. Scenarios enable us to momentarily take off these filters and reveal the blind spots, the hidden assumptions, and open new windows on the future.

2 To identify and better understand the underlying forces that are driving pivotal events. Specifically in our case, the consequences of a shift of control over money systems to various new players in society will be highlighted.

3 To work creatively with these discoveries, and use the clarity they inspire to shape a more desirable future.

'The Flight of the Flamingos'

A few years ago, Shell-trained scenario facilitators gathered representatives of all parties in South Africa. Among the participants at these confidential meetings were four of the ministers of the future Mandela government. The scenario that has been implemented in South Africa was called 'the Flight of the Flamingos', a metaphor for all parties taking off slowly, but together. Clem Sunter, currently with Anglo-American, has published parts of these scenarios.[100]

Scenarios are not academic exercises. The scenario-building process enabled Shell to forecast and prepare for the fall of the former Soviet Union, thereby avoiding billion-dollar mistakes in North Sea oil investments. Shell still updates its scenarios roughly every three years.

This process also contributed to the 'South African miracle' of the peaceful transition after Apartheid (see sidebar). These same methods were further refined by the Global Business Network founded by several Shell alumni, and later published by Peter Schwartz.[101]

■ The Official Future: 'more of the same'

The Official Future that we are told we can expect during the coming decades is usually based on an extrapolation of what has happened over the past 20 years or so.

For example, in the Official Future the same political parties are expected to continue to vie for power in the same places. Schoolchildren will continue to learn roughly the same things as did their predecessors. The same crops will be grown, harvested, sold, prepared, and eaten in much the same way as in the past. Computers will continue to become faster, cheaper, smaller. We will still pay for our purchases with our familiar dollars, pesos, pounds, francs, reales or yen. We may use 'smart cards'[102] instead of the old bills, magnetic credit cards or cheques. We may store our small change in an electronic purse instead of a leather one. Europeans will have adjusted to using a common currency instead of the national ones. But when all is said and done, how much of all this really matters?

In the more rarefied spheres of the global monetary system, we may expect an occasional crisis to shake some individual countries – such as happened for the UK in late 1991, Scandinavia in 1992, Mexico in December 1994, Thailand in June 1997, Indonesia in December 1997, Russia in September 1998 and Brazil in January 1999. Once in a while, the press may also herald a 'grand scheme'. Such schemes are given names, such as the 'Plaza Agreement'[103] or the 'Maastricht Treaty',[104] pinpointing the place where the agreement was made, but giving no indication of the pragmatic implications for the rest of us.

This Official Future[105] boils down to a continuation of what we have lived with during the past couple of decades. But the real problem with this Official Future is that it has no probability of occurring. In the words of Willis Harman: 'Our societies have reached a point where transformation is not optional anymore.'

■ Why the Official Future is not going to happen

The words of Harman are prophetic for two reasons.

The first was already synthesized in the Time-Compacting Machine of Chapter 1 (see Figure 1.3). The historically unprecedented convergence of the four megatrends – Age Wave, Information Revolution, Climate Change/Species Extinction and Monetary Instability – points out that 'business as usual' is just not a realistic possibility. Any one of these trends is sufficient to disturb significantly the familiar societal patters. In combination, they make it highly improbable that we will be able to continue undisturbed on our familiar path.

The second reason why the Official Future is not going to happen is directly concerned with the topic of this book: the future of money. Even *before* any of these megatrends have fully played out, the decade of the 1990s has revealed various significant experiments which alter the nature of money. Nobody questions that new technologies are going to change the form of our money (i.e., the ever more ethereal aspects that our 'normal' national currency can take such as electronic bits in automatic payment systems, on smart cards or on the Net). However, this is only part of what is occurring.

In parallel with these electronic money developments, something entirely different is emerging. There are those around the world who have already launched, or are experimenting with, totally different kinds of money. They are transforming what money is, who creates it, what it means, what emotions it encourages, and how people will behave towards each other and the environment when using it.

We know that the technological changes that have the most radical revolutionary impact on societies are those that change the tools by which people relate to each other. Fundamental shifts in civilization have been traced back to the invention of writing,[106] the alphabet[107] and to the printing press.[108] The breathtaking social, political and economic implications of the invention of the telephone, car, and television[109] are classic examples of such shifts that occurred during the 20th century.

Changes in the nature of money will have at least as great an impact as any of the above examples. Money is our key tool for material exchanges with people beyond our immediate intimate circle. Of all the tools that can change human relationships, what is more central in a capitalist society than money? Capitalism uses the flow of money within the marketplace to allocate resources among participants in society. Under capitalism, money is not only the means but also the objective of the overwhelming majority of the exchanges. The internal combustion engine changed only the nature of our transportation system, and look at the results! In today's capitalist society, changing money would be equivalent to altering both the fuel and the underlying motivation for most of our actions. Therefore, transforming the nature of our money is likely to have more far-reaching consequences than we can begin to imagine.

There are now hundreds of projects under way that are utilizing new kinds of money, and creating just such a transformation. Together they provide a strong indication that our very concept of money will change. Some of these schemes involve the most powerful organizations in the world and billions of dollars of investments. Others have been implemented on a shoestring by social activists in a dozen different countries, and still others were dreamed up by lonely 'cypher-punks' in lofts in Silicon Valley. My forecast is that 90-95% of all these projects will not survive; but that the remaining 5% will succeed at permanently changing our economies, our societies, our civilization, and our world.

Just as radically as gunpowder sealed the fate of the feudal system in Europe at the end of the Middle Ages, those money projects that survive will determine the direction towards which power will shift over the next century. What makes this unusually exciting – or frightening, depending on your viewpoint – is that there is no way to know which approach will prevail. It is not necessarily governments or corporations, or even the best-funded or best-staffed projects, that have the greatest chance. Some entrepreneurs in garages are succeeding where the giants have failed. Conventional wisdom has long held that only the largest corporations could attract top talent and significant financing, because size automatically ensured market clout. None of these well-established 'facts' has held true in the 1990s.

When we talk about the future of money, we cannot avoid talking about the future of our societies and of our world. This should not be interpreted as a mechanical cause-and-effect relationship between money systems and broad societal changes. Societies are extraordinarily complex systems and, therefore, impossible to understand in simple mechanical terms. This is truer now than ever before. For the first time in recorded history, our money game has become a truly global one. Now that ex-Communist countries, and even communist China of today, have irrevocably switched to money as the social motivator of choice, changing the money system may be the most powerful way available to shift our collective behaviour on a global scale. In addition, for the first time in history, the effects of any monetary changes will be multiplied by our information and communication technologies, propelling us at high speed into mostly uncharted territories.

Given that the Official Future is not going to happen, what are some of the other more plausible futures? Here are four very different directions in which changes in our money systems could take us:

- The Corporate Millennium: a world where private corporate scrip has taken over the role of the familiar bank-debt national currencies;
- Careful Communities: where a global monetary meltdown has left community-based local currencies as the dominant money-shaping force;
- Hell on Earth: where no new social or monetary order has been able to emerge after the collapse of the official money system;
- Sustainable Abundance: a world where various kinds of money innovations – described in Part Two – form a successful preventive measure against a monetary meltdown and create an 'Integral Economy' where the old and new money systems effectively balance and complement each other.

■ The Corporate Millennium

The Corporate Millennium scenario illustrates how power, including the power to create money, could shift to major multinational corporations over the next decades. This story is reported by a journalist after interviewing Britain's last Prime Minister in the year 2020.

Goodbye to the last Prime Minister[110]

London, February 7, 2020

While he gazed at the fires burning on the South Bank, I spoke to Britain's last Prime Minister in his old office at Westminster Palace. This was the most candid and informal interview I have ever had with him, perhaps because this was also his last one. 'This isn't my problem any more,' was his opening remark. He had signed the final papers earlier in the day. At midnight, Securicor was to take over the police franchise for the United Kingdom.

This was the final piece of the puzzle. Executive Solutions had already won the armed forces contract, in return for control of Cornwall's offshore oil fields. Social Services is run by Sonysoft, since Sony took over the Microsoft empire after Bill

Gates's tragic death. Consolidated Banks was in charge of the economy. NewsCorp had the Education Department franchise. Even the Houses of Parliament, no longer needed now that elected representatives had ceased to have meaningful functions, belonged to Virgin. Tomorrow the estate agents were coming to look at Number 10 Downing St, and he would slip into retirement as easily as power had slipped into the hands of corporations.

He showed me a book of old press cuttings. The first was a report of his maiden speech in the Commons in 1992. He was attacking the loss of British sovereignty to the European Union. He smiled at his own naiveté. 'I had talked about immigration, demanding greater controls. Talk about barking up the wrong tree. Getting into the country, any country, is easy now – just buy an airline ticket. But entering a corporate enclave, like Islington, Belgravia or Lower Manhattan, requires an electronic appointment and "positive identification".'

His face turned grim. 'Really efficient, this "positive ID" technology. As with most important things in history, its general acceptance was a convergence between conscious choice, accident, and necessity. The conscious choice was the initial justification to test smart cards for administrative reasons – they would include name, Social Security number, driving licence, and emergency insurance and medical information. The accident was the "credit card blitz", when a group of hackers – who had patiently created a database with credit card numbers, credit limits and approval codes – disappeared one day in 2002 after charging hundreds of millions of dollars on hundreds of thousands of accounts. After that, the smart-card payment technology imposed itself almost overnight, and the tie-in with electronic ID made a lot of sense to improve security. However, after the global social unrest of 2006, two additional types of data were added, first in the US: the PSC level and the PEC order, operating in both physical space and the cybersphere.' (See ** note.)

**In 2020 cyber-jargon, the *cybersphere* is the virtual space where all the electronic technologies – payment systems, telephone, computers, media, security systems, Internet – all converge into a single seamless system.

The *Personal Security Clearance* (PSC) defines the areas to which a person can be admitted – which areas of town, which buildings, which rooms in specific corporate buildings. This is all neatly organized through security systems that are automatically updated if you have an appointment with anybody in one of the corporate enclaves. The device reads your 'positive ID' status as you walk along. Totally unobtrusive – with the right clearances. The same PSC also controls access to the cybersphere. It became necessary to increase general security as larger segments of society – excluded from the benefits of corporate jobs – turned increasingly violent to survive (from the old petty street crime to kidnapping of executives, cyber-terrorism, extortion under the threat of mass disruptions, etc.). The *Personal Economic Clearance* (PEC) defines an individual's creditworthiness for using the various corporate scrips in which he or she participates. Without the proper 'economic clearance', one can't enter certain shops or shopping zones, whether downtown or in the cybermalls (there is not much there that anybody with a lower clearance could afford).

He continued, with some sadness in his voice: 'I remember seeing a BBC newscast back in 1996 about trends in America. It mentioned The Mall of the Americas in Minneapolis – the largest shopping mall in the world at that time – where, because of security considerations, access was prohibited to unaccompanied teenagers at the request of adult shoppers. These youngsters didn't have the economic buying power to justify their presence there anyway. I remember thinking that this could never happen in the UK. Finland, back in the last days of the 20th century, was the first country to impose general use of positive ID using smart cards. The Americans copied that experiment initially in the major metropolitan areas to cope with the spreading urban mayhem. Korea was first to legislate for the surgical embedding of electronic ID chips in the hand at birth. Now, the Securicor contract I signed this morning specifies that, in accordance with the Interpolnet agreement, implants are needed on a global level, and therefore in the UK as well. Their argument is irrefutable: how can anybody police the global cybersphere if there are security holes where people can log on without individual ID implants?'

He went on, 'An information bridge between product bar codes and personal IDs was also inevitable. In the 1990s, we already knew that the information about who purchases what was more valuable than the profits. Even Orwell did not foresee a Big Brother that could reconstruct everybody's life at that level of minutiae. Every purchase, payment and phone call made with traceable money is routinely warehoused in massive databases for future reference – the most valuable corporate marketing assets of the Information Age. But it has become even more essential to screen out anybody for dubious security connections.'

The last PM insisted that he go on record as saying that he has tried to stem the corporate tide one last time. 'But there had really not been any choice. The first warning signs were already there when "market forces" propelled Britain out of the European Monetary System back in 1991. A decade ago, the "leftist" French President tried to raise taxes to pay for essential services. Capital had fled overnight. The wealthy, even the moderately well off, had migrated to other tax bases. The multinationals took a few months to wrap up their operations, and delocated most functions performed in France to friendlier places. Back in 1996, Glen Peters, Director of the Future at Price Waterhouse, had called them nomads. "They take what they can while it's in abundance, then close up shop and move on."

'After that episode, all countries were put in competition to cut their budgets to the bone. The last items to go were subsidies used to attract foreign investments. The driving force had really been the digital revolution. Bill Gates became the new Karl Marx or George Washington, depending on who you talk to, leading us straight into the Corporate Millennium.

'Perhaps it was predictable that The Knowledge Society would become The Corporate Society. After all, the corporations that came out on top were invariably those most effective at using knowledge in an organized, strategic sense. Knowledge, power and money have always been closely linked, and now have become directly interchangeable. And governments have become irrelevant in all three.

'We should have seen it coming,' he reflected. 'As long ago as the 1990s, the Director General of the Institute of Directors, Tim Melville-Ross, had said that the possibility of the Third Millennium being ruled by the corporations was "a legitimate concern". Glen Peters had said that "all evidence is that probably the tide is unstoppable". Not everyone agreed that it would be so dramatic. Some had thought that the state would return to its traditional roles of setting rules and fighting wars. But we all expected that the Information Age would be as earth-shaking as the Industrial Revolution. And look at what that did to the old landed aristocrats, not to speak of the peasants. A host of business gurus had sounded warning bells for decades. I remember Charles Handy, author of *The Empty Raincoat,* saying "Companies are still run as totalitarian states."[111]

'The real clincher,' he noted, 'was when corporations directly issued their own currency, instead of simply competing for the currencies issued by banks under governmental supervision. It started innocently enough with "frequent-flyer miles", initially earned with and redeemable only for airline tickets. American Express simply generalized the concept by creating its "world traveler money, redeemable worldwide". When these prototypes merged with the booming cyber economy, it almost became a free for all. However, through coalitions and convertibility negotiations among the larger corporations, we created today's reality: a few dominant "hard" corporate scrips backed by real goods and services that are increasingly taking over the "unstable national currencies only backed by debt".'

The PM wiped the dust off the window ledge. No one came here any more. The Commons had held its debates on the Internet for almost a decade. That allowed the politicians to spend more time in their constituencies, or so went the reasoning. But nobody in the constituencies cared. Everybody knew that politicians had no real power to influence events.

He continued, 'The turning point for the media was when they discovered that what people really want is *to be distracted* from reality. So news increasingly became entertainment. I am willing to bet that more of the footage shot by NewsCorp at tonight's riots is going to be used as an insert for the latest episode of their series on

Cybercops and Robbers, rather than in the news report. Business reports and entertainment news have gradually replaced coverage of political issues. Turnout at elections has sunk to 5%. My government has less legitimacy than a tinpot dictatorship. When I tried to push through a law ordering the de-merger of NewsCorp and the BBC, people just laughed. The only option left was to just wind the whole thing down.

'Not everything is bad, of course. Other institutions, some high-profile charities, museums, universities, have done rather well under the new regime. Most workers work from home, or from somewhere more pleasant than big cities. London has been shrinking for almost a century now, and telecommuting gave the final push to the exodus. The streets are mostly filled with tourists. The Palace of Westminster will remain a grand old building though, now that it is an indoor park, since Disney refurbished it with the perfect theme. As the brochure says, "Representative Government as it was: from the Magna Carta to the year 2000". They take the usual liberties with the historical facts and emphasize only the most exciting episodes. But I do feel left out – they stopped the clock at the year 2000 because it made marketing easier.

'Yes, the buildings will be all right. But what about the people? It wasn't that the mega-corporations were treating them badly. In many ways, being a citizen of Goldman Sachs or Chrysler-Daimler-Benz had more advantages than being a British or German-American citizen. Certain kinds of employees are thriving like the royalty of the past. The City is paying massive salaries to those with the right skills. The problem is that nobody convinced the global giants to become socially responsible. Last century, big business was trying to bend the rules. Now, there are no rules, except the ones they create. "You have to ask whether big business and representative organizations like ours are likely to handle power in a benign way," Tim Melville-Ross had warned back in the 1990s, "and it is by no means certain that they will." He had thought disclosure and public scrutiny would be enough to ensure good behaviour. Glen Peters, too, had argued that the consumer was more powerful than the biggest company. The public had boycotted businesses they didn't like, but this inane approach could hardly work. Big business, after all, also controls most of the information people were getting – directly, by ownership of the media, or indirectly, through the influence of the advertising money. It had also managed to colonize almost all of the cybersphere.

'Then there is always the uncontrolled component, the cyber-underground, at the leading edge of the backlash. By comparison, the earlier IRA bombings in London were a picnic. Who would have thought that weapons of mass disruption would replace weapons of mass destruction? The stock market crazes launched underground by the hackers, disrupted payment systems, commercial aircraft colliding in the skies, mis-tracked commuter trains crashing into freight trains. And when any of these mass disruptions occur, no one can call an ambulance – the 999 network has been blown apart by a computer virus. And the older forms of violence still pose a threat. Even Bill Gates, with all his bodyguards, could not avoid being blown up along with his armoured car.

'But what should one expect when a third of the population, including many of our brightest kids, cannot find a job, have no room at our collective table, do not fit into the increasingly paranoid business world? The backlash against softhearted people in the business world has been harsh. Women have been singled out for not understanding that this is a tough world, that business is at war with these cyber-terrorists. "Love it, or leave it" had become the unspoken rule, very effective at generating conformity among the "Ins".'

Again the PM glanced across the river and shuddered. People on the far bank had flaming torches. 'That is the real problem, the ever growing numbers of "Outs". The underclass has been falling behind for decades. Even when I was a boy there were men living rough on the streets. Then came the kids. After that, whole families. Now it looks like hordes. Professor Handy had estimated that 20% of the population would be unemployable. He had guessed too low: with increased social uncertainty and criminality, corporations needed to be more selective than ever in hiring anybody who might be a security risk. Unemployment keeps rising for those too old, with outdated skills, or spotty security associations.'

The last PM of the UK closed his book of cuttings, put it in his red box and left the Houses of Parliament for the last time. As he walked out, he glanced up. The glowing Seiko sign on Big Ben was backlit by the glow from the fires. He said he felt a deep sense of personal failure, along with the failure of a system of governance. A page of history had been turned – irrevocably.

■ Timetable for the transition

A timetable follows detailing a plausible transition between the Information Age and the Corporate Millennium. All events up until the end of 1999 are actual, beyond that they are projected.

Timetable of the revolution

1970s: Experimental introduction of frequent-flyer miles and product bar-codes.

1980s: Generalization of fidelity cards and product bar-codes. Introduction in France of smart cards for payments purposes.

1992: Amex embarks on an alliance strategy for the 'frequent traveller' market, making membership miles convertible into 'Connect Plus' and vice versa, starting the trend of broadening the purpose of private currencies.

1994: The first Positive ID chips surgically implanted in the necks of dogs are successfully marketed in Silicon Valley.

1995: Total outstanding 'narrow purpose' corporate scrip tops $30 billion in value for the first time; 30 million rechargeable smart cards for payments in circulation in France; 88 million smart cards issued in Germany for national health record management; in Finland the central bank issues a combined payment, social security and health management smart card.

1996: Joint venture between Microsoft and Barclays to design electronic money systems. Merger of CNN and Time-Warner creating the largest 'content' empire. Introduction of Internet stations in public places in the UK. Implementation of the new World Trade Organization (WTO) Treaty, dismantling most remaining national barriers to international trade. Sensar, a pioneering biometric company, signs contracts with NCR and OKI Electric Industry for iris scanning devices in Automatic Teller Machines (ATMs).

1997: The first Britons get Internet access via home TV sets. Biometric iris scanners operational in Japan and London. A pilot project between US and Bermudan Immigration authorities uses automatic hand-reading devices to expedite the processing of frequent travellers. Mircrosoft introduces Virtual Wallet in its Internet Explorer 4.0. Worldcom merges with MCI, the largest financial deal in history so far, also the largest 'carrier' merger; 170 million smart cards in use worldwide.

1998: Citibank introduces biometric iris scanners in the US. Electronic fingerprint ID implemented. British Telecommunications (BT) merges with ATT, beating the MCI–Worldcom deal to create the largest telecom carrier.

1999: Accelerating merger trend between information 'content' and 'carrier' groups.

2000: Amex launches 'cash2000', a full-purpose corporate scrip 'for the global elite'. Microsoft and others follow suit.

2001: The volume of e-mail for the first time exceeds conventional post; 600 million smart cards in use worldwide.

2002: The first Information Rights scandal breaks out: medical information is being used to blackmail people into purchasing from one specific on-line supplier. As all relevant databases have been accumulated in a tax-haven island in the Pacific, no legal recourse is obtained.

2003: Koreans require by law 'positive ID implants' into newborn children.

2006: Repression of the 'global job riots', most violent in US cities.

2010: Private corporate scrip currencies exceed national currencies in commercial exchange volume for the first time.

2015: Tax-slashing promises are fulfilled by privatizing the remaining essential services in the UK.

2020: The last Prime Minister of the United Kingdom retires.

■ How is this possible?

This scenario describes how the Information Revolution could decisively shift power towards the corporate world, making the nation-state concept irrelevant. Instead of changing internally to adapt themselves to their expanded social role, corporations reshaped the world to their own priorities. Corporate takeovers of government functions can be a double-edged sword, depending on the field, and the way the services are handled. For instance, nobody regrets the government-owned telephone services in the countries where that was the practice. Private corporations have been supplying better and cheaper service than the government services had supplied. Similarly, the appearance of private postal services, such as Fedex or UPS, has improved quality and reliability of service.

In other areas, the outcome may be less obvious. When First Data Resources built an engineering school for the University of Nebraska at Omaha whose curriculum is specifically tailored to the needs of that corporation, the slope becomes slippery. When high school children receive their financial education from a credit card company, and they learn that it is 'good financial practice' to have 20-30% of one's income dedicated to reimbursing credit card debt, we have gone over the edge.

Specialized corporate currencies like frequent flyer miles are thinkable only because of cheap and ubiquitous computing power.

It is only a question of time before someone (American Express, Microsoft, some newly formed cyber-entity, or a consortium of corporations?) will issue a full corporate scrip, backed by its own goods and services. Even Alan Greenspan says he 'envisages proposals in the near future for issuers of electronic payment obligations, such as stored-value cards or "digital cash" to set up specialized issuing corporations with strong balance sheets and public credit ratings' and he foresees 'new private currency markets in the 21st century'.[112] In short, instead of competing for the familiar national currencies backed only by government debt, corporations could issue their own money backed by real goods and services.

Governments will, most likely, not be the only losers in such a power shift. For instance, a Corporate Millennium has the potential to erode further personal privacy and individual rights to the advantage of the large corporations. Such erosion results from a convergence of the following three trends, alluded to in the scenario:

1 The perceived need for personal identification ('positive ID') to ensure security in electronic payments. As the cyber economy expands, bringing with it a criminal cyber-underground, the rationale strengthens for this possibility.

2 Electronic forms of money – whether of the old national currencies or corporate scrip – are ideally suited to become 'traceable currency', easily used to track who purchases what. The most valuable marketing asset in the Information Age will be the massive consumer databases that result, and are already being built today, as is confirmed by the demand for unprecedented large-scale data storage devices by all major retail chains. Another sign of this trend: the South African bank Nector gives its customers a free portable telephone which automatically gives them each morning their bank balance, but also monitors all other calls to build up a profile of its customers.

3 Connecting product bar-code information to the personal identification of the purchaser. The economic incentive for this is almost irresistible, particularly for mass marketers, who thereby have available to them a complete profile of millions of consumers, including information about their preferences and lifestyles.

Privacy erosion may creep on us like the experiment with frogs that let themselves boil to death if the temperature rises very slowly. And it may all happen, thanks to giant corporations most of us have never heard of, that appear suddenly out of nowhere, like whales surfacing from the deep. This is not theory or paranoia: it can be illustrated by the actual history of the biggest Net distribution corporation of 1997-98.

■ The case of the stealth mega-store

Quiz question: Name the largest Net merchandiser in 1997 ($1.5 billion in sales). A corporation that makes available over one million different products and services on-line (as a basis of comparison, a typical super-market has 50,000 items), and that has detailed psychographic and transaction data concerning over 100 million consumers (about half of US households). An extra hint: the same corporation is also the world's largest franchiser in both hotel chains and in residential real estate.

Did you guess Cendant?

If you didn't, don't feel badly. Most of its customers don't know its name either. Cendant is the result of a merger between two just as little-known companies – Comp-U-Card (CUC) and Hospitality Franchise Systems (HFS) – which have nothing in common, except an understanding of the power of information in the Information Age. Their history is a perfect case study of how the dynamics of the Information Age can concentrate power in totally new ways.

Walter Forbes started CUC in 1976 as a computer-based shopping service. His core idea was rock-solid and simple. Instead of having manufacturers ship to wholesalers and retailers who sell to the consumer, they supply the CUC database with *information* about their goods. CUC presents that information in a palatable way to consumers who can buy at the wholesale price, plus shipping costs. When a shopper buys something, the manufacturer is notified and ships it directly to the customer. CUC makes its money, not from the merchandise, but mostly from membership fees ($69 per year) and from the vast amount of transaction information it accumulates.

CUC also launched a series of specialized on-line services: Travelers Advantage (a full-service travel agency), AutoAdvantage (purchase and maintenance of cars), Premier Dining (the first national discount dining programme), BookStacks (on-line book purchases), MusicSpot (CDs), and Shoppers' Advantage (a general on-line merchandising service that, by 1993, had 50 million members buying from a database of more than 250,000 products). CUC also acquired successively: Madison Financial Corporation (now FISI Madison, the world's largest financial marketing organization), Benefit Consultants (insurances), Entertainment Publications (publisher of discount books), Sierra On-line (a software firm) and a large European licensee.

Forbes also made deals with America On-line, Prodigy, CompuServe, Citibank, Sears, and other similar 'brandnames' to provide their on-line shopping services. So without any CUC publicity (on-line or otherwise), and with all shipping being handled directly from the manufacturer, most customers have no idea that they ever dealt with CUC. Total sales volumes don't even have to be reported because they are directly credited to the manufacturers or service suppliers.

HFS comes from a totally different world, except that most of its customers are just as ignorant of its existence as are those of CUC. It was founded in the early 1990s by Henry Silverman. The story began when he engineered the acquisition of the hotel chain licences of Ramada Inn and Howard Johnson. For these, $170 million was paid, and for Days Inn, $295 million. They became a publicly owned corporation in 1992 under the HFS name. It then further acquired Super 8 for another $120 million, making it the world's largest hotel franchiser. Silverman explains that few people understand the advantages of being a franchiser instead of an outright owner. The franchiser provides advertising for the brand name, runs the reservation systems and supplies training and inspection on the franchisees. In short, the franchiser handles only the clean information aspects and is paid a hefty, predictable fee for it. It leaves all the messy and unpredictable aspects to the franchisees, such as the changes in value of the real estate, the continuous maintenance and upgrades needed, the fluctuations of customer flows and all the labour-intensive components.

Silverman also made some other, seemingly unrelated, acquisitions, such as Century 21, ERA and Coldwell Banking in 1995. This made HFS the world's largest franchiser of residential real estate. Later he also acquired PHH, a conglomerate of corporate relocation and financial services, for $1.8 billion. But the clearest demonstration of the underlying strategy was the handling of the acquisition of Avis car rental for $800 million. Even before the deal was closed, HFS announced that it would be taking the second-largest car rental company public. It would sell off Avis's 174,000 vehicles, 20,000 employees, and 540 car rental locations to the public. The only thing that HFS kept for itself was Avis's information and reservation system, which it would run for a nice predictable charge, and of course the Avis brand name for further licensing. As Wall Street has not yet named this strategy, I propose the term 'information asset stripping'.

As a consequence, between 1992 and 1997, HFS's total revenues multiplied by a factor of 10, to $2 billion, and its net profits multiplied by twenty, to $475 million. But the most valuable asset is the psychographic, demographic, and transaction data HFS has accumulated about 100 million US consumers from all its activities, covering half of all the US households.

It was that latter asset that made the 1995 meeting between Forbes and Silverman so productive for both parties. They entered into a partnership that would match CUC's marketing muscle with HFS's client information base. Under the deal, CUC would market its travel, shopping, dining, and auto-clubs to the millions of guests of HFS. However, this is not done using mindless junk mail, primitive cold calling, or e-mail spamming. When you call any of HFS's hotels for a reservation, after the booking is completed, you are asked whether you are interested in hearing about a discount travel club that would ensure some significant savings during your trip. A free petrol coupon worth $20 is part of the incentive. If you say 'yes', you will be switched to a CUC operator to hear the special offerings available to you if you join the club. The net result: a 30% positive response (compared to the normal 1 or 2% conversion rate of direct marketing). And who could resist? 'If you fly, you may want to consider this special deal for an Avis car waiting for you at the airport.'

Similarly, if your company relocates, using the services of PHH Corporation, Century 21 will be delighted to supply your staff with excellent housing, near the new location. Your employees will, of course, have to supply all the personal financial data necessary for them to obtain mortgages from FISI Madison. But a mortgage requires life insurance for which they have to file all the relevant medical information with Benefit Consultants. When they finally buy that house, via Century 21, they will receive a list of local dining opportunities available through Premier Dining, or an offer on discount books about the area published by Entertainment Publications, as a housewarming gift from CUC's Welcome Wagon.

In 1998, the group was able supply about 20% of a typical American household's goods and services (a database of one million items). Its plans were to supply 95% of all needs (about three million types of goods and services) by 1999. However, this ambitious blueprint suffered a major setback in 1998-99. A very old-fashioned accounting scandal provoked both the resignation of Walter Forbes as Chairman, and a precipitous loss of 80% of Cendant's stock market valuation.[113] So it may not be Cendant itself, but yet another – still unknown – company that becomes the Information Baron of the cyberworld.

■ From Information Age to Corporate Millennium

What is important about the Cendant case is that it illustrates one possible outcome of the dynamics of the cyber economy. It also graphically shows that there are questions that should be raised about the implications of concentrating information power. Market concentration has led to abuses against which anti-trust laws have proved necessary. Information concentration could similarly lead to abusive use of personal information.

■ Privacy at risk

There are clearly important issues around privacy protection that the new technologies will create. While Cendant may have no intention to abuse its information power, accumulating an unending stream of personal data in any one hand, private or public, is bound to create abuses at some point. No police state has ever been able to reconstruct individual lives at the level of detail possible through an unlimited accumulation of medical, financial and transaction data. Employees have practically no constitutional privacy rights wherever their employer is involved (see sidebar). The cyber economy could extend that process to everybody else.

Big Brother = Your Boss?

Technology makes surveillance cheap and easy. According to a 1997 survey by the American Management Association, two-thirds of major US corporations routinely monitor their employees electronically.[114] The Fourth Amendment's safeguards against 'unreasonable search and seizure' apply only to government surveillance. Corporations are not tied by these constitutional rights.

- In desks, drawers, and file cabinets at the employer's premises, employees have no rights to privacy whatsoever.
- Any e-mail stored or transferred via corporate computer networks can be read by the employer for whatever reason. Similarly, bosses can listen in on any phone conversations without notifying their workers.
- Your boss may own part of your brain. Innovations you develop on or off the job can be claimed by the corporation. On the other hand, under the Economic Espionage Act of 1996, employees risk jail time for disclosing 'confidential intellectual property'.
- Employers increasingly cite healthcare costs to justify genetic testing. Workers have no right to 'genetic privacy' and no protection from random drug tests.

The most effective solution for avoiding a continuous erosion of privacy is not European-style detailed regulation, or new forms of US-style anti-trust legislation. The best way is formally to clarify ownership rights over personal data. For example, one could specify that all personal data (transaction, medical, financial) belong, by right, to the individual. Only with his or her permission could this data be sold, traded or used for purposes other than the original transaction. The right to data privacy is one right that the creators of the UN Human Rights advocates did not have to think about.

It is certain that the Information Age will deal a completely different set of cards to all the players, and modify the balance of power between governments, corporations and the population at large. This new game promises to shift power away from governments and regulatory authorities, as well as from the public. There are no direct quantitative measures for such power shifts, but the dramatic trend of privatization that is sweeping the world provides some indication of what is going on. Figure 4.1 shows the process of systematic liquidation of government-controlled assets. Before Mrs Thatcher became Prime Minister of the UK, privatization was a rare event. Since then, a worldwide trend has caught on. For the year 1997 alone, the volume reached some US$157 billion, five times what it was in 1990. Developing countries have recently embarked on the same process, representing at least 30% of the total.

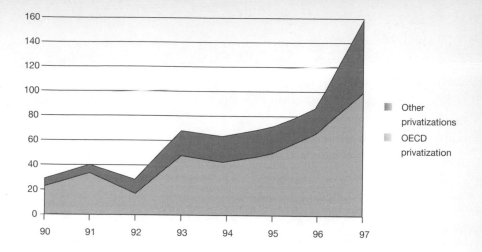

Figure 4.1 Global Privatizations 1990-96 (sources: OECD,[115] The Economist)[116]

I believe that it is rarely 'healthy' for governments to own businesses. But the point here is that this unprecedented global trend towards privatization is one indicator for the growing loss of influence that governments have over their economies.

Corporate power: some facts and figures

- Of the 100 richest economies, 51 are now corporations. For instance, sales by General Motors are greater than the GDP (Gross Domestic Product) of Denmark, or Ford than South Africa.
- The world's 200 largest corporations now control 28% of the global economy, yet need to employ only 0.3% of its population to achieve that.[117]
- The sales of the world's largest 200 corporations are equivalent to 30% of global domestic product. Their total annual sales (US$7.1 trillion) are larger than the combined GDP of 182 countries (i.e. all but the largest nine countries).
- About one-third of global trade is really intra-corporate trade, i.e. one subsidiary exporting to another subsidiary controlled by the same corporation.
- American corporations pay less in US taxes than they receive in public subsidies from US taxpayers.[118] In 1994, US corporations received $167 billion in tax breaks, to be compared with $50 billion in total federal expenditure on welfare (AFDC).[119]
- *Business Week* reports in 1997 that the compensation for American CEOs of these same publicly subsidized corporations has soared to an average of US$5.5 million per year, while the wages of the working population remained stagnant. In the 1960s, CEOs' salaries were 30 times greater than those of the average worker; compared with 200 times today.[120]
- For every dollar in total taxes (local, state and Federal) paid by individuals, corporations used to pay 76 cents in the early 1950s (1950-54). By 1980-92 corporate taxes are down to 21 cents per dollar of individual taxes.[121] In Canada, even in a year of record corporate profits, like 1996, corporate income taxes were down to 14.5 cents for each dollar of individual taxes

There are many other indicators of the plausibility of the Corporate Millennium (see sidebar).

Is it possible that this trend is the result of what Noam Chomsky has termed 'manufactured consent'? The purpose of mainstream media, Chomsky claims, is not so much to inform or report on what happens, but rather to shape public opinion in accordance with the agendas of the prevailing corporate powers. As the last Prime Minister of the UK observed, because the corporate world was also controlling the content of the media it was able to neutralize any compensating power that the media might otherwise have provided. As a result 'Virtually everywhere the mass media provide people primarily with commercial messages . . . It is hard to discover in most of today's newsmedia the kind of information that would help citizens of democratic societies to reach well-informed political decisions . . . The media have been called "Weapons of Mass Distraction".'[122]

Advertising EVERYWHERE[123]

Advertising is ubiquitous, to the point of being the cultural expression of our times. We have become accustomed to being bombarded with ads as we watch a TV programme or even movies and videos. Here are some other spaces that used to be ad-free but will not remain so:

- Giant labels on clothing transform their wearers into free billboard walkers.
- Fruit Label Company, based in California, has started placing ads on fruit: the video-release of *Jurassic Park* will be accompanied by little ad labels on 12 million Granny Smith and Fuji apples in supermarkets across America. The possibilities are endless: labelling lemons with 'if you don't want a lemon, buy a Ford', or fresh tomatoes with Campbell Soup stickers.
- Another promising new advertising medium is the beach, where for $25,000 per month a message is inscribed every day in gigantic lettering in the sand. Credit is given for rainy days because 'fewer people will be exposed to the ad'.
- Since May 1998 in Berlin, Germany, Metro Cinevision is bringing 30-second ghostlike 3D ads that appear to float outside subway trains. The subway riders are considered a prime captive viewers' target.
- The first ads have started appearing at eye level in public lavatories, taking advantage of another kind of captive market.
- With government cuts to education, more and more universities are cutting costs by marketing their students to corporations. When a Stanford University computer course is given in the Hewlett Packard auditorium of the Bill Gates Computer

Science Building, has the medium become the message? University campuses are also a main target for Cycle Stops Displays, an Ottawa-based company that provides free bicycle stands for campuses with the condition that they are adorned with eye-level ad panels. The University of Guelph has been the first to accept these racks.

- In 1995, the US Supreme Court ruled that a colour can become a registered trademark. Pepsi's next global marketing campaign called 'Project Blue' includes registering a shade of royal blue as a patented colour and a $50 million production for the first ad filmed in space in cooperation with the Russian space station Mir. Pepsi is also considering a giant permanent satellite billboard in space visible around the world as soon as the technology becomes affordable.

- Sounds can now also be patented. MGM has trademarked its 'lion's roar', NBC its 'three chimes', and Harley Davidson filed a petition on the 'hog call' or the sound of a '45-degree V-twin single crankpin motor'.

- The James Bond movie *Tomorrow Never Dies* refined the concept of 'global integrated film promotions' by marketing the movie and a series of tied-in products simultaneously. Avis Rent-A-Car, BMW, Smirnoff vodka, Visa International and Heineken have all announced tie-in promotions. For instance, panels of the 007 star will grace point-of-sales displays wherever Heineken beer is sold; and in the film, 007's BMW smashes spectacularly into a Heineken beer truck.

- 'Virtual Advertising', the use of digital computer images which are inserted in TV scenes, started in sports events (e.g. a giant Cola ad appears live in the middle of the playing court), but have now spread to entertainment programming as well. It enables an Evian bottle to be placed on a table, or a fashion retailer's shopping bag in a hotel lobby, where none were at the moment of the original shoots. These ads in live programming are more impactful than those in the breaks, because 'people pay more attention during the show than during a commercial' [124] and because the inserted ads can be changed for different reruns and markets. This makes the debate over the colouring of old black-and-white movies look quite quaint.

- The Academy of Arts and Television – the organization that hands out the Emmy awards – decided in 1997 to add a new 'Best Commercial' category. After all, the most talented people in the industry and a lot more money go into producing TV ads than into the programmes themselves.

- On the other hand, Dr Marty Rossman, director of the Academy of Guided Images, which has pioneered the use of imagery for medical purposes, claims that advertising should be considered 'pollution for the imagination'. He says that the use and abuse of the most powerful images to make people feel incomplete has

enormous consequences in social and health costs. The most powerful
archetypes, from the female body to subliminal colour combinations, are quite
effective at selling products, but at what psychological cost?

Unlike other species, over at least the last 300,000 years, humans have evolved a genetically built-in need to ponder and celebrate the mysteries of the universe they live in. During their evenings mesmerized in front of the TV, children today find the equivalent of myths, story telling and elders' chants in initiation caverns. 'One could say that the chant has been replaced by the TV show, but at the core of each show, driving the action, and determining whether or not the show will survive the season, is the advertisement. What is the effect on our children? Before a child enters first grade class, and before entering in any real way into our religious ceremonies, a child will have soaked up 30 thousand advertisements. None of us feels very good about this, but for the most part we ignore it. It's background noise. We learned to accept it so long ago that we hardly think about it any more. But at the deeper level, what we need to confront is the power of the advertiser to promulgate a world-view, a mini-cosmology based on dissatisfaction and craving. One of the clichés for how to construct an ad captures the point succinctly: 'an ad's job is to make them unhappy with what they have.'[125] In short, values are not inborn but a cultural creation, and our culture has become saturated by the corporate advertiser's agenda (see sidebar on advertising everywhere). The net result is that materialism and consumerism has become the real religion and world-view that gets inculcated in contemporary children.

Notice that here again we do not even need a dark conspiracy for any of this to happen. During the heydays of the 1950s and 1960s, broadcast technology did not enable broadcasters to charge consumers directly. So they charged advertisers for time used to expose viewers to ads interwoven with programmes. 'This created a bias towards lowest-common-denominator programming. Consider two programmes, one which will fascinate 500,000 people, and the other which 30 million people will watch as slightly preferable to watching their ceiling.' If the advertisers pay for the programme, they will prefer the mass audience because its degree of interest in the programme has little relationship to the effectiveness of the ad. If the viewers were to pay, they might very well get the niche programme. 'As a result, charging-for-advertising gives every incentive to broadcast what a mass audience would tolerate. It gives no incentive to broadcast what a niche would love.'[126]

■ Education Inc.

After graduating from commercial TV kindergarten, Education Inc. could very well become the future of schooling, all the way to the most prestigious universities. 'This is the future: universities will have to become entrepreneurs, working with corporations on curriculum and other matters or they will die' was the conclusion of Del Weber, chancellor of the University of Nebraska at Omaha,[129] after First Data Resources built an engineering school on his campus designed specifically for the needs of that corporation. Is this corporatization of the university yet another step in the direction that so many other aspects of society are already moving (see sidebar)?

EVERYTHING, Inc.

Here are some arenas in life that, traditionally, have not fallen within the corporate domain, but where new trends can be detected:

■ 'We should recognize that the architectural reconfiguration of our cities and towns has been an undemocratic event – with decisions in effect handed down from above by an assembly of corporate agents.' [127] Extreme forms of this include malls with their own rules and security force replacing public streets; or sports clubs replacing public playgrounds. Entire incorporated suburbs and 'walled communities' built and run by corporations replace cities. The number of such 'secure communities' in the US alone rose from 1,000 in 1965 to 80,000 in 1985, and this trend has accelerated recently.

■ The world's most effective peacemaking force is not run by the United Nations but by Executive Outcome, a South African mercenary company that restored, for example, relative stability in Sierra Leone in late 1995.

■ 'While governments fight against drug abuse, often with pathetic results, pharmaceutical corporations have worked through governments to receive sanction on drugs such as stimulants and anti-depressants – whose effects, it could be argued, are as great as those of outlawed drugs.'[128]

■ Many sports, churches, and religious sects have become big businesses.

■ Dennis Judd, Urban Affairs Department of the University of Missouri at St Louis, concludes, 'We have always put up with restrictions inside a corporation that we would never put up with in the public sphere. But what many do not realize is that life within some sort of corporation is what life will increasingly be about.'

There are indications that many people are becoming more aware of the risks of the Corporate Millennium. A few examples follow:

Media credibility

■ The credibility of the media in general has dropped to a historic low: a 1997 Harris Poll finds only 18% of the US public still have confidence in

TV news, and 12% in the press. This percentage has shown a steady decline; the corresponding numbers in 1990 were respectively 27% and 18%. Another poll showed that in 1985, 84% of Americans felt their newspaper did a good job of being fair; by 1996 that number had fallen to 47%. In 1985, 55% of Americans believed that news organizations 'got their facts right'. By 1997 that number had declined to 37%.[130] It has become a practice for many magazines to submit articles for prior review by the advertisers. The *Los Angeles Times* has even reorganized its management structure in order to maximize advertiser-editor cooperation.

■ However, there is also a growing awareness of the deadly trap that a Corporate Millennium means for the credibility of the media. 'Establishing credibility means developing a reputation for providing correct information, even when it may reflect badly on the information provider.'[131] In short, in an information age, credibility is the real capital. And playing to the corporate agenda for short-term financial benefits is squandering that capital, which is potentially irretrievable. Peter Bhatia, member of the Board of Directors of the American Society of Newspaper Editors, says: 'Our credibility is as low as it's ever been. There is a lot of soul-searching going on right now in our industry.'[132] The *Columbia Journalism Review* called the censorship that results from corporate-editorial cooperation 'The Big Squeeze'.[133] In a democracy, what is ultimately at stake is the legitimacy of both the media and the corporations.

■ In a remarkable exception, *Time* magazine published a whole special report on 'Corporate Welfare'.[134] It defines corporate welfare as 'any action by local, state and federal government that gives a corporation or an entire industry, a grant, real estate, a low-interest loan or a government service. It can also be a tax break.' The conclusions: 'the Federal Government alone shells out $120 billion per year in corporate welfare ... The justifcation for much of this welfare is that the US government is creating jobs ...'

But the actual numbers tell another story (see sidebar).

Subsidies per job created

The subsidies per job give an indication whether the 'job argument' for subsidies is valid.[135]

■ The State of Illinois paid $44,000 per job to Sears, Roebuck & Co. to keep its corporate headquarters from moving out of the State.
■ The State of Indiana paid $72,000 per job to United Airlines in an aircraft maintenance facility.

- The State of Alabama gave $169,000 per job to Mercedes-Benz for its automobile assembly plant in Tuscaloosa.
- The State of Pensylvania gave $323,000 per job to Kvaerner ASA, a Norwegian engineering firm, to reopen the Philadelphia Naval Shipyard.
- The State of Louisiana holds the record with subsidies to Uniroyal ($100,000 per job); Procter and Gamble ($3,100,000 per job); BP Exploration ($4,000,000 per job); Dow Chemical ($10,700,000 per job) and Mobil Oil Co. ($29,000,000 per job).

■ Autonomous corporate power

- David Korten, a Ph.D. from Stanford Business School, who also taught at Harvard Business School before serving with the Ford Foundation and the US AID programme in Asia, concludes that 'the contemporary corporation increasingly exists as an entity apart – even from the people who compose it. Every member of the corporate class, no matter how powerful his or her position within the corporation, has become expendable – as growing numbers of top executives are learning. As corporations gain in autonomous institutional power and become more detached from people and place, the human interest and the corporate interests increasingly diverge. It is almost as though we were being invaded by alien beings intent on colonizing the planet, reducing us to serfs, and then excluding as many of us as possible.'[136]

- Ian Angell, Professor of Information Systems at the London School of Economics, writes in the the *Independent*: 'The main problem of the future will be the glut of unnecessary people who will be irrelevant to the needs of corporations, and therefore will be uneducated, untrained, ageing and resentful . . . The slow redistribution of wealth to which we became accustomed after World War II is already rapidly reversed, so the future is one of inequality. We are entering an age of hopelessness, an age of resentment, an age of rage . . . The world belongs already to the global corporation. The nation state is now desperately sick.'

- Peter Montague, from the Environmental Research Foundation (Annapolis, Maryland) says: 'The corporations pretty much determine all the basics of modern life, just as the Church did in the Middle Ages. . . . Small corporate elites pretty much determine what most of us will read; what we will see in theaters and on TV; what subjects will become public issues permissible for discussion and debate; what ideas our children will absorb in the classroom; how our food and fiber will be grown, processed and marketed; what consumer products will be made by what technologies using what raw materials; whether we will have widely available, affordable health care; how work will be defined, organized, and compensated; what forms of energy will be available to us; how much toxic contamination will be present in our air, water, soil and food; who will have enough money to run an election campaign and who will not.'

■ The root cause?

While these concerns are relevant and poignant, I have come to the conclusion that they are attacking symptoms rather than causes. In modern Western history, power and influence have traditionally been shared and/or balanced between four 'estates' – the government, business, academia, and the media. Today, more blatantly and directly than ever before, money is controlling all four of these estates. Even CEOs of the most powerful corporations are obliged to do what the financial market wants, or they are fired and replaced by someone who will. Giving priority to long-term thinking over next quarter's profits is brutally punished under the present money system. At some level, we are all prisoners of the same money game.

In short, the money system is what creates the structural conflict experienced by so many CEOs between stockholders' interests, their own personal ethics, and their concerns for their grandchildren's future. My contribution to addressing this dilemma is to propose a money system that will harness corporate power and direct it towards the goal of long-term sustainability (Chapter 8: The Global Reference Currency – Making Capitalism Sustainable).

Even though it may seem that the Corporate Millennium is looming before us, this scenario is only one of the ways in which the power shift away from the nation-states could manifest itself. The next scenario – Careful Communities – reveals another very different set of dynamics.

■ Careful communities

The other night I woke up from a strange dream.

I had dreamt that I was in San Francisco, at the colourful intersection where Haight Street meets Golden Gate Park. I was sitting in a coffee shop, next to a little shop with a garish sign saying 'Tsutomo Tattoos'. I was overhearing a long monologue of a parent talking to an adolescent. There was a calendar hanging on the wall in the coffee shop – a calendar of the year 2020.

This is how the monologue went.[137]

Haight Street 2020

I got this first one at Nike. Back in '94. I was 23, a kid. I worked there delivering – get this – mail. Yeah, paper. Yeah, back when you still could cut down trees. Anyway. We all got them. Sort of started the thing, you know? The 'tatsume', tattoos to mark your jobs, your history, your path. The tat identified you as family.

This one is from Microsoft. No, I don't mean 'Sonysoft'. Microsoft, back when Gates was alive. Yeah, you've heard of him. That's the Windows 95 banner, well, reworked to be the Windows 98 banner. I did phone support. Yes, humans did that, punk. I lived in Seattle at the time. A bunch of us lived together in a house near Capitol Hill. It wasn't a commune or some other hippified label that you find in the docs. Those days, we were only sharing living space; we didn't share anything else. No, not even companions, this was before the treatment.

I met this really great woman in San Francisco – I ended up moving down here in '99. That's the logo for Java Jonestown, the coffee house where I worked in North Beach. Strange things started happening just after that. Religious nuts got the Millennium fever and[138] spread a feeling of unreality and fear of the future in almost all aspects of everyday life.

In 2000, my folks moved to Idaho to join some end-of-the-world religious group. They kept trying to get me to move out there too, but each time I went it was more and more clear that I would never really fit in. I wasn't the right age and I didn't have kids. When I finally left, the Idaho Christian Fellowship (Kuna Community) wasn't too sad to see me go. What was weird, though, was in my trips back and forth, and in mail to the home back in San Francisco, I realized the exact same thing was happening there. Everyone was locking themselves up into tight little homogeneous communities, even the hipsters and queers, and everyone was closing in on their own little niche.

Then came the Big Crash. I never really understood what the hell brought down the whole house of cards of the old money game. All I know is that it started with the banks in Japan going belly up on a trillion-dollar loss or something, and the whole thing was over before they could even print the newspapers to talk about it. Nothing was the same after that: governments, businesses, everything that depended on international contacts got into trouble at the same time.

That there is the Americorps II bar-code – one of the last things that central government managed to launch. Etzione thought of that, at HUD, and the conservatives loved it. Kept track of us; kept us safe. Kept us careful. Half of my house joined the Corps, even while we worked at Microsoft. The Big Crash had left us all shaken up in some way – jobs, friends, losing houses on mortgage payments, whatever – and we all needed some way to work it out. I did on-line counseling. That's why the Corps-code is blue.

For California, the cherry on the cake came when the Really Big One hit. Almost everybody lost someone they knew. I was among the lucky ones: that day I was out seeing some suppliers up in Sonoma. That earthquake also closed the chapter on the relevance of Washington bigwigs for us here. The Big Crash had loosened the financial grip. After the Really Big One, they had just to let go of all the rest of it.

One of the key tools that made it possible for everybody to lock themselves into such self-contained cocoons was all these local currency systems. Some had been around for 10, even 20 years, but few people took them seriously then. After the Big Crash, they started spreading like wildfire, just for survival.

When you were born, my parents really wanted us back out in Idaho, but I didn't want you growing up there. They put a lot of pressure on me, but I finally decided to stay in SF.

You may not know this, but SF used to be a pretty diversified city, with a lot of high-tech jobs, and people traveling all over the place. I still managed to move around after everybody had already locked themselves up in little community cultures. That's because we're part of a 'cosmopolite' com, a community that works with other communities, trading ideas. When you're old enough you should get out, too. Take a look at the world. The differences between communities will surprise you, because they aren't what you expect. Lots of places keep themselves safe by locking out not just people that don't fit in, but ideas that don't fit too. Even movies are altered, sometimes the language, sometimes the characters. You should see how the newsnets are changed from place to place. With these new imaging techniques, they can shape anything to order. So all information flows within a com, and from the outside world into the com, can be nicely shaped to fit the world-view of the com's inhabitants. Some places around the country are spooky, with houses that all look alike and families that all look alike. I guess people find it easier that way. Most of them seem to like it, and those coms are pretty safe.

I think I'll try to take you to Europe, if we can make it work. The patchwork is still different there. But I'll have to get permission from the council; even a cosmopolite com has rules about Europe for kids. Some coms don't even let adults go there, but those are communities that don't like to let cosmopolites in either. Sometimes I wonder how they survive.

OK, that's my last tat: a licensed teacher. I like that one the best – they're using that new holographic ink for instructor tats now. That closes as many doors as it opens, of course. Teachers bring new ideas, we're meme-carriers, and cosmopolitan memes scare people. Even with all of the community protections, with walls around the homes and minds, identities are fragile. The Nation of Islam com lost almost half of its citizens last year in a struggle over identity – were they African, Muslim, American? The remaining NOI community, in South Cal, isn't letting any outsiders in, not even for biz.

So here we are. Tsutomo is the best tattist in the area. You scared? Don't be. The first tat is the hardest, but you're getting one to be proud of. Anyway, the party tonight will take your mind off the sting. You know, I think that boy with the Rainforest tat has his eye on you. Don't give me that look! Just remember that your community cares about you. We're all very proud of you.

That is when I woke up – in a cold sweat.

Careful Communities is a modern version of what happened in Western Europe in the first centuries after the collapse of the Roman Empire (*c.* AD 500-800). It was a return to smaller-scale homogeneous communities, fragmented by the vast and dangerous European forests, that each had their own local currencies, administration and in-bred world-views. Of necessity, they had become self-sustaining. Not everything was negative; for instance, it generated a remarkable upsurge in spirituality. One of the functions of the Church and monastic orders was equivalent to a 'cosmopolitan community' in Careful Communities. Some even have considered it the high period of 'Christian Mysticism', the period in the West where the sacred and the secular sustained each other and worked in harmony. But in most other regards, the assessment that it was a comparatively 'Dark Age' remains valid.

The 'Careful Communities' scenario is triggered by a sequence of breakdowns – such as a monetary crash, and a significant earthquake in California – each of which has been forecast by many specialists. They do not *have* to occur in order to attain this scenario, but their combination would be quite devastating to most centralized governance systems. Some experts claim that, alone, a monetary meltdown would be sufficient to provoke a breakdown of our current society.

■ Assessing possibilities of breakdowns

The plausibility and consequences of some breakdowns will now be assessed separately, and the consequences of their combination evaluated.

A monetary meltdown?

The potential breakdown of a large-scale monetary crisis exists. The Mexican crash of 1994-95, the Asian crisis of 1997 and the Russian one in 1998 are certainly not going to be the last monetary crises of our times. The dwarfing of the world economy by currency speculation (see Primer) guarantees similar future episodes. However, the 'Big Monetary Crash' would occur whenever the US$ comes under attack. It is not a question of whether, but only a question of when, the instabilities of the official monetary system will assail that linchpin currency of the global money system.[139]

Professor Robert Guttman of the Economics Department of Hofstra University describes the international monetary system as the Achilles heel of the US and the global community as a whole. It is the one way whereby a true Depression could repeat itself, with massive unemployment and socio-political consequences.

Every national currency in the world[140] – even the new euro – is defined in terms of the dollar, and therefore completely dependent on the stability of this linchpin currency. In the Primer, the context for a global meltdown – in technical parlance, 'systemic risk' – is described. The probability of such a meltdown is growing year by year as the volume of speculative flows increases – at the rate of about 15 to 25% per year – while the safety net provided by the central banks becomes increasingly inconsequential relative to the ever-growing speculative volume.

Many people worry about '*how* it could really happen?' This is the less important question. Did it really matter that the Kreditanstalt bank in Vienna provided the trigger for the London market panic that spread to become the 1929 crash in New York? What really matters – then as now – is the degree of stability or instability of the system as a whole. In comparison, identifying the precise card that will bring down the whole house of cards becomes anecdotal. Whether the falling card turns out to be another crisis like the Asian one, or a financial meltdown in Japan, or in the Eurodollar market, the final result that precipitates the unravelling of our dollar-based monetary system could be quite similar.

In Careful Communities, the financial trigger was an interplay between two of the weakest links in today's global system: a failure of the Japanese banking system that provokes a panic in the Eurodollar market, and proceeds from there to challenge the US dollar market. Such a chain reaction is definitely a technical possibility.[141]

A California 'Really Big One'

In comparison with the monetary breakdown, a significant earthquake in California may appear parochial. It is also one of the most studied risks around. According to the US Geological Survey study released in July 1990, there is a 67% chance that an earthquake of magnitude 7.1 or greater (Richter scale) will occur in the San Francisco Bay Area within 30 years. It may happen today, or 20 years from now.

Consequences of a combination

This example of the 'Really Big One' is used in 'Careful Communities' not to pile up disaster upon disaster gratuitously, but to illustrate how – if the monetary breakdown is serious enough – central governments could become quite incapable of dealing with local breakdowns. People would have to reorganize their lives to be more local and self-sustaining, and very different forms of governance – like the ones reflected in this scenario – could become plausible.

■ The forces feeding 'Careful Communities'

The Careful Communities scenario is driven by a collective reaction of retreating to safety. It makes a priority of the local security and community concerns that are already evident in today's society. When money breaks down, all outstanding financial agreements – such as salaries or rents – become meaningless. Life savings are wiped away in days, leaving people suddenly exposed to a future more uncertain than they ever thought possible. In these circumstances, collective fears and shadows can surge up powerfully.

But in several parts of the world, even more extreme forms of what is described here have already happened. In Yugoslavia, what started as a monetary problem in the late 1980s swiftly became intolerance towards the 'others', whom some ethnic leaders used as scapegoats to redirect anger away from themselves, and to reassert their power in the process. Therefore 'ethnic cleansing' is a direct consequence of the IMF readjustment programme of the late 1980s, which provided the socio-political context for extreme nationalist leaders to take over. The 1998 monetary problem in Indonesia, within days, triggered mob violence, plundering and rapes directed against Chinese minorities. Similarly, in Russia, discrimination against minorities has been exacerbated by the financial collapse. Almost nobody among the intelligentsia in any of these countries would have believed these events plausible even a few months before the mayhem started. Neither are such events unprecedented. For example, the Jewish minority became the scapegoat for the consequences of the monetary collapse of the 1920s in Germany. Monetary crashes leave people in fear, despair, and anger. This is an explosive social mix that irresponsible demagogues can exploit. The rise to power of Milosevic in Serbia after the Yugoslav monetary crisis of the late 1980s is only the latest demonstration that the recipe is still operational. Similarly, it is predictable that the Russian Ruble meltdown will bring to power more violently nationalistic and militaristic figures.

In Careful Communities, control over local currencies can be used to lock people into a safety cocoon. Like everything else in this world, local currencies can be used either positively or negatively, and in this scenario their restrictive potential is revealed. Later, in Chapters 5 and 6, you will learn that when designed to *complement* the national currency, the impact of community currencies is strongly constructive. You will also learn why and how these currencies have spread to over a dozen countries around the world.

If the official global money system goes into a meltdown, such local systems could very well become – by default – the best safety net around. Under the shock, people are likely to scurry for psychological security at any price. Paradoxically, the very strength of the forces leading towards globalization is fuelling a clearly discernible new emphasis on local priorities and local cultural homogeneity. This can take place peacefully, but, as has been seen in recent years, this is not always the case. The growing trend towards smaller-scale local ethnic priorities and cultural divisions has already unchained the dogs of violence and war in places as disparate as ex-Yugoslavia, Azerbaijan and Rwanda.

Timetable of the revolution

1980s: Development of the first LETS systems, the first postwar complementary currency systems mostly in Canada, Australia, New Zealand and Northern Europe (more details in Chapter 5)

1990: Tax-free approval of the local Time Dollar systems by the IRS in the US (see Chapter 6)

1991: Beginning of the first 'ethnic cleansing' war in Yugoslavia

1992: Ithaca HOURS introduced in Ithaca, New York

1995: Survey in the US showing that 83% of population put 'rebuilding community' as top priority

1997: Decentralization of the welfare system, acceleration of devolution of power from the Federal Government to the States and municipalities in the US

2010: First year where more commercial exchanges are occurring in complementary currencies than in the old battered national currencies

2020: The girl in the nightmare on Haight Street gets her initiation tattoo

Among the plausible futures, the two described so far are neither the worst nor the most favourable. We shall now have a brief look at two more extreme possibilities. They will be called 'Hell on Earth' and 'Sustainable Abundance'.

■ Hell on Earth

The seed bed for 'Hell on Earth' is a similar combination of breakdowns as in 'Careful Communities'. The main difference in 'Hell on Earth' is that instead of people organizing themselves in self-contained communities, a highly individualistic 'free for all' ensues. It is the world that would result if enough people believed that the solution to any breakdown was to buy more bullets for their guns.

In contrast with the fictitious people described in the previous two scenarios, in 'Hell on Earth' everybody is real, actually existing in 1996. The lives of Red, Sean, Addison, Todd and Jeremy are described in the words of my friend Katherine who, at 15, was the youngest member of the audience on which I tested the ideas presented in this book during a series of conferences about the 'Future of Money'. What we learn from her is that 'Hell on Earth' is already happening. And it is less than half an hour's drive from the wealthiest counties and the fastest-growing economy in the US. 'Hell on Earth' is happening in the backyard of the world's only superpower and most advanced technological innovator. It is happening during one of the longest economic boom periods on record, during a year when the Dow Jones has broken its record high 43 times.

Katherine's friends

RED

Red was abandoned, left on the streets of Berkeley, California, by his parents when he was three years old. A young homeless couple took Red under their wing. They spent most of their winters in shelter after shelter, because three days was the limit on how long anyone was allowed to stay. In the summers they would roam around Telegraph Ave, day in and day out, searching through dumpsters and garbage cans, looking for their next meal. No one ever talked to them. No one ever bothered to stop. One day Red woke up and they were gone. He was seven years old.

When Red was ten, he met another boy in the same predicament. This boy's name was Sean. He was 15 and had been homeless since he was five. Sean arranged his hair in two turquoise Mohawks that sliced out of his skull side-by-side. The hair dye matched his eyes and pale skin. He wore a black hooded sweatshirt with drawings and patches sloppily sewn on everywhere with white dental floss. He wore chains around his neck, as well as spiked chokers and bracelets. His nails were neatly painted black. He called himself a gutter punk, an anarchist, a squatter, a member of society that everyone wanted to ignore, and for which no one wanted to take responsibility.

Red was captivated by Sean – someone who was like him, someone else who had been forgotten, erased. Sean became Red's mentor. He named him Silence Red – Silence because he was always quiet, and Red because it was his favorite color.

As Red got older, he became part of the society known as the gutter punks or squatters, the lost children who had lost their families and come together to form their own. They never fought among themselves and rarely caused any trouble. They raged against the society that had overlooked them. They hated all adults, especially parents. Most of them had either been abandoned by their parents or had run away from abusive homes. Members of the middle and upper classes spat on them, cursed at them, accused them of being drug addicts and alcoholics. They were hauled off to jail for sleeping outdoors at night, for sitting on sidewalks, even for leaning against walls. They were harassed by everyone, even though they were just fighting to stay alive.

Red and Sean squatted together as brothers for 15 years. They didn't use drugs and they didn't drink. They traveled from place to place, looking for the perfect home, but they always returned to Berkeley in the summertime.

Red was a man when he died, but he was only 25. He always said that he wanted to die by decapitation to get rid of the sickness in his head. Then he would always laugh. Before he died, he had told Sean that he had had this horrible pain in his head as long as he could remember and that it was getting unbearable. Sean took him to a friendly doctor. The doctor said that Red had a tumor in his brain and that it was too late, that without medical insurance or money, nothing could be done and that he would die within a few months. The doctor gave Sean a prescription for pain killers, drugs, but Red refused to take them. One day Sean went to a 7-11 to get a Slurpee. When he got back, he saw Red lying in the grass. He had slit his own throat to get rid of the sickness in his head.

When most people saw Red, they were terrified. He was 6′ 7″ tall. He had 8-inch red liberty spikes in his hair. He had 27 piercings in his porcelain face alone. But if you looked in his eyes, you knew he never was, nor ever would be a monster. Red would never have hurt a fly. He wouldn't even hurt those who had hurt him. He was the nicest, sweetest person you could know. He would always make sure that everyone he knew had eaten before he would eat. The only problem was that no one would or could ever look in his eyes to see the sadness and the kindness, because he was virtually invisible. Had someone seen him he might have lived just a little longer. But for most, ignorance is easier than compassion.

And when all the rich people went to sleep, Sean gathered some of the gutter punks to take Red's body to the dump and they burned him. His ashes are on your $4,000 lawn, and his body is making your flowers grow.

One of Red's favorite songs was by the Rancids; it goes:

'Red and white stripes flyin'
White for skin and Red for dyin'
Why can't I walk on through
and not feel like I am in hell.'

ADDISON

I looked at Addison, and it was death staring back at me. He stood before me, not as the beloved boy that I knew, but as the dark angel whose image haunts me in my dreams, the angel of death. His molasses skin was yellowing; his black eyes looked as if they had been sanded, left with a dull finish. His paper-thin body shook compulsively as he stepped down from the green bus toward me. He was a torrent of anxiety and sadness. He looked at his old shoes as if he were observing someone else's feet. He couldn't feel his feet, but he knew they were there because he could see them.

His skin was peeling and his hands felt like splintered cardboard as I helped him off the final gray step of the bus. Then the bus was all of a sudden gone, and we were alone, and for the first time in my life I was scared. I was scared to look at him, and it hurt to hold his hands, which were dry and felt like shards of glass. His fingernails were falling off. He pulled a comb out of his pocket and combed what was left of his hair. The comb pulled out a big chunk of gray, thin kinky hair. He didn't even notice.

He used to be so beautiful. My God, now he looked 60 years old, and he was only 16. He looked into my eyes, and he saw my pity, which I could not hide from him. He whispered, 'Don't worry, Katherine. It doesn't hurt.' I knew he was lying. All expression in his face was lost. He didn't have the muscle control.

He smelled like a rotting egg, but he was really a rotting boy. His lips were blue and cracked. I kissed my friend softly. He tasted like metal on a 90-degree day. With every step he wheezed, soft little crackles. And I didn't want to touch him for fear that he might crumble and fall beneath my stroke. I helped him sit down on a bench. It was cold, gray concrete. He looked up at the sky and then at the trees around him. 'There aren't any trees where I live,' he whispered as he tried to hide a tear rolling over his face.

And then he passed out, snared into his dark, cold, black sleep, where reality was just a fragment of his imagination and death and suffering reigned. Blood trickled down from his parched lips. His lungs were bleeding, and he reddened the bench with the serum of his suffering. The blood dripped onto his blue sweatshirt, and then the flowing stopped.

And he lay on that bench for hours in his sleep, and I held him. The blood would flow, and then it would cease. Then it would start again. But, the suffering never stopped, and it was only then that I realized that my dark angel was dying. But, in reality, he was already dead.

★★★

Addison grew up in a black ghetto called Hunters Point in San Francisco. He was beaten up for being a good student and by seventh grade had virtually dropped out of school. He showed me his homework, all neatly completed, but which he never had dared to turn in. He was forced to join a gang when he was 15, told that he would be hunted down and shot if he didn't. He began to use drugs and drink heavily, a way of numbing himself to his own pain. One of his closest friends, who was a crack baby and had been addicted to cocaine since birth, died of a massive heart attack when he was 16, trying to kick his habit. As the people around Addison began to die, he sank into a deep depression. He contracted seven different strains of HIV by the time he was 16 and developed full-blown AIDS just a few months later. He had an estimated two months to live when I sat with him that day. I met him at Pier 39 in San Francisco. I was the only white person he knew, and compared to him I was rich. We had been best friends for two years, and I tried to keep him alive as best I could. But the day before Addison's 17th birthday, he took a 9mm gun from beneath his bedding, and he shot himself in the head. He lay dead in his room. No one found his body for five days.

Addison was living in hell, and he couldn't handle it. But then again, who could? Out of the 15 people that Addison grew up with in Hunters Point, 12 died within six months of his death. Three died just months before. They were all dead within 14 months. They lived in an environment that was de-evolving because of isolation, drugs that were rumored to be supplied by the government, and because of an American people who chose to ignore the poverty, to close their eyes because they felt it wasn't their responsibility. For them, the ghettos didn't even exist.

TODD and JEREMY

Todd and Jeremy ran away from home when Todd was five and Jer was nine. They took the train to San Francisco, where they slept in Golden Gate Park. They had lived in a trailer park in San José with their father who had sexually molested them and abused them for as long as they could remember. Their mother had died in a car accident just months after the birth of Todd. Their father was unemployed, but the television, where he spent most of his time, always seemed to work. The children cooked their own meals, consisting mostly of cereal and of Tater Tots, deep fried potato scraps.

Todd's given name was Christina, but Jer, her older brother, had always wanted a younger brother, so when they packed their few possessions, Jer renamed his sister Todd. She had a thick mane of blond, almost cream-colored hair that cascaded to just below her waist. She had a small body and high cheekbones that accented her aquamarine eyes. She spoke seldom, and when she did, she was so quiet that it almost hurt to listen to her. She used small fragile words and never looked you in the eye. Jer on the other hand, when speaking, used a barrage of cuss words while frantically flailing his arms about as a way of assuring that his point was understood. He would run his grimy hands through his fluorescent blue liberty spikes, wads of hair that he glued into seven 6″ points. He talked about his dreams of getting his lip pierced and blowing up the White House with a Swiss army knife, dental floss, and a match stick like the TV hero and escape artist, McGiver.

Todd and Jeremy would sit on Haight Street for hours – Todd quietly asking the people who passed by for a nickel or dime, Jer harassing people for blocks for not giving them even a penny, screaming, 'FUCK YOU!' as mothers and daughters, fathers and sons, passed by them without even a glance. As night came they would retreat back into the park, the place where they felt the safest. For them, it was the beginning of the end of their lives.

> 'Deprived of any hope.
> Taught they couldn't cope.
> Slaves right from the start.
> 'Till death do them part.
> Poor little fuckers, what a sorry pair,
> Had their lives stolen, but they didn't really care.
> Poor little darlings, just your ordinary folks,
> Victims of the system and its cruel jokes.'
> -CRASS

'Hell on Earth' describes a world where there is a lot of work to be done, but there is simply no money around to bring the people and the work together. When children have no chance to develop themselves, the result becomes a way of life that is guaranteed to perpetuate, possibly for generations. The linkage between this situation and our topic of money may appear obvious: joblessness, bankruptcy and/or financial failure have made the parents of these kids lose their homes in the first place. Once started, the currency scarcity snowball continues. Without an education there is no prayer in hell that these kids will get a job. There will not even be money for their burial. Mental illness is another way out. A Chicago study found that 32.2% of newly admitted mental patients had a history of homelessness prior to their first hospitalization.[142]

It has proved remarkably difficult to find reliable statistics about homelessness, particularly homeless children in America. Mainstream media refer to it less and less, even as the reality of the problem grows. The number of mentions of homelessness in *Washington Post* headlines dropped from 149 in 1990, to 45 in 1995 and to 18 by 1998.[143] As one apologetic data administrator put it: 'People who have the money are not interested in finding out; those who are interested don't have the money to find out. And researchers do the studies for which they can get paid.' She explained that the best data is generated indirectly, because each county keeps track of actual numbers of families and children who seek assistance and are eligible for a particular shelter programme (the AFDC-HAP)[144] during each fiscal year.

Figure 4.5 shows that the number of homeless children in the San Francisco Bay Area alone passed the 40,000 mark in 1995: 325% higher than it was eight years earlier. These numbers reflect by definition only 'eligible recipients', so the actual numbers must be higher.

There may be many reasons why the parents of these children became homeless, but the simplest is straightforward arithmetic. The average household income in the California Bay Area increased by 34.3% between 1980 and 1990. The cost of living went up during that time by 64%, almost double that amount. The average rent for a two-bedroom unit increased by 110% over the same time period, while rent for a vacant studio increased by a whopping 288%.[146] This explains why 20% of the homeless families have at least one parent with a full-time job. In short, the fastest-rising component of the homeless is the families of the 'working poor' of yesteryear.

San Francisco is in no way a strange anomaly. Because the US Department of Education funds a project tracking schooling problems

Thousands

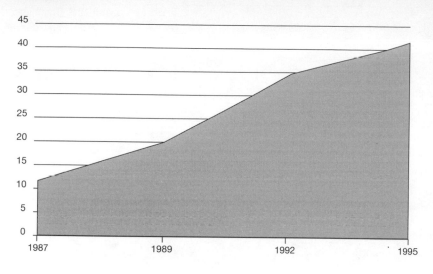

Figure 4.5 Thousands of homeless children in San Francisco Bay Area [145]

experienced by homeless children, it has prepared a report for the US Congress identifying the different ages of homeless children. Here again, only eligible recipients are counted, which means these children still have to be 'in the system' enough to actually try to go to school. For instance, it is unlikely that any of Katherine's friends would be picked up by these statistics. Here too the graph illustrates really a *minimum* level of the problem at hand. The most striking aspect of these statistics is the dramatic increase of homeless children in the lowest age brackets (less than six years old).

'Trickle down theory' or 'hoping for better economic times' is clearly not addressing the problem. In parallel, the number of families getting federal housing help dropped from 400,000 in the 1970s to 40,000 in the Reagan years (mid 1980s) to zero after the National Housing Act was passed in September 1996.

Having a full-time job at minimum wage does not provide someone a home anywhere in America. In 1996, the US Conference of Mayors found that nationwide 19% of the homeless population were employed.[148] Declining wages have put housing out of reach of many workers: in no state can a full-time minimum wage earner afford the costs of a one-bedroom unit at fair market rent.[149] In 45 states and the District of Columbia, families would need to earn at least double the minimum wage in order to afford a

Thousands

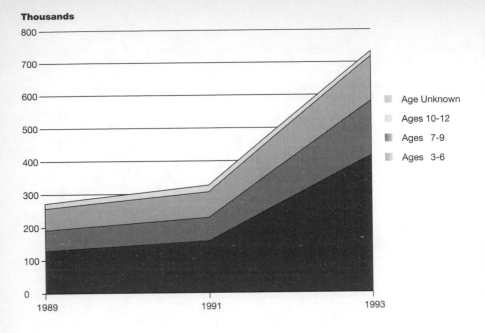

Figure 4.6: Thousands of homeless children in the US, by age group (US Department of Education, July 1995)[147]

two-bedroom apartment at fair market prices.[150] The fastest-growing segment of the homeless population is families with children, now about 40% of the people who become homeless. Requests for emergency shelter by families with children in 29 US cities are increasing at a rate of 7% per year. The same study found that 24% of the requests for shelter by homeless families were being denied due to lack of resources. The net result: children currently account for 27% of the total homeless population, and their average age has been steadily dropping.[151] While in 1987, the average age of a homeless child in New York was nine years old, as of 1992, it was down to four years old.[152]

All this occurred *before* 1996, when the responsibility of the US welfare system was transferred to the states and municipalities. On the second anniversary of this welfare reform, the media and politicians from both parties announced it a success due to large declines in the welfare rolls, and an increase of recipients finding employment. But an independent study released in December 1998[153] revealed that the number of children living in extreme poverty (below one-half of the poverty line of $6,401 per year for a family of three) grew by 400,000 between 1995 and 1997. Many families are being 'bumped off' the welfare lists through little or no fault of their own. For example, a state-funded study of Utah families who were denied assistance because of failing to participate in required activities found that 23% failed to participate because of lack of transportation, 43% due to a health condition, 18% due to lack of child care, and 20% due to mental health issues.

This is happening while the US economy is in its longest boom in history . . .

■ Sustainable Abundance

My strongest motivation for researching and writing this book has been my increasing belief that it is possible for us to create a Golden Age of Sustainable Abundance within our lifetimes. This letter to my best friend from high school days, now a Benedictine monk living at Lake Titicaca in Southern Peru, explains why.

Letter to a friend

My dear friend Pierre,

I am in the process of writing my next book about a topic that you – in your monk's retreat near your lake at the edge of the world – will probably consider of little relevance. Nevertheless, of all the people I know, you are one of the very few who live in the ultimate luxury – to be able to dedicate your full time and energy to following your bliss, your calling, to being who you want to be, without any concern over money. It is ironic that only monks, who don't own anything, or possibly the *very* rich, or the extraordinarily gifted, can afford your equanimity about money. The rest of us, the vast majority of humans, even in the richest countries in the world, have succumbed to the obligation – or you might say the temptation? – of 'making a living' that does not really coincide with what we really would like to be doing or being.

How much have we had to give up of our being, of who we really want to be, in this process of making a living? Many have not even dared to find out what they really would like to do, out of the fear that it would be too painful to go back to the 'normal' job after that. The game we play is that – later, when we retire, when we have put enough money aside – then we will take care of our dreams. Some take it in little instalments. We rush through our week, looking forward to the weekend or a vacation, when we will do what we really want to do.

You know that I have not always been optimistic about the future of humankind. You know that I was 'realistic' enough to choose not to have any children if they have to live in periodic fear of atomic annihilation, as was the case during the Cold War. So what I have dreamt about may come as a surprise to you. I have seen the possibility of a Golden Age of Sustainable Abundance, where the money we use will enable us to be ourselves. I have dared to dream that each child born into this world will have as a main concern the discovery what his or her calling really is, and have the opportunity to become a master in that endeavor. What if the main reason geniuses are so rare is that we kill the genius even before anybody knows in what field she is a genius? And how many of those who find out what they really want to be have the opportunity or the resources to learn how to realize their full potential? Maybe the human race will need all the geniuses it can produce to get out of the collective corner into which we have painted ourselves.

What if the scarcity is not mostly 'out there' in nature, as we all have believed for centuries? What if the money system we have been using, by which we have been collectively hypnotized, was continuously creating that very scarcity that we most fear? Is there a limit to the amount of learning we can do, to the amount of passion, creativity or beauty we can generate and enjoy? What if every garden could be cared for with the love and attention to minutiae that have created traditional Japanese tea gardens? What if every child could be encouraged by the best mentors in her field of bliss? What if every street in our cities could become a work of beauty? What if the limitations arise when we change 'work' into 'jobs', i.e. when we need to exchange our work for an artificially scarce currency? Why could we not design a money system that works *for us*, rather than having us work *for it*? Walter Wriston, ex-Chairman of Citibank, defined money as information. Why should information be scarce, particularly at a time when the technologies of the Information Age are spreading like wildfire all over the world?

Yes, I'll concede to you that it is not quite *that* simple. Before you conclude that I have gone completely crazy, I ask you to hear me out, to accompany me in exploring some new possibilities. I hope you will find them as surprising and as much fun as I do.

Your friend,

Bernard

For starters, a definition of the term Sustainable Abundance may be useful.

Of all the definitions of Sustainability, the one I prefer is the instruction of my scoutmaster whenever we arrived at a new campsite: 'Leave the place in better shape than you found it.' A more formal definition is the one used by the Gro Brundlandt Report for the United Nations (1987): Sustainability is characteristic of a society that 'satisfies its needs without diminishing the prospects of future generations'. Such a society, I believe, should also respect the needs and diversity of other life forms in the process.

Abundance does not refer to a mechanical accumulation of more 'stuff', or a Porsche in every garage. Abundance is what provides enough freedom of choice in the material domain to as many people as possible, so that they can express their passion and creativity. Such creativity is the expression of their highest form of consciousness, their highest calling, and provides a true sense of meaning in their life. Someone who is starving, and whose child is dying from hunger, will simply not have the opportunity to express creativity in a positive way.

Later in this book, you will discover the evidence upon which the scenario for Sustainable Abundance is grounded, and why it is not a Pollyanna dream. You will learn about the pragmatically tested mechanisms, at monetary and other levels, that make 'Sustainable Abundance' available to us as realistically, and with the same probabilities, as the previous scenarios.

One simple way to express the core thesis of Sustainable Abundance is that it is now possible to make capitalism truly sustainable through initiatives in the money system, sustainable not only ecologically but socio-politically as well. In short, capitalism with a human face does not have to remain an oxymoron.

An important common key to developing sustainable capitalism is the implementation of money systems that support such objectives. We will see how at least three of the most critical problems of today's societies can be addressed effectively by using new kinds of currencies that could operate as a complement to the existing national money, and that are *already* operating in such a way in small-scale, prototype form in a dozen countries around the world.

■ The four scenarios in perspective

The difference in the length and detail of our different futures does not reflect their relative importance or likelihood. What these differences do reflect is the complexity of ideas that can be presented now, without the background that will be covered in the coming chapters. All four scenarios have just about the same chance of occurring. And they are not the only possible outcomes. In fact, the most probable outcome is likely to be some mixture of several or all of these stories. Outcomes will also play out differently in different parts of the world. Remember these scenarios were designed to focus your attention on the driving forces that could lead to any of the four outcomes, as well as to surface the variety of choices that are available, and to illustrate the implications of those choices. The next step is to look more closely at these key driving forces that are behind each scenario.

■ The two driving forces

The following diagram (see Figure 4.8) is an overview of the scenarios that highlights their relationship to one another.

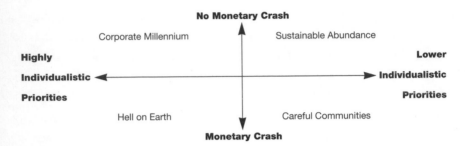

Figure 4.8 First approximation of relationships between the four scenarios

What the two lower scenarios ('Hell on Earth' and 'Careful Communities') have in common is one specific event: a global monetary crash. The two top scenarios (Corporate Millennium and Sustainable Abundance) do not include such an event. Similarly, the two scenarios on the left give top priority to individualistic and competitive tendencies; the two on the right do not.

Focusing upon these driving forces, however, only allows us a relatively superficial view of the dynamics involved. The real agents of change are people. Figure 4.9 suggests what we can do, individually and collectively, to improve the chances of Sustainable Abundance.

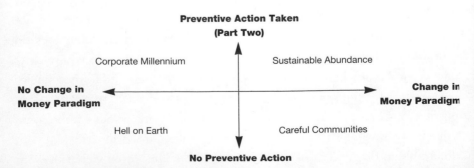

Figure 4.9 Relationships between the four scenarios

The monetary crash of the vertical axis in Figure 4.8 is not a random natural catastrophe – like a thunderstorm – that we may or may not be lucky enough to avoid. The reason no crash is occurring in the two top scenarios is because preventive actions have been consciously taken. The nature of these preventive actions is the recurrent theme of the four chapters that constitute Part Two: Money Choices.

Similarly, the left-right divide of the grid (i.e., whether highly individualistic priorities prevail in a society or not) should not be considered as a mechanical collective switch that just happens to be turned on or off. Instead, as discussed in Chapter 1, the key will be whether we are willing or not to revisit the money paradigm. The cartoon on the next page depicts in another way the costs of remaining locked in the prevailing interpretation of money. It is only if we choose to become aware that we can walk out of the money box, to the sides where no bars are blocking us, that Sustainable Abundance will become available.

■ One last question: where is the 'Official Future Scenario' on this map?

Looking down at the page, imagine that you are suspended above the crossing of the two axes of Figure 4.9. That point in space is where the Official Future is temporarily suspended. Imagine yourself with an open parachute on your back, moving slowly down towards the page, expecting to manoeuvre a safe landing. One thing is for certain: gravity will pull you down to a landing, somewhere. The Official Future has no probability of keeping us suspended indefinitely. Let us hope that we have the time, and the patience, to learn how to use the ropes of our parachute to make a landing in the future of our choice.

While all four scenarios are equally plausible, I believe that the most preferable is Sustainable Abundance. The balance of this text is like a guide to using the ropes of our money system to make a smooth landing in that upper right corner, in a future where Sustainable Abundance is the norm, as well as the ongoing goal. There is still much to learn about the many strands and facets of these ropes, learning that we all will be doing together. Whatever happens, the ride over the next couple of decades promises to be an extraordinary one. Susan Watkins has said it well: 'I think that wherever our journey takes us, there are Gods waiting there, with divine patience and laughter.'[154]

'Remaining stuck within the conventional interpretation of money'

In Part Two: Choosing Your Future of Money, we will explore pragmatic options that are currently available for changing the money paradigm. Each of these systems can operate in parallel with, and complementary to the prevailing national currencies. The shift in paradigm is not about abandoning the previous system, but complementing it with new money systems that support different sets of values. Together with the conventional system, these currency innovations can bring about Sustainable Abundance.

Part Two:

Part Two: Choosing Your Future of Money

■ *'Sure, money's all wrong,*
  and the devil decreed it;
  It doesn't belong
  to the people who need it.'

  PIET HEIN, DANISH PHYSICIST

■ *'Money is a mode of organizing our life in the material world;*
  money is an invention, a mental device, very necessary, very ingenious,
  but, in the end, a product of the mind.'

  JACOB NEEDLEMAN[155]

■ *'Money to be money [. . .] does not have to be legal tender. It can be what*
  one might call "common tender", i.e. commonly accepted in payment of
  debt without coercion through legal means.'

  RICHARD TIMBERLAKE[156]

In Part One we looked at the old money story; in Part Two we will explore some new ones.

The Time-Compacting Machine of Chapter 1 made obvious that the transition from the Industrial Age to the Information Age will be one of rapid change entailing a whole range of adjustment problems for everybody in society. The core idea of Part Two is simple: *the possibilities offered by money innovations to tackle some of the key problems in this transition are extensive, and have remained so far mostly untapped.*

This does not mean that we should expect the national currencies to disappear, replaced with another kind of money. Instead, what is already happening is that other parallel currency systems are developing to complement the existing system, to fulfil roles that the national currencies do not, cannot, were never designed to play.

A Note for Economists

This book was written for the general public, not for economists. However, as the solutions presented here affect economic processes, objections by economists are relevant, and a few of the sidebars will be dedicated to providing answers to such potential objections.

One objection to complementary currencies is that their introduction may be *economically less efficient* for the price formation process than a single national currency. This objection is valid from a purely economic viewpoint. However, the economy is only a subpart of society, and human society a small part of the global ecosystem. *Not* the other way around. In any system, the optimization of a subpart should take into account its impact on the larger system. If your stomach were to optimize its throughput regardless of the impact on the rest of your body, it would kill you. Not a good outcome for yourself or – for that matter – your stomach in the long run. In short, transdisciplinary trade-offs between pure economic optimality and other priorities need to be considered. And this is why a whole systems approach was chosen as underlying logic for this book.

There are ample historical precedents for this approach, including in the monetary field. For instance, on the basis of economic efficiency alone, one could argue that we should have been using all along only one single global currency, instead of the 170 different national currencies currently in operation. However, the priority of creating a privileged geographical area for exchanges that builds national consciousness was deemed more important that the pure economic efficiency of a single global currency.

The monetary innovations decribed in Part Two illustrate a similar give and take. They therefore should be evaluated as prototypes of social tools that facilitate a trade-off between their broader social and community benefits and pure economic efficiency.

CHAPTER 5

Work-Enabling Currencies

- *'Change occurs when there is a confluence of both changing values and economic necessity, not before.'*

  JOHN NAISBITT[157]

- *'The lack of money is the source of all evil.'*

  BERNARD SHAW

- *'Life and livelihood ought not to be separated but to flow from the same source, which is spirit. Spirit means life, and both life and livelihood are about living in depth, living with a meaning, purpose, joy, and a sense of contributing to the greater community.'*

  MATTHEW FOX

- *'People who say it cannot be done*
  Should not interrupt those who are doing it.'

  JACK CANFIELD AND MARK VICTOR HANSEN[158]

The 'money question' of our Time-Compacting Machine that is being addressed here is 'how can we provide work to billions in an era of jobless growth?' (Chapter 1).

This topic will be tackled by exploring the following five core ideas:

- The nature of unemployment has changed over the past decades, and this process will accelerate as the Information Age takes further hold.
- The traditional ways to handle unemployment are increasingly going to fail.
- In areas with high unemployment, people have already demonstrated that living conditions can be improved by creating their own complementary currencies instead of just relying on welfare. Surprisingly, it is not the first

time that such solutions have been successfully implemented in the modern world. During the 1930s many thousands of such initiatives were operational in the US, Canada, Western Europe and other areas affected by the Depression.

■ Complementary currencies could become a key tool to buffer a region from the shocks caused by failures and crises in the official money system.

■ Finally, this approach is a win/win for both locally owned businesses and society at large.

■ An important distinction

There is definitely enough work for everybody on the planet, but jobs are another matter.

I will use the term 'job' to mean any activity that people do primarily to obtain money, 'simply to make a living'. 'Employment' will be used as a synonym for jobs in this context. 'Work' in contrast is an activity that is performed primarily for its own sake, for the pleasure derived from the giving, or the passion expressed in the activity itself (see sidebar).

Jobs vs. Work

■ The word 'Job' is recent; it dates only from the Industrial Revolution. It was initially defined as a 'pile of things to be done', or even more precisely 'something done for hire, with a view for monetary profit.'[159]

■ 'Work', in contrast, is a very old word. Its first appearance in English dates from the Aelfric Homilies (11th century): 'That work was begun under God's will.'[160] It still has that connotation when referring to a 'work of Love', a 'work of Art', a 'work of Mercy'.

Many signs point to the idea that a 'job' for everybody, which became prevalent only during the Industrial Age, may be dying with that age.

A lucky minority has jobs which are also their work. Successful artists always combined the two. Similarly, the real geniuses in any field – whether it is in business or healing, the military, education, academics or politics – always 'followed their bliss', as Joseph Campbell put it so eloquently. However, these cases still remain exceptions to the rule.

Would you continue doing what you are doing if you had all the money you would ever need? If the answer is yes, you are among the fortunate ones whose work and job coincide. What is the percentage of people you know who would continue their job, if they didn't need the money?

Anything that may help people enjoy what they are doing should be welcome. As a Chinese proverb puts it:

If a person has joy in what he does
There will be harmony in the work
If there is harmony in the work
There will be order in the nation
If there is order in the nation
There will be peace in the world.

The connection to public health

There are two ways by which our health relates to money and work. Evidence points out that jobs without meaning can make you sick and even kill you. The prestigious Canadian Institute for Advanced Research reached the startling conclusion that 'medical services have little if any effect on national health levels'. Instead, what most influences health is a work situation where people are in control of their lives. The difference in life expectancy between rich and poor is explained primarily by the different control they have over their lives and work. 'Something is killing the great lower classes of the modern world, grinding them down before their time. The statistics show it's also killing the middle classes, who live longer than the poor but not as long as the rich.'[161]

■ The money connection

The problem with work is finding someone who will pay you pounds for it, i.e. make it a paid job as well. The scarcity in jobs is therefore money scarcity, as economists since Keynes have known. But does money have to remain scarce? Why not create your own money in sufficiency to complement the scarce national currency, to enable more work to be paid? Sounds crazy? Too simple?

It is nevertheless what many communities in various parts of the world have already done. I will show later that the results of such money innovations prove that this process is effective in practice, why it does not create inflation, and which prototypes are the best candidates for generalization.

But at this point, let us first establish the nature of the job problem, and why it has irrevocably changed over the past decade.

■ Unemployed? who? me?: today's job problem

Conventional wisdom states that unemployment is mostly a blue-collar problem, and only a temporary one at that. But these assumption are now hopelessly out of date, even in activities which have long been considered immune to technological obsolescence or corporate layoffs (see sidebar):[162]

Information Age unemployment in the making

- ■ A robot is being tested to perform hip replacement surgery.
- ■ The first novel written in its entirety by a computer program – a torrid romance rated no better or worse than average – was published in New York in 1993.
- ■ The latest performance by the Washington Opera Company of *Don Carlos* had only the conductor, two pianists and a synthesizer in the pit.
- ■ In 1993, Sears eliminated 50,000 jobs from its merchandising division, reducing its workforce by 14%. That same year sales went up a nice 10%. This was before the emerging trend towards electronic home shopping even started.
- ■ The electronic home shopping cyber-malls are expected to take over 20% of the two trillion-dollar-a-year retail market by 2007 (the largest of the service sectors, where all the new jobs are supposed to come from).
- ■ The frontal attack against government bureaucracies closes off another place where jobs were created in the past.

As far as the 'temporary' nature of unemployment is concerned, it is often implicitly assumed that – as in previous business cycles – the economy will pick up and the demand for labour will follow. Theory predicts that 'frictional' unemployment is indeed to be expected. It is part of the market allocation system that even in a booming economy, some people will be in-between jobs.

However, millions of people around the world are starting to wonder.

What is less normal, for example, is that the 'frictional' unemployment level is slowly creeping up decade after decade. This is even more alarming if one takes into account that people's ability to move around and the efficiency of our information systems to match jobs with people has *increased* over the same time period.

For instance, the US average unemployment for the decade of the 1950s stood at 4.5%. In the 1960s it crept up to 4.8%, in the 1970s it reached 6.2% and in the 1980s it stepped a further notch to 7.3%.

For the 1990s, the official statistics of American unemployment are clearly bucking this trend, returning to the level of the 1950s. However, the 'dirty secret' of this exception is that the global scramble for jobs is reflected in a substantial deterioration of working conditions and pay. US wages peaked in real terms in 1973 and have been declining ever since, compounded by the fact that Americans work longer hours than they did two decades ago. 'Bill Clinton has created ten million jobs – and two of them are mine' was one complaint heard in workers' circles during Clinton's 1996 re-election campaign. Predictably, there is a lot of dispute about whether the US became competitive with the Third World by forcing Third World standards of living on its workers.

Even *Fortune* Magazine has been wondering why 'nearly half of all the new full-time jobs created in the 1980's paid less than $13,000 a year, which is below the poverty level for a family of four'. Also, education levels don't necessarily help any more. As reported by the *Wall Street Journal*, one college graduate out of three is now obliged to take a job which doesn't require a college degree.[163]

In Western Europe, the unemployment rate has been stubbornly stuck at a very uncomfortable 10% level for almost a decade. At the end of 1998, in Germany the official number was 10.8%, in Italy 12.3%, in France 11.5%, in Belgium 12.2.1%, and in Spain a mind-boggling 18.2%. The main difference between America and Europe is that in America, people end up accepting employment below their competence and training. Is a college graduate flipping hamburgers to be interpreted as a sign of a healthy economy and the high-tech society of the future? One graduate of the class of 1996 summarized his friends' experience of the 'real working world' as follows: 'Half of us are ridiculously overworked, and the other half are seriously under-employed. It seems like a choice between workaholism or depression, and nothing in between. And this is supposed to be a good year for the economy!'

Even in Japan, where employment by the same company is practically considered a birthright, unemployment keeps inching up.

What *is* going on?

■ The age of downsizing

Most of us have been trained to believe that we learn a profession, are hired by a company to perform a job in that profession, and – if we do all the right things – we will move up through the ranks until retirement. But this whole idea has already become as obsolete as the dodo.

For the past three decades businesses have invested billions of dollars in information-processing equipment. The rate of growth of such investments has been higher than any technology in history. For instance, the share of Information Technology investments in US firms has jumped from 7% of total investments in 1970 to 40% in 1996. Add the billions of dollars spent on software, and the amount spent on Information Technology, annually, now exceeds investments in all other production equipment combined.[164]

To understand the true scale of this, one needs to multiply this extraordinary increase in dollar investments by the even more remarkable drop in unit cost. Computer processing costs have continued to drop by 30% per year for the past two decades, and all experts agree this will continue for at least another decade or two.

Initially repetitive tasks were computerized in one area after another of the corporation. However, all computer applications were really being built around the existing organizational structure and management procedures. One day someone thought to reverse the process by asking the simple question: 'how should we organize ourselves to best take advantage of the available information technologies?'[165]

Re-engineering was born. So were 'strategic layoffs'.

In all fairness, such layoffs were not the intent of the original re-engineering inventors. One of the earlier pioneers was Thomas Davenport, research VP at CSC Index (the 'home' of re-engineering). In an article in *Fast Company*, Davenport reported that: 'Re-engineering did not start out as a code word for mindless corporate bloodletting. It wasn't supposed to be the last gasp of Industrial Age management. I know because I was there at the beginning. I was one of the creators . . . But the fact is, once out of the bottle, the re-engineering genie quickly turned ugly.'[166]

And like all genies, it cannot be put back into the bottle.

Oswald Huber in Rolf Kübel: Resonance Mensch (Munich: C.H. Beck'sch Verlag, 1990).

Large corporations worldwide have been shedding people at a rate of between one and two million people per year. And this is happening for the first time at all levels in the corporation. When Kodak reduced its number of management layers from thirteen to four, a lot of people who never thought it could happen to them found themselves out of a job. Of course, a lot of new jobs are being created outside these corporations, but they usually do not measure up in terms of income level or security that people were used to and had grown to expect.

What is important to realize is that these 'strategic layoffs' are of a totally different nature from the traditional cyclical layoffs. It was considered normal for example that factory workers would be let go whenever inventories of finished goods piled up as the business cycle moved into low gear. They would also be re-employed as soon as those inventories were absorbed and the good days of the cycle returned. But with strategic layoffs, there is no reason to expect that the business cycle will reverse the trend. What is going is gone for ever. Growth without increased employment is not a forecast; it is an established fact. William Greider's statistic is worth repeating: the world's 500 largest corporations make and sell seven times more goods and services than 20 years ago, but have managed simultaneously to reduce their overall workforce.

Even the people who remain or are hired in these corporations face a very different process from previous times. The old criteria for hiring used to be the matching of job specifications to the classical three Es: Experience, Endorsements and Education.

Today everything is different at the pace-setting corporations such as CNN, Intel or Microsoft: 'Nobody has a job. Even if someone is hired for a job, we forget about that as soon as he or she is in. The work is being done mostly in project teams which may often include outsiders. People have assignments, 'own' a problem or an opportunity, but not a job.'[167]

In addition to straightforward layoffs, the need for additional flexibility has pushed corporations to redefine their own boundaries by:

- Outsourcing: Xerox machines are being installed by Ryder truck drivers; Commodore computers are being repaired by the Fedex personnel who used to only deliver the parts.
- Delocalization: One of the largest US insurance companies, Metropolitan Life, is billing from Ireland; British Airways is handling its accounting in Bangladesh; California software companies are debugging from India.
- Temping: probably the most significant of all these new trends from a society viewpoint. The single largest employer in the US is now Manpower, whose business is to place *temporary* personnel in corporate jobs.

If you believe that all this is happening only in 'greedy private businesses', think again. Even the military – historically a rather eager employer of able bodies – is embracing the new way of thinking. The 1997 strategic review of America's defence capabilities concluded that as many as 50,000 active-duty troops should be cut, especially in the army, to help pay for weapons such as computerized artillery systems and electronic detectors of biological weapons. The Quadrennial Defense Review, analysing what will be needed from now to 2010, has focused on cutting 'infrastructure costs' (now 40% of total Defense Department appropriations). This covers everything not directly related to its 'core competence' of fighting wars: from the military bases' cafeteria managers to schoolteachers, day-care centres to accountants. You guessed it: they are now 'privatizing' and 'outsourcing' these functions.

None of this should be seen as a short-term fad. A UK survey funded by the Department of Education and Employment and published by Business Strategies, a consultant company with close links to the Treasury, concludes that no new full-time employment is to be expected in Britain during the next ten years.[168] While an optimistic forecast is supplied for self-employment and part-time jobs totalling 1.5 million over that time period, none is expected to come from what was once considered 'normal' full-time jobs.

Nor should any of this be considered as a purely Anglo-Saxon trend. A survey of 4,720 organizations in 14 European countries performed by the Cranfield School of Management on behalf of the European Commission reports a staggering increase in part-time or fixed-term (up to three months) employment even just in the past year. The largest increase was in The Netherlands, where 70% of the corporations increased their use of part-timers. More than 50% of the German, Italian, Finnish and Swedish corporations are now doing the same. The rest of Europe has registered an increase in 'only' 30% to 50% of the corporations.[169]

Dr William Bridges, an expert on employment trends, asks the question: 'What is the percentage of jobs which are performed by temporary labor?' Most people's estimates fall in the range between 2% and 20%.

His answer: 'In fact, it is 100%; 85% of us still happen to be in denial.'[170]

■ Economic consequences

The International Metalworkers Federation in Geneva forecasts that 'within 30 years, as little as 2 percent of the world's current labor force will be needed to produce all the goods necessary for total demand'. The interesting question is, of course, what will the other 98% do?

Some may argue, so what, jobs are disappearing? It has all happened before:

- in 1800 over 80% of the US population was occupied in farming;
- by 1900 this was down to 48%;
- by 1950 to 11%,
- and now to an insignificant 2.9%.

And that 2.9% not only feeds the entire nation better than the 80% ever did, but it feeds a good deal of the rest of the world as well! All these people who moved out of farming found jobs in the cities in industry, the trades, and services.

Paul Krugman vs. Wiliam Greider and Robert Reich

In a series of witty essays[171] Paul Krugman has sent a broadside to the best-selling books[172] of a famous journalist (William Greider) and a Secretary of Labor of the Clinton Administration (Robert Reich). He attacks what he calls 'emotionally satisfying myths' relating to a potential job crisis due to technology changes. Krugman's punches fall in two categories:

- He attacks the 'lump of labor fallacy' i.e. the idea that there is only a limited quantity of jobs in the world, and therefore as productivity rises the number of jobs available automatically is reduced. He counters with the argument that while productivity gains in one sector may indeed provoke job losses in that sector, it stimulates even more job creation in other parts of the economy. And he provides the classical example of productivity increases and job losses in the manufacturing sector over the past thirty years being more than compensated by new jobs in the service sector.

- Much of the debate about the relationships between globalisation, trade, technology and jobs is really irrelevant because 'if you want a simple model for predicting the unemployment rate in the United States over the next few years, here it is: It will be what Greenspan wants it to be, plus or minus a random error reflecting the fact that he is not quite God'.[173] This is so, because Greenspan can take all the impacts of changes in trade or technology into account, and adapt his monetary policy accordingly.

★★★

I fully agree with both these points. But I remain nevertheless concerned about the issue of jobs because of the following two questions:

- Losing jobs in one sector while creating jobs in another sector may be OK from an overall statistical viewpoint, but it is not quite as simple for the individuals involved. If such change occurs over a generation, it is realistic and even quite consistent with the American dream that the child of a steelworker becomes an electronic engineer or a lawyer. But how realistic is it to hope that the laid-off steelworker himself will have the financial resources or acumen to recycle to the high-tech jobs which the new economy is creating? As the speed of change accelerates, the number of people caught between the old and the new growth sectors will predictably rise. What should these people do?

- Why has roughly a third of humanity (most of it in the so-called Third World) been under- or unemployed for as long as we have data about it? An estimated 700 million people worldwide have been unemployed for decades. Krugman's answer may be that this is not Greenspan's concern. Nevertheless the Federal Reserve decisions directly affect millions of jobs around the world because of the dollar's global role. When Paul Volcker decided to stamp out inflation in the US in the 1980s he sent all Latin America into a tailspin. In other words, I claim that the issue on global employment is not an economic management problem but an *institutional* predicament.

I also allege that the approach recommended later in this chapter could alleviate that issue by giving a role for currencies complementary to the national currencies that Greenspan and his colleagues manage. Furthermore, if such currencies are well designed they can help rather than hinder the aim of lower inflation on the national currencies (as will be shown in Chapter 7).

This is, of course, true. However, there is a structural difference when we are dealing with an Information Revolution instead of an Industrial Revolution. A farmer became a stagecoach maker, and the stagecoach maker could learn how to make automobiles. Every time he changed jobs he also earned more money than before. But what is a no-longer-needed information handler to do, flip hamburgers (see sidebar)?

This time we may well remain stuck between a rock and a hard place. Because – while it makes sense for each corporation to improve its competitiveness by downsizing – this time all the pieces just don't add up. When Henry Ford decided to make a car that was so cheap that his factory workers could buy it, he put in motion a virtuous cycle between more cars, more workers, more cars, more workers.

Jobless growth may very well turn this virtuous cycle into a vicious one, operating in the other direction. Every time people are laid off, or are forced to reduce their income, they are going to drop out of the market for at least some of these great new widgets that the corporations keep producing. Even if each corporation is better off at each step, the total market pie is shrinking, so cumulatively we may suddenly find everyone worse off, even the corporation itself.

The fact that this is a global game further complicates the picture. Plants that are being built in the Third World use technologies which are just as effective as those applied in the First World. And a decade of 'structural adjustment' policies implemented by the International Monetary Fund have stripped away many of their skimpy social safety nets as well.

■ Keynes's foresight

John Maynard Keynes, in his *Essay on Persuasion*,[174] predicted over sixty years ago with remarkable foresight that a time would come when the production problem would be solved, but that the transition was likely to be a painful one:

> If the economic problem [the struggle for subsistence] is solved, mankind will be deprived of its traditional purpose. [. . .] Thus for the first time since his creation man will be faced by his real, his permanent problem [. . .] There is no country and no people, I think, who can look forward to the age of leisure and abundance without a dread. It is a fearful problem for the ordinary person, with no special talents to occupy himself, especially if he no longer has roots to the soil or in custom or in the beloved conventions of a traditional society.

The writing is on the wall: we are in this predicament *now*.

From as far back in history as anyone can trace, people have been identifying with their jobs. We still describe ourselves as stone cutters, professors, bankers, computer experts. In fact, many of our most common family names are derived from various jobs and professions: Smith, Fletcher (arrow maker), Potter or similar titles in living or dead languages. It goes back all the way to the stone age. In the earliest Sumerian tablets, the writer identifies himself as 'So-and-so, the Scribe'.

If Keynes is right, we will for the first time in history be forced to reinvent ourselves, to find other ways to identify who we are. We won't any longer be able to identify ourselves with these 'production labels'. In other words, we will be forced to seek other identities, other reasons that give a purpose to our lives. Keynes concluded that 'no country can look forward . . . without a dread' to this unprecedented historic shift.

Nor was Keynes the only one to foresee such problems. Norbert Wiener, the originator of cybernetics, was also one of the very first to warn us of the social implications of computers: 'Let us remember that the automatic machine [i.e. computer-driven production equipment] . . . is the precise economic equivalent of slave labor. Any labor which competes with slave labor must accept economic conditions of slave labor. It is perfectly clear that this will produce an unemployment situation in comparison with which the present recession and even the depression of the thirties will seem a pleasant joke.'[175]

But are there not already some telltale signs of what that may look like?

■ Socio-political consequences

Within the existing framework, we can have a fairly good idea of what is going to happen. We just have to look around us: it is already happening. I call it the 'vicious circle of unemployment'.

It involves a six-step feedback loop as follows (see Figure 5.1)
1 Unemployment creates a feeling of economic exclusion;
2 Part of those touched express it through violence;
3 Most ordinary people react to the violence with fear;
4 Community breaks down, society becomes unstable, political polarization increases;
5 Fewer investments take place, fewer things are bought;
6 The investment climate deteriorates. More unemployment is created.
And the whole process starts all over again from the beginning.

Figure 5.1: Vicious circle of unemployment within existing framework

Let us visit this vicious circle step by step.

Economic exclusion

'From the standpoint of the market, the ever-swelling ranks of the [unemployed] face a fate worse than colonialism: economic irrelevance . . . We don't need what they have and they can't buy what we sell.' This is how Nathan Gardels, editor of *New Perspectives Quarterly*, summarizes the linkage between unemployment and economic exclusion. It translates into the increasing realization by those concerned that there is no room for them in this society, that they don't belong here.

When this happens to an individual, he or she usually becomes depressed (is it a coincidence that the many industrialised countries have declared depression a national epidemic?). When it happens to a group (as is typically the case for the younger generation where unemployment is always higher than in the population at large), it is normally expressed as anger. Such anger accumulates until it explodes into a violent rage lashing out randomly at society at large, or at some specific scapegoats.

Violence

Niccolo Machiavelli (1469-1527) thought that: 'It is necessary and useful that the laws of a republic give to the masses a legal way to express their anger. When this isn't available, extraordinary outlets manifest. And there is no doubt that such events produce more harm than anything else.'[176] Indeed, violence is usually the expression of frustration and impotence.

In a suburb of Lyon, France, a police car runs over and kills a teenager. Such a regrettable accident would normally make the news only in the local papers. But this was Vaux-en-Velain, a depressed working-class neighbourhood where unemployment among the young is particularly high. Hundreds of young people took to the streets, clashed first with the police, then with the CRS (the special riot troops). The fighting lasted three days, and caused over £120 million in property damage. The one point the residents and the government officials agreed on was that the root cause of all the mayhem was the high unemployment levels of the youth.

The French sociologist, Loic Wacquant, made a systematic study of urban rioting in the developed world. The majority of urban rioters – independently of the country involved – have a common profile: they are formerly working-class youth which has given up on finding a job in the brave new world of the Information Age.

Fear by the majority

The next step is an easy guess. How do most people react to random acts of violence against property and people? Fear is the answer.

Fear of what will depend on the interpretation given to the events, and this will vary in turn with the location, age, origin, social background, nationality of the observer.

It ranges from fear of all young people, fear of punks, fear of all immigrants, fear of blacks in America, fear of Arabs in France, fear of Turks in Germany, to fear of . . . . (please fill in the blanks for your area).

Political polarization

Fear is to politics what the ocean is to an island. It draws the boundaries of the constituency, whom you want to exclude and whom you want to attract.

This is why politicians everywhere tend to blame another country whenever possible when there are particularly tough situations to deal with. Nobody can vote for them there. But unemployment and violence usually result in a need to focus blame to situations closer to home.

For example, one cannot distinguish whether the campaign slogan 'These immigrants are the cause of your job problems' comes from Pat Buchanan in the US, Zhirinofski in Russia, Gianfredo Fini in Italy, or Jean Marie Le Pen in France. All have recently started a political movement, and already attract between 10 and 20% of the voters. Finally, as unemployment and violence increases, these more extremist parties can be expected to grow.

On election night 1994 in Italy, the neo-fascist leader Gianfredo Fini was greeted by young people (mostly unemployed) with chants of 'Duce! Duce!' while his party won an unexpected 13.5% of the national votes. Commentators were amazed as to why young people – too young to have known Mussolini or experience nostalgia for his time – somehow spontaneously reinvented the same values and slogans used by their grandparents. It is, in fact, predictable.

As more extremist parties play a bigger role in our political systems, it gets harder and harder to 'hold the centre'. Positions become more polarized across the political spectrum, and maintaining a consensus becomes almost impossible. This can be fertile ground for extreme nationalism, all the way to 'ethnic cleansing' such as what happened in Yugoslavia in the 1990s after the IMF imposed economic restructuring, or in Indonesia with killings of various minorities after the collapse of the rupiah in 1998-99. Furthermore, these problems can even spread when populations flee the mayhem to take refuge in neighbouring countries, and create new unemployment problems there.

Imagine what all that does to an investment climate.

Feedback to increased unemployment

Everybody takes a defensive position, reduces investments, and therefore the employment opportunities drop further.

This increasing unemployment will make us go through the entire loop once again: it is a vicious circle which – once started – is particularly difficult to break.

■ Case studies

There are many historic and contemporary examples of this process. Entire countries have gone through it with devastating results. We could take several examples in Latin America, where political instability not only caused foreigners to take their money out of the country, but the citizens themselves would not invest in their own country (e.g.: Peru, Bolivia or Argentina in the 1970s). Unemployment levels skyrocketed, and massive internal migrations occurred to the larger cities in hopes of finding jobs – which weren't there either. Their descendants are still there in the *barrios*, *barriadas*, *villas*, *favelas*, and other shanty towns. An even more telling tale is how many African-Americans congregated in the slums of the largest cities of the northern United States in less than one generation.[177] After the mechanization of cotton picking in the South, for the first time the black population became economically irrelevant. The result: 'One of the largest and most rapid mass internal movements of people in history started.'[178] Between 1950 and 1970, over five million black men, women and children migrated from the South to the larger industrial towns in the North in search of jobs. One generation later, a significant minority managed to take advantage of the loosening grip of race discrimination and become middle-class mainstream Americans. But millions went down the spiral: from economic exclusion to violence and fear, from extremist political positions to burned neighbourhoods where nobody wants to invest. These neighbourhoods spawn what is now called the underclass – a permanently unemployed part of the population who live at the margin of society, where the only remaining choices are either to become a welfare recipient or make a living in the underground economy of drugs and crime.

This could very well become the blueprint of what happens with First World workers when technology makes significant portions of the population obsolete. The main difference is that the Information Age would make that process geographically universal. This time we are all potential victims.

This picture may appear too grim. After all, racism was an exacerbating element. But this case study remains a stark illustration of what normally happens within this framework when large groups of people become economically irrelevant, at least if we remain within the framework of the existing money system.

■ Traditional solutions

It should not come as a surprise that the solutions most commonly presented for today's unemployment problem fall into different camps, depending on from where the recommendation comes in the political spectrum. The old political divide between right and left still provides the easiest classification of the traditional solutions.

Solutions from the political right

The Conservatives claim that employment is not something the government should get involved in, and that over time free markets will take care of this rather messy problem. They did so in the past, and will do it again.

When Milton Friedman was asked whether the Information Age might not outdate this approach, he answered – only half jokingly – that we can always create jobs by psychoanalysing each other to deal with the breakdown.

In practice, the Conservatives tend to deny the existence of any structural employment problem. When faced with the social tensions which result indirectly from unemployment, they will often deal with the symptoms in the sequence in which they appear. This amounts to clipping the branches while the roots remain intact. For instance, one slogan on the right is that jobs are gone because immigrants take them from you, therefore let us crack down on immigration. Another solution is tougher laws on crime. As a consequence, prison building has become one of the biggest growth industries in the US.

Learning from the past on the right?

Building more prisons may well be seen in retrospect as the most expensive welfare system in history: paying $20,000 per person per year to keep someone in prison for ever is unlikely to prove to be the most cost-effective method of tackling the vicious circle of unemployment.

The most likely outcome of this scenario is what has already happened in many Third World countries. Instead of indefinitely putting more people in prison, what happens is that those who can afford it lock themselves up in 'golden ghettos', or other gated communities. Whatever the level of luxury or comfort that these golden ghettos can provide, it still boils down to a self-imposed prison system. In parallel, the majority of society – those who cannot afford the golden ghettos – is left to fend for itself in a gang-infested urban jungle. Is that really an acceptable evolution for a democratic society?

Solutions from the political left

A typical analysis of the unemployment problem by the Left is that of Jeremy Rifkin.[179] His solution to build 'social capital' has three main components:
- reducing the working week from 40-hours to 35- or 30-hours (a strategy which France is testing)
- taxing the new high-tech production technologies
- using the proceeds of such taxes to pay for vouchers which can be issued to those working in the non-profit world.

Learning from the past on the left?

The solutions recommended from the left have also been tested recently. Some of the remnants of the New Deal and the Great Society projects in the US and the welfare states in Europe are still around in the form of youth job creation programmes and the like.

Government-created jobs have left an aftertaste of failure, as well as a legacy of heavy taxes and bureaucracies, not to speak of unmanageable deficits and debts which will still have to be paid off well into the 21st century. No society, however generous, can indefinitely afford to keep a growing number of people on welfare; i.e., it is not a realistic option if the unemployment losses are not cyclical, but structural. The real problem is that these welfare programmes have failed to lift people out of poverty. Worse still, the people who are being helped in this way on a long-term basis lose self-respect and dignity as well.

Why traditional solutions won't work this time

However well intended the proposals are from both sides of the political spectrum, neither will solve the problem at hand.

The big strategic question is whether the current unemployment problem – or in America employment at levels below one's skill or training – is a short-term problem that will disappear with the next business boom cycle, or whether we are dealing with a structural process, which will systematically grow over time. Much academic ink has been spilt on trying to distinguish which of the two we are dealing with. In truth we may be dealing with both.

I will distinguish between three types of unemployment.

1 The so-called 'frictional' unemployment. Even under the best of economic circumstances in a free market there will be some people who are fired or who leave and who remain for a few weeks or months 'in between jobs'. We should expect that there will always be some small percentage of people in such a transition.
2 Unemployment due to the 'inventory adjustments' in the normal business cycle. This occurs when stockpiles of finished goods grow in an industry. While this inventory is being gradually liquidated, businesses quite often tend to reduce their production workforce temporarily. Again, we should expect that as long as there is a business cycle, demand for labour will also fluctuate between the good and the bad years.
3 However, we now have evidence that in addition to both well-known types of unemployment described above, a long-term structural trend has also started to build up. This explains why the 'frictional' unemployment seems to get worse decade after decade. This structural trend turns out to be just the job market consequence of the shift in the production processes from the Industrial Age to the Information Age. To the extent that this is true, none of the solutions proposed within the traditional left-right political divide framework will be capable of dealing with the structural nature of this problem. As we are only just starting to enter the Information Age, we should expect a further acceleration of the corresponding trends.

For instance, breakthroughs in nano-technology – processes which enable objects to be built atom-by-atom – promise to make obsolete the very idea that direct human labour is a necessary ingredient in production processes (see sidebar).

The 'two-week revolution' [180]

As soon as the 'first nano-assembler works, we could order it to build another one. Then we could tell them to build other things. A great flourishing of new nano-technologies would follow – as fast as we could design them... When the first assembler works, a stampede of working machines could follow. This sudden surge of working nano-technologies has been called the "two-week revolution". In the first two weeks after the assembler breakthrough, the world will change radically. For some, this is not a metaphor but a prediction. Entire new system of fully functional technology will emerge, ready to transform the world.'

Expert consensus is that this breakthrough is to be expected some time during the first decade of the 21st century. Even if it takes longer than two weeks – as it most likely will – the long-term implications should be clear: production without human input is a realistic possibility.

■ Our next leading socio-political problem

As several futurists predicted a couple of decades ago,[181] accelerating technology is finally catching up with us. Therefore jobs promise to become one of the hottest international political issues. In a global market system, no country or area can really opt out of world 'progress', without running the risk of also sliding into a downward spiral of underdevelopment. On the other hand, we have not developed institutions or mechanisms to deal with the social dislocations that our new technologies lead us to.

'Here we stand, confronted by insurmountable opportunities!'[182]

■ Neither left, nor right, but forward?

The traditional left-right debate is itself an inheritance of the Industrial Age economic framework. The origin of that debate had to do with private or public ownership of the 'means of production', i.e. the factories and machines. As the means of production are becoming knowledge, the new political and economic vocabulary to deal with these new realities doesn't yet exist.

But how about changing the monetary framework itself? To understand this, let's first play a very simple game called the 'Sufficiency of Money Game'.

The Sufficiency of Money Game

The game can be played with one or several people. You can do it by yourself, with your family or a group of friends or strangers. You may learn a lot about yourself and others in the process. There are no losers in this game; but the one who has most fun wins.

Just pretend that there is no scarcity of money. It has happened by magic. You have become the founder of a large financial institution or foundation and the rules of the game require you to spend your money within your community. It can be a neighbourhood, a group of friends or your family, a whole region, or a non-geographic community like a sub-group on the Internet. You then decide what you want to do with your money in this community. You can realize your dreams, and create a community of your dreams.

Then you answer these three questions.

1   What talent would you like to develop and offer to your community?
2   What is the vision of your newly formed community? What would you like to accomplish as a group?
3   Who are the other people or organizations you need to realize this vision?

If you play this game with others, get everyone to explain their answers.

In a second round, see how your different dreams can help each other, how some of your initiatives can mesh with those of others. You will often find that they strengthen and synergize each other in unexpected ways.

Some of the goals for communities that have come up when this game has been played include:

* Quality child care
* Teaching
* Youth mentoring
* Elderly care
* Infrastructure repair
* Housing rehabilitation
* Environmental cleanup
* The greening of towns
* Arts, entertainment, music, dance, theatre, fun
* Public transportation
* Crime prevention
* Preventive healthcare

We can see that there is a lot of work to be done in our communities, in our cities, among the people and the families that we live with and around.

There are people capable of and willing to do the work – people who have the skills and the knowledge to achieve these things. Our problems are not caused by a scarcity of people or ideas. There are even organizations who have the skills to hire the people and put them to work. This could all be done. What is missing?

■ Waiting for money, or is it Godot?

What is missing is money. *Everyone is waiting for money.*

If one stops to think about it, it is a fascinating phenomenon. Imagine a Martian landing in a poor neighbourhood and seeing rundown communities, people sleeping in the streets, children without mentors or going hungry, trees and rivers dying from lack of care, ecological breakdowns and all of the other problems we face. He would also discover that we know exactly what to do about all these things. Finally, he would see that many people willing to work are either unemployed, or use only a part of their skills. He would see that many have jobs but are not doing the work they are passionate about. And that they are all waiting for money. Imagine the Martian asking us to explain what is that strange 'money' thing we seem to be waiting for. Could you tell him with a straight face that we are waiting for an 'agreement within a community to use something – really almost anything – as a medium of exchange'?

And keep waiting?

Our Martian might leave wondering whether there is intelligent life on this planet.

But how about changing the monetary framework itself?

What this game illustrates is what Edgar Cahn, the creator of Time Dollars, means when he says: 'The real price we pay for money is the hold that money has on our sense of what is possible – the prison it builds for our imagination.'[183]

The fact is that there is enough work to be done for everyone in your community to keep busy for the rest of his or her life. Work that expresses our specific creativity. Have we become so hypnotized by our fear of the scarcity of money that we are also fearing lack of work?

So what can we do? The short answer is: create complementary currencies designed to fulfil social functions that the national currency does not or cannot fulfil. A variety of such non-traditional currencies already in operation in over a dozen countries will be described below. Here I will just outline the new possibilities such a strategy would create.

Imagine what becomes possible when two complementary economic systems are allowed to operate in parallel. On the one side a competitive global economy driven by the mainstream existing national money system, and a cooperative local economy fuelled by the complementary currencies. The competitive economy would be the familiar 'jobs' of today paid in scarce national currency, while the cooperative economy could encompass all kinds of activities that people are happy to pay for in a complementary currency always available in sufficiency. Unemployment and underemployment could be resolved by people doing work at improving their communities, and payable in local currency.

As in the vignette story 'A world in balance' (Chapter 1) most people would be involved part of their time in both economies. Or within a given family some members would be employed mostly in the global competitive economic loop, while another might be active mostly in the local economy. Hopefully both might be 'following their bliss', ideally both having the opportunity for their work also to become their job.

Such an outcome is possible within what I will call the 'Integral Economy' (explained in detail in Chapter 9), which consists of the traditional competitive economy on one side, and a local cooperative economy on the other. The former produces financial capital, and the latter social capital. They can operate in symbiosis with each other, as represented in Figure 5.2.

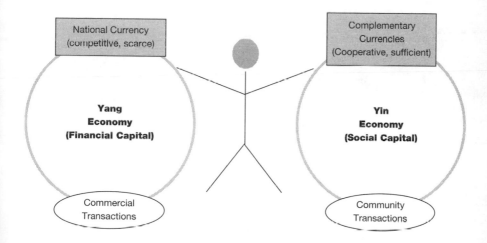

Figure 5.2 Integral economy with complementary currency systems.

I call it 'Integral' because it aims at integrating dimensions that the official economy has tended to downplay or ignore. But before understanding how the Integral Economy operates, we need to become more familiar with the non-traditional currencies which would complement the usual national currencies.

What was most surprising to me was to discover how remarkably close we were to implementing such a solution once before, back in the 1930s. However, governments at the time did not seem ready to give this approach a real chance. The *Zeitgeist* of the 1930s favoured strongly hierarchical and centralized solutions to all problems. You will also see that these experiments were stopped by governments, not because they were not working, but because they were working too well without the need for central government involvement.

■ The path not taken in the 1930s

If your family lived in the 1930s in Western Europe, the US, Canada or Northern Mexico (i.e. the area where the Great Depression hit hardest), you may have heard about the path not taken. In the aftermath of the German hyperinflation period of the 1920s, or of the Crash of 1929 in the other countries, literally thousands of communities started their own currency systems. Your village or town probably used one.[184]

The interesting solutions which were implemented at that time include a now almost forgotten movement of 'emergency currencies'.

There was one overriding objective in all the 1930s complementary currency systems: ensuring that people had the medium of exchange necessary for their activities, to give each other work. Two means were used to attain that single objective:

■ people compensated for the scarcity of the national currency by creating their own complementary currencies;

■ In the more sophisticated implementations, they also built in an incentive to avoid hoarding of currency. This aimed at conteracting the tendency for people who had any money to hoard it out of fear of the future, thereby worsening the crunch for everybody else. (A similar problem has been observed in Japan in the late 1990s.)

Compensating for the scarcity of national currency

Unemployed people don't earn money. If enough of your clients are unemployed, your business also fails, increasing the number of unemployed further, which brings down even bigger businesses, and so on. This is the snowball effect that was happening throughout the Western world as the shocks of the crash of the 1920s were being absorbed.

'When someone knows he is going to be hanged in a fortnight, it concentrates his mind wonderfully.' Suddenly people realized that, after all, money is only 'an agreement within a community to use something – almost anything – as a means of payment'. So they agreed to accept pieces of paper issued locally, metal tokens, or whatever else they could settle on. Among the more exotic outcomes of this creative brain storm of the 1930s I found

- rabbit tails used in Olney, Texas (issued by the local Chamber of Commerce in 1936) – it apparently also had the beneficial side effect of reducing an excess of jackrabbits in the area
- sea shells marked with the seal of Harter Drug Company in Pismo Beach, CA (issued March 8, 1933)[105]
- the wooden discs engraved with 'In God we Trust' manufactured by the Cochrane Lumber Company as medium of exchange for Petaluma, CA (1933).

Circulation incentive

Silvio Gesell (1862-1930): prophet, crank, or just unlucky?

Silvio Gesell was born on March 17, 1862 as the seventh of nine children in Rhenish Prussia of a Walloon mother and German father. In 1887 he emigrated to Argentina where he became a successful businessman. He left his businesses to his brother and returned to Europe to settle on a farm in Switzerland. He practised what Keynes called 'the two most delightful occupations open to those who do not have to earn a living, authorship and experimental farming'. In 1911, he moved to an agricultural cooperative near Berlin, founded by Franz Oppenheimer (1864-1934) whose ideas later shaped the kibbutz movement in Palestine. His business experience with highly unstable currency in Argentina had convinced him that the key to socially responsible capitalism is money and land reform. In 1891 he described the role of velocity of money as a decisive factor in determining the level of prices, preparing the ground for Irving Fisher's celebrated work of the 1920s.

At the end of WWI in 1918, he published a prophetic warning in the Berlin newspaper *Zeitung am Mittag*: 'In spite of the sacred promise of the nations to reject war for ever more, in spite of the cry of the masses "Never again war!" in the face of all hopes for a better future, I must state the following: If the present monetary system – the interest-driven economy – is maintained I dare to predict even today that it will not take 25 years before we are faced with another even more terrible war. As in former times, attempts will be made to annex foreign territory and for this purpose arms will be manufactured with the justification that this at least provides work for the unemployed. Wild revolutionary movements will form among the discontented masses and the poisonous plant of extreme nationalism will flourish. There will no longer be any mutual understanding between nations and in the end this can only lead to war.'

In 1919 he was named Finance Minister in the government of Gustav Landauer in the *Rätterrepublik* of Bavaria, but Landauer was brutally murdered within a week by a right-wing paramilitary group, and Gesell was arrested. Immediately thereafter, hard-line Marxists took over in Bavaria, and arrested Gesell again to court-martial him for high treason. Even after his acquittal, he had become *persona non grata* to the Swiss and could not return to his farm. He died in 1930, just before his 68th birthday. His death was pointedly ignored in the German press.

Gesell's monetary theories on 'Free Economics' have been summarily dismissed by the right and the left almost ever since, sometimes through misunderstanding, more often because these ideas were trying to 'hold the centre' in a Marxist-Capitalist ideological battlefield. Indeed his work has been considered a 'great reconciliation of individualism and collectivism'. Many German economists consider that his work is becoming more relevant today.[186] Two non-German Nobel Prize-winners in economics , Maurice Allais and Lawrence Klein, have now joined in the earlier praise by Keynes and Fisher of Gesell's contributions.

Once the currency was created, the next problem was ensuring that people did not hoard it. Every time someone hoards currency, by definition its lack of circulation deprives other people in the community of being able to perform transactions. The more sophisticated forms of complementary currency of the 1930s included a circulation incentive feature recommended by the Argentinean-German businessman and economist Silvio Gesell (see sidebar). We will talk more about Gesell's ideas later.[187] At this point, let us limit ourselves to the 'stamp scrip' mechanism he recommended. The core idea was to encourage people to circulate the money through an anti-hoarding fee (technically called 'demurrage', a word dating back to the railroads' practice of charging a fee for leaving a railroad car inactive). The back of each note typically had 12 boxes (one for each month) where a stamp could be affixed. Any bill, to remain valid, had to have its stamps up to date. These stamps could be purchased with local currency at shops participating in the scheme.

Let us now see how this generic scheme was implemented in practice in three key countries: Germany, Austria and the US.

■ The German 'Wara' system

By 1923 the German official currency situation was out of control. The exchange rate of the Weimar currency against the US dollar exemplifies this. Before World War I (1913) the value of one US dollar was 4.2 marks. By the end of the war it had risen to 8. In 1921 it was worth 184, and a year later 7,350. In the summer of 1923, a United States Congressman, A.P. Andrew, reported that he had received 4 billion marks in exchange for seven dollars, then paid 1.5 billion marks in a restaurant for a meal and leaving a 400-million-mark tip.[34]

The game stopped when, on 18 November 1923, one dollar bought 4.2 trillion marks. By then, 92,844,720 trillion marks were in circulation.[35] Postage stamps cost billions, paying for a loaf of bread required a wheelbarrow full of money. Daily wage negotiations preceded work, and salaries were paid twice a day and spent within the hour.

It is in this context that the 'Wara' experiment took place. The hero of this story is Dr Hebecker, the owner of a coal mine in the small town of Schwanenkirchen. He gathered all of his workers and explained that they had a simple choice: either they accepted 90% of their wages in 'Wara' backed by the coal they were extracting or he would have to close the mine. After a predictably lively exchange, they finally accepted the new currency when Hebecker arranged for vital foodstuffs to become available in Swanenkirchen which could be purchased with Wara.

The 'Wara' is a compound term in German meaning 'commodity money'. The Wara was a piece of paper fully backed by the coal inventory, and – to cover the storage costs – it also had a small monthly stamp fee. This fee was a form of demurrage tax which ensured that the money would not be hoarded, but would circulate within the community.

It not only saved Dr Hebecker's coal mine and the whole town of Schwanenkirchen, but it started circulating in wider and wider areas. It became a centrepiece of the *'Freiwirtschaft'* ('Free Economy') movement, whose theoretical underpinnings came from Silvio Gesell's work. Over 2,000 corporations throughout Germany started to use this alternative currency. Although, by definition, it would not become inflationary (given that its value was tied to the value of coal), it was considered much too successful by the central bank. It exerted pressure on the Ministry of Finance, which decreed in October 1931 that the Wara was illegal.

The next thing that transpired was that Hebecker's mine had to close, and the men went back into unemployment. As it had become impossible for people to help themselves on a local level, there only remained one option: a strong centralized solution. In the *Bierhallen* of Bavaria, an obscure Austrian immigrant began attracting increasingly interested audiences for his fiery speeches.

His name was Adolf Hitler.

The graph shows the direct correlation between the level of unemployment and the percentage of seats captured by National-Socialism in Germany in the successive elections between 1924 and 1933 (Figure 5.1). This graph also serves to illustrate one of the key steps in the 'vicious circle of unemployment' – the feeding of political extremism.

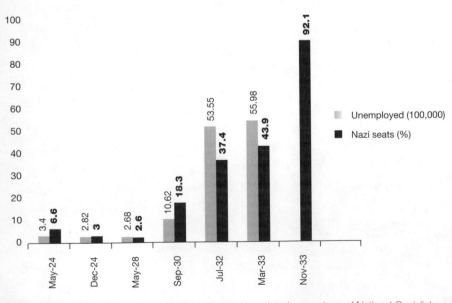

Figure 5.1 Relationship between number of unemployed and percentage of National-Socialist seats in German election 1924-33[36]

Between 1924 and 1928, unemployment in Germany fell gradually from 340,711 to 268,443. The percentage of seats obtained during the elections by the National-Socialist party declined in parallel from 6.6% to 2.6%. In contrast, from 1930 to 1933, as unemployment shot up first to 1,061,570 and then to 5,598,855, the percentage of seats obtained by the National-Socialist Party climbed first to 18.3%, then to 43.7%, to culminate with 92.1% by the end of that last year.

■ Wörgl stamp scrip

Meanwhile, elsewhere . . .

One of the best-known applications of the stamp scrip idea was applied in the small town of Wörgl, Austria, with a population of about 4,500 people at the time. When Michael Unterguggenberger (1884-1936) was elected mayor of Wörgl, the city had 500 jobless people and another 1,000 in the immediate vicinity. Furthermore, 200 families were absolutely penniless. The mayor-with-the-long-name (as Professor Irving Fisher from Yale would call him) was also familiar with Silvio Gesell's work and decided to put it to the test.

He had a long list of projects he wanted to accomplish (re-paving the streets, making the water distribution system available for the entire town, planting trees along the streets and other needed repairs). Many people were willing and able to do all of those things, but he had only 40,000 Austrian schillings in the bank, a pittance compared to what needed to be done.

Instead of spending the 40,000 schillings on starting the first of his long list of projects, he decided to put the money on deposit with a local savings bank as a guarantee for issuing Wörgl's own 40,000 schillings' worth of stamp scrip.

He then used the stamp scrip to pay for his first project. Because a stamp needed to be applied each month (at 1% of face value), everybody who was paid with the stamp scrip made sure he or she was spending it quickly, automatically providing work for others. When people had run out of ideas of what to spend their stamp scrip on, they even decided to pay their taxes, *early*.

Wörgl was the first town in Austria which effectively managed to redress the extreme levels of unemployment. They not only re-paved the streets and rebuilt the water system and all of the other projects on Mayor Unter-guggenberger's long list, they even built new houses, a ski jump and a bridge with a plaque proudly reminding us that 'This bridge was built with our own Free Money' (see photographs). Six villages in the neighbourhood copied the system, one of which built the municipal swimming pool with the proceeds. Even the French Prime Minister, Édouard Dalladier, made a special visit to see first hand the 'miracle of Wörgl'.

It is essential to understand that the majority of this additional employment was not due directly to the mayor's projects as would be the case, for example, in Roosevelt's contract work programmes described below. The bulk of the work was provided by the circulation of the stamp scrip *after* the first people contracted by the mayor spent it. In fact, every one of the schillings in stamp scrip created between 12 and 14 times more employment than the normal schillings circulating in parallel (see sidebar)! The anti-hoarding device proved extremely effective as a spontaneous work-generating device.

Wörgl's demonstration was so successful that it was replicated, first in the neighbouring city of Kirchbichl in January 1933. In June of that year, Unterguggenberger addressed a meeting with representatives of 170 other towns and villages. Soon afterwards 200 townships in Austria wanted to copy it. It was at that point that the central bank panicked and decided to assert its monopoly rights. The people sued the central bank, but lost the case in November 1933. The case went all the way to the Austrian Supreme Court, but was lost again. After that it became a criminal offence in Austria to issue 'emergency currency'.

Wörgl's experiment: facts, figures, and fiction[37]

The experiment lasted from July 5, 1932 to November 21, 1933. The 'work notes' were issued in three denominations valued respectively at 1, 5 and 10 schillings. An average of only 5,500 schillings of the stamp scrip were outstanding, but they circulated 416 times over the 13.5 months that the experiment was allowed to develop, producing 2,547,360 schillings of economic activity (equivalent to approximately 64 million of today's schillings or US $7.5 million). As a result, the investment in productive assets in Wörgl jumped by 219% over the previous year.

In addition, the monthly demurrage fee was used for a soup kitchen that fed 220 families.

Mr Unterguggenberger's political programme would be considered today as middle-of-the-road social-democratic, as he vigorously campaigned '*against both fascism and communism and their utopian economic theories, State capitalism, bureaucracy and lack of economic freedom; and for private initiative and economic freedom'.*[192]

Nevertheless, during the 1930s his experiment was branded by monetary authorities first as an '*unfug*' ('craziness'); then as a communist idea; and after the war as a fascist one...

So Wörgl had to go back to 30 per cent unemployment. In 1934, widespread social unrest exploded throughout Austria. During the crackdown against the civil disorder, all political parties to the left were outlawed. Michael Unterguggenberger's party was identified with that group, so he was removed from office at that point. He died in 1936, still much loved by the local population.

Does it sound familiar? Only a central authority saviour can help people who are not allowed to help themselves locally. And as all economists will point out, when there is enough demand, supply always manifests in some way. Even if you have to import it.

During the Anschluss of 1938, a large percentage of the population of Austria welcomed Adolf Hitler as their economic and political saviour.

The rest is well-known history . . .

■ US Depression scrips

In the 1930s there were complementary currency issues all round the world; in the Baltics, in Bulgaria, Canada, Denmark, Ecuador, France (the 'Valor' project), Italy, Mexico, The Netherlands, Romania, Spain, Sweden, Switzerland, even China and Finland. Not all of them were suppressed, either. As we shall see later, at least one of these systems survived the war and is successful to this day (the WIR system in Switzerland, described below).

But the 'mother of all stamp scrip applications', and the place where the implementation came the closest to become official public policy was in the US.

The US, in fact, has a much longer history of issuing complementary currencies than is generally known. With clockwork regularity people under similar circumstances of duress seem spontaneously to reinvent the same solution. Complementary currencies sprung up during the Panic of 1837, the Civil War years, and the Panics of 1873, 1893 and particularly of 1907.

Professor Irving Fisher of Yale, author of a classic book on interest rates, and widely considered the most prominent American economist of his time, heard about the Wörgl experiment and published several articles about it in the US. At the time he was advising several communities on starting their own stamp scrip systems and was so inundated with additional requests that he quickly decided to publish a little monograph to meet the demand.[193]

He counselled against poor applications, such as the one implemented in 1932 by Charles J. Zylstra in Hawarden, Iowa, which erroneously applied Gesell's theory. In his case, the stamps were to be applied to the scrip at each transaction, instead of every month or every week, as it should be. This transaction-based taxation was effectively a sales tax, which in actuality encouraged hoarding, instead of discouraging it. It did not have the desired effects and users ended up hating it. As Zylstra was also a member of the Iowa House of Representatives, he had become a very active and prominent salesman for – unfortunately – the wrong approach. This erroneous application has been described by some detractors of the complementary currency systems as 'typical', while in reality it was an exception.

However, notwithstanding such mishaps, the majority of the applications in the US were correctly designed and successful. There even exists a remarkable catalogue which illustrates several thousand examples of local scrip from every state in the Union.[194]

This sets the scene for some key conversations between Professor Irving Fisher and Dean Acheson, then Undersecretary of the Treasury. Fisher was convinced that stamp scrip was *the* way out of the Depression, and brought his considerable knowledge to bear to prove this. He went on record with the statement that 'The correct application of stamp scrip would solve the Depression crisis in the US in three weeks!'[195] Dean Acheson, a prudent man, decided to refer the whole concept to one of his own economics professors at Harvard, the well-respected Professor Russel Sprague. The answer came back that in his opinion this approach would indeed succeed in bringing America back to work out of the Depression. But it also had some political implications about decentralization that he might want to check with the President . . .

We know what President Roosevelt's final reaction was from a speech he made a few weeks later. This is probably his most famous address, the one including the phrase 'The only thing we need to fear is fear itself'. In it, he announced a series of impressive centralized new initiatives to counter the crisis: the expansion of the Reconstruction Finance Corporation, and a series of large-scale Federal government-managed work-creation projects basically, what became known as the New Deal, completed in 1934 by the first US Export-Import Bank. He also announced that by executive decree he would henceforth prohibit 'emergency currencies'. This was the code name for all the complementary currencies already in existence, and all those in preparation around the country.

This is how the road was not taken in the US in the 1930s. It was a close call, but the *Zeitgeist* of the time seemed definitely in favour of spectacular centralized decisions for which political credit can more easily be claimed.

What is most interesting is that there is a growing consensus among economic historians that these centralized initiatives did not really get the US out of the Great Depression after all. They were better than nothing, and a lot of hard-working people produced a lot of valuable work under the programmes. But the majority of economic historians agree today that – for the US as for Germany – the spectre of the Great Depression was only vanquished by shifting the economy to prepare for World War II.

■ Some political lessons

The main lesson is that what appear to be boring technical decisions relating to banking and currency regulations are probably some of the biggest political time bombs around. We cannot prove that Hitler would not have been elected, or that the Anschluss would not have happened if the Wara and other stamp scrip grass-roots initiatives had been left to flourish. We cannot prove either that World War II would not have happened if the path not taken in the 1930s had been given a chance. There are obviously many other variables affecting such sweeping phenomena. History is not a laboratory experiment in which we can try again from scratch, and neatly change only one variable each time.

The historical record shows, however, that stamping out the popular grass-roots initiatives where people tried to solve their problems on a local level helped push a sophisticated and educated society into violently supressing its minorities, towards less and less democracy and, ultimately, towards war. That such suppressions have this power should not amaze us, given the cumulative nature of 'the vicious circle of unemployment' we saw earlier in Figure 5.1. Mussolini was right when he claimed that 'fascism is not a doctrine, it is a response to the need for action'.

The 1930s were one more demonstration of the 'vicious circle of unemployment' connecting unemployment, violence, fear, political polarization and instability. The closing of the loop back to higher unemployment was only avoided by the biggest instability of them all: war.

Given this historical record, we can make the next three observations:

- Whoever makes the decision to stamp out complementary currency initiatives should also be held accountable for providing alternative solutions and finding the money to pay for the services that they render. It just won't do to block them on some technicality and leave the subsequent social and political mess and despair to take care of itself, because we know exactly where this leads. We have been there before.
- Impeding individuals or groups from solving their own problems at a local level automatically creates demand for a saviour. Such a saviour invariably appears, whether called the Central Government, the Führer, the Duce, Zhirinofski, Buchanan, Le Pen or Fini, or any one of their successors.
- The record also shows that the only really effective way for large-scale centralized approaches to reduce serious structural unemployment is to prepare for war. Such economic reasons for war have been found not only for World War II, but for many other conflicts as well.

■ Today's systems

Very few complementary currencies survived the turmoil and reconstruction processes of World War II and the booming postwar years. As we would expect, it is only when economic duress knocks on the door that suddenly, like mushrooms under the appropriate weather conditions, local systems reappear. Today's systems have, therefore, reappeared primarily where unemployment has become abnormally high for local reasons.

Figure 5.3 best summarizes the dramatic growth of all types of complementary currencies over the past decade. As recently as the 1980s, there were fewer than 100 such currency systems in the world. They have multiplied by a factor of twenty over the past decade.

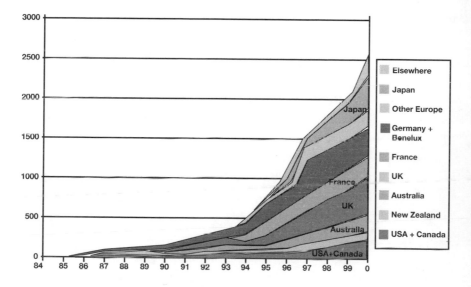

Figure 5.3 Number of community currency systems operational in twelve countries 1984-1998[196]

In the balance of this chapter and the next one we will have a look at the different types of such complementary currencies as are currently operational, and how they have been implemented in specific countries.

■ Clarifying some distinctions

Before describing some of the contemporary examples of non-traditional currencies, it is important to clarify some money distinctions. In some of the literature on new currencies, confusion has sometimes arisen between barter and complementary currencies. Occasionally, **barter** is erroneously described as any exchange that does not involve the 'normal' national currency. By definition, barter is the exchange of goods or services without any form of currency. Barter requires as a prerequisite that the two people involved each have something that the other wants. In technical terms, the parties need to have 'matching needs and resources'. This is a strong constraint to the fluidity of exchanges. It is also why money was invented as a medium of exchange in the first place.

In contrast, a **complementary currency** refers to an agreement within a community to accept a non-national currency as a means of payment. Such currencies are called complementary because their intent is not to replace the conventional national currency but to perform social functions that the official currency was not designed to fulfil. It is also complementary because most participants use the normal national currency and a complementary currency in parallel. It is often the case that a single transaction includes partial payments in both currencies at the same time.

Another useful differentiation is the one between fiat money and mutual credit currencies. A **fiat** currency, as we saw earlier (Chapter 2), is a currency which is created out of nothing by an authority. For instance, all our national currencies (including the euro) are fiat currencies. In contrast, **mutual credit** currencies are created by the participants themselves in a transaction as a simultaneous debit and credit. A more detailed description on how such currencies operate will be provided hereafter in the case of LETS or Time Dollars, both mutual credit currencies. Thomas Greco found references to such mutual credit systems in colonial Massachusetts.[196] Mutual credit systems are simply a monetary formalization of the tradition of helping each other that is embedded in almost all traditional societies. In Southern France, for example, it used to be called *aller aux aïdats* and in Ireland *meithal*.

These distinctions will help to identify the kinds of currency which encourage reciprocity and cooperation, instead of destroying them. Complementary currencies, particularly of the mutual credit variety, have proved effective in achieving that goal. This is so because, in contrast with fiat national currencies, they are compatible with a gift economy. They sometimes even spontaneously fuel a rebirth of a tradition of gift exchanges among neighbours.

Finally, it is notable that none of the currencies which have been most effective at fostering community bear interest. Remember, interest is one of the 'obvious' features of our familiar national money systems. It is also the hidden mechanism which was shown to generate competition instead of cooperation among participants ('The Eleventh Round' of Chapter 2).

■ LETS

By far the most frequent complementary currency system currently operating in the world is the Local Exchange Trading System (LETS). It was re-invented in the early 1980s by Michael Linton in British Colombia (Canada).[197]

Canadian prototypes

In 1983, Michael Linton and David Weston had implemented in Vancouver, Canada, a very simple but effective way to stretch the remaining scarce dollars circulating in high-unemployment communities. He incorporated a local non-profit corporation which is basically a mutual credit company, whose only indispensable asset was a personal computer. It is a membership organization, and a small entrance fee is paid to cover the set-up costs.

Just after this pilot episode, in the north-eastern provinces of Canada, years of over-fishing created a sudden necessity for fishing quotas to try to replenish the stocks. Just as suddenly, this brought to a halt entire fishing communities in the Maritime Provinces. Previously prosperous villages suddenly found themselves on the brink of disaster with 30-40% unemployment levels. The LETS model became a way to address this crisis.

So let us follow Amy who has decided to participate in her local LETS-Happyville system after she had paid her $5 set-up fee and $10 yearly membership fee.[198] Amy's account begins at zero balances. She sees from the (electronic and/or physical) notice board that Sarah is offering automobile tune-ups, and John is the local dentist participating in the system. She also sees that Harold wants freshly baked wholewheat bread. Amy sees potential trades in all of these. She negotiates with Sarah for her car tune-up for 30 'green dollars' plus $20 in cash for the new spark plugs. She receives her dental treatment from John for 50 'green dollars' and $10 in cash. She agrees to provide Harold with two deliveries of bread this week for 10 'green dollars' and finds out that he also would like some of the vegetables from her garden for another 30 'green dollars'.

The cash component is handled by all the participants directly as in any ordinary sales transaction, and only the 'green dollars' component is called in by phone or by a note to the LETS system. At the end, Amy obtains what she needs for only $30 in cash for a total value of $110 of goods and services. She also ends up still owing another 40 'green dollars' to the community as a whole. The 'green dollars' are not a scarce currency; as soon as people agree on a trade the currency is available. Neither do they pitch the participants against each other the way the normal dollar does (remember the Eleventh Round?). In most systems, there is no interest charge on any balances. Finally, the information about any individual's outstanding debit or credit balance is available to all participants so that there is a self-policing process to avoid abuse of the system by attempts to accumulate unreasonable debits.

Canada has between 25 and 30 operating LETS systems at this point. However, LETS became much bigger in the UK than in its country of origin. From there it spread to a dozen other countries, primarily in regions where high unemployment levels prevailed.

UK

In 1994, Alan Wheatley, a Reuters journalist, filed a report (see box).

Manchester, England

Warminster has its 'link'. Tomes its 'acorn' and Manchester its 'bobbin'.

They are the currencies of some of the 200 or so local exchanges trading schemes (LETS) that have sprung up in Britain, most of them in the past 18 months, as self-help initiatives to revive economic activity in communities ravaged by recession. 'I think they've become so popular because cash is short. That's the common story everywhere,' says Siobhan Harpur, who works at the National Museum for Labour History in Manchester, and who helped set up a scheme in that city of 3 million people . . .

'At least 40 per cent of the economy of a city like Manchester should be in complementary currency by the year 2000,' Harpur says. 'No one should have to work in sterling terms more than 20 hours a week at the most.'

The local council is encouraging the scheme by extending a £10,000 loan to be repaid in bobbins, which the council will use to buy child-minding and other services . . .

Ed Mayo, director of the New Economics Foundation, an 'alternative economics' think tank, says complementary currency schemes could be particularly useful in greasing the wheels of commerce between cash-strapped small businesses. 'They have tight credit lines and could well benefit from local schemes to trade between themselves,' says Mayo, who is founding a LETS in Greenwich, south-east London. [. . .]

It would be wrong to dismiss complementary currencies as the passing fad of misty-eyed do-gooders. 'Some people get involved because they're interested in recreating a community,' Mayo says. 'But for others it's not a hobby, it's a livelihood. It gives them access to goods and services they might not otherwise be able to get hold of.'

Geoff Mulgan, director of the Demos think tank, believes parallel economies such as LETS could provide jobs for many people without the skills or competence to participate in what he calls the money-based 'first economy'. 'Moreover, they may turn out to fit better within the culture of much of modern Britain, and in particular the culture of the young unemployed, than traditional solutions,' Mulgan says.

A group of dedicated volunteers were behind the remarkable community information campaign which made the UK a fertile ground for complementary currency efforts. In 1991, a group centred around LETSLINK UK including Liz Shephard and Harry Turner, were key agents in this process. Several innovations or expansions on the original model resulted from all this, such as the increased importance of the 'Directory of Wants and Offers', or new software developments. The Schumacher Award for 'triumph of individual effort' formally recognized all these efforts. The role of the New Economics Foundation, a spin-off from The Other Economic Summit (TOES) meetings should also be mentioned. Some specialized LETS project have also been successfully developed around healthcare issues (see sidebar).

A mental healthcare project based on LETS

The 'Creative Living Centre' in Manchester is a charitable company that supports people with emotional distress (patients with light mental health problems). It is based in a building owned by a health trust which was part of a huge mental hospital, and is operated in cooperation with National MIND (a mental health charity) and a group of people with personal experience of their own distress. A LETSystem is one of the mechanisms that provides networking support.

About 100 people per week come in for support. The Creative Living LETS has 150 members. There is a LETS shop, people can hire rooms and space for LETS and there are regular markets and auctions. There is a community gardening project which has an allotment and uses the garden around the centre, a coffee shop, and regular arts classes are offered through LETS. Complementary therapists offer some of their services through LETS, and there is the usual mix of services and goods sold through the system entirely independently of the centre.

As a result of this experiment, a national LETS and Mental Health Conference was held in Manchester which attracted hundreds of people. There are now a number of health trusts in the UK incorporating a LETSystem into their designs for 'Healthy Living Centres' as part of a government initiative for bringing communities together around health issues.

The Minister for Social Security of the Conservative government, Peter Baldwin, announced on December 8, 1993, that 'LETS type credits will not be counted as income for the purpose of the Social Security income test. LETS type schemes are a useful community initiative which should not be artificially discouraged by Social Security arrangements. I believe there is a strong case for giving Social Security clients the flexibility to participate in such schemes. In particular, LETS type schemes represent a form of activity that assists our clients in keeping in contact with labour market skills and habits, and indeed, in contact with the labour market itself.'

More recently, several UK government entities have further recognized the positive social role that these systems play.[199] Research has indeed shown that LETS can play an important role for the socially excluded in inner cities.[200] Prime Minister Blair endorsed LETS as 'showing the way' towards rebuilding human capital and 'making the links between rebuilding communities and rebuilding economic opportunity'.[201] Nevertheless, at the same time tax ambiguities are reported as a continuing impediment for small businesses or professionals to provide services in LETS, reducing both employment creation opportunities and the variety of what is available in this environment.

As of 1999, there are an estimated 450 LETS systems operational in the UK, more than a 100% growth since Alan Wheatley's report in 1994. City Councils – such as those in Bradford, Greenwich, Redditch, Shepway, Liverpool or Leicester – now have LETS development teams. In total over 100 local authorities are funding LETS development schemes via the Single Regeneration Budget, as part of their anti-poverty strategies. It should be noted, however, that impressive as this may all seem, in the big picture of economic things, the whole process remains marginal. An estimated 30,000 people are involved with a total annual turnover of only £2.2 million.[202]

Another indication of the depth of the social experimentation with money that is taking place in the UK is that there are now 500 credit unions (community created pools of 'normal' national currency to lend among members) operational in the country.[203]

New Zealand

David James, a Quaker from Whangarei, and Vivian Hutchinson, a community activist from New Plymouth, both in New Zealand, participated in a Quaker-organized alternative economics workshop in London in 1984.

Back home, the new Lange-Douglas government had commenced the most significant restructuring of economic policies since the Depression. These new policies, combined with a global economic slowdown, created high unemployment throughout New Zealand, particularly in the rural/forestry areas.

By 1986, both the ideas and the social stress had reached critical mass, and David James launched the first New Zealand 'green dollar' scheme: the Whangarei Exchange and Barter System (WEBS for short). He further conducted workshops to disseminate the idea. A government official, Hilary Allison, Regional Manager of the Alternative Employment Program of the Department of Internal Affairs in Dunedin, decided to fund an information tour of Otago and Southland in 1988. The national television news broadcast (TVNZ) covered the success story of Whangarei, and the process spread like wildfire across the country.

We know more about the New Zealand situation than many others thanks to the first Ph.D. thesis about LETS systems, by Mark Jackson.[204] He started off with an inventory of 61 green dollar systems as listed in the spring 1993 issue of the *New Zealand Green Dollar Quarterly*. He found 47 of these systems functioning well, and 14 moribund or deceased.

The backgrounds of the 'movers and shakers' who were instrumental in getting green dollar systems successful in New Zealand provide an insight into the amazing variety of people who are pioneering complementary currency technologies. They include government officials, Christian fundamentalists, hippies, mainstream political reformers as well as ordinary citizens.

One of the most intriguing findings of this survey is that the involvement of women in the process is also increasing with time, independently of their social or political background. In fact, in communities using the green dollar, women often have the highest participation rate.

Last but not least, there have been substantial debates and evaluations in New Zealand within the Internal Revenue Department (IRD, the tax authority) and the Department of Social Welfare (DSW, the administrator of the welfare and unemployment support system).

The tax authority in New Zealand has followed a general ruling that whenever systematic professional services are involved (e.g. a plumber doing a plumbing job), the green dollar income should be accounted for as regular income; taxes are therefore due, and remain payable in NZ$.

However, when the activity is outside normal activity (e.g. that same plumber repairing a car and getting paid in green dollars), then no taxes are due.

The Department of Social Welfare has been directly instrumental in funding a number of start-up projects in LETS systems because:

(a) The green dollar systems help the beneficiaries to maintain and acquire skills;

(b) Participation helps maintain motivation to search for 'normal' jobs; and

(c) These systems are often a springboard to self-employment.

Australia

Currently, Australia has the highest ratio of complementary currency systems *per capita*. Although the government has not been as actively involved as in New Zealand in supporting LETS systems, the latest estimate is that there are over 200 systems operational today. In 1991 there were 45 systems in Australia, and only three years later four times that amount. One of the best known is the Blue Mountains LETS near Sydney, with well over 1,000 members.

Among the reasons for this blossoming is that, after evaluating the results in the field, provincial governments, such as the one of Western Australia, help launch new LETS systems. The Australian Social Security Office has formally endorsed this approach since 1993.[205]

The French case: 'Le Grain de Sel'

We could cover every Northern European country: Scandinavia, Germany, the Low Countries, and make an inventory of what is happening in each.

Instead we will take the story of two more countries, France, because it illustrates the explosive nature of the multiplication process of complementary currencies when the unemployment conditions are serious enough, and Switzerland. As the French unemployment level shot up in the early 1990s, Claude Freysonnet, an organic farming specialist from Ariège, decided to take an initiative. In 1993, she heard about complementary currencies from Phillip Forrer, a Dutch friend. And *presto*, here comes *le Grain de Sel* (literally the 'grain of salt', which in French, as in English, has the double meaning of something not taken quite seriously). SEL is also the acronym for *Système d'Échange Local* (Local Exchange System).

Today, Claude sells her production of organic cheeses to the 300 participants of her *Grain de Sel* network in Ariège. She has spent her own *Grain de Sel* income on fruit trees for her garden, bicycles for her children, even the car she drives. Another participant in her network, Eric, unemployed, lives in a house which he rents in exchange for doing the repairs it needs, he eats organic food, drives around on his motorcycle, and acquired a new kitten. Everything is paid in *Grains de Sel*. He in turn trades his skills as an accountant and handyman, which are used by Chantal, 35, who in exchange, lodges a group of children during weekends and summer holidays in her big house. Marcel, 65, claims that 'he finally has been able to implement some dreams which never came to fruition under the normal money system'. In addition to the one-to-one deals typically found in LETS systems, every fortnight in Ariège there is a new tradition: a very special big party in the marketplace of Poix. People come to trade not only their cheeses, fruit and cakes, as in the normal market days, but also hours of plumbing, hair cuts, sailing or English lessons. Only *Grains de Sel* accepted!

Many people from all around the area come just 'because it is more fun this way'.

Two and a half years later, Claude Freysonnet has imitators in France. A lot of imitators. There are now over 200 *Sel* networks in France. Some have decided to call their unit of account '*la Truffe*' or '*Le Coquillage*' (the truffle, the seashell).

In addition, there are some 350 centres specializing exclusively in trading knowledge and information (*Réseaux d'Échange de Savoir*). That concept has been around in neighbouring countries as well. A typical example is what happens in *La Maison de l'Amitié* ('the house of friendship') in the sleepy town of Beauraing, Belgium. Their little brochure has the title 'I teach you, you teach me, we learn together'. Bernardette exchanges lessons in accounting for a special jam recipe, Jean exchanges information about how to keep chickens for the way to bake traditional breads, Dominique and Sophie receive cooking lessons from Marie who is interested in learning Dutch. 'It's a way to have relations which go beyond the simple "good morning". It's a great way to make friends. I have noticed that – once I understood the underlying principle – I dared more freely to ask for what I need. The other day I organized a workshop on Thai cuisine at home, and I just went out to invite my neighbours. It even has spread to the children. My daughter told me "Caroline is a bit weak in spelling . . . I could help her". I have been able to break the traditional barriers and treat everybody as an equal.'

This process has spawned a book on how to start your own information exchange centre.[206]

Every Saturday at 12.30 p.m. on the television network 'France 2' there is a programme entitled *Troc Moi Tout* (Barter Everything), which is the electronic version of a periodical called *Troc Tout*. Three cable television programmes (*Paris Première*, *MCM-Euromusiques* and *Eurosport*) are providing a support system to advertise available barter exchange opportunities between individuals.

According to a survey made in December 1994 by the CREDOC (*Centre de Recherche pour l'Étude et l'Observation des Conditions de vie*) one out of four French people are now performing exchanges not using the official French franc: 2% of all the French now trade mostly that way, 10% regularly, another 13% occasionally.

'There was a time when the people from the villages went *"aux aïdats"*. It was a reciprocal aid custom which became essential at harvest time. What if these old customs became the hottest modern thing to do?' wonders Dorothée Werner in an article about 'Trends for the Future' in *Elle*. She may be right: remember the Australian story of the 'Eleventh Round' (Chapter 2)? Here is a pragmatic demonstration that whenever the competitive undertow generated by the normal national currency disappears, people spontaneously rediscover the pleasures of cooperatively working with each other.

Even in France, there are professional party poopers. The 'Fisc' (the tax authority) is interested in its cut on exchanges over 20,000 FF per year, or if the exchange occurs in the normal professional activity of the person (as we saw in the UK).

WIR

'WIR'[207] is a Swiss example of a complementary currency run by and for a community of individuals and small business people. It is interesting for three reasons. First, it is the oldest continuous system in the modern Western world. It was founded in 1934 by 16 members in Zurich, and has continuously grown in both number of participants and volume of business for over 60 years. Second, it illustrates that complementary currencies make sense, even in the most conservative and hard-nosed capitalist country with one of the highest standards of living in the world. Finally, it is a system which has grown to a respectable size. In 1994, on the sixtieth anniversary of the WIR system, annual volume reached 2.5 billion Swiss francs (i.e., over two billion dollars). Its 80,000 members come from all areas of the country. It operates in four languages and owns its own bank building, as well as six impressive regional offices.

'WIR' is an abbreviation of *Wirtschaftsring-Genossenschaft* (roughly translated as 'Economic Mutual Support Circle'), and also means the pronoun 'We' in German.

Two of its key founding members – Werner Zimmerman and Paul Enz – were true visionaries for their time (see sidebar).

WIR's founders

In 1933, Werner Zimmerman published a paper on 'The liberation of women' where he demanded 'monetary compensation for the work of mothers'. Note that this is Switzerland, the last European country to have given the right to vote to women (1971). In 1935 he gave speeches on 'Dying forests and rivers – the issue of living water', and in 1972 published *Nuclear Energy – Blessing or Curse?*.

Paul Enz established in 1931 a horticulture foundation whose mission was the 'care and promotion of the physical and ethical recovery of the whole nation'. He also managed a chain of natural food stores in Zurich.

Zimmerman and Enz had studied the theories of Silvio Gesell and decided to copy two 'circles' which had applied these theories in Scandinavia and the Baltic during the early 1930s.

In their own words: 'What do we want? – Satisfying work, fair earnings and secured prosperity. This is what all working people strive for economically, and what they could and should all have . . .'[208] The name 'WIR' was explained by Zimmerman in opposition to 'Ich' (German for 'I') 'because together as a community, we better protect the interests of the individual'.[209]

The start was rocky, given that the creation of this complementary currency was heavily attacked by the press, the banks, and the more traditional business circles. But they managed to raise some 140,000 SF of working capital, mostly in amounts of 50 and 100 SF. Given that this was in the middle of the Depression, this was an extraordinary achievement in its own right.

The WIR system was started with about 2,950 members in 1935, and its low point was in 1945, when the turmoil of the war had brought membership down to only 624. After the war, it gradually picked up year after year, reaching 12,567 members in 1960, 24,227 members by 1980 and over 80,000 members now. Most are middle-class individuals and small- to medium-sized businesses. The volume of business has grown remarkably. Total turnover was still only 196 million SF in 1973, reached close to 1 billion SF by 1980, and is valued now at over 2.5 billion SF. The volume of credits outstanding in 1994 was the equivalent of about 1 billion SF.

There are two ways by which a member can obtain WIR: either by selling goods or services to someone else in the circle, or by obtaining a WIR credit from the coordinating centre. In other words, the WIR is a hybrid of mutual credit (whenever trading occurs by selling goods directly) and fiat currency (whenever a loan is made from the centre). Such credit has a very low interest rate (1.75% per annum). In practice, these credits are often guaranteed by real estate or another asset. As is true with all currencies, trust remains the key. The WIR credits are automatically removed from circulation whenever a member reimburses a loan to the centre.

The value of the WIR is pegged to the Swiss franc (i.e., 1 WIR = 1 Swiss franc), but all payments have to be made in WIR. (In technical language, the unit of account is the Swiss franc and the medium of exchange the WIR.)

Members report that they participate in WIR exchanges for the following reasons:

- it is a very cost-effective way of doing business: commission on sales is limited to 0.6% on deals completed in WIR;
- it gives access to a pre-screened and loyal client base; credit is much cheaper than in national currency;
- other services are provided (direct-mail, publicity among members, publications, etc.);
- it offers a buffer against exterior shock, such as a sudden increase in the national currency interest rate, or other economic disasters;
- it is a way for small businesses to gain some of the advantages to which otherwise only big businesses have access.

WIR, therefore, provides an idea of the economic potential of a complementary currency system when it can reach full maturity.

■ Regional development currencies

One of the most promising applications of complementary currencies – also one of its most recent ones – is its application to regional economic development. It is also an important sign that some significant governmental authorities are starting to take complementary currencies seriously. Two case studies will be presented briefly here: an initiative by the European Commission and perhaps the most impressive one of all by the Japanese Ministry of International Trade and Industry (MITI).

Europe

The European Commission (DG V) has been co-financing four pilot regional projects, jointly defined as the 'Barataria' projects (described in the website www.barataria.org). The four prototypes were purposely chosen to be of a different nature from each other. They are:

- the Scottish SOCS (www.socsystem.org.uk)
- the ROMA project in the Connaught area, Ireland

■ Amstelnet in Amsterdam, The Netherlands (email info@amstelnet.nl)
■ and '3er Sector' project organized by the non-profit La Kalle in the Vallecas district of Madrid, Spain.

The first two were developed in the countryside, while the two latter are for city dwellers. The Irish system is a paper scrip currency, while the three others are purely electronic money. In all cases, the normal taxes are due on local currency transactions, including Value Added Taxes (VAT). A few words about each give a flavour of the range of these applications.

1 The Scottish experiment is an adaptation of the WIR precedent adapted for regional development purposes. It was launched by Ruth Anderson of the Scottish Rural Forum in 1997. Membership to the SOCSystem is restricted to organizations, such as businesses, governmental agencies and non-profit organizations. Each member has an interest-free (unsecured) line of credit, which is determined on the basis of the number of trading partners and volumes. Additional credit can be granted when the organization can provide some guarantees (secured line credit). The SOCS directory is maintained on a website as well as in periodic print form. Payments are made using credit cheques, but other instruments are planned in the future. Membership dues are payable quarterly, and cover administrative overhead and a reserve account for bad debts.

2 The Irish experiment is operational in what is called the 'Black Triangle' in Ireland, the region bordering County Mayo and Roscommon, where economic decline continued even during the 1990s boom period in the rest of the country. It is an area with low density and diminishing population (about 25,000 people) spread over many small farm units. The unit of account is the ROMA which has been issued since January 1999, and it operates like a LETS system but with fairly strict credit rules. This particular project involves Richard Douthwaite, author of *Short Circuit: Strenghtening Local Economies for Security in an Unstable World*.[210] This book develops convincingly the reasons for specific regions to create their own currency systems.

3 Amstelnet is an initiative of the Strohalm Foundation in Amsterdam, The Netherlands. The area covered has one of the highest population densities in the world. It is a business network for companies, professionals and organizations and uses the *Amstelnet Eenheden* (AE 'Amstelnet Units' equivalent to one guilder) as unit of account and means of payment. The non-profit Strohalm is specifically focused on research and implementation of non-traditional currency systems. It has been active for a decade, has in 1999 a full-time staff of 47 people, and has been pioneering several other projects in The Netherlands.

4 Finally, the Spanish 'La Kalle' project is implemented in Vallecas, near Madrid. With 200,000 inhabitants, this is one of the largest working-class neighbourhoods in the country. The unit of account is the BICS equivalent to 100 pesetas. Interest-free loans are available automatically up to the equivalent of 50,000 pesetas, and after approval from a credit committee for larger amounts. One operating rule is that at least 25% of any trade has to involve BICS units.

Japan

Toshiharu Kato, the Director of Service Industries Division of the Ministry of International Trade and Industry (MITI) – the powerful coordination mechanism between government and the corporate world in Japan – completed personally a three-year study in the US of two types of high-tech development models: the 'Route 128 model' and the 'Silicon Valley model'. The former is named after the development of high-tech companies around a nucleus of large corporations (e.g. Raytheon and Hewlett Packard) and universities (e.g. MIT) in the Boston area; the latter refers to the proliferation of small high-tech computer companies and venture capital firms south-east of San Francisco near Stanford University. He concluded that the 'Silicon Valley Wave', based on high-density contacts among hundreds of small corporations (without large companies at the centre), is the wave of the future for Japan. More impressive still, he pushed his regional development strategy to its logical conclusion by introducing a new concept of regional currencies, which he called 'eco-money' (see sidebar).

Japan's next development model and 'eco-money'

(Extracts from Memoranda by Tashiharu Kato, MITI)[64]

'Using the Silicon Valley as a model, *Japan needs to actively create diversity in its different regions in order to promote a new socio-economic system based on the local community* . . . In Japan's movement toward an information society, it must make innovations in its economy and community to take the lead as a front-runner type society. Japan should implement a concrete action plan to carry out its shift to be a part of the next generation information society. This involves a coordination of business, government, education and community, to work together as one organization. Individual regions will develop their own unique industrial clusters, resulting in specific economic bases with entrepreneurial environments and creative communities . . . When we look to academia, modern economics does not provide us with any clear-cut solutions. The traditional world-view of economics deduces the total movement of the economy from a simple sum of component elements. With this world-view, it is impossible to analyze and understand the changes associated with economic shifts from one attractor to another attractor . . . The true task of an economic policy is to shift the attractor at the core of the economic movement, and through this effort, to put the economy on the track of solving the problems. In order to do this, we must not only note the decisions made by individuals and corporations who are the constituents of society at the macro-level, we also need to look at the interactions among these . . .

'The Japanese type new development model will be based on regions, and *it has the characteristic of a dual structure of regional economy and community.*'[212]

One of the key tools Kato introduces to create the dynamic of simultaneously activating a regional economy and a community is 'eco-money'.

'Eco-money is money for the 21st century which can be used in the exchange of varied and "soft" forms of information covering such areas as the environment, social welfare, communities and culture . . . Eco-money is always used in the direct exchange of items and services so that it does not accelerate any money creation functions. Therefore there is no risk of inflation, creating a bubble economy, or the shrinking of money circulation after the burst of the bubble . . .

'People can use standard money in parallel with "eco-money" and make efficient use of one or the other to create the most appropriate life-style . . . The ultimate objective in implementing eco-money is to nurture trust among people, so that a sense of community can be cultivated.'[213]

From four initial pilot projects the experiment has now expanded to ten different implementation models. They vary from a small village (Yamada in the Toyama prefecture) to a town of 16,000 people (Kuriyama in Hokkaido) and whole prefectures (equivalent to a county, specifically Shizuoka, Chiba and Shiga). Some include LETS type currencies, others *Hureai Kippu* (described in the next chapter) and still others integrate various services into a single smart-card system. An impressive list of 27 different types of activities are being integrated by using eco-money, including welfare, education, disaster prevention, environmental protection, services promoting the understanding of cultural assets, as well as a series of 'civil businesses' such as enterprises providing natural foods for children with allergies to chemicals, production of soap made from recycled cooking oil, and at-home care for the sick and elderly.

As of October 1999, besides the ten pilot projects, another thirty are in an 'assessment' stage (designing the specifications of their own systems, while evaluating the results of the ten pilot projects).

These projects are being combined with the generalization of the use of smart cards by the Ministry of Health and Welfare. Already one of the smart-card pilots in Yokosuka combines health insurance data with eco-money and normal national currency usable for everyday shopping. Plans for a 'Next Generation Info-Community Network' expand that concept to include medical care support and allergies data, safety confirmation systems for natural disasters, various licences, public ID, Internet as well as physical mall shopping, phone card and discount services for long-distance phone calls, petrol and other services available at discount rates, public transport and travel mileage services. Whether all these functions will end up on a single smart card or not, the main point remains valid: Japan is determined to be a leader in regional development strategies for the Information Age, and is using the appropriate tool of complementary currencies to achieve it.

Some big corporations are getting involved in this eco-money process: for instance Nippon Telegraph and Telephone (NTT) is developing software systems in the context of its 'Daily Life Welfare Information Network' project (which includes city governance, local businesses and non-profits, healthcare and welfare information, job training and volunteer information, etc.) Similarly, Oracle Japan has expressed interest in getting involved as well.

■ Financing small businesses

To illustrate further the flexibility of these local-currency concepts, here are examples of small businesses which have obtained financing through the use of complementary currencies. In this category fall the Berkshire experiments in Massachusetts or the 'Dining Dinero' issued by Café de la Paz in Berkeley.

None of the following complementary currencies was designed to be used as a general means of payment, but rather as an alternative financing mechanism for specific predetermined purposes, supported by the community.

The four main Berkshire experiments are Deli Dollars, Berkshire Farm Preserve Notes, Monterey General Store Scrip and Knitter Restaurant scrip.[214] Normal banking sources were not interested in providing such financing. All these experiments follow a similar pattern to that of the Farm Preserve Notes. The Farm Preserve Notes – officially sanctioned by the Massachusetts State Agricultural Department – provide working capital for some small farmers who sell them against normal US dollars. These certificates are redeemable at the next crop against merchandise and produce. A discount is built into the price of this future produce to provide an incentive to the buyer to purchase now what will become available only months from now. This approach was very well received by the clients, and enabled the farmer to raise working capital immediately, while ensuring him in advance the sale of part of his crop with reliable clients in the future.

The Café de la Paz in Berkeley, CA, needed capital for refurbishing a community meeting room at the side of the main restaurant. It approached several banks with a request for financing. When none was forthcoming, the Café de la Paz issued a scrip which was redeemable against lunches and dinners in the future. The accounting works as follows: a client buys for $100 the value of 120 'Dining Dinero' (so the client gets a 20% discount on the corresponding meals). As the cost of goods sold is about $40, Café de la Paz still makes a $60 profit on the transaction. It also obtains the financing needed, and in addition has increased the loyalty of its clients. It is a win-win for everybody.

■ Local loyalty schemes

Saving downtown: the case of Leominster[215]

The local butcher Graham Hurley decided to fight back against the superstores in his small town of Leominster when 17% of local downtown shops had already closed down. Local unemployment had risen in parallel to 8.1%.

He invented a scheme which he called 'Loyal to Leominster'. Local businesses paid £20 to join, and received in exchange 'Loyal to Leominster' cards and posters. Within a year, 63 businesses had joined and 8,000 loyalty cards had been issued (which later grew to 15,000 cards). Temporary 'Visitor to Leominster' cards were also issued to attract tourist trade. Some businesses reported as much as a 30% increase in sales. The scheme was so successful that several new businesses moved to town to take advantage of it.

Leominster's idea was copied the next year by nearby Midsummer Norton and Radstock, which attracted 8,000 customers and increased its turnover by 15%. Bath followed the same year with a 'Bath Shopping Card'. Newcastle, Wilmslow, New Milton, Havant and Harlesden all did the same thing somewhat later.

The full potential of these schemes has definitely not been exploited so far, as there has been no effort to collect the names and addresses of members or to cross-market additional services to them.

The last examples of a special type of complementary currency aiming at creating local employment are local loyalty schemes. It is now generally recognized that small businesses are the major source of future employment. However, the development of superstores and American-style shopping malls has continued unabated over the past decades. For instance, in the UK, superstores have increased their share of retail space from 12.9% to 23% over the ten years to 1996. In some areas 70% of the grocery market is accounted for by just two surperchains.[216] The net result: systematic death of the local retail outlets, and the transformation of dowtown areas into ghost towns with high unemployment and crime rates. This doesn't have to remain so, as was proved by a butcher's initiative in a small English town (see sidebar). The possibilities for local loyalty schemes to revitalize local downtowns, stimulate small business employment, compete more effectively against the larger distribution systems and improve the quality of life generally have only been barely tapped so far. With the growth of Internet businesses, expected to become one-fifth of European company sales in five years time,[217] the importance for groups of smaller businesses to learn the sophisticated use of complementary currencies can only increase over time.

■ Conclusion: complementary currencies as 'Early Prototypes'.

In conclusion, complementary currencies make sense socially, economically and from a business viewpoint. It should also be noted that many of the current complementary currency systems should be considered as being at the stage where aeronautical engineering was when the Wright Brothers made their first flying attempts. The remarkable feat of the Wright Brothers was that their contraption flew at all. But it was nevertheless their and their 'crazy' colleagues' pragmatic demonstrations that ultimately has made possible that we and our most perishable products today fly routinely around the world. It is also significant that *The New York Times* mentioned the Wright Brothers' achievement for the first time only four years after the fact, and then only because the President of the United States was present at such a demonstration. The real understanding of the theory of why these contraptions could fly had to wait for many more years after that.

There should be no shame attached to considering the current versions of complementary currencies as 'early prototypes'. Almost all of today's systems remain obviously marginal in terms of total economic volume, for instance. Just like the Wright Brothers, they are typically being ignored, or when noticed sometimes ridiculed, by mainstream academic or media pundits. Most are still waiting to be recognized by some 'Presidential witness' to be taken seriously. But what matters for us here is that they have already proved that they can 'fly', that they actually produce the intended effects at the scale for which they were designed.

Specifically, the following findings have already been demonstrated in practice:

1 Complementary currencies make possible transactions and exchanges that otherwise would not occur. This means in practice that more economic activity – implying more work and wealth – is being created than would otherwise be the case. In one field survey, more than half of the people interviewed actually started to provide their services as a direct result of availability of the complementary currencies in their community.[218]

2 This additional work and wealth is being generated where it is most needed without the need for taxes, government bureaucracy and without creating the risk of inflation in the mainstream economy (this last point will be developed in detail in Chapter 7). Note that this is *additional* wealth, not a result of redistribution of existing wealth. Therefore, complementary currencies are *not* a new form of welfare. Welfare is a compulsory transfer of resources from the rich to the poor via taxes. In contrast, the use of complementary currencies is voluntary for everyone; it creates new wealth, and – once started – becomes a completely self-funding mechanism to address many social problems without requiring permanent subsidies or taxes.

3 Complementary currencies make not only social sense, but also business sense. They enable locally owned businesses to compete better against the large chain distribution systems. Small local businesses can more easily accept the local currency, because they can spend them in the community – as is the case for small farmers who can use local labour at harvest time. In contrast, large chains have suppliers that are typically far away, and are therefore less likely to be interested in local currency participation. In this sense, complementary currencies can also contribute to making the local economy more self-reliant, a modest but healthy counterweight to the relentless globalization of the economy. This creates a more level economic playing field, ensures better competition and therefore overall benefits to the consumers and society.

4 The WIR case and the one of Curitiba show that complementary currency systems can be scaled up to quite substantial volumes – in the first case to 80,000 members and several billion Euros of annual trade, and in the latter to a city of several million people even in Third World conditions.

5 Nevertheless, I do not claim that complementary currencies are a sufficient solution to the complex problems of unemployment in the Information Age. I specifically do not claim that more traditional forms of employment encouragement should not be implemented. My point is simply that complementary currencies are potentially an important tool – one that has often been overlooked – and that they deserve more attention than has been the case so far. Given the foreseeable scale of the employment problem during the transition period of the next decades, can we afford to ignore tools that have shown that they can be effective?

CHAPTER 6

Community Currencies

- *'Money symbolized the loving giving and taking among individuals which gave men the feeling of having emotional roots in their community [. . .] Money originated as a symbol of man's soul.'*

  WILLIAM S. DESMONDE[219]

- *'The economy of the future is based on relationships rather than possession.'*

  JOHN PERRY BARLOW

- *'What idealists have dreamt about,
  What hippies used to talk about,
  Now people are just doing.'*

  ANONYMOUS

This chapter addresses another 'money question' of our Time-Compacting Machine; the one relating to the Age Wave; i.e. 'how will society provide the elderly with the money to match their longevity?' But it also goes beyond that specific topic by tackling the broader issue of community breakdown. Problems in elderly and child care, education, reduction of criminality, and improvement of the general quality of life are all symptoms of the same phenomenon of community crises. Community breakdown has become a universal pattern all over the modern world. Although it is usually not perceived that this trend relates to money, this chapter will show that both the cause of the problem and its solution can be found in money systems.

■ Community breakdown

Around the world, in rich and poor countries alike, the structure of family life is undergoing accelerated and fundamental changes. 'The idea that the family is a stable and cohesive unit . . . is a myth. The reality is that trends like unwed motherhood, rising divorce rates, smaller households, and the feminization of poverty are occurring worldwide,' a recent study demonstrates.[220] Only Japan has remained virtually unchanged over the last 30 years.[221]

The world over, we can hear the same complaint. 'Things aren't the way they used to be. We used to have a better sense of community.' What is referred to may be different in each culture, but the trend is identical. Its consequences are also similar, including vandalism against common property and criminality, particularly among the younger generation.

The more 'developed' the country, the more this trend has advanced (see sidebar). For instance, in Northern Europe and the US, the extended family was considered the norm during the 19th century. By the 1950s, the nuclear family was standard. Today, the median of social identity in the US has already moved from the nuclear family to the single parent family as 51% of all US children now live in a single parent home.[222] What is even more enigmatic is that the same movement – although with different starting points – seems to happen almost everywhere.

Definition of 'family' by an Australian Aboriginal Elder[223]

'You white people don't understand what we mean by "family". When a baby is born, it is given to its "mothers". That means, the mother who bore it, all her sisters and all her aunties. They are responsible for nurturing and loving it. It is also given to all its "fathers". That means its natural father, all his brothers and all his uncles. They are responsible for caring for it and teaching it. Everyone else in the tribe is brother and sister. *We think it is really primitive for a baby to have only one mother and one father!'*

Many children, in Western society, don't even have two parents! Imagine the love, support, and caring they would experience with a whole group of mothers and fathers!

Are we, indeed, 'primitive' in our assumption that two parents are enough for one child? Maybe 'existential angst' is only part of Western culture – not necessarily a given of the human condition.

In Italy, for instance, a few decades ago *la famiglia* still referred to the extended family: 60 or 80 people, including, of course, several generations, such as grandparents, parents, uncles, cousins, nieces and in-laws. Now, the norm has moved towards the nuclear family, particularly in the more 'modern' northern half of the country. Other Southern European and Latin American cultures are following an identical trend.

From the Hopi in Arizona to the Kogi in Colombia and the Chipibo in the Peruvian Amazon, we hear the comment that the young are losing their connection to the tribe and identifying themselves with smaller subgroups, or even just blood relatives, 'as white people do'.

All of this is usually written off – depending on the age and political persuasion of the observer – as the price of progress or the signs of decadence of society. But could community breakdown be a contagious disease? Is it thinkable that they all may have a deeper common cause? What could it be?

To understand how community is lost, we must find out how it is created. Of all the disciplines which have studied community, the most useful insights come from anthropology. Anthropologists discovered that community does not necessarily arise out of proximity (otherwise, a 200-apartment high-rise building in a big city would produce community). Similarly, common language, religion, culture, even blood, doesn't automatically produce community either. All of these factors can clearly play a secondary support role in the process, but the key ingredient is something else.

Anthropologists have found that community is based on reciprocity in gift exchanges.[224]

Community building and the 'gift economy'

If community were a fabric, what would be the individual thread? Or, to use another metaphor, if community were a molecule, what would be its constitutive atom, the smallest act that creates it?

If you need a box of nails, you go to the hardware store and buy one. There is no expectation by either you or the shop assistant that any future reciprocity is involved. This is one of the main reasons why monetary exchanges are so efficient. Each transaction stands on its own. However, no community has been created either.

Gift economy as an evolutionary social survival skill

Gift giving was developed as the earliest form of social security according to anthropologist Stanley Ambrose of the University of Illinois at Urbana-Champaign. 'Social ties, established by gift giving, would have helped people in tough times, particularly important in a difficult or unpredictable environment.' The San hunter-gatherers from Kenya still maintain such networks today by exchanging ostrich eggshell beads, the gift helping secure future favours. The age of this eggshell bead gift tradition was established when Dr Ambrose discovered in a rock shelter called Enkapune Ya Muto in Kenya's rift the remains of an ostrich eggshell bead workshop with over 600 shell fragments and completed beads, dating back 40,000 years!

'It gave the African people an advantage over Neanderthals, who may not have had such symbolic mechanism for social solidarity.'[225]

Now, assume that you go out for another box of nails, and that your neighbour is sitting on his porch. When you tell him you are going to buy a box of nails, he responds, 'Oh, I bought six boxes just the other day. Here is one, it will save you the trip to the hardware store.' He also refuses your offer to pay. What has happened?

From a purely material viewpoint, in both cases you end up with your box of nails. But an anthropologist would point out that in the second case, something else has happened as well. When you meet that neighbour again, you will definitely say hello. And if ever on a Saturday night he rings your doorbell because he forgot to buy some butter, you will most likely share some of yours. The gift of the box of nails is a community-building transaction. Its purchase is not.

A commercial transaction is a closed system, the nails versus the money. In contrast, a gift is an open system. It leaves an imbalance in the transaction that some possible future transaction completes. The gift process creates something that the monetary exchange does not. A new thread has been woven into the community fabric.

The evidence for this relationship between gifts and community is overwhelming. It has been documented all over the world and at all times.

■ Some examples

It is odd that I needed anthropologists to discover the relationship between gifts and community building. The etymology of the word 'community' could have provided even more explicit information about the link, without all that hard field work by anthropologists. 'Community' derives from the two Latin roots: *cum*, meaning *together, among each other* and *munus*, meaning *the gift*, or the corresponding verb *munere, to give*.

Hence *'community'* = *'to give among each other'*.

Could it have been more obvious?

I will now provide three examples of communities where this unwritten rule – that community is built over time as a result of gift exchanges – has been operational since time immemorial.

Monastic communities

Benedictus of Aniane introduced some Celtic concepts into early Christianity and founded the Benedictine Order during the fifth century AD, the first Christian monastic organization in the West. Its rule book specifies that *communitas* is created by the way one organizes the economic necessities of these monasteries. The monks should be self-sufficient as a group, but totally inter-dependent between themselves. Everybody has a function – from abbot to doorkeeper, from cook to scribe, from ironmonger to cheese maker. But each job has to be contributed as a gift to the community. Monasteries knew all about monetary exchanges, as these regularly occurred between the monastery and the rest of the world. It is, therefore, quite intentional and significant that the Benedictine rule explicitly prohibits any monetary exchanges among members of the community.

Non-Christian monastic traditions have gone even further in the same direction, without the benefit of knowing the Latin etymology for the word 'community'.

For instance, 'According to the Buddhist monastic code, monks and nuns are not allowed to accept money or even to engage in barter or trade with lay people. They live entirely in an economy of gifts. Lay supporters provide gifts of material requisites for the monastery, while the monastics provide their supporters with the gift of teaching. Ideally this is an exchange that comes from the heart, something totally voluntary. The returns in this economy do not depend on the material value of the object given but in the purity of heart of the donor or the recipient.'[226]

Traditional societies

In the early 1950s Lorna Marshall and her husband lived with a band of Bushmen in South Africa. As a farewell gift, they gave to each of the women in the band a bracelet of cowrie shells. Cowries are not available in the area, and had been bought in New York. Marshall wondered what that might do to future archaeological research in the area.

When the Marshalls returned a year later, they were surprised to find none of the cowries in the original group. 'They appeared, not as whole necklaces, but in ones and twos in other people's ornaments at the edges of the region.'[227] The gifts of the cowrie seashells had spread like water through the wider community.

While we often tend to think of gift societies as primitive and dismiss them in a condescending way, some of these gift rituals are extraordinarily complex and sophisticated. In traditional societies, gift rituals are considered among the most important social activities within the community. Their very complexity is a sign of the significance given to them.

For example, the Tikopia who live in an archipelago in Polynesia engage in no less than 24 different kinds of ritual gift exchanges to complete one single wedding.[228] The whole process requires several days.

In another island group, the Massim archipelago, otherwise totally useless ornaments called the Kula are always moving as ceremonial gifts from one island to the other. Specific 'soulava' necklaces – worn only by women – circulate in a counterclockwise sequence among the islands, while the male 'mwali' armshells circulate among the men in clockwise sequence.[229]

The North-western American Indians had great meetings of all neighbouring tribes to celebrate *potlatch* (literally to nourish, to give). Status was marked by the quality and quantity of objects given. We consider people famous because they have accumulated a lot of money, or because they bear a title such as 'Her Royal Highness'. In contrast, the Kwakiutl honorific titles characterize the generosity of the giving in which people have engaged: e.g., 'Whose Property was Eaten in Feasts' or 'For Whom Property Flows'.[230]

Modern societies and scientific communities

What is left of our Western world family communities still occurs around Christmas and birthday reunions, and – as all retailers will tell you – around gift exchanges. Today's marriages – the ritual where two families formally join to create a single larger community – are still marked by the exchanges of gifts.

Japan is the one developed country which has been bucking the trends in community breakdown. This is usually attributed to a mysterious peculiarity in the Japanese social structure or psyche. However, here too our universal key of gift exchanges is applicable. The Japanese tradition of *Butsu Butsu Kokan* refers to the reciprocal nature of gift exchanges, which explicitly exclude monetary exchanges. The name itself reflects that point, its literal translation being 'Object-Object-Exchange'. These gifts are a key ritual in practically all aspects of the Japanese culture. Gifts are constantly exchanged not only within the extended family, but between co-workers, esteemed individuals, social and work superiors and elders. It takes often the form of sharing one's talents in art, calligraphy, culture or other social graces. It is not the monetary value of the gift that matters; what counts is the intention, the quality of the personal touch.

Even the most 'modern' of all communities – the worldwide scientific community – is nurtured by the same unwritten rule. Indeed, scientists who give their ideas to the community receive recognition and status. In contrast, those who do it for the money, or who write only textbooks (a commercial activity) have no recognition, or may even be scorned. 'One reason why the publication of textbooks tends to be a despised form of scientific communication [is that] the textbook author appropriates community property for his personal profit.'[231] In short, to the extent you want to belong to the scientific community, you can get credit for your ideas, on the express condition you present them as gifts to the community; i.e., do not get monetary fees for them.

A contemporary German scientist, Almut Kowalski, has developed a complete alternative theory based on gifts to explain how physical reality operates. Her claim is that from atoms to galaxies, from plants to organs in our own body, all exhibit processes which she describes as 'tuning in and gently giving' as the core exchange mechanism. For instance, your kidneys are 'tuning in' on what the rest of your organism needs, and 'gently give' what they can for the benefit of the whole. Ken Wilber's *holon* theory develops a similar idea.[232]

■ How communities break down

It should not come as a surprise that to unravel the fabric of a community you do the opposite of what helped create it in the first place. Therefore, I propose as a general rule that communities break down whenever non-reciprocal monetary exchanges replace gift exchanges.

Let us revisit specific examples of community building described above, starting with the last one, the scientific community. They all show that community unravels every time exchanges involving the 'normal' national currencies replace gifts.

Dr Jonathan Kind, Professor of Genetics at MIT, says, 'In the past, one of the strengths of American bio-medical science was the freedom of exchange of materials, strains of organisms, and information . . . But now [that the universities are trying to make money from the commercial potential of recombinant DNA], if you sanction and institutionalize private gain and patenting of micro-organisms, then you don't send out your strains because you don't want them in the public sector. That's already happening now. People are no longer sharing their strains of bacteria and their results as freely as they did in the past.'[233] The fabric of one corner of the scientific community has started unravelling.

The first significant contact with north-western American Indians was made by Captain Cook around the time of the American Revolution. Pelt traders moved in thereafter, and the Hudson Bay Company established its first outposts in the 1830s. All of these people were only interested in the furs, and otherwise left the Indians alone. But decades before the missionaries arrived to try to change the 'pagan' traditions of the indigenous people, some communities started to unravel because of their contact with the traders' commercial exchanges. Tribes that had replaced the gift exchanges within their community with monetary exchanges were those that fell apart within a generation.

This process has repeated itself all over the world whenever traditional societies start interacting commercially with the Western world. As soon as non-reciprocal monetary exchanges begin to occur within these traditional societies, their communities start breaking down. I have seen this happen at first hand in the 1970s in the Peruvian Amazon when the Peruvian national currency started circulating within some tribes.

In light of all of the above, we should consider community not as a state, but as a process. If it is not nourished by regular reciprocal exchanges, it will tend to decay or die. That is why I define a community as a group of people who honour each other's gifts, who can trust that their gifts will be reciprocated some day, in some way.

Revisiting the strange global epidemic of community breakdown, we can now see what may be a common mechanism behind the breakdown of Amazon tribes, the transformation of Italian extended family into nuclear families, or the Western nuclear family crisis. While other factors certainly play a role, there is one key that fits all of these phenomena. Non-reciprocal monetary exchanges have started taking place within each of these community systems. Some economic theories consider the monetization of all transactions as a key sign of 'development', because from that moment they are captured in the national statistical system. No wonder that the process of community decay is also the highest in the more 'developed' countries.

As Hazel Henderson puts it: 'If you want to have breakfast prepared by Mom, go to McDonald's where she is serving it.' In a society where you need to pay your son to cut the grass, the nuclear family breakdown is on its way. And when you decide to put Grandpa in a nursing home, not only is the extended family gone, but you will also have to pay for the day care centre.

In a recent survey of the priorities of the American population, the desire to 'rebuild neighborhoods and communities' received the highest ranking for an astounding 86% of the population.[234] This is one priority that everybody seems to agree on.

But how can community be rebuilt in today's world?

■ Currencies that build community

We just learned the apparently general rule that whenever money gets involved, community breaks down. However, this turns out to be true only when scarce, competition-inducing currencies, such as our official national currencies are involved. In fact, the use of some other types of currencies can have exactly the opposite effect of building community.

None of this is theory. We are dealing with real-life experiments which have been going on in a wide variety of countries, in some cases for decades. Theory is way behind practice in this field (see sidebar).

Complementary currencies and economic theory

One traditional economic hypothesis which this chapter on Community Currencies challenges is that "money is value neutral", i.e. that money is simply a passive medium of exchange which does not affect the transaction or the users of a currency. Under such an assumption, a currency simply facilitates an exchange, but does not otherwise modify the transaction. In contrast, the claim here is that the characteristics of a currency (such as how it is issued, whether the users themselves can create it or not, and whether it bears interest or not) can affect the nature of the exchange and ultimately the nature of the relationship between the people which use it. My arguments in favour of this view do not come from economic theory, but from two other sources of evidence: empirical observation and the most solid psychological theory.

Empirically, users of some types of the complementary currencies claim that they experience such a difference; they even claim that they do so specifically for that reason. Some conventional economic theorists have tried to explain away the whole non-traditional currency phenomenon on the basis of tax dodging. However, the complementary currency phenomenon cannot be explained away on such a simple basis. The proof is that by far the most prevailing types of complementary currency are electronic, where all transactions are stored in a central computer. It is therefore very easy for a tax authority to find out what is going on in - in fact much easier than when conventional cash is used. So why else than the community building difference claimed by its users would explain people accepting the inconveniences of dealing with complementary currencies and the national currency in parallel? A sampling of such testimonials' is provided in chapters 5 and 6.

The traditional psychological hypothesis that underlies economics is that of a totally rational "economic man", which dates back to Adam Smith, a century before the discovery of the unconscious by Freud and Jung. I propose that this simplistic model should be completed with a more comprehensive emotional map of human motivations. The empirical evidence that this is justified includes the repeated "irrational" financial manias ("boom and bust cycles") which have been periodically plaguing our Modern financial systems for several centuries, and which economic theory has not been able to explain in a satisfactory way. It also includes substantial historical evidence on how different monetary systems have contributed to shaping values and relationships in other societies. Given its importance, it is fully developed elsewhere.

(See *The Mystery of Money*, originally written as an integral part of *The Future of Money*.)

There are indeed currencies which have reciprocity built in, which are more compatible with a gift economy than our national currencies. Practice has demonstrated that such currencies build community instead of destroying it.

What kind of money could that be?

■ Some real-life examples

The balance of this chapter will provide seven case studies. The first three are US applications, the others are respectively from Brazil, Japan, Mexico and Thailand. Each one depicts a very different approach. You will learn something different from each, but you can also get the core concept by choosing from among the seven only those examples you find most intriguing.

1 Time Dollars, invented by a prominent Washington lawyer, and applied now in several hundred communities in the US. Thirty different states have recently started promoting this approach to pragmatically solve local issues.

2 Ithaca HOURS, a paper currency launched by a community activist in the small university town of Ithaca, New York. Ithaca is a relatively low-income community of about 27,000 inhabitants. Similar types of paper currency systems are now operational in 39 different communities in the US.

3 The PEN Exchange, illustrating how a complementary paper currency helped build community in Takoma Park, Maryland, a well-off suburb of Washington DC.

4 Curitiba, a provincial capital of 2.3 million inhabitants in Brazil, where a mayor used complementary currencies for 25 years, propelling this Third World city to First World standards in less than one generation. In 1992, Curitiba was awarded the title of 'the most ecological city in the world' by the United Nations. Its mayor has become a nationally recognized political hero.

5 A remarkably successful application of a specialized 'Healthcare Currency' operating at the national level in Japan which provides an innovative way to improve the quality of healthcare at no costs to the government.

6 Tlaloc: a Mexican popular neighbourhood currency provides another version of low-tech complementary currency. It operates without

individual users needing access to either a computer or even a telephone.

7 Bia Kud Chum: the first South-East Asian community currency, a remarkable synthesis which is the result of cooperative efforts from Holland, Canada, Mexico and Japan.

This chapter concludes with two examples of hi-tech integrated payment systems, enabling dual payments in both national currency and complementary currency in one single transaction.

1 Time Dollars

Edgar S. Cahn, professor at the District of Columbia Law School, developed his Time Dollar concept in 1986, initially for retirement homes in Florida, a school district in Chicago and a social project in Washington DC. Now it has spread into hundreds of applications. One incentive is that the Internal Revenue Service (IRS, the US tax authority) has ruled that Time Dollar transactions are tax free.

The system has an elegant simplicity. Here is how it works. Joe doesn't have good eyesight and can't drive a car any more. But he needs a special pair of new slippers from the other side of town. Julia agrees to make the one-hour drive to get the slippers. Julia gets a credit for one hour, while Joe gets a one-hour debit, which they can mark on the blackboard near the superintendent's office.

Julia can spend her credit on the biscuits baked by another neighbour, while Joe will offset his debit by tending the community garden, or something else that his bad eyesight allows him to do. If Joe was going to spend one hour working in Julia's garden, that would be simple barter. However, the fact that Joe can work for an hour in the garden of someone else in the community to cancel his Time Dollar debit, and that Julia can use her credit to buy Jane's biscuits, makes Time Dollar exchanges much easier to complete than barter. Joe and Julia do not need to have 'matching needs and resources' to complete the transaction.

That is why Time Dollars is real money as we defined it earlier: an agreement within a community to use something (in this case, hours of service) as a means of payment. In other words, Joe and Julia have created money. It is as simple as that.

'Einstein discovers that time is actually money'

The costs of starting such a system are almost nil. For small-scale communities, one can use a blackboard or a piece of paper. For larger scale projects, a 'Timekeeper' computer program can be downloaded for free on the Internet (www.timedollar.org). All participants' names are listed with little pluses and minuses. It expands automatically to record whatever number of participants and person-hours are needed.

Furthermore, whenever someone gets a credit, someone else automatically creates a debit. The sum of all the Time Dollars in the system is, therefore, always zero at any point in time. But Joe got his slippers, Julia her biscuits, and the community a vegetable garden, and not one dollar was needed to make it all happen.

The goods and services exchanged are only the tip of the iceberg. A comparative survey was made of retirement homes: those using the Time Dollar approach compared with those that didn't.[235] In the retirement homes using the Time Dollar approach, they found that using this money knits the group together. People say hello to each other. When someone has a birthday, there is a big party for the entire home. People look out for each other. There is an informal dinner once a week. They start a communal garden. In short, community has been created.

This simple device has changed the way people relate to each other. People feel that their contributions are rewarded. They feel valued. One totally unexpected side effect appeared. Participants got healthier! In Brooklyn, New York, a health insurance company called Elderplan has decided to accept 25% of the premiums for its senior health programmes in Time Dollars. Elderplan has even created its own 'Care Bank' where participants log an average of over a thousand hours per month. It started as a home repair service by which potential problems are fixed *before* they cause accidents. The Care Bank has as motto: A broken towel rail is a broken hip waiting to happen.[236] For the insurance company, this is clever marketing. But Elderplan also took these unusual initiatives because it had noticed that pensioners participating in Time Dollar systems were experiencing fewer health problems. The bottom line was that their health care is less expensive for the insurance company. The Elderplan system is expanding during the year 2000 to include various boroughs of New York. A special new programme focusing on diabetics and which includes a major component of self-help is being launched by the same time bank. The time credits are now also redeemable against cinema and theatre tickets, transport vouchers, healthcare products, supermarket and luncheon vouchers throughout Brooklyn.

UK applications of Time Dollars

The first application of Time Dollars was Fair Shares which opened in three sites in Gloucestershire.[237] The New Economics Foundation is launching some additional ones in Newcastle and Lewisham. The Watford Council included a Time Dollar scheme in its Better Government for Older People programme announced in March 1998.[238]

What these systems have in common is to provide a framework for elderly people to take care of other, worse off, elderly people. Older people earn the credits by visiting, giving lifts or helping with meals on wheels and other neighbourhood tasks which help other people remain healthy and in their own houses.

They also receive them for their work evaluating council services. In turn, the councils let them spend these credits on special privileges in council-run facilities.

In a world where pensioners are becoming an ever-increasing proportion of society, to the point that medical expenses may bankrupt entire countries, is anybody taking any notice?

The good news is that in the UK, more and more people have started doing so (see sidebar). Research has also proved with hard data the value of this model. Time Dollars systems have proved effective not only in boosting healthcare systems, but in other social problems such as youth crime, and lawlessness in run-down neighbourhoods. Research has also proved the validity of this model in various domains.

Time Dollars can now be exchanged not only for services, but also for food, clothes, home mortgages (through Habitat International), health insurance, computers and student loans.

It is also clear that the full potential for cross-fertilization between Time Dollar systems and local businesses has barely been tapped, and would provide important benefits to both sides (see sidebar).

Potentials for cross-fertilization between business loyalty schemes and Time Dollar systems

More and more businesses have started loyalty schemes (the largest in the UK being Tesco, and there are many smaller ones started by downtown communities, both explained elsewhere). Why not cross-fertilize such commercial loyalty schemes with Time Dollar systems?[239]

- Businesses would thereby show that they are active supporters of local communities; and it would bring in customers that they otherwise would not have.
- Time Dollar systems are always looking for additional ways of giving value to their credits, and the potential for such credits to be cashed in with local businesses is a definite plus.
- Most loyalty credits end up not being spent. Why not set up a local charity pot, where they are bundled up and used to back the value of the local Time Dollar systems? They could even be auctioned off against conventional currency to support the national currency requirements of the charities using the Time Dollar systems.

By the year 2000, more than 300 townships and social service programmes have started Time Dollar systems, most of them in Anglo-Saxon countries.

2 Ithaca HOURS

Ithaca is a small university town with a population of about 27,000 in upstate New York. It is not a rich town. It has, for example, the highest percentage of 'working poor' in the state of New York (people who are fully employed, but whose income is so low that they still remain eligible for food stamps).

Paul Glover, a local community activist, felt that the proximity of New York City kept diverting the community energy into the vastness of the big city. He decided to do something about this problem. In November of 1991, he launched a complementary currency designed to encourage people to spend their money and time in the community. Although it requires a little more infrastructure than Time Dollars, it still remains remarkably simple.

The core of the system is a bimonthly tabloid-style newspaper that advertises the products and services of people and businesses who accept Ithaca HOURS. One Ithaca HOUR is equivalent to $10, and represents roughly one hour's work at a generous minimum wage in the area. There are bills in denominations of two, one, one half and one quarter of an hour. Most Ithaca HOUR bills are issued initially via the advertisers in the tabloid newspaper. Each advertiser receives four HOURS' worth in bills when they place an advertisement in the newspaper. The community in which Ithaca HOURS can be spent is voluntarily limited to a geographical radius of 20 miles around the centre of town.

The bimonthly tabloid typically includes about 1,200 listings, including over 200 businesses. These include a local supermarket, all three cinemas, the farmer's market, medical care, lawyers, business consulting and the best restaurant in town. The local bank also accepts accounts in complementary currency, and has been able to attract a very loyal local customer base as a consequence.

One of the keys here is that the advertisers provide their quote in a combination of the two currencies. For example, a house painter advertises that he wants US$10 per hour, 60-40 (meaning 60% is payable in Ithaca HOURS, and 40% in regular US dollar currency for the paint, brushes, petrol, taxes, etc.). Another painter may advertise at $11 per hour, 90-10 (he is willing to accept up to 90% in Ithaca HOURS). So, if you happen to have more Ithaca HOURS available than dollars, you may prefer to go to the latter painter, even if his nominal rate is a bit higher.

Ithaca's cinemas, for example, accept up to 100% in Ithaca HOURS in the afternoon because the cost of projecting a movie is a fixed cost, independent of how many people are present (i.e., the marginal cost of one more viewer as long as seats are empty is, in fact, zero).

Over one thousand people use the complementary currency regularly, and many pay rent or other services with it.

Finally, 9.5% of all Ithaca HOURS issued are being given to local non-profit organizations who perform various tasks for the community at large. So far, 19 different non-profits have benefited from these donations.

Paul Glover summarizes the benefits. 'Thousands of purchases and many new friendships have been made with our own money, and hundreds of thousands of local trading has been added to what we call our Grass-roots National Product.' The big decisions concerning the system as a whole (printing, denominations, manner of issue, grants) are made during twice-monthly informal dinners, which acts as the 'Ithaca Reserve Board'.

The system has been featured on national TV, first in Japan, and more recently in the United States. The participants are happy with the results, and the businesses have seen more locals stay around to spend both their regular dollars and their Ithaca HOURS. Even the people who don't like Paul Glover's activist style or politics have come to like his system. This system has also started spreading around the country. Paul Glover sells a kit describing how to set up such a system for $25 or two and a half Ithaca HOURS. As of 1997, there were 39 HOURS systems operational in the world.

Bottom line: it is a successful model with very low start-up costs, and it works. However, it has one drawback common to all fiat currencies: Ithaca HOURS require someone to decide centrally how much currency to issue. While this is done in a democratic way by the 'Ithaca Reserve Board', all central bankers will confirm that managing a fiat currency supply remains a tricky decision. The biggest risk is that if more currency is issued than people want to use, there will be inflation and devaluation of the complementary currency. This will not happen as long as Ithaca HOUR managers follow Paul Glover's and his colleagues' lead in remaining wisely conservative in their money supply decisions. But this risk precludes me from recommending this approach for general use.

3   The PEN Exchange

Olaf Egeberg lives in Takoma Park, Maryland, on the borders of
Washington DC, where the US Treasury and the Federal Reserve
headquarters are located. After he retired, he wanted to give something back
to his community. 'In this day and age, we lose sight of the most valuable
resources: each other. We can have a walking-distance society right here,
where we already are. I think neighborhoods are the most important society
for us to build now,' was his reasoning.

In contrast with Ithaca, this is a decidedly middle-class community with a
very low unemployment level (about 1%). Olaf decided to define his neighbourhood as all families within five minutes' walking distance from the centre
of town, roughly 450 families in total. Hence the name 'Philadelphia-Eastern
Neighborhood' (PEN for short) for the streets at the limit of these blocks.

He sent out 50 letters, describing how the PEN Exchange would
contribute to 'building a more supportive society for us here. There's more
human contact, more communication, more getting to know each other
than before.' He did not have a single reply.

Puzzled by this lack of response, he decided to visit all the houses in person. The mystery was cleared up immediately: nobody thought they had
something to offer in the Exchange. They all thought that the activities
involved in the Exchange would be like normal commercial transactions. For
instance, an accountant who loves to hunt for mushrooms at weekends had
not thought that other people might be interested in learning about mushrooms. A retired person who had lived ten years in Europe never thought of
exchanging her knowledge of the area for something she might need.

There is quite a difference between the normal commercial yellow pages
and the PEN Directory. Lots of goods and services are offered for trade in
the PEN Directory for which people wouldn't be spending US dollars. Also,
many of these listings are for things that people like to do for the fun of it.
This is fun work, not boring jobs.

As a consequence, something else happens in Takoma Park. It turns out
that the complementary currency and the directory are just the oil to
lubricate the imagination, an excuse to make the first contacts. Most actual
exchanges use the complementary currency only for part of the transaction,
sometimes not at all, and involve exchanges that weren't even thought of as
items to be listed initially in the directory. Gradually, neighbours get into the
habit of just helping each other out as gifts, without any currency exchange.

Notice that, as Olaf's purpose was to reconnect people, such an evolution is a positive sign.

The *Washington Post*[239] covered the story. It quoted Mary Rodriguez, 89, who has lived in Takoma Park for over 40 years, and has never seen anything like it. 'There are so many neighborhoods where you never get to know the people next to you. Here the neighbors do things for one another. It gives a small-town feel.' After only three years, the community fabric is already strong and goes way beyond what an economic analysis might show about people exchanging goods or services in another way. Neighbours keep abreast of local issues by e-mail, and computer-literate residents offer free Internet lessons to any neighbour wishing to join. Nikolai Vishnesky, 40, who started the e-mail system last year says, 'Now folks can take technology that is usually used for global interaction and make it a local resource.'

Neighbours deter crime by patrolling the streets at night, publish a neighbourhood Newsletter, take turns looking after each other's children in play groups, help housebound seniors, grow food on a community farm in Upper Marlboro and greet new neighbours.

Martha Monroe, 38, believes, 'We are unique because in most Washington suburban neighborhoods, people get home from their job in the city, watch television and go to bed.'

4 Curitiba: the Brazilian city which left the Third World[240]

In 1971, Jaime Lerner became mayor of Curitiba, the capital of the southeastern state of Paraná, Brazil. He was an architect by profession. Quite typical of the region, the urban population had mushroomed from 120,000 people in 1942 to over a million when Jaime became mayor. By 1997, the population had reached 2.3 million. Again, quite typically, the majority of these people lived in *favelas*, shanty towns made out of cardboard and corrugated metal.

One of Jaime Lerner's first big headaches was rubbish. The town rubbish collection trucks could not even get into the *favelas* because there were no streets wide enough for them. As a consequence, the rubbish just piled up, rodents got into it, and all kinds of diseases broke out. A mountain-sized mess.

Because they didn't have the money to apply 'normal' solutions, such as bulldozing the area and building streets, Lerner's team invented another way. Large metallic bins were placed on the streets at the edge of the *favelas*.

The bins had big labels on them which said glass, paper, plastics, biodegradable material and so on. They were also colour coded for those who couldn't read. Anyone who brought down a bag full of presorted rubbish was given a bus token. A school-based rubbish collection programme also supplied the poorer students with notebooks. Soon the neighbourhoods were picked clean by tens of thousands of children, who learned quickly to distinguish even different types of plastic. The parents use the tokens to take the bus to the centre of town, where the jobs are.

What Jaime Lerner did, from my perspective, is invent Curitiba money. His bus tokens are a form of complementary currency. His programme, 'Garbage which is Not Garbage', could just as well have been baptized 'Garbage which is Your Money'.[241]

Today, 70% of all Curitiba households participate in this process. The 62 poorer neighbourhoods alone exchanged 11,000 tons of rubbish for nearly a million bus tokens and 1,200 tons of food. In the past three years, more than 100 schools have exchanged 200 tons of garbage for 1.9 million notebooks. The paper-recycling component alone saves the equivalent of 1,200 trees each *day*.

Let it be clear that Lerner's team did not start off with the idea of creating a complementary currency. What happened instead is that they used an integrated systems analysis for all the major issues in the area and spontaneously ended up creating a complementary currency to solve them.

Nor is the rubbish cycle the only form of local money in Curitiba which has resulted from this approach. For instance, another system has been designed specifically to finance the restoration of historical buildings, create green areas, and social housing in a way that would not financially burden the municipality. It is called *sol criado* (literally, 'created surface') and works as follows.

Like most cities, Curitiba has a detailed zoning plan which specifies the number of floors that can be built in each zone. In Curitiba, however, there are two standards: the normal allowable standard and the maximum level. For instance, a hotel with a ground plan of 10,000 square metres is being built in an area where the normal allowable level is ten floors and the maximum 15. If the hotel owner wants to build 15 floors he has to buy 50,000 square metres (5x 10,000 sq.m.) in the *sol criado* market. The city itself only plays the role of an intermediary matching demand with supply in that market.

But where is the supply for these *sol criado* surfaces generated?

One source is historical buildings. For instance the *Club Italiano* owns a beautiful historic building called the Garibaldi House. The property has a total ground surface of 25,000 square metres, but it needed a serious restoration job. The Club did not have the money to restore the building, but because it is located in an area where up to two floors could theoretically be built, it sold 50,000 square metres (2 floors x 25,000 sq. m.) to the highest bidder, for instance, the hotel owner mentioned above. The proceeds belong to the Club to administer, but have to be used to restore the property. Therefore, the hotel owner ends up paying for restoring of the historic edifice to obtain the right to build the extra floors of the hotel, without financial intervention from the city. Other sources of supply for such 'created surfaces' are green areas where trees are protected and the construction of social housing in other parts of the town.

Several of the more recent of the 16 extensive parks, open to the public, have been completely financed in this way. The owner of a large plot of land obtained the right to develop one side of the street on the condition that the other side becomes a public park. The new housing has an extra value because it is located at walking distance from the park, the people of Curitiba have another park for their weekend strolls, and the township does not have to go into debt or raise taxes to obtain all of that. Everybody wins.

What is most interesting from our perspective is that this market for 'created surfaces' is another type of specialized complementary currency, which enables Curitiba to obtain public goods for which other cities have to obtain traditional financing.

By now, this should sound familiar. Whenever a well-designed new currency system is implemented, something much bigger than the money and the economic activities it generates starts to happen. What began as a rubbish and public health problem has become a way to solve public transport and unemployment difficulties in a uniquely innovative way. By creating the *sol criado* market system, significant public advantages are obtained at no cost to the city itself. The secret is not that this city or population has something unique, but that an integrated systems approach has created complementary currencies to tackle the problems at hand. The net result is a city where many things run against conventional wisdom (see box).

Curitiba: another development strategy

- Public transport is encouraged over individual car usage. This is accomplished by making the public transport better and more convenient than the private variety. For example, it is speedier because of an original speed-loading process: the bus tokens enable the users to enter specially designed raised-tube bus stops; when the bus arrives, entire sections of both the bus and the unit open so that people can move in and out in large groups in a few seconds. No time is lost collecting money or tokens. Similarly, the special express lanes for public transport have made the bus the fastest and most convenient way to move around anywhere. A single fare of .65 R$ (about 50 US cents) enables someone to move over the entire system, regardless of distance covered. This includes any connections to feeder and inter-district public transport systems. The real proof is that this public transport system has become the preferred way. One out of four people using public transport own cars, but prefer not to use them to get around town. Because of the efficiency of the public transport system, it has been possible to create several town centre pedestrian streets, including the Main Boulevard. These pedestrian streets are now used for local music, popular theatre performances and children's art festivals. There are also arcades of shops and restaurants which stay open 24 hours per day and maintain the vitality of the downtown area, instead of the ghost towns that most city centres become.

- Conventional city planning claims that any city with more than one million inhabitants must have an underground railway system to prevent traffic congestion. Similarly, cities that generate more than 1,000 tons of solid waste per day need expensive mechanical rubbish-separation plants. Curitiba has neither. And the investment needed for their public transport system costs only 5% of an equivalent underground system. The savings have allowed Curitiba to keep its fleet of buses among the more up to date in the world.

- There is a Free University for the Environment offering practical short courses at no cost for homemakers, building superintendents, shopkeepers, and taxi-drivers. They are taught the environmental implications of their daily activities. The building is a breathtaking architectural landmark made mostly out of recycled telephone poles, in what is now an idyllic setting near a lake. The location used to be an abandoned industrial stone mine.

- Curitiba is the only town in Brazil that now has a significantly lower pollution level than in the 1950s; it also has a lower crime rate and a higher educational level than comparative Brazilian cities. It is the only city in Brazil that has actually turned down grants from the federal government, because they have solutions which involve less red tape.

- A botanical garden has been planted on what was once the inner city dump, which now serves as a recreation and research centre. In addition, there are currently 16 different nature parks around the city, based on different themes. As a consequence, Curitiba has 52 square metres of nature per inhabitant. The UN ideal standard is 48 square metres of green surface per city inhabitant, a level rarely, if ever, reached by cities in either the developed First or the Third World. Furthermore, all these parks are easily accessible from the transport network, so that the ordinary people can – and do – fully take advantage of them.

■ Curitiba was recognized in 1992 by the United Nations as the world's model ecological town. And Jaime Lerner has received international recognition for his initiatives. Some other cities have started to take notice. About 20 cities in Brazil have started to implement the integrated public transport system. Cape Town has copied several features of it. City planners from Buenos Aires, Santiago de Chile, Montreal, Paris, Prague, Mexico and Lagos have been impressed by what they saw.

Perhaps the clearest political signal that all this works is that every time Jaime Lerner presented himself for election, he was re-elected by a landslide. Today, he is Governor of the State of Paraná. A movement has started to draft him as next President of Brazil.

The Curitiba story demonstrates that there are political careers to be made in relation to complementary currency. Jaime Lerner's success cannot be attributed simply to personal charisma or ethnic background. The proof is that not one but at least three political careers have already been launched on the strength of these ideas. The two mayors who succeeded Lerner – Rafael Greca and Cassio Inaguchi, each with a quite different personality and ethnic background – started as staff members in Jaime Lerner's planning team. What is required for succeeding on this path is imagination and an ability to get things done.

Finally, the impact of the complementary systems is identifiable in economic terms. The average Curitibano makes about 3.3 times the country's minimum salary, but his real total income is at least 30% higher than that (i.e., about five times the minimum salary). This 30% difference is income directly derived in non-traditional monetary forms, such as the food for rubbish systems. Another indication is that Curitiba has by far the most developed social support system in Brazil, and one of its most vibrant cultural and educational programmes, and still doesn't have a higher tax rate than the rest of the country.

Even at the traditional macro-economic statistical level there are clear indications that something unusual is going on in Curitiba. Between 1980 and 1995, Curitiba's Domestic Product *per capita* grew 45% faster than those of the state of Paraná or Brazil as a whole.[243]

Curitiba is a practical case study where 25 years of experience show that a whole-system approach using both the traditional national currency and well-designed complementary currencies is beneficial to everybody, including people who are focused exclusively on the traditional economy denominated in national currencies. It enabled one Third World city to join First World living standards within one generation.

5 Japanese Healthcare Currency

The Japanese population is the second-fastest ageing one in the entire world. There are already 800,000 retired people needing periodic help and another million handicapped people, and the Japanese Ministry of Health forecasts a vast increase in these numbers in the foreseeable future. In order to face this rapidly rising problem, the Japanese have implemented a new type of Healthcare Currency.[244] In this system, the hours that a volunteer spends helping older or handicapped persons in their daily routines is credited to that volunteer's 'Time Account'. This Time Account is managed exactly like a savings account, except that the unit of account is hours of service instead of yen. The Time Account Credits are available to complement normal health insurance programmes.

Different values apply to different kinds of tasks. For instance, a meal served between 9 a.m. and 5 p.m. has a lower credit value than those served outside that time slot; household chores and shopping have a lower credit value than personal body care. This was the currency which was behind the vignette of 'Mr Yamada's Retirement Plan' in Chapter 1.

These Healthcare Credits are guaranteed to be available to the volunteers themselves, or to someone else of their choice, within or outside of the family, whenever they may need similar help. Some private services ensure that if someone can provide help in Tokyo, the time credits become available to his or her parents anywhere else in the country. Many people just volunteer the work and hope they will never need it. Others not only volunteer, but also give their time credits away to people who they think need them. To them, it amounts to doubling their time. It works like a matching grant: for every credit hour of service, the amount of care provided to society is two hours.

Most significantly, this type of service is also preferred by the elderly themselves, because the caring quality of the service turns out to be higher than those obtained from yen-paid social service workers. One of the names of this currency *Hureai Kippu* ('Caring Relationship Ticket') spells out the agenda. It also provides a more comfortable emotional space for the elderly, who might otherwise be embarrassed to ask for free services.

The Japanese also report a significant increase in volunteer help, even by people who do not bother to open their own Time Accounts. The reason may be that with this system, all volunteers feel more acknowledged. This precedent should put to rest concerns that paying volunteers with complementary currency might inhibit those not getting paid from volunteering.

As of end 1998 there are over 300 municipal level healthcare time credit systems in Japan, mostly run by private initiatives such as the Sawayaka Welfare Institute, or the 'Wac Ac' (Wonderful Ageing Club, Active Club) and the Japan Care System (a non-profit with some governmental funding).

In summary, the Japanese Healthcare Currency has proved both more cost effective and compassionate than the system which prevails in the West. As the US and Europe embark on an identical trend of an ageing population, why not learn from the Japanese experience?

6 Tlaloc

Tlaloc is the old Aztec rain god, important in the pre-Hispanic pantheon. It is also the name of a street in a populous neighbourhood of Colonia Tlaxpana in today's Mexican capital city. This street is the home of a cooperative development centre *Promoción del Desarollo Popular A.C.* which, in 1987 under the impulse of the Architect Luis Lopezllera started its own currency system to which the name Tlaloc was given. What is particularly interesting in the Tlaloc example is its mixing of high-tech and low-tech operation, given that it does not require access to a computer or even a telephone to operate effectively. But it has nevertheless its own website (www.laneta.apc.org), its own periodic publication (*La Otra Bolsa de Valores*), and even a whole range of other community services.

The Tlaloc is a mutual credit system where the currency is issued in the form of paper cheques. A number of trusted users have chequebooks and always issue the cheques in round amounts (e.g. 1, 2, 5, 10, 50). These cheques have a number of endorsement spaces on the back, so that the first recipient can endorse it for the next user, and so on. The cheques circulate as currency, and periodically someone can bring in the cheque to the centre when the last user is credited and the issuer is debited. In short, this system has the advantages of being both a mutual credit system and a paper currency. It requires only one personal computer in the system to keep the accounts. And it can circulate as paper currency without needing access even to a telephone to call in the transaction. Other communities have started to emulate this model. For instance, the *compromisos* cheques circulate in the neighbourhood of Toctiuco in Quito, Ecuador.

7 "Bia Kud Chum", Southeast Asia's First Community Currency System

Synthesis of a report by Powell & Menno Salverda (tccs@Ioxinfo.co.th) in cooperation with Stephen DeMeulenaere (stephenlets.net and web site http : //ccdev.lets.net/asia.html)

On March 29, 2000 villagers from Kud Chum district in Yasothon, about 10 hours bus trip from Bangkok in northeast Thailand, began trading in bia, an interest-free community currency.

At first glance, the small, rural market in the village of Santisuk looks just like any other Thai rural market. But when a customer asks: 'How much is the bottle of liquid soap made by a village homemakers' group?' The woman behind the table casts a broad grin, her teeth stained a betel-nut red, and replies: '30 baht and five bia'.

Bia is the name of a currency which is equal in value to, and used together with, the Thai baht. Bia notes are available in denominations of one, five, 10, 20 and 50 bia. The notes are made available to community members of the Bia Bank in Santisuk. Ms Buatong Boonsri, manager of the Bia Bank, explains community members can borrow up to a maximum of 500 bia. She said: 'They must pay back the amount of bia which they borrow' but the important difference is, there is no interest charged. Similarly, there is no interest earned for deposits made to the bank. 'Only community members who have registered at the Bia Bank have access to these services. Unregistered villagers may still use the bia if they wish to do so, simply by accepting it from other community members.'

Use of the bia as an exchange medium is restricted to six neighbouring villages. This being the case, one visitor asked: 'So what good is bia if I cannot pay for my bus ticket to Bangkok with it?' Pranomporn Tetthai, a member of the Bia Kud Chum working group from Kud Hin Village, said: 'That is exactly the point! We are trying to reduce the number of things villagers buy from outside the community and encourage the support of locally produced goods and services.' He adds: 'Our agricultural income (from the sale of jasmine rice) will still be in baht. Therefore, we will still have baht for necessary expenses such as hospital care. However, for local goods and services we can reduce our expenses by exchanging in bia.'

Earlier after an alms-giving ceremony, Pra Supajarawatr, abbot of Talad Temple, gave a sermon which touched on these same issues. 'Our ancestors were self-reliant,' he said. 'They exchanged with one another based on kindness and mutual respect. The natural environment was abundant and community relations were strong.' Pra Supajarawatr has been very active in community development in the region for three decades. His efforts have helped to conserve area forests, revive knowledge of traditional medicine, and preserve local culture. He said: 'Today we are increasingly dependent on others with whom we have no community bonds, only commercial relations. Even within the community we take advantage of one another rather than supporting one another. The environment gets worse. Community relations break down. I hope that the Bia Kud Chum can be a part of the process of reducing destructive dependence, and strengthening our community.'

During a break from the market, noted social activist and founder of the Spirit in Education Movement, Sulak Sivaraksa, stated: 'Wealth does not mean that one owns many cars. True wealth is community stability. Consumerism, which has trapped villagers in a never-ending debt cycle, is destroying this stability.' The answer, asserted Mr Sulak, lies in a return to greater self-reliance. He said: 'Self-reliance means a return to the precepts of Buddhism. This process must begin with the community. It cannot be implemented from above.'

By the end of the launch day, 112 households, out of some 600 households in the community, had registered as members of the Bia Kud Chum system. More than 8,000 bia had been taken out as interest-free loans.

Origins of Bia Kud Chum

The Thai Community Currency Systems project (TCCS) was started in 1997 as a collaboration of various Thai NGOs, including the Local Development Institute, Thai Volunteer Service, Focus on the Global South and the Spirit in Education Movement. Canadian and Dutch volunteers, acted as advisers–facilitating the exchange of information between Thai organisations and community currency groups worldwide. Funding came from the Japan Foundation Asia Centre.

In September 1998, a community currency workshop was held at the Northeastern Thai (NET) Foundation Training Centre in Surin. More than

50 representatives of peoples' organisations from across the northeastern region attended – including four villagers from Kud Chum. These representatives decided to invite the TCSS people to their area.

Initially, TCCS project staff spent several months in Kud Chum, learning about the community, its development activities, and the history of exchange in that area. Two interested individuals from each of six villages formed an organizing committee. Monthly meetings were held to discuss the how-to details of establishing a system. After a notes-based system was decided upon, a competition was held to create the pictures which would adorn the bia. The front of the note bears drawings of the various stages of rice planting and harvesting; on the back are traditional festivals. Also, on each note is a spirit poem, or kam kwan, written in the local dialect.

This emphasis on such local traits was partly a result of the urgings of Luis Lopezllera, one of the organisers of the Tlaloc community currency system in Mexico City. Mr. Lopezllera visited Kud Chum in April 1999 to begin a dialogue which would allow the two communities to learn from one another.

How the Bia Kud Chum Community Currency System Works

The community currency is issued as interest-free credit to account-holding units of the Bia Kud Chum Community Bank, managed by two female community members with a core group of about 10 individuals.

Each account is considered a Unit, and each Unit can have many members. Thus, one family can have one Unit with each family member as a sub-participant in the system. The Unit has an opening credit limit of 500 Bia, which must be repaid before more can be withdrawn. Each month, Unit account information is transferred to a system ledger for transparent accounting. The system ledger is always in balance, providing accurate and transparent information about the state of the system.

The Bia currency is intended to replace the Thai Baht for local purchases, increasing possibilities for import substitution and local production activities. For example, discussion with the villagers revealed that a significant amount of money was being spent on non-locally produced snack food, whereas more healthy snacks could be produced locally.

Through participatory and cooperative activities, a system has been designed that reflects community needs, desires and most certainly input. It uses a sound and simple accounting system that suits the community into which it was introduced. It has the support of important individuals in the community as well as broad community interest. Although future developments of the system are for the community itself to decide, the system even at this stage allows for a substantial development in import substitution, interest-free banking, micro-credits, and funding of health programs and education through the Bia Bank.

The Bia Kud Chum Community Currency System is the first system of its type in South East Asia. What is technically original here is the combination of a paper currency technology with a group system of mutual credits (each account Unit represents in fact a group of co-responsible individuals). What is also significant is that this Thai NGO project is a direct result of cooperation and cross-fertilization of Dutch, Canadian and Mexican complementary currency expertise, funded by a Japanese non-profit. It symbolizes thereby the rising sophistication and globalization of the complementary currency movement.

■ Complementary currencies in the Information Age

Payment systems for complementary currencies at this point tend to function in parallel with the existing national currency. Although many transactions involve simultaneous payment by both types of currency, their execution will typically require two different interventions. I think that the best route will be the convenience of simultaneous transactions in both types of currency using the same media. This would automatically provide the same level of security for both payments, and cost about the same as setting up automatic payments in a single currency.

An integrated currency design: Commonweal Inc. of Minneapolis

Joel Hodroff, founder of Commonweal Inc. in Minneapolis, Minnesota has created what I suspect is the first design formally integrating the national and the complementary currency systems.[245] He has also obtained impressive endorsements from the business community (including presidents of several banks and of the largest shopping mall in the country), city and labour union leaders, a county board of commissioners, community activists, technology experts and other opinion leaders.

The Commonweal Community Herocard system is consciously designed as a win-win proposition for all participants. Businesses gain new customers and improve their profitability. Non-profits attract more volunteers and stretch their dollars at little cost, and earn referral fees ('cause-related marketing') every time one of their members makes a purchase with Herocard (the initial system is a simple debit card, but the design is ideal for dual-currency smart cards whenever merchants are equipped with smart-card readers). And, perhaps most importantly, communities have a way to mobilize otherwise underutilized human and other resources to solve their local problems.

All the pieces of the puzzle, including the technologies, are currently available and have all been successfully market-tested separately. What is new is putting them all together in an integrated design. The secret is a dual-currency system, where the national currency and the complementary currency operate simultaneously.

This is how it works.

The concept

In the Minneapolis case, two currencies are utilized: the normal US$ and C$D. C$D is an acronym for Community Service Dollars. Its unit of account is 1 C$D = 1 US$, and one service hour is valued at 10 C$D.

The process of C$D creation starts in the business world. Practically all businesses have spare capacity in order to be able to deal with peak seasons or hours. This is lying idle most of the time: cinemas in matinées, even the most popular restaurants in the earlier hours, resort hotels during weekdays. Most manufacturing processes similarly lend themselves to making a few extra runs whose marginal costs are only a fraction of the normal costs. For example, furniture makers or clothing manufacturers can produce at a low marginal cost extra items of a series, and often do so. Today, in most cases this extra capacity just lies idle. The more entrepreneurial businesses try to make something extra from it by off-loading the surplus items in barter or discount deals. This is already a very common business practice in many types of businesses from hotel rooms to two-for-one dining in restaurants, from textiles to sporting goods.

In Minneapolis, businesses have an additional option: joining the Commonweal Community Herocard programme and accepting C$Ds. (For example, a restaurant could decide to accept C$D for up to 50% of the bill for any customer before 7 p.m. instead of the usual two-for-one early dining discount. Or a cinema could accept up to 90% in C$D during matinées because the marginal dollar cost once it projects a film is, in fact, zero for additional customers as long as seats are available.)

The C$Ds are issued to non-profit organizations who provide services to the community, and who pay their volunteers with them.

One important feature of the Minneapolis approach is that after a C$D has been redeemed in a business, it disappears (in this respect C$Ds are similar to frequent-flyer miles or discount coupons). New C$Ds are then issued to reward new community service. This limits the problems that can arise in decisions of quantities of money to be issued, given that they automatically self-destruct after each use.

Advantages of the dual-currency approach

This design enables people who have more time and less money to fully participate in the economy (as with TimeDollars). It is also very effective marketing, because it increases new customer traffic and loyalty without having to cannibalize their normal dollar-based clients.

It is really a win-win for the entire community, as shown for each type of stakeholder.

FOR PARTICIPATING BUSINESSES

From the participating businesses' viewpoint, there is one significant advantage even beyond those already mentioned: customer loyalty and the label of good 'community supporter'. Businesses gain clients they would not gain without this system, and they still make a dollar profit on each transaction (because the dollar component should always more than cover the marginal dollar costs, including taxes).

Finally, there is an improvement in the neighbourhoods where services are provided that otherwise would not occur, which is good for business overall.

FOR NON-PROFIT ORGANIZATIONS

They are also among the big winners in this new game. They can increase their volunteer activities. The community involvement in the selection and allocation of C$D also gives the more active non-profits wider recognition.

FOR MEMBER PARTICIPANTS

Members who participate have an easier way to blend their two lifestyles together. Those who choose to do so can have their jobs *and* their work. Their work contributions are more acknowledged than before, and the general improvements in the quality of their community also benefit them.

FOR THE UNEMPLOYED AND ECONOMICALLY DISADVANTAGED

This system enables people to turn time into money. Economically disadvantaged people can therefore more fully participate in the economic system, as they are typically those who have more time than money to spend. It also provides them with a second career chance in the non-profit world which would otherwise not exist. The discreet nature of the payment system (nobody but themselves has to know whether they are paying in dollars or C$D) also ensures more dignity than food stamps or social security cheques. It is also free of the hassles of these bureaucratic programmes.

FOR THE REST OF THE COMMUNITY

Even the people who do not participate at all in any part of the system derive a significant benefit from this approach. If the Commonweal programme did not exist, a number of functions in their community would either not happen at all or would have to be subsidized by their taxes.

What the Commonweal system offers is to mobilize otherwise unused resources in the community to solve problems that need solving. It does this using the market system every step of the way without taxes.

As of 1998, the Commonweal system is in its pilot phase in the Lyndale neighbourhood of Minneapolis. Besides the non-profit sector, the Mall of the Americas and other mainstream businesses are involved, including National City Bank which provides the accounting system and statements in C$Ds.

Internet Money for Virtual Communities

One of the most intriguing and encouraging aspects of Internet developments has been the mushrooming of 'virtual communities' compellingly documented in Howard Rheingold's *Virtual Communities: Homesteading on the Electronic Frontier*.[246]

Community has become such a scarce resource in our societies that the appearance of a new way to create it is indeed remarkable.

Virtual communities versus a monopoly of national currencies on the Net

The process by which this miracle has occurred is often not fully understood. Even some of the people who created virtual communities have not always been aware that the secret of their success relates to the fact that they had created a gift economy on the Net. 'I'll help you today, and someone else will help me if needed some other day' has been the common pattern wherever successful virtual communities have sprung up. In short, it is one more application of the principles underlying communities as described at the beginning of this chapter. Virtual communities today are 'communities' only because social bonds have sprouted up around a 'gift economy' of an open information exchange. Recently the business world has also discovered the importance of this phenomenon.[247]

However, there seems to be little awareness either in business or on the Net that unless some precautions are taken in the way this is done, it may kill the proverbial goose that lays the golden eggs, and virtual communities will simply disappear as have most traditional 'primitive' communities operating on the basis of 'gift economies'. Just as traditional communities have unwittingly suffered from the competition-inducing process built in to our 'normal' national currencies, communities on the Net similarly may be torn apart if the new payment systems developed for the Internet rely exclusively on these types of currencies.

As the Net becomes home to the growing number of commercial enterprises, those who value the Net as community space may want to take some precautions lest virtual communities meet the same fate as almost all the gift economies that preceded them.

The Net: an ideal yin space for economic symbiosis

It so happens that some characteristics of the Net may make it an ideal space where the community-supporting currencies could happily thrive next to the traditional national currencies, enabling a new symbiosis between the two approaches.

Because Internet offers unlimited 'space' and transcends natural and cultural boundaries, the electronic marketplace need not be limited to one exclusive currency system. New synergies between virtual communities and local communities would become possible, improving the quality of life of the participating Netizens.

Desirable characteristics of Internet currencies

I propose that the following five characteristics would be desirable for Internet currencies for use by virtual communities:

- efficient and secure in an electronic payment system
- convertible into local expenses (i.e. answering the key question: how can I use credits earned on the Net to pay for my food and daily needs?)
- non-national (one key characteristic of the Net is its lack of national boundaries while national currencies are specifically designed to foster national consciousness. Why should a German buying a product offered by an Indian company on the Net have to pay in Deutschmarks, dollars or rupees?)
- self-regulating on the Net itself
- supporting the creation of community.

None of the currencies and payment systems currently offered on the Net meets all these requirements. Specifically, payment systems using the existing national currencies clearly meet the first two characteristics but none of the others.

A solution: A Complementary Currency Clearing House on the Net?

Of course, all these characteristics are met by complementary currencies (particularly the Mutual Credit Currencies), except that they are currently not available for trading on the Net. The only additional step needed to create the Internet currency meeting our specifications is to have an automatic electronic clearing house for such complementary currency systems, a clearing house which could operate on the Net itself. Such a Complementary Currency Clearing House would allow someone in Manchester, UK, for instance, to 'earn' credits by providing a service on the Internet, and exchange them for use in his or her local LETS system. Conversely, the credits earned in Manchester's local economy would be more valuable by becoming exchangeable for goods and services on the Internet. 'Think globally, act locally' would gain some added pragmatic reality in this approach.

Note that I do *not* claim that no national currencies should be used on the Net, or that community currencies of the type described above could or should replace the national currencies. But I do claim that the time is ripe to ensure that community is not squashed by ignorance of the power of currency to shape our relationships.

■ Conclusions

*'A true community is inclusive, and its greatest enemy is exclusivity.
Groups who exclude others because of religious, ethnic or more subtle differences are
not communities.'*

FOUNDATION FOR COMMUNITY ENCOURAGEMENT

One wish that a vast majority of people can agree upon is to rebuild community. All the above examples confirm that implementing complementary currencies can significantly help in reaching that goal. I do not claim them to be a panacea, but they have definitely proved once again that they enrich our social toolkit to face issues raised by our Time-Compacting Machine.

CHAPTER 7

Some Practical Issues

■ *'When a great innovation appears, it will almost certainly be in a muddled, incomplete, and confusing form . . .*
For any speculation which does not at first glance look crazy, there is no hope.'

FREEMAN DYSON

■ *'Chaos is creativity in search of form.'*

JOHN WELWOOD

■ *'The future is like everything else,*
It isn't what it used to be.'

CHARLES KETTERING

It is not sufficient to invent or even implement a new currency. Because of money's central role in our societies, a lot of different and powerful organizations and people have their say in this domain. As long as the complementary currency movement has remained marginal, it has been largely ignored by the powers that be, such as tax authorities or central banks. However, if this process goes mainstream as recommended here, if we want to use complementary currencies as a systematic tool to address the issues raised by the Time-Compacting Machine, it would be unwise just to ignore the concerns and objections that these organizations may want to express. This chapter will address these issues. It will also identify some elements for a European social policy using complementary currencies, and provide some pragmatic advice for people who may be interested in implementing their own complementary currency project.

Why not a Radical Money Reform?

Given the problems of the conventional currency system, why not simply replace it? Why propose only 'complementary currencies' which are designed to function in parallel with conventional money, leaving intact the prevailing bank-debt system?

The short answer is that in every generation of economists, there have been unsuccessful proposals for replacing the official money system with 'better' ones. The lock-in between the political, legal, banking and institutionalized monetary system has proven invariably too tight to break, even when the proposals came from the most influential economist of his time (such as Keynes' proposal for his *bancor*) or when they were supported by substantial popular movements (such as Gesells' *Freiwirtschaft* ('Free Economy') movement between the two wars).

Just a reminder: the objective here is not to design a therotically perfect system, but more modestly to identify potentially useful monetary tools that have a fighting chance to be implemented.

■ Complementary currencies, legal and tax authorities

The short answer to the relationship between complementary currencies and both the legal and taxation systems is that there are no insurmountable obstacles. However, a few more words are warranted to support such a blanket claim.

Are complementary currencies legal?

Most countries in the world have no legislation making it illegal for anybody to 'agree within a community to use something as a medium of exchange'. On the other hand, most countries have also assigned the monopoly of 'legal tender' to their banking sector under supervision of the central bank. All this means from a pragmatic standpoint is that you cannot force anybody to accept complementary currency to repay lawful debts, and that you should pay your taxes in the national currency.

What about taxes?

A general taxation rule is that it is not the currency used which determines whether a transaction is taxable, but the nature of the transaction itself.

Whenever an activity is performed on a professional basis (a plumber doing plumbing), most countries will consider it as taxable, independently of the kind of currency used. And the currency in which taxes need to be paid is the 'legal tender', i.e. national currency. In contrast, if a transaction is simply people helping other people, most countries consider it as non-taxable. An important precedent has been set in the US, widely regarded as the toughest tax country in the world. Because of this predominantly social purpose, all transactions in Time Dollars are now officially tax-exempt.

Complementary currencies, central banks and inflationary pressures

Central banks as well as most people currently involved in the complementary currency movement have tended to ignore each other. The former have tended to disregard local currencies as 'beneath contempt' because of their marginal status and scale. As for the latter, few community activists seem fully aware of the exact role and powers of central banks.

Some of the brightest and most public-service-minded professionals I have ever met were in central banks. However, they have both the power and history to snuff out anything as unorthodox as complementary currencies, as soon as too many people catch on to the idea. But this time there is a strong argument for them not to succumb to this reaction. There are now arguments proving that central banks have in fact an interest in tolerating – and in some circumstances even supporting – well-designed complementary currencies.

Central bank reactions to complementary currencies

Historically, central bankers have reacted to local currencies in three different ways:

1 Most of the time – as long as they remain marginal, including now – they have simply ignored them.
2 Whenever they have become 'too successful' for whatever reason, they have suppressed them by legal recourse if needed (this is what occurred in the 1930s in Austria, Germany and the US, as described in Chapter 5).
3 For the first time, one central bank – the one in New Zealand – has gone exactly the other way by not only tolerating them, but seeing them as a device to reduce unemployment while keeping a tight rein on inflation in the national currency. The reasons for this important exception will explain my claim that central banks actually now have an interest in accepting well-designed complementary currencies, even from their own perspective.

At this point, the vast majority of central banks may not even have noticed the phenomenon – the current developments are still below the radar beam of the official system. But that is just a matter of time. If the Information Age creates more structural unemployment and, therefore, more demand for complementary currencies, and as new technologies will soon increase the means to implement them, an explosion of complementary currencies could be expected (see sidebar).

The European Central Bank and 'electronic money'

A critical battle is being played out between the priorities of the banking sector and those of the rest of society around the deceptively 'technical' issue of the European Parliament Directive on e-money, planned to be operational as early as 2001. Understandably the banking sector is trying to protect at all costs its traditional monopoly of issuance of currency, a monopoly which is threatened by new e-money technologies. The new European Central Bank (ECB) has therefore been lobbying particularly powerfully in this domain.

The position of the ECB has been made most succinctly clear by Prof. Issing, Member of the Executive Board of the ECB:

'The ECB considers it essential that the following minimum requirements [on e-money issuance] be fulfilled:

- issuers of electronic money must be subject to prudential supervision;
- the possibility must exist for central banks to impose reserve requirements on all issuers of electronic money;
- issuers of electronic money must be legally obliged, at the request of the holders, to redeem electronic money against central bank money, at par.'[248]

This last feature – sounding almost innocuous – is technically justified in the ECB's annual report as follows: 'The redeemability requirement is, inter alia, necessary . . . to maintain price stability by avoiding any unconstrained issuance of electronic money, and to safeguard the controllability of the liquidity conditions and short term interest rates set by the ECB.' [249] However, this feature was also the most effective device used by Hjalmar Schacht's German central bank in the 1930s to eliminate any form of 'emergency money', whether these had potential inflationary implications or not (see Chapter 5). Indeed, as it requires any currency issuer to have available 100% bank-debt money to back its issuance, it *de facto* hinders anybody else than banks from being in this business.

If the banking lobby obtains European legislation including this feature, it would lock in its monopoly advantage in whatever type of e-money is included in its definition. This could potentially seriously handicap European business's competitiveness in the cyber economy; and – as in the 1930s – kill any attempt at solving Europe's problems with complementary currency strategies.

I fully respect the need for the ECB to be able to control inflation in the euro, which is why in any European legislation on e-money a critical distinction should be made between electronic currencies which contribute directly to inflationary pressures on the euro (or the pound sterling for the UK) and those that would not, such as mutual credit systems – as explained in the main text.

From a central bank viewpoint, the critical concern is the relationship between complementary currencies and inflation. If large-scale use of complementary currency fuels inflation, legitimately they should block such development. However, if complementary currencies are not creating inflation, they should not. My thesis here is that well-designed complementary currencies do not contribute to inflation, and can even be used to reduce inflationary pressures on the national currency.

A good starting point for the relationship between money issuance and inflation is Robert Lucas's synthesis in his recent Nobel Lecture: 'The prediction that prices respond proportionally to changes in money in the long run, deduced by Hume in 1752 (and by many other theorists, by many different routes, since) has received ample – I would say decisive confirmation, in data from many times and places.'[250]

However, all this excellent work has invariably been based on the implicit assumption that there is only a single currency system in a country. For example, within that frame of mind, the appearance of a second complementary currency may be interpreted as a simple local increase in money supply. All economists would immediately understand why such a process would create employment, but also (erroneously) conclude that complementary currencies would automatically add to inflationary pressures on the economy as a whole.

This reasoning would be valid if and only if the complementary currencies were all fiat currencies as are the dollar, the euro or any other national currencies of today. There is indeed one type of complementary currency (the Ithaca HOUR described in Chapter 6) which is such a fiat currency, and which could pose such a risk if its use became widespread. However, it will be shown that other designs, including all mutual credit systems (e.g. LETS, Time Dollars) do not contribute to inflationary pressures.

Rather than argue from theory to prove this point, let us take three practical examples of increasing complexity.

In the case of simple barter exchanges, where no currency is involved at all, the only effect of such an exchange is who owns what. No inflationary pressures arise from barter exchanges given that the overall quantity of goods and currency in circulation remain unchanged.

In the case of mutual credit systems (e.g. LETS or Time Dollars) the situation is in some respects similar to barter, because for every credit generated there is a simultaneous creation of a debit within the same community of consumers. The net amount of currency in circulation is therefore still the same, exactly as in the case of straightforward barter. In fact, from a monetary perspective, mutual credit systems simply facilitate multilateral barter, and have the same overall effect as a group engaging in triangular or multilateral barter.

In the case of well-designed integrated payment systems – such as the Minneapolis Community Exchange Network system which was described in the previous chapter – the argument is a bit more complex. In that case the currency is issued in proportion to the spare capacity of the businesses participating in the system. The existing precedent is the well-known corporate scrip issued by airlines, the so-called frequent-flyer miles.

Does issuing frequent-flyer miles increase the number of times a passenger will fly? The answer is, of course, yes. Does it create inflationary pressure on the airline air fares? The surprising answer is no. Not because the marginal cost for an additional passenger is virtually nil (which is why they give these free tickets in the first place), but because any airline manager worth his or her salt will ensure that anybody using the free frequent-flyer ticket is sitting in a seat that would otherwise be empty. That is why there are restrictions such as 'no frequent flyers at Christmas or holiday seasons, or on this route at weekends', etc.

This is exactly what happens with the Minneapolis C$D issued. For instance, a restaurant might accept 50-50 national currency-comple-mentary currency before 7 p.m. So there is no inflationary pressure on the restaurant's prices, because it just uses space that would otherwise remain idle. In a competitive market, a restaurant would theoretically be able to afford to increase prices only when operating above capacity. This feature of enabling the businesses themselves to better manage the problem of their excess capacity – from a theoretical inflation control viewpoint – is one of the intriguing aspects of the complementary currency approach. Within a single-currency environment there is no easy way for businesses to differentiate among customers to improve the use of their spare capacity in order to increase their productivity. For instance, what tends to happen with discount offers is that they end up cannibalizing the income from normal national currency customers.

This is not to say that the problem of inflation has been solved with this process. But we have shown at the very least that the normal monetary equations mislead us whenever complementary currencies instead of a single national currency are involved. It is clearly another game.

One could even argue that it will be possible to reduce inflation risks if well-designed community currencies are encouraged in an economy. That this is not just theory is demonstrated by the case of New Zealand. One would expect central bankers to react with suspicion when complementary currencies are appearing. The Governor of the central bank of New Zealand has an unusual contract with government. It stipulates that the Governor will automatically lose his job if the inflation rate on the national currency exceeds 2.5% per annum. This stipulation is one of the many original initiatives created when New Zealand decided to modernize its social and institutional systems a decade ago.

This contract has the advantage of concentrating the mind of the Governor on the main objective of his job: keeping inflation in control. The New Zealand central bank suddenly discovered that complementary currencies are useful in attaining its inflation control objective. If in the pockets of highest unemployment people create a complementary currency to alleviate their own problems, then the political pressure to lower interest rates and potentially fuel inflation would also be reduced. Suddenly, the first central banker in favour of complementary currencies was born ... In central banks whose main objective is to keep inflation in check, rather than to protect by principle or monetary dogma a monopoly of currency issuance, then a conclusion similar to the one in New Zealand should prevail.

Why New Zealand is right

There are several significant reasons to claim that the New Zealanders are on the right track. Several of these reasons are new: they reflect a changed political and technological environment.

THE ISSUE OF GEOGRAPHIC SCALE FOR MONETARY POLICY

Let us assume for a moment that Governor Greenspan of the Federal Reserve becomes responsible for the economic well-being of the poorest depressed area in Washington DC, instead of the country as a whole. Would he follow a different monetary policy from the one he does today?

He certainly would, and justifiably so.

One of the main problems when a central bank has to make decisions about the money supply is that it needs to look at the economic situation over the entire country. From this perspective, complementary currencies make it possible to fine-tune the medium of exchange to the local needs. This is why the New Zealand and Australian governments are involved in creating complementary currencies in the worst unemployment areas of the country. This is also why the introduction of the euro provides an additional incentive to promote local currencies.

Information Age unemployment

Monetary policy has been one of the main tools used to counteract the effects of the well-known short-term business cycle over the past half-century.

But if today's unemployment issues are the result of a structural adjustment to the new production technologies of the Information Age, this puts us in a very different ball game. Central banks have an interest in experimenting with new ways to solve this problem. It is clearly what New Zealand has decided to do, and it chose the right tool to do it. Historically, complementary currencies are the only tool that has proved to have worked when the situation was at its worst, like it was in the 1930s. Today, with the new information technologies and what we already know about the way complementary currencies operate, we can make such experimentation safer than ever before.

Back to the future of private money?

History shows that it is easy for central banks to stamp out local community currencies. However, trying to protect the money monopoly in this way may resemble killing one small fox to protect the chickens, while leaving a hungry pride of lions roaming around.

Consider the following observations by the *Washington Post:*

In fact, one of the most intriguing financial phenomena of this decade will be the inexorable rise in the importance of 'private money' issued by companies to lock their customers into their 'economic systems'. Once upon a time, this kind of private money – or scrip – was associated with railroad towns, the armed forces and the Great Depression. Today, think of these shadow currencies as the 'scrip of the elite' . . .

The issue is no longer individual or frequent-purchaser programs to buy brand loyalty – it's the gradual fusion of these plans to create a new kind of consumer-credit economy. It's only a matter of time before a new generation of 'central bankers' emerges to coordinate the exchange-rate issues. Citicorp credit card holders can 'buy' frequent-flier miles on American Airlines as well as hotel and rental car discounts. Selected

American Express card holders can buy 'membership miles' on other frequent-flier programs or purchase phone time on MCI or Sprint via the Connect-Plus programs. Corporate Scrips – frequent-flier points and frequent-traveler credits – are becoming ever more convertible to one another. This is an economy that is now worth billions – and growing. 'In the customer's mind, it may well be currency,' said Alfred J. Kelly Jr., vice-president of frequent-traveler marketing at American Express Travel Related Services. 'There is no question that you'll see more partnerships between organizations as they try to provide additional value to customers. We're trying to create segment-specific programs that not only provide value to our customers but also instill loyalty to us and our partners.'

For example, Kelly noted, if American Express customers want to have 'convertibility' between Membership Miles credits and Connect-Plus, that's something Amex's 'central bank' might be prepared to arrange. All of a sudden, Amex credits begin to rival dollars as a means of payment to purchase both travel and communication. Private currencies are on the rise not just because companies are pushing them, but because they are what the customers want. If the ruble can be convertible, why not the American Airlines frequent-miles program?

Indeed, as sophisticated information technology continues to seep through the economy, the ability to grow and manage private currencies increases. It becomes both cheap and easy to track individual purchases and credits. 'Just as people try to manage their credit cards, they will soon be managing their 'credits' to handle a variety of shadow currencies.'[251]

What will a central bank do about such private corporate scrip, or those that will appear on the Net – such as the already available NetMarket currency of Cendant?

Should we not recognize that the Information Age has already created a much more fundamental question about the way national currencies will play their role in the future? The danger is that central banks may be tempted to clam down on what they can reach (i.e. the small-scale, politically unprotected complementary currencies) rather than tackle the big changes which are politically better protected (i.e. corporate currencies).

An appeal

The biggest threat to the experimentation and successful resolution of the issues revealed by the Time-Compacting Machine through the creative use of work-enabling and/or community currencies is that their continual growth will be interpreted as a dangerous and contagious phenomenon by central banks.

The central banks have the power to crush these complementary currencies, and/or could muster the legal backing to enforce this power. One of my reasons for writing this book was to make the case for central banks not to follow their first technical instincts in this particular case. There is more at stake here than meets the technical eye. This is a time where public service may require us to rethink business as usual. Another reason is to request the academic community to start evaluating the implications of multiple and, particularly, complementary currency systems. This is somewhat virgin territory, and we need a lot more knowledge about how dual-currency systems (whether they are local or corporate scrip) will affect our economic processes. Part of the complexity is that each currency creates a market allocation system in its own sphere of activity, but in addition, they all interact in the same marketplace.

In contrast, multiple national currencies did not do that. Each country had its own privileged market area where its national currency reigned alone. The classical theories of multiple currencies within the same country, such as Gresham's laws, suppose that one of the currencies is 'good' and the other 'bad', but what happens when both are 'good' within overlapping market segments? This is one of the many fields today where 'there has been an alarming increase in things we know nothing about'.

What is at stake is quite substantial. If the cooperative economy is squashed – as it has been repeatedly in the past – we will be condemned to choose between two comparatively unpleasant possible futures: Hell on Earth or the Corporate Millennium. If on the other hand social experimentation with complementary currencies is allowed to happen, I believe we are halfway to Sustainable Abundance.

■ Elements of a European Social Policy for the Information Age

Of all the areas in the developed world, Europe is the one that has the strongest incentive to innovate on a large scale in the social domain. The industrial age social safety net which Europe pioneered in the past, is now going to come under unprecedented pressure.

Three powerful forces converge to make unemployment one of the key issues that Europe will have to face for the next decades:

– A long-term trend, already observable over at least the past two decades, points to fewer and fewer manpower needs to meet the production requirements on a global level.

– The advent of the cyber economy will further extend this same process to the distribution, retail and part of the services industries.

– Finally, the introduction of the euro will reduce the traditional options available to mitigate unemployment.

Whatever can be salvaged from the previous safety net, it is important to understand that new thinking will be required whether Europe embraces the cyber economy or not. The European unemployment issue existed before the Internet became a factor. The advent of the cyber economy just makes addressing the issue more starkly urgent.

The development of a European Social Policy for the Information Age falls beyond the scope of this book. However, one important component of it – the creative use of complementary currency systems – is relevant here. In fact, such systems have already emerged spontaneously at the grass-roots levels in every European country. The introduction of the euro provides an additional strong incentive to move in that direction now.

The introduction of the euro

The Treaty on European Union, signed in Maastricht on February 7, 1992 (the 'Maastricht Treaty'), called upon the member states of the European Union to form an economic and monetary union (EMU) in three stages by the turn of the century. The new single currency – the euro – is managed by a single monetary policy defined by the European Central Bank (ECB). An important step in this process was reached on January 1, 1999, when 11 countries officially began to use the euro as their own currency.

The EMU project is both ambitious and far-reaching. Nothing has been tried on this scale in monetary history.

The euro quandary

While important positive reasons existed to introduce the euro now, there is one significant negative in doing it at this time: it coincides with a high level of unemployment as described in Chapter 5. Such levels of unemployment are unprecedented since the Treaty of Rome created the European Common Market in 1958. For several countries including Germany the current level is even the highest since the Depression of the 1930s.

Furthermore, there is a growing consensus that this unemployment situation will not be solved through economic growth. 'Full employment can no longer be taken for granted as the automatic outcome of growth-creating economic policies' concludes a European green paper.[252] A French study showed that even the high postwar rates of growth of 5% resulted in an annual employment increase of just 0.2%, and that this trend for jobless growth is getting stronger over time.[253] The introduction of the euro will further reduce the room of manoeuvre for participating countries to decrease their unemployment levels in three converging ways.

1 Each government participating in the EMU is giving the levers of control over the euro money supply to the European Central Bank. The ECB will by definition be less responsive to the requirements of any one country's unemployment situation.
2 The Maastricht Treaty gives the ECB a single objective: to ensure price stability. Full employment is specifically not one of its official priorities.
3 Finally, the only other traditional tool available – the fiscal one – has similarly been put under severe constraints. The maximum limit of 3% of government deficit financing is supposed to be a permanent one, and most governments are adopting the euro with their spending at or close to this straitjacket target limit. In practice this means again that little room for manoeuvre exists to reduce unemployment via the fiscal tools.

To summarize, an unprecedented set of circumstances will converge over the next decade. The shift towards an Information Age and the budgetary constraints imposed by the Maastricht Treaty are at this point inevitable, and have powerful and valid arguments in their favour.

Bottom line: all signs are that the introduction of the euro in such circumstances amounts to European governments painting themselves into a corner of untenably high unemployment levels without any of the traditional tools to do something about it.

Social and political consequences

Even before the introduction of the euro the socio-political temperature in many European countries was uncomfortably high. If the job situation does not miraculously improve, one should expect the tensions to rise further, to the benefit of only the more extremist and nationalist political parties.

It is also to be expected that the European Union will be blamed for the growing unemployment situation – and if the European Central Bank feels obliged to follow the policies described above, the blame will at least partially be valid.

What is at stake ranges from an escalation of social unrest and political extremism to a loss of legitimacy of the European project.

■ The need for a permanent solution for regional differences

Some people have argued on a theoretical basis that with the introduction of the single European currency business conditions – and specifically the business cycle – will slowly become uniform across Europe. Therefore, it is argued, the negative employment effect of the introduction of the euro would be only temporary.

However, studies by the US Federal Reserve based on actual data show the opposite to be true. They found that sub-national economies in the USA still behave at different speeds in reaction to similar impetus, after centuries of having a single currency. They also show why different European regions will continue for ever to have different reactions to the same common monetary policies.[254] This means in practice that there is a currently generally unperceived need to find a structural, permanent strategy for the problems which will result from regional differentials in unemployment, and from permanent differences in business cycles in different European regions. The longer we will remain in denial of such need, the stronger the political backlash is likely to become.

A proposal

In parallel with the introduction of the euro, it would be very beneficial to include a formal role for complementary currencies in a new European Social Policy for the Information Age. Such an approach could be achieved at practically no cost to European governments simply by removing administrative barriers from the creation and use of such currencies.

There are three different levels by which such a policy could be implemented.

Passive tolerance

A policy of passive tolerance towards complementary currencies is basically what has been apparent so far in most European countries. Continuing such a policy simply means avoiding introducing new or additional administrative hurdles. A group of people agreeing to use something else than national currency as a medium of exchange among themselves does not break any laws anywhere. From a tax viewpoint any income obtained in complementary currencies is treated as if it were income in national currency, and the taxes are due in 'legal tender', i.e. the national currency. And from an unemployment benefit perspective, an unemployed person who starts making money in complementary currency could lose his unemployment benefits as if such income was in national currency.

Mildly supportive

This is the level of support that the New Zealand government and more than 30 states in the US have been providing to complementary currencies (in the New Zealand case to LETS type 'green dollar' systems, in the US to Time Dollar systems). In the UK, the government of Tony Blair seems to be moving towards this direction as well.

In both the US and New Zealand the local governments have been directly instrumental in funding a number of start-up projects in complementary currency systems. The main justification for doing this is that for a given amount of social support provided to the end-user, setting up a complementary currency system costs only a fraction of the more traditional support to unemployed people. Complementary currency systems provide a mechanism for people to help themselves on a permanent basis, at no permanent cost to the taxpayers.

In New Zealand, Australia and several states in America, governmental entities pay full-time administrators and promoters of Time Dollar systems. In Britain, some local governments have been doing the same thing. Their salaries have been justified because complementary currencies – respectively 'green dollars' and Time Dollars – have proved to be an effective complement to social programmes which were failing without them. It has been proved time and again, for instance, that crime cannot be reduced just by adding more police, or that failing education cannot be remedied by throwing money at the problem. Nothing can replace a community where people watch out for each other, or where older children mentor younger ones. And complementary currencies have been able to build community and other social capital in a way that national currency simply fails to do.

The US went one step further by having the IRS rule that any income in Time Dollars is automatically tax-exempt.

Strongly supportive

What this would involve is to provide systematic funding for complementary currency initiatives that provide better social results at a lower governmental cost. This would include funding the start-up of complementary currency systems and all the other features described in the 'mildly supportive' policy.

The Japanese go beyond that with their healthcare system, and in regional development based on 'eco-money' projects. The Japanese government is completely funding eco-money activities and is considering paying for the accounting and clearing systems for Healthcare Time Accounts. They justify it because it reduces the need for other yen-based expenses, and provides a better service as well.

Besides automatic tax-exemption for income in complementary currency as is the case for Time Dollars in the US, the most productive tax incentive would be one that gives an incentive for professionals and businesses to accept complementary currencies. Such an incentive would increase the quality and diversity of services and goods becoming available in complementary currencies. As most complementary currency systems are already set up as non-profit membership organizations, one could simply allow businesses to treat complementary currency income as a contribution to a non-profit organization. Community Way, a multimillion dollar project in Vancouver, Canada, is currently experimenting with this approach, using smart cards to deal with the complementary currency component.

Another important incentive which would not burden government budgets would be the acceptance of complementary currency in payment for local taxes. The main purpose of such local taxes is to provide local services, and there is no reason why the local authorities should not be able to use complementary currencies in partial payment of such local services.

For instance, in Manchester, England, local authorities have paid for the start-up costs of a LETS system through a loan in pounds sterling, but accept repayments in 'bobins', the local currency itself. There may also be other reasons, such as promoting local sustainability, which would justify such a policy (see sidebar).

Sustainability and the choice of the tax currency

Local governments who are in favour of promoting local sustainability at their own scale often forget that the most effective tool used to destroy local sustainability has been the introduction of a national currency.

There was a time when this was done on purpose. For instance, during the 19th century in Africa, when Britain wanted to 'open up' the colonial economies to British imports, it introduced a 'hut tax' in the national currency. The simple fact that each family unit was obliged to pay annually a tax denominated in 'national currency' also meant that each family had to start earning an income in that currency, and therefore trade outside its traditional local circles. The 'hut tax' by itself was enough to attain in a few years' time the objective of breaking up local trading patterns which had kept the local economies self-sufficient for many centuries.

A city or region which desires to improve its local sustainability, but keeps raising its local taxes exclusively in national currency, is like a doctor who claims to cure an alcoholic by prescribing more alcohol.

Which policy?

The choice among the different policies above – tolerance, mildly or strongly supportive – would best be decided on the basis of the level of unemployment of the region involved. If unemployment levels remain at the current uncomfortably high level a strongly supportive policy would be justified in the most affected regions. If a significant recovery occurs, a mildly supportive or even a continuation of a passive tolerance policy could be warranted.

Projects such as the funding of the 'Barataria' projects in four different member countries by the European Union (Chapter 6) should be encouraged. By fostering the emergence of well-designed complementary currencies in Europe in parallel with the introduction of the euro the following advantages could be gained:

1 It has already been pragmatically demonstrated that issues of unemployment, healthcare and other social problems have been effectively mitigated by using complementary currencies;
2 Such improvements do not require additional governmental budgets or bureaucracies, on the contrary they have proved most effective when self-organizing at the grass-roots level.

■ Some objections to a multiple currency strategy

One might expect that different types of objections could be levied against the strategy proposed above. Among the more predictable ones one could mention:

1 From the traditional left: this proposal may be criticized because it would reduce the pressure on the governments to maintain the 'acquired benefits' and 'social safety nets'.

2 From the central banks and the banking sector: that this will reduce the power of the monopoly of conventional money.

3 From economists: that a multiple currency approach could reduce the efficiency of price formation, and therefore lessen the effectiveness of the market system.[255]

4 From idealists: that volunteering should always be a gift, and that therefore attempts at providing volunteers with a compensation in complementary currencies are counterproductive.

Some brief specific responses

Each of those objections could be argued extensively: however there is room here only for a few lines as a first answer to each one:

1 If the prevailing forecasts on the 'Age Wave' and unemployment are valid (see Chapters 1 and 5), the existing social safety nets will have to be modified, regardless of the political pressure exerted. Blocking a solution such as the use of complementary currencies will only make the final result worse for the people who can least afford it.

2 It is understandable that organizations who benefited from the advantages of a monopoly would prefer the maintenance of the *status quo*. However, neither the technologies coming on-line in cyberspace, nor the pressures of the 'Time-Compacting Machine' leave any of us the luxury of the *status quo*. As well-designed and managed complementary currencies do not create inflationary pressures on the conventional currency, they should at least be tolerated, if not welcomed, even from a central banking viewpoint.

3 This criticism is the strongest objection raised against Hayek's proposals for multiple private currencies. However, my proposal for complementary currencies does not question the primary role of the conventional currencies in the competitive economy, thereby reducing the applicability of this argument in this case.

4 In an ideal world, maybe this argument would be valid. In the real world, a majority of people never volunteer for anything, and those who do suffer a 'burn-out' or 'drop-out' rate of 40% per annum according to research by the University of Maryland Center of Aging. In contrast, that same research has shown that about a third of the people taking part in Time Dollars had never volunteered for anything before. It also showed that the annual 'drop-out' rate declines to a remarkably low 3%.[256] Similar results were discovered in Japan with the use of *Hureai Kippu*.

Each one of these objections deserves a more detailed response than can be provided here (see sidebar). There is however a common response valid for these and other objections. It refers to the four 'money questions' formulated at the beginning of this book (see 'the Time-Compacting Machine' of Chapter 1). Specifically, I would ask any objector to the above proposal the following four straightforward questions:

- How does he or she plan to provide the money to the growing population of elderly so that it would match their longevity, without either raising taxes unduly or bankrupting the governmental budgets?
- How does (s)he plan to deal realistically with the issue of jobless growth, particularly as we should expect another doubling of the human population over the next 50 years, and a continuation of the technological trend that makes human input in the production processes less and less relevant?
- How does (s)he plan to deal effectively with the conflict between financial priorities which determine decisions in the real world, and long-term ecological sustainability?
- How does (s)he propose to deal with global monetary instability?

If these four questions are valid, they deserve a response (my own responses to the last two of these questions are still to be fully developed in the next two chapters). I sincerely hope that as a result of such responses a better solution than the one proposed here will emerge . . .

Until that is the case, we should proceed on the basis of the limited knowledge accumulated so far about what has been demonstrated to work pragmatically somewhere in the world. I am the first to acknowledge that these solutions are still primitive prototypes – to return to the early 'flying machines' metaphor of Chapter 6 – but they have shown themselves to be capable of flying. And they do so by empowering grass-root organizations to solve problems which centralized government solutions have patently failed to address effectively.

■ How to start your own complementary currency

The hard part of creating currency is not conceiving a new variation of complementary currency, nor even starting it. The hard part is having it accepted and used in your community. The national currencies have history and habit on their side, not to speak of the law as 'legal tender for all debts public or private'. Your local currency does not have these factors on its side, so it requires credibility of another nature.

As for all currencies, what is most needed is credibility – without it nothing will happen.

Three keys to successful implementation

There are three key ingredients in the successful implementation of a complementary currency system: good timing, quality of local leadership and a valid design. A few words about each follows.

GOOD TIMING

The Greeks had a special word for it: *Kairos* ('perfect time') which they distinguished from ordinary *Chronos* (time). The same initiatives by the same people can have very different results depending on timing. These 'good timings' can be positive or negative.

For instance, as mentioned earlier, sudden increases in unemployment have created perfect timing for the rapid expansion of the complementary currency movement in Britain and France. The shocks to the national currencies in Argentina or Mexico have resulted in the creation of complementary currencies in these countries.

On the other hand, the 'right moment' may be simply the coalescence of the right group of people who decide to do something positive for their community, which brings us to the next key ingredient.

QUALITY OF LOCAL LEADERSHIP

Perhaps the most important factor to start a local currency is local leadership. Someone, or some group, is needed with the combination of vision, entrepreneurial capability and charisma. Vision to see that another way is possible, and to adapt whatever model is used to local circumstances. Entrepreneurial capability to decide to do something about the situation, and be effective at it. And finally, charisma to convince your community to follow you. If one of these three leadership characteristics is missing, it ends up as either 'just talk' or a failed project, of which there are many. However, when these three capabilities are gathered in one team, they can generate the credibility that is crucial for a successful complementary currency system.

Remember, money ultimately is about trust, and thus about the trustworthiness of the people who will be promoting the system. It will also automatically determine the scale and nature of the project that becomes possible. If the leadership has credibility only within a small area of town, work at that scale. If it has the capacity to mobilize a whole region, then a complementary currency system of the size of the region becomes possible.

To conclude with this aspect, Lao-Tzu's comment is particularly relevant for grass-root movements: 'The best leadership is when at the end people claim they did it themselves.'

VALID COMPLEMENTARY CURRENCIES DESIGN

The last critical step is to choose among the wide variety of complementary currency systems that are available as prototypes today, the one that best fits your own requirements. The following table should help in such a selection. It provides a synthetic overview of the main characteristics of various currency systems reviewed so far.

	Unit	Issuance	Details	Main Benefit
National Currencies	US$, euro, yen pound (mediated via US$)	Fiat currency issued by banks supervised by central bank	Debt-based Bearing interest	Legal tender
LETS	1 Green $ = 1$	Mutual Credit	Most prevalent current system	Easy pricing (because unit = $)
Time Dollars	Hours of Service	Mutual Credit	Fixed exchange rate: 1 hour = 1 hour	Simplest system
WIR	1 WIR = 1 SF	Mutual Credit+ Loans from Centre	Fiat currency	Most mature system ($2 billion/year)
Ithaca HOURS	1 HOUR = $10	Fiat currency issued by community 'pot luck' centre	Quantity must be managed	Ease of use (paper bills)
Japanese Healthcare	Hour of Service	Non-profits Local governments	National Clearing House	Caring Service at no taxpayers' cost
Tlaloc	1 Tlaloc = 1 Mexican peso	Mutual Credit	Issuance by cheques	Low tech (no computer or telephone needed)
ROCS (Robust Currency Systems)	Hour of Service	Mutual Credit	Negotiated exchange rate Demurrage charges	Synthesis of most robust features

Figure 7.1 Comparative table of various currency systems

The only new complementary currency system in this table is the ROCS (Robust Currency System) which synthesizes the most robust features of all the different systems. It is designed to be able to resist best any shocks in the monetary system, and will be described in more detail at the end of this section.

Each of these systems has characteristics which can be considered as advantages or defects depending on the circumstances. For example, tying the unit of the complementary currency to the national currency (as is the case for most LETS systems, WIR and Tlaloc) has the advantage of making pricing easy for everybody including merchants, given that any product or service has the same numeric value assigned in both currencies. On the other hand, if the national currency is in crisis, the value of the complementary currency would depreciate in parallel. In this sense, the complementary currency's role as back-up system, as 'spare tyre', is clearly less effective.

Depending on your priority, it may make sense to choose a currency that ties in with the national one, or one that does not. In the latter case, the unit that makes most sense is the hour. The hour is a universal standard, and almost all contemporary systems which do not tie their unit to the national currency are using it.

Another key decision is whether to use a fiat currency model (as Ithaca HOURS or WIR) or a mutual credit system (as LETS, Time Dollars, Tlaloc, or ROCS). There are two important reasons why a mutual credit system will generally be preferable, particularly for systems that are designed to be able to be scaled up or replicated in large numbers.

1 All fiat currencies by definition are issued by a central authority, whether it is a community central bank, an individual person or a 'pot luck' committee. The trickiest decision – as all central bankers will confirm – is to decide how much currency to issue. If too much is issued, inflation in the currency will be an immediate result, and people will resist accepting it. If too little is issued, the complementary currency can only perform part of its function. In contrast, the main advantage of mutual credit systems is that the quantity of money is always perfectly self-regulating. As participants themselves create the currency at the moment of each transaction, there is by definition always the exact quantity in circulation. Furthermore, this quantity will automatically reduce as people engage in transactions in the opposite direction of their initial trade (i.e. someone who had a credit in one transaction, and uses the credit to purchase a good or service brings his or her balance back to zero). This self-regulating feature is important, because it eliminates the most tricky and treacherous decision in currency management.

2 The second reason is strategic. As mentioned above, the biggest danger to the complementary currency movement is a repression by central banks, as has happened in the 1930s. Central banks have a legitimate role in keeping the inflation rate on the national currency in check. If there was a proliferation of fiat complementary currencies, this would indeed potentially impact the management of inflation on the national currency, as we saw in the section on central banks. Mutual credit complementary currencies do not pose such a threat, and therefore could grow in importance over time without interfering with central bank duties.

We are still in the very early days of the Information Age, and it is far too early to determine which is the 'ideal' complementary currency system. Creativity and experimentation should therefore be encouraged. My personal favourite complementary currency system is the ROCS, because it brings together all the best features that provide robustness to the system. As of this writing, this currency has not yet been implemented to my knowledge.

Its choice of the hour as unit of account makes it pretty universal, and safe against shocks to the national currency system. Its mutual credit aspect eliminates the risks of over-issuing that is intrinsic to all fiat currencies. What differentiates the ROCS from Time Dollars is that the rate of exchange of the hour is negotiated between the participants. Some people may consider that everybody's time should be equally valued. But this is Utopian, as in practice it simply means that people whose services are significantly more valuable in the 'normal' marketplace, such as dentists or surgeons, simply will not accept Time Dollars in exchange for their services.

Finally, ROCS would include the demurrage feature for reasons explained next.

■ Some technical lessons from the 1930s usable today

One of the more interesting features successfully tested in hundreds of cases in the 1930s (including Wörgl, described in Chapter 5) – which has not been copied in the more recent systems is the idea of demurrage. This feature has nevertheless some very important and desirable effects. First of all, it would advantageously replace the transaction costs (which have the built-in incentive to discourage trading) necessary to fund overhead expenses. It could also be used to fund some collective project that the community agrees should be supported.

One pragmatic disadvantage experienced in today's complementary currency systems is that they typically have to depend on continuous sales efforts by the originators of the system. Many systems have simply died when the originators got tired of performing this task on a continuous basis. When a time-related demurrage system is used, every participant in the system potentially becomes a motivated sales person.

There have been some valid technical criticisms to the stamp scrip process of the 1930s. Handling stamps is inconvenient for everyone involved. Furthermore, there was a tendency in the 1930s that the day before a monthly stamp was due, shops would suddenly receive a massive inflow of the stamp scrip from people who preferred not to pay the stamp themselves. Weekly stamps were designed to reduce that tendency, but it still happened on a smaller scale.

However, with today's computer technologies, both of these inconveniences can be easily and efficiently eliminated. The vast majority of complementary currency systems today are computerized. It would be very simple to apply a small, continuous, time-related charge on either only credits or on all balances (credits and debits) in the list. For example, one could impose a charge cumulatively equivalent to 1% per month or more on a daily or even an hourly basis. With smart-card technology, this can easily be built into the card programme itself.

One last reason to apply demurrage to currency systems is that it also helps in switching the attention to longer-term concerns. The next chapter will develop that aspect of demurrage in full detail.

CHAPTER 8

A Global Reference Currency – Making Money Sustainable

FRANK AND ERNEST by Bob Thaves

FRANK AND ERNEST reprinted by permission of Newspaper Enterprise Association, Inc.

■ *'NO PLANET, NO BUSINESS'*

BUMPER STICKER

■ *'Faced with widespread destruction of the environment, people everywhere are coming to understand that we cannot continue to use the goods of the earth as we have in the past. A new ecological awareness is beginning to emerge, which rather than being downplayed, ought to be encouraged and developed into concrete programmes and initiatives.'*

POPE JOHN PAUL II

■ *'It's good business to anticipate the inevitable, and it seems to me inevitable, whether we like it or not, that we are moving toward an economy which must be limited and selective in its growth pattern. The earth has finite limits – a difficult idea for Americans to adjust to.'*

JOHN D. ROCKEFELLER III

■ *'On the bleached bones of dead civilizations are written the words: "too late".'*

MARTIN LUTHER KING JR.

One last time, we will play our game of 'tell me what your objectives are, and we can design a currency that supports it'. This chapter deals with the 'money question': 'how can financial interests become compatible with long-term sustainability?' Another way to ask the same question: is a win-win approach possible for finance, business and society?

This issue may be the most important because even the survival of our own and many other species is at stake. As the prominent French monetary theorist Jacques Rueff claimed, 'Money will decide the fate of mankind.'[257] Will we have to see the last fish die, or the last rainforest cut down, before we realize that we will not be able to eat money?

It is presented in this late chapter because – in contrast with the new currency designs presented in the previous chapters – this proposal breaks new ground and has therefore no contemporary case to demonstrate it.

This chapter starts with a brief status report on both the positive achievements of the Industrial Age and its negative impact on 'Biosphere Earth'. This balance sheet makes clear the relevance of the question identified above.

Next, the limits of being able to convince business to do things which are not financially motivated are identified ('Three Tools of Persuasion').

Then I'll show the direct relationship between one particular feature of the official national currency system – namely interest – and the phenomenon of short-term vision of the business world and Western society at large. A solution to the dilemma is then proposed both as a metaphor ('Far-Seeing Glasses') and as a sound technical possibility.

■ Long-term sustainability

There is a growing consensus that our current path is unsustainable. It has become unsustainable ecologically, socially and politically.

After a lifetime of study of the causes of the demise of civilizations, the historian Arnold Toynbee concluded that only two common causes explain the collapse of 21 past civilizations: extreme concentration of wealth and inflexibility in the face of changing conditions. Over the past decades our civilization seems to have embarked on a path combining both those causes of collapse. But before looking at the role of the money system in these issues, one should first look at the positive side of the ledger.

■ Positive results of the modern money system

We should start by acknowledging that the modern monetary system has played a key role in the extraordinary achievements of the Industrial Age.

If you want to industrialize, you need to concentrate enough resources for industry. Steel plants are not built on a small scale in a backyard – the Chinese tried and failed as late as the 1970s. And to concentrate resources – to paraphrase Churchill's quip about democracy – competition among private players is the worst system, with the exception of all others. Would you prefer to buy your next car, meal, or computer from *non*-competing producers?

This system has been highly effective in instigating and propagating the Industrial Age around the world.

The truly exceptional achievements of the Industrial Age can best be appreciated by observing its impact on our species as a whole. Human life has been totally transformed by the process of industrialization. Just to bring into perspective what is so unique about the last two and a half centuries, consider Figure 8.1.

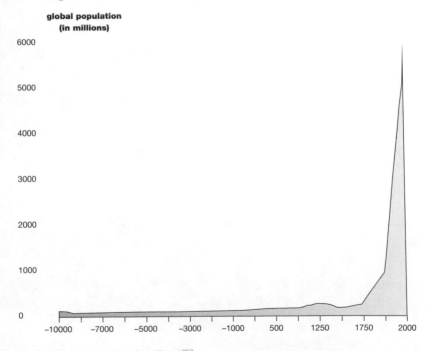

Figure 8.1 World population (in millions)[258]

The human population remained below the level of 400 million for many thousands of years. There were several periods with significant population decreases: for instance in the period between roughly 10000 to 8000 BC; and at the end of the Middle Ages, when the Black Death killed at least 75 million people (including about a quarter of the European population). Human population grew to one billion for the first time during the first half of the 19th century. Then it took off.

We reached the second billion in 1925, the third in 1962, the fourth in 1975, the fifth in 1986, and the sixth in 1999. At this point it is clearly good news that the rate of growth has started to taper off. Most experts forecast that we are now doubling for the last time. We should attain the seventh billion in 2009 and the eighth billion in 2019. Global population is supposed to stabilize around 10 to 12 billion some time around 2050.[259]

What has made this population explosion possible (again for better and for worse) has clearly been the Industrial Revolution, when human and animal power was replaced for the first time by fossil-fuel energy. The production of goods follows an even steeper curve than the population. Gross Domestic Product (GDP) *per capita* in the developed world multiplied by a factor of 20 between 1800 and today.

The standard of living has soared from bare subsistence to what our ancestors would have considered extraordinary affluence for many people in Europe, North America and industrialized Asia. These are immense accomplishments which, whatever drawbacks they may entail, should still be recognized. However, there is also another side to this balance sheet, which should be looked at squarely as well.

■ Status report on Biosphere Earth

Until last century, Nature was perceived as a big, powerful, awe-inspiring force on which humans had very little if any impact. This has now dramatically changed. In 1996, the World Conservation Union, in collaboration with more than 600 scientists, published the most comprehensive survey so far on the status of animal life on earth. Their conclusion: 25% of mammals and amphibians, 11% of birds, 20% of reptiles and 34% of fish species surveyed so far are threatened with extinction. Another 5% to 14% of all species are 'nearing threatened status'. A 1998 survey concluded that 6,000 tree species, ten per cent of all existing tree species, are now endangered as well.[260]

A report released by the United Nations in September 1999 based on assessments by 850 specialists around the world concludes that the rate at which humanity destroys the biosphere is still accelerating. 'The full extent of the damage is only now becoming apparent as we begin to piece together a comprehensive overview of the extremely complex, interconnected web that is our life support system.'[261]

The big question that should be asked is: 'Is economic progress killing the planet?'

My personal balance sheet of all the above can be summarized in three points as follows:

- The encouraging results on the positive side prove clearly that we can reverse the ecological degradation process if we so choose, but our window of time in which to do so is closing down.
- The means used to encourage businesses and people to do so (i.e. mostly regulation and moral persuasion) are too narrow in both geography and scope to achieve sustainability.
- Finally, the rest of this chapter shows that a change in our money system offers a pragmatic possibility to harness the massive energy of the global economy towards long-term sustainability.

■ The three tools of persuasion

Why change our monetary system to attain long-term sustainability? Isn't there a more direct way to attain this objective?

There are only three ways to persuade people or institutions to engage in any non-spontaneous change in behaviour:

- education and moral persuasion;
- regulation;
- and financial interest.

Over the past decades, as people started focusing on the issues of the environment, the first two ways have been emphasized almost exclusively.

History has shown that whenever financial interests contradict regulations, financial interests almost always end up as the winners. The permanent and mostly losing battles to enforce anti-smuggling or anti-drug regulations provide many case histories of what we should expect from relying exclusively on a regulatory approach.

Similarly, whenever financial interests run up against moral pressure, the battle is often even harder. Many people just decide that they either cannot afford, or do not care enough, to follow the moral advice when it personally costs them something.

It is apparent that large-scale changes in behaviour should only be expected when all of these motivating forces are lined up in the same direction. For instance, recycling glass bottles or aluminium cans has become really effective whenever there were simultaneously:

- regulations requiring people to recycle;
- a public information campaign about the reasons to do so;
- and last but not least, a small refundable deposit per unit.

In short, the realigning of financial interests with long-term concerns is a necessary condition, but not a sufficient one, for a truly successful sustainability strategy.

The importance of realigning financial interests with long-term sustainability is even more critical because many of the issues involved need to be addressed on a global level (e.g. global climate changes, acid rain, ozone layer, etc.) or it just won't make much of a difference. And there is little chance that we can regulate or morally persuade the whole world. For example: by the year 2015, the Chinese are planning to emit as much carbon dioxide by themselves as the whole world does today. This forecast is based on coal-fuelled electric power plants currently being built or already on the drawing boards in China. What can we do?

Some Questions for CEO's

If you are a CEO or know one, obtain honest answers on the following two sets of questions:

1. Will there be more monetary crises?
2. Do such monetary crises affect your business?
3. What do you plan to do about it?
4. What is the time horizon you use to plan for your children?
5. What is the time horizon you use in your business?
6. What world will your and all other businesses leave to your children, given the difference in time horizon between question 4 and 5?

If the answers to these questions raise concerns, then the Terra project described in this chapter is for you.

The well-known architect William McDonough claims that 'Regulation is a signal that you have a design failure'. He asks the question: 'Who is in charge of a ship?' The answer is the designer, who has already built into the ship ninety per cent of what the captain can do. I claim the same is happening to the business world: the design of the money system is preordaining ninety per cent of the investment decisions made or not made in the world. And regulations aiming at sustainability just try to correct the flaws built into our money system. Furthermore, regulations have proved so far mostly ineffective in reaching that goal.

Our economics textbooks claim that corporations and individuals are competing for markets or resources. In reality, they compete for money, using markets and resources in this process. If we were able to redesign money in a way that favours long-term vision, we could harness the massive resources of the global corporations in a direction of a more sustainable future.

■ Relationship between money systems, time perception and sustainability

Monetary specialists and Greens alike typically see no connection between the money system and sustainability. What follows will show that this is an oversight.

The gentlest way to acquaint ourselves with that connection is through another short fairy tale for my godchild.

The man with the near-seeing glasses

(Fairy tale for Kamir, seven years old)

Once upon a time, in a very near place, there was a man who had been wearing glasses for so long that he even forgot he had them on. The main problem, however, was that his glasses, instead of correcting his vision, were making him so near-sighted that he couldn't see anything further than his nose.

So he would bump against everybody or everything because they would always suddenly appear to him without warning, when it was too late to avoid the obstacle. He was getting worried enough about the problem that he went to consult a Scientist.

The Scientist listened to the problem carefully, then pulled out a very thick book about Optics filled with equations and diagrams. And he showed him that it was very normal to see better closer-up than far away. He explained something about the number of light particles decreasing by the square of the distance from which he saw them. The Man with the Near-Seeing Glasses did not quite understand the explanation, but he was very relieved to hear that there was a scientific reason which made it all very normal.

So he went on bumping against people, trees, even his own green front door and everything else which popped up suddenly when he was hitting them with his nose. After he hit a particularly hard red brick wall with his forehead, he was getting worried again and felt depressed about all the bumps he kept collecting. So he went to see a Psychiatrist.

The Psychiatrist told him to lie down on a big couch, and started asking him a lot of questions – how he got along with his father, with his mother and his brothers and sisters. After he answered all these questions, the Psychiatrist told him that it was very normal that he was depressed, and asked him to come back every week for some in-depth treatment about all that.

One day, much later, as the Man with the Near-Seeing Glasses came back from his appointment with the Psychiatrist more depressed than ever, he bumped against his little five-year-old granddaughter who was waiting for him in front of his house. He was very happy to see her again, and they went into the house to play together.

As the little girl was playing horsy on her grandfather's knees, she suddenly grabbed at the horse's bridle and ripped off the Near-Seeing Glasses from her grandfather's nose. Just as suddenly the Man discovered that he could see much further than his nose after all. His granddaughter's smiling face was clear. The green door he'd smashed into last week was clear. He even noticed that the red brick wall needed some repairs where he had hit his head. Seeing things beyond his own nose before bumping into them made a lot of sense after all.

We can now rephrase the relationship as follows: interest rates create a built-in tendency to disregard the future, to create a world-view with 'near-seeing glasses'. Furthermore, the higher the interest rate, the more that tendency prevails.

We have seen in Chapter 2 how interest rates are deeply woven into the very process of creating money in our prevailing money system.

Understanding the relationship between interest rates and time perception will be accomplished in the three following steps:

- comprehend how capital allocation decisions are generally made through the financial technique of 'Discounted Cash Flow';
- how such discounting of the future is one of the key underlying causes which create a direct conflict between financial criteria and ecological sustainability under our present money system;
- and how the discount rate used in the Discounted Cash Flow technique is directly affected by the interest rate of the currency used in the cash flow analysis.

■ 'Discounted Cash Flow' = 'Discounting the Future'

'Discounted Cash Flow' is the financial technique generally used to decide on whether to invest in a given project, or to compare different projects. It is presented in full detail in any finance textbook.

What we need to understand about it here can be explained by a simple example. Let us assume that a particular project requires a $1,000 investment today, and that it will produce a net profit of $100 on the first day of each subsequent year for the next 15 years. Let us further make the assumption that there is no inflation during that period of time. Figure 8.3 shows what the real cash flow of that project would look like: it starts with a negative –1,000 when the cash outflow occurs today, and for each of the next 15 years we have the same amount of $100 shown on the positive side.

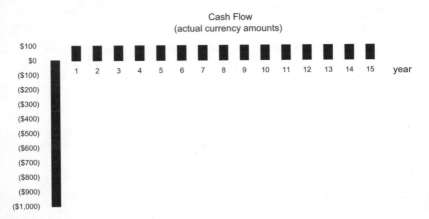

Figure 8.3: Actual annual currency flow of a project

By financial analysts, however, that same project will be viewed differently (Figure 8.4).

Figure 8.4 Discounted cash flow as seen by financial analyst

He will still see the same negative $1,000 in year 0.

But the income of $100 after the first year will only be worth $91 assuming the interest rate is a flat 10% per year for the entire duration of the project. (All values are rounded to the nearest dollar for illustration purposes, since carrying lots of decimals would not modify the argument presented.)[116]

We all know that money in the future is worth less than money today. How much less depends critically on the 'discount rate' applied to the project.

Our analyst knows he could deposit $91 in a bank today at a 10% risk-free rate of return, and automatically get $100 a year from now. Therefore the $100 a year from now is identical to $91 today. By the same reasoning, the second year's $100 would only be worth $83, the third's $75, etc. By the tenth year, the $100 inflow only represents to him $39; and in the fifteenth year a paltry $24.

So what looked like a perfectly reasonable investment, getting back $1,500 on a $1,000 investment of Figure 8.3, turns out as a lacklustre project when looked at through the Near-Seeing Glasses of our financial analyst.

If we projected this forwards for a century, the last $100 would really be worth only seven cents. Two centuries out we are looking at a few hundredths of a cent. No wonder that in our societies we do not usually think about the effect on our decisions 'for the seventh generation', a process which would require us to take into account two centuries in the future . . .

There is nothing wrong with the financial analyst's eyesight or his reasoning. He just applies straightforward financial logic to a currency which has a positive interest rate.

Short-term vision versus sustainability

As this same reasoning applies to all financially motivated investments, it collectively creates the well-known pressure by the financial system for short-term returns at the expense of any longer-term consideration – including long-term sustainability.

When a corporate executive complains that financial pressures force him to focus only on the next quarter's results, he is the victim of the Near-Seeing Glasses. When the Chinese say they cannot afford cleaner energy production technologies, they are really saying the costs of the long-term future economic consequences discounted to today are negligible compared with the immediate cost savings made possible with the 'dirty' technologies they are planning to use. When a homeowner decides it is too expensive to install solar panels for heating the household water, she is implicitly saying that the cost of purchasing electricity or gas from the grid in the long run discounted to today is cheaper than the initial capital outlay required. When we build a house cheaply without appropriate insulation, we are really making the trade-off between the higher heating costs in the future discounted to today and the higher construction costs.

Relationship with interest rates

In the explanation of the Discounted Cash Flow technique, we made an assumption that the discount rate used is identical to the interest rate of the currency. In reality, the discount rate which should be used is the 'cost of capital of the project'. Without getting unduly technical, there is not one but three components to that cost of capital:

■ the interest rate of the currency involved;
■ the cost of equity;
■ and an adjustment reflecting the uncertainty about the cash flow of the project itself.

The third component is completely project-related and therefore unaffected by the currency used. It would remain identical whatever the monetary system, and for the purposes of our discussion here will be ignored.

The first two, in contrast, are directly affected by the monetary system of the currency involved.

Here is the root cause of the proverbial 'short-sightedness' of the financial markets, which forces corporations into making decisions which they know may hurt society and even business itself in the long run.

If a CEO of a corporation were tempted to think in longer-term social or ecological ways, he would soon be removed either by his board, or – if needed – by a new board after raiders have taken over. 'A special breed of investors, the corporate raiders, specializes in preying on established corporations. The basic process is simple, though the details are complex and the power struggles often nasty. The raider identifies a company traded on a public stock exchange that has a "break-up" value in excess of the current market price of the shares. Sometimes they are troubled companies. More often, they are well-managed, fiscally sound companies that are being good citizens and looking to the future. They may have substantial cash reserves to cushion an economic downturn and may have natural resources they are managing on a sustainable yield basis.'[263] After the takeover, they change the policies to suit short-term gains, ironically often to service the interest on the enormous loans used to make the takeover in the first place. The net result: one more company has put on Near-Seeing Glasses . . .

In summary, under the existing money system, longer-term thinking is not only less profitable, it is severely punished.

However, it is possible to design a monetary system which would dramatically lower the cost of capital through simultaneously reducing both interest rates and the cost of equity. And you will see how this process realigns financial interests with the long-term sustainability objectives.

Far-Seeing Glasses?

What happens when you reverse the way you look into binoculars? Suddenly, instead of bringing distant objects closer, it makes everything look far away.

In our metaphor of the Near-Seeing Glasses positive interest rates were the feature of our current monetary system which created a generalized financial myopia, and made the future appear less relevant. And the higher the interest rates, the stronger the myopia. In other words, the result of positive interest rates is similar to what happens when one looks through the wrong end of binoculars.

What would happen if we reversed the financial analyst's glasses?

Remember the demurrage charges mentioned at the end of the previous chapter? Demurrage was the brainchild of Silvio Gesell (1862-1930), and was most recently used as an anti-hoarding device for the stamp scrip currencies of the 1930s. Gesell's starting premise was that money is a kind of public service, like a bus ride. And that a small fee is charged for the time one hoards it . . .

From a financial perspective, a demurrage charge on money is mathematically equivalent to a negative interest rate. For reasons that will become clear soon, I will call this time-related charge a 'sustainability fee'. Now, what would such a sustainability fee or demurrage charge do to the eyesight of our financial analyst?

The project described in Figure 8.3 would suddenly appear to him as described in Figure 8.5.

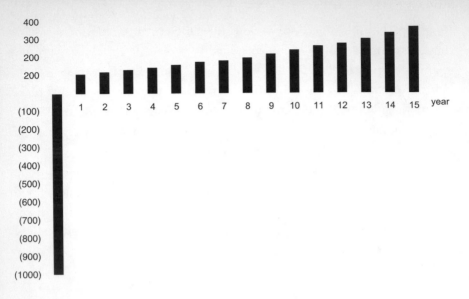

Figure 8.5: Financial analyst's view of Figure 8.3 with a cash flow expressed in a currency with a sustainability fee (or demurrage charge)

This is not just true because of a mechanical application of the equations of Discounted Cash Flow. Even if it looks strange at first sight, even if it contradicts what we are used to with our normal currencies, it still makes perfect financial sense.

Let us assume that I give you a choice between 100 units of an inflation-proof currency charged by a sustainability fee, today or a year from now. If you do not need the money for immediate consumption, and you have guarantees about my creditworthiness over the next year, you should logically prefer the money a year from now. The reason is that by receiving the money only in a year's time, you will not have to pay the sustainability fee for that year. In technical terms, discounted to today's value, the 100 units will be more valuable a year from now than if you received them now. They will be worth exactly 100 plus the sustainability fees.

When sustainability-fee-charged currencies are used, the future becomes more valuable with time, exactly the opposite of what happens with our normal positive-interest-rate currencies.

There remain two fundamental issues to be addressed :

- How could such an idea be implemented? Who could take the initiative for such a new global currency system in the foreseeable future?
- Is such an unorthodox money system sound? What would be its economic consequences?

■ A Global Reference Currency (GRC) and the Terra unit

I will call a Global Reference Currency (GRC) the generic concept of a currency which is not tied to any particular nation state, and whose main purpose is to provide a stable and reliable reference currency for international contracts and trade.

Furthermore, I will propose as unit of account for one particular type of GRC the Terra, which aims at firmly anchoring that currency to the material/physical world. Remember, one of the reasons that the global currency casino can churn as wildly as it does is the disconnection between the financial world and physical reality, a link which was severed by President Nixon in 1971. In this role, the Terra would be akin to the gold standard in the 19th century.

The Terra is defined as a standard basket of commodities and services particularly important for international trade, and their relative weight in the standard basket would ideally reflect their relative importance in global trade.

For instance, the value of the Terra could be defined as:

1 Terra = 1/10 barrel of oil (for example Brent quality and delivery)

+ 1 bushel of wheat (Chicago Mercantile Exchange delivery)

+ 2 pounds of copper (London Metal Exchange delivery)

+ . . . etc.

+ 1/100 ounce of gold (New York delivery)

(Note: the specific commodities, their quality, delivery standards, and their respective weights in the Terra unit are proposed here as simple examples. In practice, this would be part of a negotiated agreement among participants. This standard could also include services, or indices aiming at increasing further its stability.)

The Terra has the following main characteristics and effects:

- This currency can be made inflation-proof by definition. Inflation is always defined as the change in value of a basket of goods and services, therefore to the extent that the basket composing the Terra can be made representative of global trade automatic inflation-proofing is obtained.
- The value of this new Terra currency could easily be translated into any existing national currency. Anybody who wants to value the Terra in his own national currency just has to look up the prices of those internationally traded commodities which are part of the basket. These

prices are already published in the financial sections of all the major newspapers in the world, and are available in real-time on the Net everywhere.

■ More importantly, this currency is also automatically convertible in any existing national currency without the need for any new international treaty or agreement. Anybody who is paid in this currency would have the option just to receive the basket of commodities delivered in pre-arranged facilities (such as the already existing delivery places for the different futures markets, for example). These existing commodity markets could also be used to obtain cash in the conventional national currencies for the products delivered, if this is desired. We should expect that – as the system proves reliable and credible – fewer and fewer people would feel the need to go through this process of cashing in the receipts.

■ The system would automatically tend to counteract the prevailing business cycle. It would tend to activate the economy when the business cycle worsens, and dampen inflationary tendencies when a boom prevails (see box on 'Economic tech talk' for details).

■ But the most important reason for our purposes here is that the sustainability fee is 'naturally' embedded in the money system. It therefore guarantees the full integration of the proposed currency in the existing market system of the 'real' economy in all its aspects.

There are indeed real costs associated with storing commodities, and the sustainability fee would simply be the cost of storing the basket of commodities agreed upon. These storage costs (and therefore the sustainability fees) have been estimated in a detailed study for a Commodity Reserve Currency at 3 to 3.5% per annum.[118]

Note that these costs are not new additional costs to the economy as a whole. They are indeed already factored in the current economy. What is proposed is simply transferring these existing costs to the bearer of the Terra, thereby giving them the useful social function of a sustainability fee.

Economic tech talk

Economic textbooks define money in terms of its functions, the three most important of which are: Standard of Value, Medium of Exchange and Store of Value (definitions in Appendix A).

Since 1971, there has been no international standard of value. In this sense, a GRC simply restores that function for those who choose to use it as a contractual currency.

The role of medium of exchange would be played by either the GRC or conventional national currencies at the choice of the parties – just as today's decision of which national currency is to be used for an international payment.

Finally, the store of value function would *not* be played by the GRC. It could be played by instruments in conventional national currencies, or by new specialized financial products which would create liquidity from investments in productive assets.

This functional specialization shows how the GRC plays a role *complementary* to the conventional national currencies.

The behaviour dynamic that a GRC induces is similar to the 'good' aspects of inflation while avoiding its 'bad' ones. Economists have noted that a moderate amount of inflation can actually have a good impact on the economy. For instance, the 1980s inflation in the US provoked a negative net return on fixed income instruments, thereby encouraging investments in productive projects. However, inflation also implies regressive effects such as the erosion of all price agreements and the redistribution of wealth from the financially unsophisticated majority to a sophisticated minority.

The demurrage fees of the GRC therefore obtain the positive effects of inflation, while avoiding its negative ones.

Fisher's classical velocity of money equation provides another way to illustrate the impact of the GRC.

$$T = Sum (PG) = QV$$

(where T = total economic exchanges; P = prices; G = goods and services exchanged; Q= quantity of money and V = velocity of money circulation).

For a given quantity of money in circulation (a given Q), the demurrage feature of the GRC increases V. To the extent that the Terra unit is expressed in terms of a representative basket of commodities and services, it keeps P constant by definition. Fisher's equation therefore shows that G, the total goods and services exchanged, would necessarily increase with the introduction of a GRC, thereby improving overall economic well-being.

Last but not least, the use of a GRC in complement with conventional national currencies would automatically tend to counteract the prevalent business cycle, thereby improving the overall stability and predictability of the world's economic system. This is so because there is always an excess of raw materials when the business cycle is weakening (weakening of raw material prices is one of the key indicators of a recession). Corporations would therefore tend at this point of the business cycle to sell more raw materials for storage to GRC Inc., which would pay for them with Terra. The Terra would be used immediately by these corporations to pay their suppliers, so as to avoid the demurrage charges. These suppliers in turn would have a similar incentive to pass on the Terra as medium of payment. The spread of this increased incentive to trade would therefore automatically activate the economy at this point in the cycle. On the contrary, when the business cycle is in a boom period, corporations have a systematic incentive not only not to sell new inventories to the Countertrade Alliance, but even to cash them in to have access to the raw materials themselves. This would reduce the amounts of Terra in circulation when the business cycle is at its highest thereby cooling off the economy at this point. At the peak of the cycle, it is even possible that no Terra remain in circulation at all (which does not preclude their continued use as contractual reference currency).

Both Keynes and Friedman have shown that with conventional money, the velocity of money is pro-cyclical (each for different reasons: the former on the basis of changes in interest rates, the latter on the basis of the predominant role of Friedman's 'Permanent Revenue' in determining the demand for money). The fact that the quantity of Terra in circulation would be counter-cyclical to the business cycle would therefore tend to counteract the pro-cyclical nature of the conventional money system.

In summary, the introduction of a GRC would tend automatically to dampen the business cycle by providing additional monetary liquidity in counter-cycle with the business cycle relating to the conventional national currencies.

■ Theoretical and practical soundness

The box on 'Economic tech talk' synthesizes some key effects of the Terra for those who prefer a purely economic language.

Conceptually, the Terra is the combination of two ideas: a currency backed by a basket of raw materials which has been proposed by many top economists of every generation,[265] including the contemporary Economic Nobel Prize-winner Jan Tinbergen on the one side; and sustainability fees as originally proposed by Silvio Gesell under the name of demurrage charges on the other.

This second idea – demurrage charge on currency – was formally endorsed by no less an authority than John Maynard Keynes. He claimed that demurrage not only makes sense from a theoretical viewpoint, but is actually preferably to our normal currencies. Chapter 27 of Keynes's principal work, the *General Theory of Employment, Interest and Money* explicitly states that: 'Those reformers, who look for a remedy by creating artificial carrying cost for money through the device of requiring legal-tender currency to be periodically stamped at a prescribed cost in order to retain its quality as money, have been on the right track, and the practical value of their proposal deserves consideration.'[266]

Keynes concluded with the amazing statement that 'the future would learn more from Gesell than from Marx'.[267] At least some officials at the Federal Reserve seem to have their own reasons to agree with him (see sidebar). The best recent contemporary analysis of Gesell's thesis is provided by Dietrich Suhr.[268] He proves that our normal positive interest rate currencies create systematic misallocation of resources, while zero-interest-rate or sustainability-fee-charged currencies do not. He also provides solid answers to some of the criticisms levelled against sustainability-fee-charged currencies.

A Federal Reserve official recommending demurrage?

The US currency should include tracking devices that let the government tax private possession of dollar bills, recommends Marvin Goodfriend, a senior vice-president and policy adviser at the Federal Reserve of Richmond. In a 34-page paper he argues that this demurrage charge will discourage 'hoarding' currency, deter black market and criminal activities, and boost economic activity during deflationary periods when interest rates hover near zero.[269]

The motivation and the mechanism for this application is obviously different from the ones I propose here. I also think that the likelihood that Mr Goodfriend's idea will be acceptable to Congress is low, but this shows that the concept of demurrage is at least starting to attract renewed attention.

These people were in favour of different parts of the GRC proposal for a variety of valid reasons – other than sustainability – such as monetary stability, reducing the volatility of business cycles, and reduction of international inequalities. A Global Reference Currency such as the Terra would also cumulate these advantages, in addition to the benefits of the sustainability fee idea with its long-term sustainability aim.

It is also important to understand that people would not need to handle the commodities themselves when making or receiving payments in Terra, exactly as someone owning a futures contract in copper does not have to handle copper itself. A Terra is simply a warehouse receipt giving the right to receive the *value* of the basket of commodities in whatever currency he or she deals in. The Terra would therefore be capable of being transferred electronically just like today's national currencies; it would simply be stable and inflation-proof, something which today's national currencies have proved not to be.

Historical precedents

Note that the idea of a commodity-backed currency combined with a sustainability fee is not really new. An early form of it was applied as early as Pharaonic Egypt. It was the secret of the remarkable stability of the Egyptian monetary system, which has not been reproduced by any civilization ever since.[270] It created economic stability and abundance for over a thousand years This historical record also demonstrates the remarkable capacity of sustainability fees to foster sustainable growth which can last over several centuries. This topic will be discussed elsewhere.[271]

■ Implementation options

There are several ways in which a Global Reference Currency could be implemented. For instance, one could theoretically attempt to obtain a consensus for a GRC reform among the governments of the world via a new Bretton Woods Agreement or via a reform of the International Monetary Fund (IMF).

However, the political realities today are such that it is highly unlikely that such a new consensus could be reached by governments. Private conversations with top executives at the Bank of International Settlements (BIS) and the IMF have confirmed that a fundamentally new monetary initiative could only be taken by the private sector in today's geopolitical circumstances.

Furthermore, real decision-making power today lies more with multi-national corporations than with governments anyway. The most important time priorities that require shifting if sustainability is to be achieved are those of the global corporations, and therefore a buy-in from the corporate world would be necessary. This is why the strategy proposed here is to convince a group of key corporations to set up the Global Reference Currency themselves as a service for anybody who wants to trade internationally.

■ Terra as a business initiative

The Terra makes sense as a business initiative for a number of reasons which will be presented next.

The world has been living without an international standard of value for decades, a situation which should be considered as inefficient as operating without a standard of length or weight. Furthermore, as the Asian, Russian and Latin American currency crises of the past few years have demonstrated, currency instability can take a dramatic toll on international business contracts and transactions. The cost of these foreign exchange risks to business and society are quite substantial (see sidebar).

Business costs of currency instability

In a survey of US *Fortune* 500 corporations, all participants in the survey reported that foreign exchange risks is now one of their main concerns.[272] Furthermore, 85% reported that they needed to use expensive derivative strategies to attempt to reduce this foreign exchange risk. It is significant that the firms engaging most in such hedging were also the largest and most sophisticated.[273]

One important aspect about which no surveys have been made is that many foreign investments end up not being made at all, simply because the currency risk cannot be covered, or its coverage is too expensive. These opportunity costs are detrimental not only to the corporation involved but to society at large as well.

One way in which corporations have learned to adapt to this lack of an international standard of value is by resorting to barter. The volume of countertrade (international barter) was estimated at $650 billion in 1997 by the IRTA (International Reciprocal Trade Association) and is growing at 15% per year, three times the rate of conventional-currency-denominated transactions. As this was before the effect of any of the recent currency crises, countertrade is likely to be over $1 trillion for the first time in the year 2000. Two out of three of the *Fortune* 500 corporations are regularly involved in such transactions.[274] Such transactions are expensive in legal and operating costs, because of a lack of standardization. The Terra, from this perspective is simply a standardization of an international barter unit. Such a standardization has already started within certain business sectors (see sidebar on sectorial barter standards), but so far no cross-industry standard has been set up. Furthermore, this could be achieved in a way that it would provide substantial additional benefits not only for business but also for society in general.

Sectorial barter standards

Some business sectors have already developed standard units of exchange specific to their business. For instance the International Air Transport Association (IATA) has been using for more than two decades its own global unit of account (Iata10) to settle payments among its member airline corporations. Similarly, 'hotel-rooms' and 'TV Spots' are gradually evolving as standard industry-specific barter units. In this sense, the Terra or any other GRC unit would simply be the next logical step of a cross-industry barter unit, operated on the Net. It could even include such sectorial standards as components to the Terra itself.

Because it is designed to be by definition inflation proof, it would be ideally suited for long-term planning and longer-term contractual and international trading purposes. It would be issued on the basis of physical inventories of the products incorporated in the basket, therefore be fully backed, ensuring maximum security and stability of the unit involved. In this sense, the Terra is simply a standardized inventory receipt useable as medium of exchange.

In summary, the Terra would reduce operational costs under normal monetary circumstances, and in addition constitute a very robust back-up system in case of further major monetary instabilities.

A specialized business entity called the Countertrade Alliance would issue this 'currency' in exchange for deposits of inventories of the goods in the basket. It would also be in a position to pay back Terras on request in national currency against a small fee, by delivering the corresponding raw materials to existing commodity exchanges and thereby transforming them into conventional national currency when needed. The commodity exchanges involved would be the same ones as those used for commodity futures trading today. Because its liabilities are fully covered in this way, the Countertrade Alliance would benefit from an AAA rated security risk.

Finally, by passing the storage costs of the basket to the bearer of the Terra, one ends up with a currency with a built-in demurrage charge (i.e. a time-related charge on currency holdings, conceptually similar to a negative interest rate) estimated at 3-4% per annum. This combination in a currency of the features of inflation security and a demurrage charge provides this trading currency with the two unusually interesting attributes already explained earlier.

1 The use of the Terra would automatically tend to counteract the prevalent business cycle, thereby improving the overall stability and predictability of the world's economic system and business conditions. For the first time in over 60 years, the possibility of a global recession beyond the control of monetary authorities cannot be dismissed. As Paul Krugman put it, 'Problems we thought we knew how to cure have once again become intractable, like temporarily suppressed bacteria that eventually evolve a resistance to antibiotics ... There is, in short, a definite whiff of the 1930s in the air.[275]

As shown earlier, the Terra system could be managed in such a way as to have a powerful counter-cyclical economic effect with the official money system. It would thereby contribute to reducing economic instability and unpredictability by reducing the risks of both major global recession now, as well as future inflationary booms.

2 Last but not least, the use of a demurrage-charged currency like the Terra for planning and contractual purposes would eliminate the conflict which currently prevails between financial priorities and long-term (e.g. ecological) priorities. By doing so, it reduces the needs for regulations to attain the objective of long-term sustainability.

In summary, a Countertrade Alliance approach to the Terra would enable a private initiative to address five key problems international businesses are experiencing today:

1 It makes available to businesses an international standard of value;
2 It reduces the cost of completing some countertrade transactions;
3 It provides an insurance against uncertainties deriving from international currency instability;
4 It systemically reduces the possibility or seriousness of a global recession;
5 And it structurally resolves the conflict between long-term ecological sustainability and financial priorities built in by the conventional currency system.

Such a strategy can be initiated as a small-scale Internet-based pilot project among a core group of multinational corporations. It can be expanded to include more participants into the Alliance when the system has proved its operational value, and if the international monetary conditions warrant it. It would be a significant contribution that a business initiative can make to make this planet more prosperous, more stable and more sustainable.

■ Business and the environment: A business viewpoint

A Global Business Network special report on Sustainability concluded that:

Industry and environment can no longer be compartmentalized. The global environment system and the socioeconomic system are now coupled – the fate of one is tied to the fate of the other. If conventional industrialization keeps growing, it risks bringing down the ecosystem; if the ecosystem crashes, it will bring down the economy.

The industrial system is highly vulnerable if there is a serious ecological breakdown. Multinational companies are tuned like Grand Prix racing cars for better and better lap times. They assume the racetrack will be perfectly smooth, without obstructions. Industrial installations, buildings, plant, energy transmission lines, are all designed for a narrow set of climatic and ecosystem assumptions – conservative maximum wind loading, moderate earthquake resistance, a steady flow of resources. But we now know, from studies of such things as Arctic ice cores, that nature is certainly capable of far more severe disturbances than the recent, relatively narrow range of climatic variation has led us to assume. This puts the operational basis of today's industrial society directly at risk from possible global ecological breakdowns and accompanying widespread natural disaster.[276]

As we saw earlier (Chapter 1), the insurance industry has been the first major sector to have its profits directly affected by this connection. But while it is the first, it is clearly not the only sector concerned.

■ Conclusions

It may sound strange initially to have businesses perform this function of creating a currency as a public good. However, it is useful to remember that the so-called 'national' currencies are in reality also a form of corporate currencies, issued by private banks as explained in the Primer and Chapter 2. Note also that the banking and financial services industry are not excluded from the GRC process: financial institutions would be providing Terra-denominated services, exactly as they do today for any foreign exchange account.

There is a historical precedent for an international initiative taken by business people: the Hanseatic League (1367-1500) (see sidebar).

However, the contemporary version of such a function would also be significantly different from the historical *Hansa*. It should be global rather than regional, it should be an open public service system rather than a cartel, and it should be using contemporary legal and financial concepts and communication technologies (i.e. the Internet) to implement it.

Historical precedent for business creating multinational framework (1367-1500)

At a time of strong fragmentation in Northern Europe, merchants in different independent cities (Bremen, Cologne, Hamburg, Bruges, the Baltic cities, etc.) got together to create their own legal trading framework (the *Hansa*), complete with its own standard currencies and even its own international courts of justice to settle disputes. All of this was outside of the official political/governmental system. That system lasted for well over a century, six times longer than the current floating exchange experiment.

The *Hansa* was defined as an official institutional structure in 1367, after more informal experiments covering more than a century. This system was remarkably successful in attaining its objectives. However, the merchants in each harbour would spend as much energy impeding access to the system for other merchants competing with them in their own market, as working at expanding their markets overseas. It also purposely excluded traders from specific countries. It finally fell apart at the end of the 15th century when Dutch and English traders, shippers and fishing fleets – originally excluded from the system – successfully challenged the monopoly.

If a private initiative is taken to implement a GRC of some kind, it would therefore be important to set up from the beginning guarantees for a truly open market access for all participants in international trade, independently of size or origin, to avoid having to repeat that part of the *Hansa* history.

What it really boils down to is the question of whether business leaders are willing or capable to take responsibility to reform the current monetary system by a private initiative that would help make business truly sustainable. The word 'business' in Swedish is *Näring Liv* (literally 'Nourishment of Life'). A Terra initiative by an alliance among businesses would be one way whereby it also could be made more true. It would also be a deeply effective way for business leaders to escape the perpetual conflict between stockholders' priorities and their own personal concerns for long-term sustainability, whether these concerns arise from public pressure, personal ethics, or their own grandchildren's future.

'The world is not given to us by our parents.

It is loaned to us by our children.'

(PANEL AT THE BIODIVERSITY HALL OF THE NY MUSEUM OF NATURAL HISTORY)

The proposal of a corporate Global Reference Currency may be perceived at first sight as a direct contradiction with the 'Corporate Millennium' (chapter 4) where a de facto monopoly of private corporate currencies was shown to entail significant risks for our societies. However, my proposal is *not* to create such a monopoly. Instead a global corporate currency is recommended *at the same time* as the introduction of local complementary currencies with social aims (chapters 5, 6 and 7). The issue here is one of *balance*, and such a balance will not be achieved by excluding some of the most active components of our society.

How all the pieces of the puzzle, including the Global Reference Currency, fit together to create such a balance aiming at generating Sustainable Abundance, is the topic of the next and last chapter.

CHAPTER 9

Sustainable Abundance

■ *'History is a race between education and catastrophe.'*

H.G. WELLS

■ *'Because of the interconnectedness of all minds,
affirming a positive vision may be about the most sophisticated action
any one of us can take.'*

WILLIS HARMAN (1918-1997)

■ *'Let us be of good cheer, remembering that misfortunes hardest to bear
are those that never come.'*

JAMES RUSSELL LOWELL (1819-1891)

■ *'Let's be optimistic.
Pessimism is for better times.'*

ANONYMOUS

Sustainable Abundance is not a forecast, but a possibility, a scenario that will follow the same format as the other scenarios described in Chapter 4. It assembles all the pieces of the puzzle identified up to this point. Sustainable Abundance will be explored through 'A Visit to the Stanford Campus'. This story highlights the role of three overlapping waves – a Value-Shift Wave, an Information Wave and a Money Wave – in creating Sustainable Abundance. In conclusion, the relationships between Sustainable Abundance and the other scenarios outlined earlier are analysed.

■ A Visit to the Stanford Campus

The other day, I was fiddling with some of the unfamiliar handles of the Time-Compacting Machine (Chapter One), and suddenly something quite unexpected happened. I ended up doing some accidental time travel to the campus of Stanford University on the first day of the academic year. Here is a report of what I found.

A Time Travel Report

The site was familiar – I could perceive the emblematic Hoover tower and the surrounding neo-Spanish buildings immersed in the atmosphere of excitement and hesitancy typical of large groups of first-day Freshmen milling around.

I went into the Economics Department building. A sign in the hallway in front of the first classroom door stopped me dead in my tracks. It read:

Fall Semester 2020

Ecosophy 101

That is when I started to suspect that I had somehow ended up in the future . . .

In the room, a very attractive mature woman was starting to lecture.

'Once upon a time people actually graduated with degrees such as Economics, Business Administration, Monetary Theory, Psychology, or even Sociology and Political Science without having a firm foundation in Ecosophy. It seems that at that time there was no awareness that this would be as dangerous as having a "Doctoral Degree in Stomachs" for example without any understanding about food, blood circulation or the nervous system.

'The origin of the word "ecosophy" is similar to the etymology of the words "ecology" and "economy".' She started writing with what looked like a small laser-light pen, and the text appeared simultaneously floating in the air a few feet in front of three walls. I thought 'some holographic laser technology: I am definitely in the future . . . ' Three neat columns of words appeared as follows:

Greek Roots	Contemporary Words	Initial Meaning
oikos = household	Ecosophy	Wisdom of the household
Sophia = Wisdom		
logos = knowledge	Ecology	Knowledge of the household
nomos = rule	Economy	Rules of the household

'Ecosophy is about how to live wisely on this planet. How our economic, monetary, business, political, sociological, psychological and ecological constructs and activities all interact and affect our collective presence on this planet. It constitutes the indispensable common foundation underlying any one of the fields of knowledge mentioned earlier. It looks at the human species within the context of the broader biosphere with which we are interdependent.

'Ecosophy is only one of the signs that our civilization has moved from Modernism to what we now call the Age of Integration. The main seeds for this shift can be traced to changes in interpretations of the physical universe which started over a century ago. Exactly like what happened with previous mutations in world-views – as for instance the Copernican revolution five centuries ago – it is the interpretation of the physical universe which has provided the leading indicator of a shift in civilization.

'For many centuries people had seen Mother Nature as an orderly extrapolation of the human mind. Descartes saw her as spiritless matter which could be apprehended only by analysis of smaller and smaller parts. Newton saw her as a well-behaved inert machine set in motion by God and driven by eternal laws, the knowledge of which would deliver her to our control. All this started to change when the theories of relativity, quantum physics of the first half of the century, and the theories of non-duality and complexity of the second half, became accepted as valid interpretations of reality. They provided the mental framework for our era. The works of Einstein, Heisenberg, Bohr, and later in last century Bohm, Feynman, Prigogine and the dozens of names involved in Chaos and Complexity theories were all key milestones in that process.

'The old metaphors of the world as a soulless machine with humans as separate "objective" observers have been replaced by a living and learning world with which humans communicate and share part of the responsibility for its evolution. Some say that we have been forced into this new world-view to be able to deal with global issues such as pollution, deforestation, climate changes or the weakening of the ozone layer.

'One key integration catalyst was also a paradox. It arose when one of the most Yang technologies of the entire Industrial Age – the computer – spawned for the first time a perfectly Yin space where such an integration could flourish without constraints. I am referring to the "cybersphere" which succeeded the old Internet. The paradox is even stronger when taking into account that all this was developed initially for the US military at the end of the Cold War. New synergies between the virtual world and the physical world gave rise to the Integral Economy.'

[As a reminder, the cybersphere is the virtual space where all earlier communications technologies such as telephone, TV, computers and payment systems converged into a coherent whole (Chapters 3 and 4). The concepts of Yin and Yang, and of the *Integral Economy* will be explained below.]

The professor continued: 'To understand the full scope of that process, a framework initially coined by the mid-20th-century anthropologist Teilhard de Chardin will prove useful.'

Suddenly a crisp diagram appeared as if floating in vibrant primary colours a few feet in front of all four white walls of the room. The professor moved in between the front graph and the wall. I became aware at that point that she seemed to address a larger audience than the students sitting in the class. 'Some form of distant learning technology' flashed through my mind.

- **Lithosphere** (from *lithos=stone*)
  - inert mass of planet Earth
- **Biosphere** (*bios = life*)
  - all life forms
  - from a few feet below surface to a few hundred feet in the atmosphere
- **Noosphere** (*nous=consciousness*)
  - field of consciousness generated by humanity
  - would evolve towards 'Point Omega'
- **Point Omega**
  - Consciousness of Unity of All that Is
  - (unknown final(?) destination of human evolution

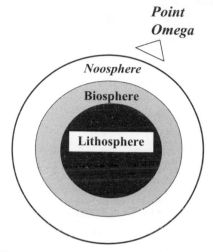

The vision of Teilhard de Chardin (mid-twentieth century)

She moved close to the diagram and commented, 'Teilhard got inspired by a little-known work entitled *The Biosphere* by V.I. Vernadsky, a Russian biologist of the 1920s. Teilhard generalized that concept by seeing the evolution of our planet in embedded "spheres". First the lithosphere which represents all the inert matter of this planet; then the biosphere which regroups all life-forms. It looks like a more or less dense "biomass-crust" around the inert matter, represented here in green. It is physically located in a thin layer including a few feet below and a few thousand feet above earth's surface, including the water and the lower reaches of the atmosphere for birds, airborne insects and micro-organisms. It is only during the 21st century that humans finally shed the illusion that they can disconnect from Nature. Only recently have they truly understood that there is only *one* life-form on earth – the biosphere – and that the entire human species plays a role similar to an organ in our own body.

'The next layer up, the noosphere, represented here in blue' – she pointed to an almost diaphanous zone in the graph – 'is more etheric. It is the space where all forms of consciousness interplay, including human consciousness. What Teilhard saw was that – as humanity became more conscious of its interdependence – it would also grow in the awareness of its Unity. He thought that the objective of human evolution would be what he called "Point Omega", a cosmic consciousness of Unity respectful of all diversity.

'However, what Teilhard did not see is *how* such a mysterious process could occur. Remember, he wrote his major works around the time of World War II and its aftermath. It is amazing that – under these circumstances – he could foresee even the direction of the next evolutionary step. Well, to us now the means by which this consciousness shift would accelerate has become obvious.'

She approached the diagram and touched the diaphanous edge between the biosphere and the noosphere circles, and it smoothly transformed into a vibrant violet edge so that the full diagram ended up as follows:

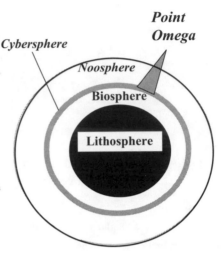

- **Lithosphere** (from *lithos=stone*)
  - inert mass of planet Earth
- **Biosphere** (*bios = life*)
  - all life forms
  - from a few feet below surface to a few hundred feet in the atmosphere
- **Noosphere** (*nous=consciousness*)
  - field of consciousness generated by humanity
  - would evolve towards 'Point Omega'
- **Point Omega**
  - Consciousness of Unity of All that Is
  - (unknown final(?) destination of human evolution
- **Cybersphere** = Virtual Space in which integration towards Point Omega is occurring

The vision of Teilhard de Chardin
Role of the Cybersphere

'The cybersphere is simply the link between Teilhard's noosphere and its destination, it is the virtual space in which human consciousness towards Integration has been able to manifest itself. It plays a role similar to the one the lithosphere has been playing for the biosphere. All life forms use inert chemical components of the lithosphere and reorganize them to create their physical life support systems. When computer technicians in the 20th century thought they were just creating a computer network, they were in fact creating an additional dimension and a new type of space.

'In retrospect, the last decades of the 20th century play a role similar to what biologist have called the Cambrian explosion. Five hundred and fifty million years ago a sudden mutation occurred in the biomass: single-cell life saw a burst of biological diversity and complex multi-cellular organisms proliferated. Hundreds of million years later, the emergence of photosynthesis, and later still the joint appearance of sexual reproduction and individual death were similar milestones. Evolution apparently undergoes such quantum transformations. From this perspective, life has entered digital space using humanity as a surrogate. In the cybersphere life is freed from the confines of slow molecular recombination, can travel at the speed of light, even off this planet as needed . . .'

I moved to the classroom next door, overhearing what appeared to be an introductory course in Economic History.

'During the early stone age, humans used the same tool for many different purposes: a broken stone fragment would be used for everything from killing prey to cleaning one's nails afterwards. During the 19th and 20th centuries there seems to have been a similar fixation with trying to use the same monetary tool – national currencies – for everything from global trade to paying for someone's education or for elderly care. To use another metaphor, this would be similar to assuming that the nervous system is the only information carrier in the human body, ignoring the role of the circulation of the blood, the lymphatic system and a wealth of biochemical links.

'This idea of "one fits all" in monetary systems finally had to be abandoned when information and nano-production technologies ensured that the majority of the population had no production-related "jobs". Today, less than 30% of the world's population still has full-time jobs of that type. This has freed the vast majority of the people to dedicate themselves instead to whatever they feel most passionate about – their "work" – mostly in their local or virtual communities. The old scarce national currencies had never been designed to support such an explosion of random creativity.

'Of course, many of the Industrial Age economic concepts such as Gross National Product (GNP) had to be revised. It originated as ways of measuring military potential in the earlier decades of the 20th century. Among other flaws, GNP measured only those activities which involved exchanges in national currencies. This led to increasingly strange anomalies. For instance, identical activities (e.g. someone taking care of a sick child) would be classified as "employed" and part of the GNP – or not – simply because in one case the carer was paid for the service in national currency and in the other she wasn't. This amounted to a straight denial of the reality of the actual service rendered for free.

'The old measures of GNP were still confusing crude growth with smart and wise growth. The Information Age objective of "Full Potential" has now replaced the Industrial Age idea of "full Employment". "Full Potential" refers to the use of someone's learning capacity and the opportunity fully to develop one's gifts. Just as was the case with Full Employment, one can never reach 100% of the Full Potential for a population.

'In retrospect, it was only by liberating the extraordinary potential of human creativity, of all humans, that there was any hope for Planet Earth. Human creativity was something which in past generations was the privilege of only a tiny minority: a few artists, scientists and some other members of the intelligentsia. Even on the basis of the old narrow definition of "employment" at least 700 million adults were routinely "jobless" on the planet in the 1990s. In terms of evaluating their "Full Potential" at the same time, estimates by our economic historians say that less than one per thousand of humanity reached it. They were considered rare "geniuses". Add to this the extraordinary fact that only two of the nine forms of intelligence were being recognized, and therefore developed and measured in the education system; i.e. the verbal/linguistic and the logical/mathematical, both with a *Yang* bias. The other seven forms of intelligence used to be simply ignored. So it was very rare that the development of a child took into account these other seven modes of learning : i.e. the musical, spatial, bodily/kinesthetic, intrapersonal, interpersonal, pattern recognition and mystical.[277]

'In short, human potential used to be dramatically underestimated, not to speak of developed and used to address our challenges. It is amazing that humanity made it as far as it did back in the 20th-century. From today's perspective it really looks as if our species was asked to engage in a race blindfolded with feet and hands bound. A 20th-century pioneer, Duane Elgin, claimed that humanity has always been at its best when its capacities are challenged to the maximum. We either radically and consciously changed toward sustainability in all domains, or we just would have to disappear like the great lizards did before us.

'The secret of the shift has been a succession of three waves which overlapped in time around the turn of the century. These three waves were:
– a Value-Shift Wave in which the old Modernist values were gradually commuted into the values of the Age of Integration;
– the Information Wave which enabled unprecedented access to knowledge for vast numbers of people;
– and the Money Wave whereby new money systems complemented the old national currency system.

'In the 1990s most people only were aware of the Information Wave. It was the one that the media focused on at that time. But in reality, all three mutations were in fact already well on their way if one was willing to peek beyond the reports from officialdom.

'Together, these three waves have given rise to accelerated change in our economic system, where the cyber economy has become what it is today: the largest and still the fastest-growing economy in the world. That is why the cybersphere is the best place to observe the current status of our monetary system. As you know, our continuously evolving money system operates simultaneously on different levels, ranging from the global to the local. The main advantage of such a multiple-level money system is that each type of activity is supported by the kind of currency best adapted to the circumstance. Convertibility among the different currencies is ensured on the Net whenever that is needed. These different systems interact as an organic whole, where each component continually evolves to adapt to the demands and opportunities of the environment in which it operates.

'Now let us see some of the main milestones which get us from the last century's quandaries to what is being hailed at the Age of Sustainable Abundance for humanity . . . '

Suddenly I saw the scene fading away in front of my eyes, and found myself in a daze back in our own time. Much to my great frustration, I may never know for sure how we got there . . .

Oh well, I should remain open to life's many surprises, I suppose . . .

The rest of this chapter provides the evidence supporting the claims of the professors of 2020, evidence that is already available in 1999.

■ Defining Sustainable Abundance

Sustainable Abundance was defined earlier as the characteristics of a society that satisfies its needs without diminishing the prospects of future generations, while simultaneously providing freedom of choice and creativity to as many people as possible (Chapter 4). Notice that humanity is bound willy nilly to reach *some day* at least one of the two components – sustainability. One can only argue over how much time that will take, whether it will be achieved by design or after a major breakdown, and whether conscious change can be mobilized for this purpose.

The planet itself is sustainable. The open question is whether it will include us.

Sustainability: A synthesis of views

Sustainability is a rallying cry for hope. It postulates that there can be a future design of society in which environmental degradation and extremes of social inequity are avoided on an ongoing basis. As an agenda, it implicitly calls for a sense of responsibility and action sincerely aimed at improving or changing our current way of living, and adverting what many feel is a looming social, ecological and economic crisis.

Global Business Network Report on Sustainability[278]

Sustainable development is growth in welfare without physical growth. It is a process and not a state, and therefore does not necessarily imply that the population or the economy are static or stagnant.

Brundtland Report: *Our Common Future*[279]

Former World Bank Economist Herman Daly[280] proposes three conditions for a society to be physically sustainable:

1   The rates of use of renewable resources do not exceed their rates of regeneration.
2   Its rates of use of unrenewable resources do not exceed the rate at which sustainable renewable substitutes are developed.
3   The rates of pollution emission do not exceed the assimilative capacity of the environment.

Biologists Paul and Anne Ehrlich[281] propose a simple equation showing the role of technology in reducing the overall ecological impact:

$$\text{Ecological Impact} = \text{Population} \times \text{Affluence} \times \text{Technology}$$

If Population doubles one last time over the next 50 years, and Affluence quadruples, then Technology needs to reduce the impact by at least 1/8 to maintain an impact similar to today.

What I am proposing here is that humanity reaches sustainability within a time span of one generation, rather than later (see sidebar). The monetary component of such a strategy aims at unleashing the extraordinary creativity of which humans are capable, and tapping the capacities of the technologies of abundance that are now becoming available. The strategy proposed would also avoid the massive suffering that a monetary collapse would entail. Taking some precautionary measures now will be infinitely cheaper than trying to repair damages later. A spare tyre may look useless most of the time, until one has a puncture in an awkward place . . .

Many people/organizations focus on either sustainability (e.g. the ecological movement) or abundance (e.g. the corporate world), but not both. Of course there are many activities where sustainability and abundance are genuinely in conflict. If you want an abundance of timber, you will have to cut more trees; if you have an abundance of cars, expect pollution and traffic jams. However, such intrinsic conflict is fortunately not valid in all domains. Specifically, the three waves described by the Stanford professor of 2020 happen to be activities where sustainability and abundance are not only compatible but synergistic.

That is why I became so curious to discover what is already visible now of what the Stanford professor of 2020 credited for the shift towards Sustainable Abundance. Here is a synthesis of the evidence I have found so far.

■ Towards an Integral Economy?

To begin, we should clarify some cryptic notions such as a Yin, Yang or an Integral Economy casually referred to by the professor of 2020. What can we discover now about these concepts?

A Taoist viewpoint: All is about balance

'Every explicit duality is an implicit unity.'

ALAN WATTS[282]

The first concept has been available for several millennia. It is the Taoist view of the available synergy when we cease to oppose polarities.

Our modern culture, our information sources, our values, even the words with which we communicate and think, always tend to polarize things. Whenever we make a distinction, 'it rests on an assumption of opposition and a logic of negation'.[283] For instance, in any Indo-European language when we think 'cold', we are automatically implying 'not warm' . The word 'health' means the absence of disease and so on.

The Taoists, in contrast, do not view opposites as inevitably mutually exclusive. For instance, their best-known polarity is Yin-Yang. We tend to translate this oriental concept as an expression of our familiar opposites. We, therefore, assume Yin-Yang to represent opposites: black or white, cold or warm, night or day, female or male, etc. Our normal interpretation is that black excludes the white, cold excludes warm, night is when it is not day, etc.

Taoists see Yin-Yang as *connected* to each other, as *necessary components to make the whole possible.* That is why they never refer to 'Yin *or* Yang', but always to 'Yin-Yang'. In this way, they point to the link between them rather than the space that separates them. Yin is black only to the extent that Yang is white. Yin is cold only to the extent that Yang is warm. Yin is night only to the extent that Yang is day, etc. This difference in world-view is subtle, but critical. The Taoists look at the whole at the same time as the parts. Each part exists only because of the interface they create in the whole. In contrast, we tend to take one part and oppose it to the other.

The same distinction is made in martial arts, where Eastern traditions talk about the 'soft eyes' which enable you to see at the same time your protagonist and the surroundings. Fly-fishing requires similar 'soft eyes' encompassing both the spot where the line is dropped and the entire river, in contrast with the 'hard eyes' used for bait-fishing where the focus remains only on the float. People who are good at bird or whale watching report exactly the same process. In short, Taoists are fly-fishing, while our very language tends to keep us stuck with bait-fishing (see sidebar on Lao-Tzu).

Lao-Tzu for the 21st century

Taoism was founded by the Chinese scholar Lao-Tzu, about whom very little hard historical facts are known. Tradition describes him as the curator of the emperor's Imperial Library some time in the 6th century BC. In his old age, he became disgusted with courtly chicanery, resigned from his respected post and decided to live as a recluse, leaving most of his belongings behind. He mounted a water buffalo to leave town when a gate guardian asked him whether he would please sum up all he had learned from a life spent with the best book collections of the Empire. Lao-Tzu is said to have written then on the spot the shortest treatise on good living in existence, the *Tao Te Ching,* totalling only 5,000 ideograms. (In fact, even this is now considered legendary, given that research has now proved that this text was written after the 5th century BC.)

It starts with 'The Tao that can be spoken is not the real Tao. The Name that can be named is not the Eternal Name.' In other words, he is saying that language is the first barrier that prevents us from knowing the Way. He insists on the importance of living in a balanced flow, on valuing both the feminine and masculine, on equality between men and women. He emphasizes intuition, relationship with Nature and silence.

Lao-Tzu was an elderly colleague of Confucius, then an earnest, ambitious young teacher. Confucius proposed that men should learn to control their desires first, their wives second and their children third. Confucius formalized the patriarchal family control system in China, emphasized hierarchy, intellectual pursuits through reason and scholarly reading of the classics. All this was exactly at the opposite end of Lao Tzu's world-view.

Chinese history has seen several alternations between Lao-Tzu's and Confucian priorities. The final switch occurred during the Sung dynasty – some 1,800 years after both founders' deaths – under the intellectual influence of the neo-Confucian scholar Chu Shi (AD 1130-1200). Confucianism won decisively to become the official social system in China from then on.

I propose that we now have more to learn from Lao-Tzu than from Confucius, at least for the transition period in which we are currently engaged.

For example, how many of you have read correctly the title of this section: 'All is about balance'. Have you automatically read 'it is all about balance', which has a different meaning? Or did you just decide that it was a typo?

If this text were written in Chinese ideograms, its readers would immediately understand what is referred to: the whole exists only because of the balance between the two parts. 'All is about balance' is illustrated by the classical T'ai Chi symbol (see Figure 9.4) where the black and white create a single whole through their balanced interaction. Notice that not only does each opposite shape the other, but that at the heart of each polarity, the opposite is also present (the little white dot in the black side of the symbol) (Figure 9.3).

On a lighter note, a similar point is made in the pun about a Buddhist monk requesting a food vendor: 'Make me one with everything.'

Figure 9.3: T'ai Chi Symbol

The point here is to illustrate the subliminal power of our language which automatically makes us read what we expect, rather than what is there. Our very words will automatically make us project and see polarities where, in fact, harmonious interaction may be present as well, or even predominantly present.

■ The Yin-Yang coherences

I will now integrate the Taoist vocabulary of Yin-Yang into economic systems. This aims not at exoticism, but is included because it is hoped that this terminology will remind us to think in holistic ways, instead of in the polarities which our Indo-European languages have embedded in our consciousness. Humans create coherence: they feel, think and perceive realities according to the coherence in which they live. For instance, a Yang coherence shapes thoughts, actions and emotions ranging from the perception of God and the world to daily minutiae. Figure 9.4 synthesizes some aspects of these Yin-Yang coherences. It can be read vertically to see each internal coherence, or horizontally to grasp what the Taoists would call the connective contrasts between the two world-views.

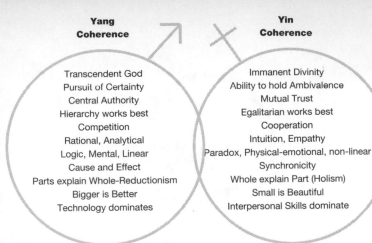

Yang Coherence	Yin Coherence
Transcendent God	Immanent Divinity
Pursuit of Certainty	Ability to hold Ambivalence
Central Authority	Mutual Trust
Hierarchy works best	Egalitarian works best
Competition	Cooperation
Rational, Analytical	Intuition, Empathy
Logic, Mental, Linear	Paradox, Physical-emotional, non-linear
Cause and Effect	Synchronicity
Parts explain Whole-Reductionism	Whole explain Part (Holism)
Bigger is Better	Small is Beautiful
Technology dominates	Interpersonal Skills dominate

Figure 9.4 Map of Yin-Yang Coherences

Modern societies have tended to acknowledge the legitimacy of only one of these polarities: the Yang coherence. This Yang coherence has been embodied in a patriarchal control system in all aspects of life – from organized religions to science, from military power and politics to day-to-day jokes. Specifically, our prevailing money system is saturated with these Yang values, and has been one of the main ways by which 'the real world' has been made to fit this viewpoint. What is being questioned here is not the validity of this Yang coherence, but its claim to a monopoly of valid interpretations.

In contrast, what is proposed is to take both concerns into account simultaneously. Notice that sustainability is coherent with the Yin coherence, while abundance is Yang. This is why the Taoist viewpoint – which always insists on proper balance between the two coherences – provides us with a useful framework. It can even contribute some handy economic distinctions concerning the different forms taken by capital.

	Yang	Yin
Non-material Level	Financial capital	Social capital
Martial Level	Physical capital	Natural capital

Traditional economics acknowledges the existence of only the two Yang forms of capital: financial capital (stocks, bonds, cash, and 'intellectual property' such as patents and trademarks); and physical capital (e.g. plant, equipment, inventions, real estate). It therefore ignores the role of the two forms of Yin capital: and social capital (e.g. family or group solidarity, peace, quality of life, etc.) and natural capital (e.g. clean water or air, biodiversity, etc.). This denial is remarkable, given that Yang capital would simply not survive without a continuous input from the Yin capital forms.

One sign of a shift in awareness is the growing talk about 'knowledge capital' – which is in fact a bridge between financial and social capital – and the discussions about 'green taxes' which aim at compensating for our blindness to the scarce resources obtained from the pool of Natural capital.

Finally, Taoist wisdom would warn us that the tendencies of a dominant Yang to suppress the other will be dangerous to the whole, and ultimately deadly harmful to the Yang itself.[138]

■ A map of complementary Yin-Yang currency types

One useful way to look at all the different currency systems described in this book is to classify them according to the strength of their Yin or Yang influence. The following table sets out the criteria applied to classify the different currency types that enables us to map them in Figure 9.5.

	Yang	Yin
Effects on Relationships	Scarce/Competition -inducing	Sufficient/Cooperation -promoting
Manner of Creation	'Fiat', created by a Central Authority	'mutual credit', created by the participants themselves

Just a reminder: 'fiat' currencies are by definition those that require a central authority to be created and maintained, and therefore require a Yang type hierarchy.

Mutual credit currencies in contrast are those created by the users themselves at the moment of a transaction, and are therefore more Yin in nature.

Figure 9.5 describes the resulting framework.

Complementary Roles of Different Currency Systems

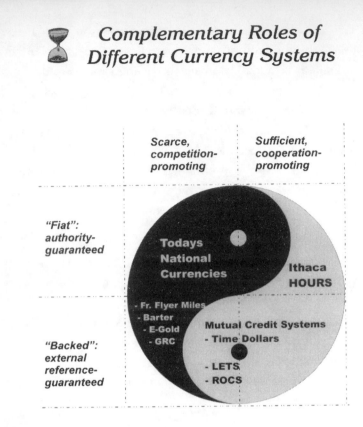

Figure 9.5 Map of Yin-Yang currency types.

Social capital is best nurtured by cooperation-inducing Yin currencies, while global industrial trade would be best handled by competition-generating Yang currencies. This graph also illustrates the way that each of these currency systems can complement the others.

Another way of using this map is by becoming aware of the way relationships will be shaped by the different monies used. Currency is always about relationships. All other things being equal, different kinds of currency will tend to induce different kinds of relationships among its users.

In groups where you want to create a cooperative, egalitarian, Yin type of relationship, use Yin type currencies. In contrast, trading with Yang currencies will tend to shape competitive, hierarchical relationships, perfectly appropriate for certain contexts like business. Both types of relationship have their appropriate role in everybody's life.

When reciprocity is built into the very process of currency creation, and when the currency is available in sufficiency – both conditions being fulfilled in mutual credit currency systems – the exchanges using this currency will tend to be more compatible with community creation (Chapter 6).

This logic is not to be taken to ridiculous extremes, like believing that it would be sufficient to give a Yin currency to a gang of murderers in order for them to transform into lambs. 'All other things being equal' is a relevant *caveat* here. However, how many apparently loving families do you know where competition for a scarce currency created havoc?

Integral Economy or Complementary Yin-Yang Economies

The concepts of Yin-Yang coherence (Figure 9.6) can now be overlaid with the competitive and cooperative economic circuits (Figure 5.2). This overlay produces the combination shown in Figure 9.8. It illustrates the potential role of a fully developed Yin economic cycle as a necessary complement to the traditional Yang economy. The graph illustrates how each perspective, the Yang or the Yin side of the economy, can be in Tarnas's words 'both affirmed and transcended, recognized as part of a larger whole; for each polarity requires the other for its fulfillment'. [205]

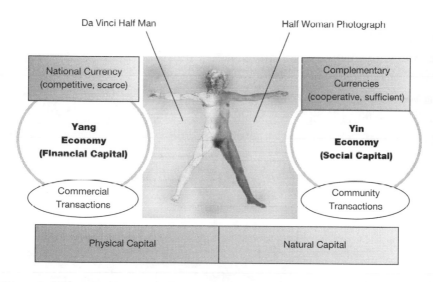

Figure 9.6 Integral Economics and the Yin-Yang Complementary Economic circuits

The human figure facing you at the centre of Figure 9.6 represents our collective energy, all of our economic activities. The circuit on its right-hand side (left on the image) is the Yang economy, fuelled by the conventional national currencies, which automatically generate competition among the participants as we have seen in the 'Eleventh Round' (Chapter 2). This is the dominant economy. To most economists, it is the *only* economic system. It recognizes physical capital, and aims at generating financial capital.

The circuit on its left side would include either the gift economies of yesterday, or the emerging cooperative community-building currencies of today. It acknowledges natural capital, and aims at generating social capital.

If it is true that the unemployment process in the Information Age has a structural component, I claim that it is in everybody's interest, including the participants in the Yang economy, to see a stronger development of the Yin economy through all means at our disposal, including the formal encouragement of complementary currencies; even through tax incentives. Why?

Remember the vicious circle of unemployment (Chapter 5)? When a growing number of people are structurally unemployed, they don't just disappear. They will either become 'economically irrelevant', and therefore a permanent potential source of violence and problems for the rest of society, which can be very expensive indeed (including 'pensions for life' in prisons). Or they will, as proposed by Jeremy Rifkin, be supported by taxes on the Yang economy (see Figure 9.7).

Either way, the Yang economy is shooting itself in the foot whenever it tries to stifle Yin type initiatives as it historically has tended to do. By blocking a Yin currency and economy, by insisting on a monopoly of Yang economy, the Yang economy also has to transfer resources via taxation to the Yin economy. From a Yin economy viewpoint, these transfers have proved invariably insufficient for the needs at hand. Would it not make more sense for both sides to enable a Yin economy to blossom fully with its own complementary currency in sufficiency?

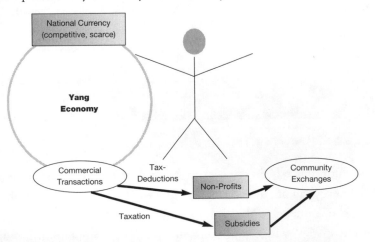

Figure 9.7 Classical approach within single currency framework

"Oh, come on back, Yin.
I was only kidding."

There is a growing awareness of the need for 'social capital' in a healthy society. Cooperative currencies are simply a tool to foster it. Exactly as the Yang cycle is the space where financial capital is taken care of, in the Yin cycle the social capital is being nurtured and developed. It is time to recognize that both types of capital – financial and social – are indispensable for human activity to flourish.

To summarize: the Integral Economy has as purpose to make available Integral Wealth. I therefore define wealth *not* as an accumulation of money. Integral Wealth is developed only when all four types of capital – natural, social, financial and physical – are in appropriate balance (see sidebar). By confusing wealth with only financial capital, we run the risk to believe that we can run down our natural or our social capital indefinitely. Below a certain level of natural or social capital, however, it is obvious that financial capital has no relevance any more: a huge bank account in a wasteland of social disorder or ecological collapse is meaningless and would soon become worthless.

Complementary currencies and wealth creation
A note for economists

When real estate was the main form of wealth, banks would issue money almost exclusively on the basis of collateral of land or buildings. Over the past 50 years, new forms of wealth have gradually been recognized and then used as a source of collateral. For instance, one can now borrow money for a university education, and the increased level of income that the graduate will get in the future is used as collateral for that loan. Note that even from a traditional economic viewpoint additional financial wealth is created in this process. The money issued on the basis of that future collateral enables exchanges to occur (i.e. economic activities) and investments to be made (i.e. an education) that would otherwise not occur.

What complementary currencies make possible is a similar additional wealth creation process: the recognition of another form of capital (social capital) is the implicit basis of mutual credit systems. The money is created by people who recognize each other's social capital, the 'backing' of mutual credit systems. This enables in turn exchanges to occur that otherwise would not happen, which means again that wealth is created, this time both financial wealth and social wealth. Furthermore, well-designed complementary currencies make it possible to engage in this process without creating inflationary pressures on the national currency itself.

Economic development can be defined as the capacity to transform resources into capital. In this sense, complementary currencies could become an important form of development.

■ The Three Waves towards Sustainable Abundance

Opportunities seem to come in bunches, like grapes or bananas. The three waves are indeed building on each other. The Value-Shift Wave has been until now largely unreported, but underlies the entire process. It provides the fuel for the mutation, while the Information and Money Waves contribute the technological means to unleash the necessary creativity.

Two important studies on Sustainability – *Beyond the Limits*[286] and the Global Business Network's 'Sustainability'[287] – have shown that both a value shift and technological shifts will be needed concurrently. After evaluating and modelling in detail the relationships between global resources, population, industrial output and pollution, the authors concluded:

> The potential for technological innovations only buys time – there is still a collapse, but it is delayed until the middle of the twenty-first century. Radical behavioral and attitudinal changes are explored too, but it turns out that these alone are not enough either – there is *still* a crash in the mid twenty-first century. It is only when both these kinds of changes are applied together that a crash is avoided.[288]

It is precisely such a combination which is in fact already happening today.

■ 1. The Value-Shift Wave

'First they ignore you;
Then they ridicule you;
Then they attack you;
Then you win.'

MAHATMA GANDHI

The most detailed data set about changes in values over the past 20 years relates to the US. But there are preliminary indications that this process is in fact going on in the entire Western world, and possibly even globally.

Paul Ray has carried out the largest up-to-date surveys of the changes in values over the past 20 years. These surveys covered scientific samples of 100,000 Americans, and were further refined with over 500 focus groups. This included a benchmark study in December 1994, focusing on emerging new values among a representative national sample of the American population.[289] It has provided an invaluable set of hard data about the current state of values in that country. Ray found that there are in fact three subcultures cohabiting in the US today. Each is a different world of meaning, and has its own world-view. They are respectively the 'Traditionalists', the 'Modernists' and the 'Cultural Creatives'.

Here is a thumb-nail sketch of each:

The 'Traditionalists' are the religious conservatives, Pre-Modern, about 29% of the population and shrinking in relative importance since World War II, with a slight higher density in the Midwest. Until recently they used to share the scene only with the next group: the Modernists.

The 'Modernists': the dominant subculture embodying the official 'Western Way of Life', dropping from a triumphant majority in the 1950s down today to 47% of the US population (88 million adults). It is the viewpoint that has shaped the Industrial Age. But even as their percentages slowly fall over time, the Modernist viewpoint remains exclusively the one reflected in mass media.

Historically, Modernism developed during the Renaissance in reaction to the 'Traditionalist' societies, as a rejection of the religion-dominated world-view which had been the almost exclusive viewpoint until that time. It therefore considers as 'modern' (treated as synonymous with 'sophisticated,

advanced, urbane and/or inevitable') the values, technologies and interpretations which oppose themselves to the 'backward', 'under-developed'
societies which preceded it. The Modernists kept intact, however, one of the
key premises of the previous religion-dominated world-view: the biblical
premise that 'Man is to be Master over the rest of creation'.

The 'Cultural Creatives': the only group growing in numbers over the
past decades. While they were still statistically undetectable 20 years ago
(less than 3%), they now represent 23.6% of the population (44 million
adults in the US). Figure 9.8 shows the relative growth in numbers of this
subculture compared to the others.

(millions of adults, US, 1965-2000)

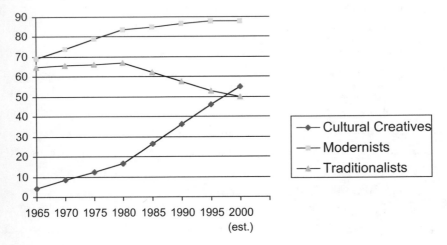

Figure 9.8 Relative growth of the three subcultures (US, 1965-2000)

This is a historically extraordinary shift in values in less than one
generation. It is this last subculture that constitutes the Value-Shift Wave
referred to by the 2020 professor. Therefore more details will be provided
about their world-view and current status. It will be shown later that this
trend may actually be a global one.

World-view of the Cultural Creative subculture

Exactly as the Modernist view developed in reaction to what was considered
the over-simplifications and excesses of the religion-dominated world-view

of the late Middle Ages, the Cultural Creative subculture has emerged in reaction to the blindness and excesses of the Modernist tradition.

At the personal level, their main concern is self-actualization, i.e. inner growth, as opposed to exterior social prestige.

At the collective level one of their main concerns is the deterioration of the community and the environment (92% want to rebuild community; 87% believe in ecological sustainability).

What is surprising?

The size of the numbers of Cultural Creatives which have appeared out of the woodwork in less than one generation may be surprising to many. It certainly surprised me. Even people who are part of this subculture consider themselves to be isolated exceptions.

Two reasons converge to create that impression of isolation:
– there is no organization that identifies them;
– there is no media mirror.

NO ORGANIZATION

One of the main reasons for its relative invisibility is that this subculture has not spawned a mass political party, a mass religious movement, or even a separately identifiable publication market. Cultural Creatives are by definition eclectics who pick and choose as their interests lead them, from mainstream to marginal publications, national as well as foreign. So there is no place or group where they can actually meet and be counted.

NO MIRROR

Even more important, the mass media and the political debate, our mirrors in society, are still completely immersed in the Modernist subculture, and almost exclusively reflect that viewpoint. Whenever they refer to the subculture of the Cultural Creatives, they tend to present as typical a caricature of the whole group: the marginal fringe of 'New Agers', who represent less than 2% of the population (four million adults). So even when this is reflected, the majority of the 44 million Cultural Creatives do not recognize themselves in this image either.

This invisibility – even to the members themselves – may be the most unusual feature of this new subculture.

When Modernism came into fashion from the Renaissance onwards, the 'Modernizers' knew very well that they were a movement. Erasmus of

Rotterdam and the French Encyclopaedists had the media of their respective times focusing on every one of their doings. They were known as a movement by others, and they also knew each other. All of this was true even as they represented only 1% or 2% of the population in their time, compared to 24% that the Cultural Creative subculture represents today. So whenever the socio-political reality of these trends finally sinks in, we can expect a much swifter shift than when Modernism was born.

'Green' and 'Integrative' Cultural Creatives

Ray goes on by distinguishing between two types of Cultural Creatives: the 'Green' Cultural Creatives and the 'Core' ones.

- Green Cultural Creatives (13% or 24 million in the US) are concerned with the environment and social concerns from a secular viewpoint. They tend to be activists in the public arena. They focus on solving problems 'out there' and are less interested in personal change.
- Core Cultural Creatives (10.6% or 20 million in Ray's survey) have both personal evolution and green values. They are seriously engaged in psychology, spiritual life, self-actualization, self-expression. They enjoy mastering new ideas and are concerned socially and interested in ecological sustainability. Two out of three Core Cultural Creatives are women, and explain the importance of 'women's issues' in contemporary debates.

The Cultural Creatives: A global shift?

No detailed survey similar to Paul Ray's has covered the entire globe. However, in September 1997 the secretariat of the European Union used Ray's values questionnaire identifying Cultural Creatives in its monthly *Euro-Barometer* survey of all 15 nations (800 interviews per country) and found to its surprise that the percentage of Cultural Creatives is as high in Europe as in the US.

In another study by Duane Elgin, all data available globally further indicate that this shift is in fact a global phenomenon. His conclusion: 'considered together, trends do seem to indicate that a global paradigm shift is underway.'[144] The global population at large is everywhere ahead in the transition compared to both their official leaders and their media. For instance, a majority worldwide gives priority to protecting the environment over economic growth (see Graph A of Figure 9.9), and are willing to pay higher prices to do so (Graph B). There is also a growing majority – stridently contested by fundamentalists everywhere – that women and men should have equal opportunities, and that having more women involved in political office would improve the general situation (Graph C). What is perhaps most striking is that this trend prevails almost as strongly in developing countries as in developed ones.

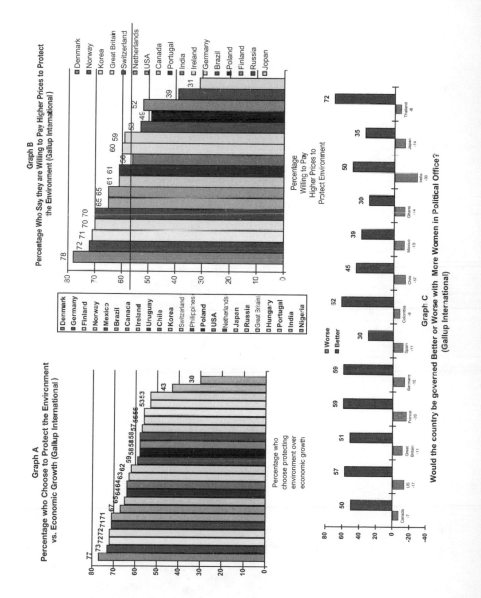

Figure 9.9 Some global indicators of Integrative Value shifts

Elgin reports also another interesting and under-reported indicator: a shift toward holistic medicine, away from the Modernist conventional medicine. In a 1993 study 'Unconventional medicine in the United States' published in the *New England Journal of Medicine*[291] Dr Eisenberg concluded that unconventional therapy in the US is far higher than previously reported. There were actually *more* visits to US providers of unconventional therapy than visits to all primary care physicians (425 million visits to 388 million visits). Another study published in the *Journal of the American Medical Association (JAMA)* in 1998 found that the trend further accelerated since that time, doubling the out-of-pocket expenses on alternative medicine to between $27 and $34 billion per year. Responding to this shift in consumer demand, 64% of US medical schools now offer courses in what used to be described as alternative medicine. Most significant, these medical practices are now becoming acknowledged as complementary to the conventional Western medicine.

In Europe, the trend for doctors to include complementary medicine is 'overwhelming' according to a *Time* magazine article: 'Out of 88,000 practicing acupuncturists in Europe, 62,000 are medical doctors.'[292] In Britain, 42% of all doctors routinely make referrals to homeopaths. In France, one third of all family doctors prescribe homeopathic remedies, as do 20% of all German doctors. In most European chemists, there is now at least as much shelf-space dedicated to herbal medicines as to pharmaceutical drugs. In Asia, scientific and public health interest in acupuncture had already started in the 1950s. More recently other traditional approaches such as the Ayur-Vedic medicine are growing in popularity, again as complement to Western Modernist techniques.

In short, each one of these trends separately is often dismissed as a 'quirk' or an insignificant 'fashion' by Modernist opinion leaders. However, when considered together, the pattern reveals a major shift towards a re-honouring of Yin values in all aspects of society. It affects all domains. The pattern includes such disparate phenomena as the growing concerns about the environment, holistic health practices; chaos theory in physics, the replacement of hierarchical structures with networks (such as the Internet and virtual organizations); the bridging the Cartesian split between matter and spirit, and the women's emancipation movement.

These shifts can be observed in men and women alike. But again, the most striking of all is that in each of these domains the pattern is repeated, while the meaning of the whole is missed. Thereby the significance, the speed and the scale of this mutation is often missed.

■ 2. The Information Wave

This is the one wave which does not require us to look below the radar beams: all mainstream media channels are saturated with news about it. No further explanations about it are therefore necessary, beyond what was already discussed earlier (Chapter 3). Suffice it to remember that the 'cybersphere' was defined as the ideal space where the Money Wave will be able to develop fully.

■ 3. The Money Wave

This entire book is about this third wave. This 'Money Wave' has been chronicled here as the birth of currency systems which complement the official national currency system. Our official money system was shown to be an extreme Yang construct and the monopoly of such currency has locked our societies into an extreme Yang value system. What is proposed here in Taoist medical terminology is 'to calm the Yang and activate the Yin'. Pragmatically, the Global Reference Currency is a device that would 'calm the Yang', and the activation of local complementary currencies a means to 'activate the Yin'.

The ongoing money innovations are more compatible with cooperative, feminine-type interactions. Far from being anecdotal curiosities, these new money systems turn out to be an integral part of the broad societal Value-Shift Wave described above. Seen from this perspective, these currency innovations fit into the general shift towards Yin priorities highlighted earlier which includes changes in the paradigms in science to in medicine, politics and gender relations.

I claim that if we make available to people stable currencies in sufficiency, they will move towards Sustainable Abundance as predictably as water flows downhill.

How the 'Money Wave' could pragmatically play itself out in a multiple-level currency system will be described in the next section.

■ A monetary system for Sustainable Abundance

This section will deal with the details of the monetary system that would best support Sustainable Abundance. To traditional monetary thinking, one currency per country has always appeared adequate. Therefore a multi-level system would be criticized for its undue complexity and inefficiency. This criticism will be answered first, followed by a portrayal of how the different levels of currencies could fit together in 2020.

Yap Islanders in Fort Knox

Milton Friedman noticed an intriguing parallelism between the 'primitive' currency system of the Yap Islanders and our contemporary one.

In 1903 an American anthropologist named William Henry Furness III was so fascinated by the money system of the Uap or Yap island – one of the Caroline Islands in Micronesia and at the time a small German colony of about five thousand people – that he entitled his book *The Island of Stone Money* (1910). 'Their medium of exchange they call *fei,* and it consists of large, solid, thick, stone wheels, having at the center a hole varying in size with the diameter of the stone, wherein a pole may be inserted sufficiently large and strong to bear the weight and facilitate transportation. These stone 'coins' were made from limestone found on an island some four hundred miles distant. They were originally brought to Yap by some venturesome native navigators, in canoes and on rafts . . . After concluding a bargain which involves the price of a *fei* too large to be conveniently moved, the new owner is quite content to accept the bare acknowledgment of ownership and without so much as a mark to indicate the exchange, the coin remains undisturbed on the former owner's premises.

'When the German Government assumed the ownership of the Caroline Islands in 1898, many of the paths were in bad condition, and the indigenous people were told to repair them. Some refused, and it was decided to impose a fine on the disobedient districts. The fine was exacted by sending a man who marked some of the most valuable *fei* with a cross in black paint to show that the stones were claimed by the government. This worked like a charm; the people, thus dolefully impoverished, turned to and repaired the highways to good effect. Then the government dispatched its agents and erased the crosses. Presto! The fine was paid, the happy islanders resumed possession of their capital stock, and rolled in wealth.'[293]

In 1932-33 and again in 1971, the Banque de France (the French central bank) asked the Federal Reserve to change some of its excess dollars into gold. This would mean in practice simply replacing some of the 'Federal Reserve' labels at Fort Knox with 'Banque de France' labels. This was described in US financial newspapers as 'loss of gold', the markets considered the dollar as weaker, the French franc as stronger.

Milton Friedman asks: 'Is there really a difference between the Federal Reserve Bank's believing that it was in a weaker position because of some marks on drawers in its basement and the Yap islanders' belief that they were poorer because of some marks on their stone money? The Yap islanders regarded as a concrete manifestation of their wealth stones quarried and shaped on a distant island and brought to their own. For a century and more, the civilized world regarded as a concrete manifestation of wealth a metal dug from deep in the ground, refined at great labor, transported great distances, and buried again in elaborate vaults deep in the ground. Is the one practice really more rational than the other?'[294]

■ Why a multi-level currency system?

The criticism of 'undue complexity' is valid only if habit makes us overlook the inefficiencies and complexities of the money system of 1999. This system involves some 170 different national currencies, disorganized in eight different types of monetary systems according to the IMF's own reports.[149] In any case, the record of the post-Bretton Woods monetary *modus vivendi* is clearly unsatisfactory.

> During the nearly three decades since the demise of the Bretton Woods arrangements, the annual rate of economic growth in developed countries has fallen by a third, and the incidents of international financial crises have increased sharply – to the point where even countries that follow sound economic policies are often stricken along with the profligate. According to figures cited by the World Bank no fewer than 69 countries have endured serious banking crises since the late nineteen-seventies, and 87 nations have seen runs on their currency since 1975.[296]

It is also likely that seen from a longer-term historical perspective some of the features of our prevailing money system will be seen as strange anomalies. (See sidebar on Yap Islanders in Fort Knox).

Organizational requirements

The fundamental monetary shift that is needed is an organizational one. The proposal here is that in addition to the command-and-control hierarchical (Yang) national money systems, more flexible, open, adaptive systems (Yin) should be allowed to develop during the post-Industrial transition period we have now entered. The reasons for this are best understood by comparing the characteristics of a mature industrial society with a post-Industrial one, as in the table.

Old Environment (Mature Industrial Age)	*New Environment (Post-Industrial Age)*
Predictability and Control Assumed	Fundamental Structural Changes Assumed
Intelligence and Information Centralized	Intelligence and Information Distributed
Expert-driven solutions	Many agents experimenting with new patterns
Command and Control Structures	Complex Adaptive Structures

As long as the assumption was valid that we are living in an environment which is both predictable and controllable (both key Yang assumptions), it made sense to centralize information and leave the decisions to 'experts'. The most coherent management structure in such circumstances is the traditional command and control hierarchical structure, which is now almost ubiquitous. However, as breakdowns and crises spread to many domains (e.g. global monetary system, government, education, environment, jobs, etc.) if the transition towards an information economy becomes indeed an 'Age of Uncertainty'[151] – then the time is ripe to reconsider the old organizational assumptions. Under such circumstances, holding on to the old expert-driven, hierarchical command and control structures will predictably kill the very innovations that the circumstances require.

Tony Judge, whom Alvin Toffler described as 'one of our most brilliant organization theorists', claims that the organizations of the future will take the form of 'networks not coordinated by anybody; the participating bodies coordinate themselves'.

The first large-scale contemporary implementation of such principles was accomplished by Dee Hock, when he founded the VISA credit card system in the 1970s.[298] VISA has grown spectacularly to become the largest business organization in the world: it has a sales volume of $1.3 trillion per year and serves 600 million clients. And yet can you tell where its headquarters are? Or on which stock market you can buy its shares? The surprising answer is that it has *no* headquarters or stock available anywhere. And yet it works efficiently, and has grown to a staff of 3,000 in 21 offices on four continents. It is structured as an alliance among over 20,000 financial institutions in more than 200 countries and territories. It is a structure where all relevant decision-making flows through the entire system rather than only from the top. Dee Hock calls it the first business 'chaord' (a term he coined to describe an organization that is both 'chaotic' and 'orderly'). 'Show me the Chairman of the Board of the forest, show me the chief financial fish in the pond, show me' (tapping his head) 'the Chief Executive neuron of the brain.'[299]

It is indeed true that all this is not applicable just to monetary or business matters. The work pioneered by the Santa Fe Institute on complex adaptive systems has verified these principles in all types of systems (physical, biological, social, economic, etc.) which are reaching a certain level of complexity. Complexity theory predicts that contrary to Newtonian logic, complexity does not grow linearly, but occurs in non-linear jumps in episodic stages of 'surfing at the edge of chaos'. These 'near-chaos' periods are when systems regenerate and restructure at the next level of complexity, according to Nobel Prize-winners Ilya Prigogine.

I believe we have now started to 'surf at the edge of chaos', that the current crisis of the dominant institutions of modern society is the sign that humanity has started to reorganize at the next level of complexity (see sidebar on the butterfly metaphor). This is why we are now in the transition period, the period 'in between stories' of the Time-Compacting Machine of Chapter 1.

The butterfly metaphor

The biology of the metamorphosis of a caterpillar into a butterfly has been used by Norie Huddle as a metaphor for our times.[300] When the caterpillar starts its metamorphosis, special cells – called imaginal cells – literally dissolve from within the body of the caterpillar into an amorphous-looking liquid. Then these imaginal cells start inter-connecting with each other, building new networks; and they end up restructuring the whole into the miracle of the butterfly

Modern civilization has now entered the dissolution phase, and the imaginal cells have started interconnecting outside the traditional communication channels by using the cybersphere. Sustainable Abundance is the butterfly, an available outcome as originally described in the 'Four Seasons of 2020' (Chapter 1)

The major danger in the monetary field is that some of the spontaneously emerging new monetary levels will be blocked off (historically the most likely one is the local one, because it is the easiest to stamp out), while others will be left to thrive (e.g. private corporate currencies, because they are beyond the control capacity of individual central banks). Such an outcome would perpetuate the imbalance towards Yang currencies and values in our economic system, just when a Yin influx is needed. Traditional command and control structures may not be able to avoid the chaos in the existing old order, but one should not underestimate their power to choke off embryonic attempts at a new order.

Beyond 2020?

In the long run – some time after 2020 – I expect that new economic and governance structures will emerge at the next order of complexity, and that a new era of predictable patterns will return. Other monetary systems than the ones described in this book will most likely be necessary at that point. Maybe at some time in the future we will not need money at all. If we believe Jean-Luc Godard of *Star Trek* fame, 'money does not exist in the 24th century'. Meanwhile, I think we will need transitional money systems, which can be used as crutches to re-educate atrophied collective behaviour patterns.

My purpose in this book has been to focus only on these transitional money systems appropriate for the phase we have already entered. And the main point bears repetition: during the current transition period a lot of violent disruption and pain can be avoided by encouraging social experimentation, by letting embryonic forms have a chance to thrive, by allowing them to reproduce in new patterns which have already proved effective at dealing with structural change in other parts of the world. This is the way nature has been doing it successfully for five billion years. Can we afford not to learn from it?

What follows next is a description of the development of a four-level monetary system. One already exists – the conventional bank-debt national currency system. The development of the three new money systems is synthesized in three timetables, revealing that the emergence of these new systems is in fact an organic development of trends which have been prevailing for decades, each pushed by its own logic. In parallel to these three new levels, it is assumed that the conventional national currency systems will be able to operate roughly as they do today. The only significant difference is that they are not any more perceived as the only game in town.

■ The monetary system of 2020: a four-level gear box

Let us imagine that we are living in 2020. Almost all corporations and many individuals are dealing routinely in currencies at different levels. For a small transaction fee, it has become very simple to exchange any of these currencies for most others somewhere on the Net. Just as with today's frequent-flyer miles, mixed payments are common (you can buy a ticket in national currency and pay for an upgrade in frequent-flyer miles).

The four levels operational in 2020 would be the following:
– A Global Reference Currency
– Three main Multinational Currencies
– Some National Currencies
– Local Complementary Currencies

1 A Global Reference Currency

Several corporate scrips are competing on the Net, issued by the likes of Amex, Microsoft, and an alliance of European and Asian corporations. Some have created special subsidiaries – with strong and liquid balance sheets – to issue these currencies and provide them with stronger credibility. One such currency has taken the form of a Global Reference Currency as described in Chapter 8, and arose from a systematization of corporate barter.

Barter – the exchange of goods or services without the use of any currency – has been around since the dawn of mankind. Because of this, barter has often been seen as an 'inferior' or 'primitive' form of exchange, sometimes associated with the underground economy. All this has completely changed over the past decades, and the barter industry has now two major trade organizations, the International Reciprocal Trade Association (IRTA, website www.irta.net) and the Corporate Barter Council (CBC).

What follows is the timetable of the growth of both barter and the cyber economy, and how their convergence created a corporate-initiated Global Reference Currency (all data until 1999 inclusive is actual, and is projected thereafter).

Emergence of a Global Corporate Scrip (1960-2020)

1960s: Development of large-scale professional barter by Western corporations with the Comecon ('Communist Bloc') countries.

1970s: Extension of barter to Less Developed Countries whenever 'hard currencies' are in scarce supply.

1974: In the US, 100 small barter exchanges facilitate trade valued at $45 million, among 17,000 corporations.

1980s: Generalization of barter in international exchanges, as consequence of the Latin American debt crisis.

1982: The US Congress recognizes barter as a legitimate domestic commercial process, and sets up reporting requirements. All barter income is treated as normal income by the IRS.

1990s: Expansion of barter within all developed countries. In parallel, Internet commerce starts taking off.1997: Alan Greenspan, Chairman of the Federal Reserve Board, gives implicit OK to corporate currency initiatives: 'If we wish to foster financial innovation, we must be careful not to impose rules that inhibit it.'[301] The cyber economy is estimated at $35.6 billion per year.

1998: In the US no fewer than 400,000 businesses are members of 686 barter exchanges, totalling a volume of $8.5 billion in domestic exchanges. Annual growth rate is 15%, three times faster than commercial exchanges facilitated by dollars.

1999: Internet traffic doubles every 100 days.

2000: The cyber economy reaches $200 billion per year, about half of which is between corporations. Barter business starts moving onto the Net, and begins to merge with the cyber economy.

2001: Standardization of barter contracts by some corporations.

2002: Internet commerce among businesses alone reaches $300 billion.[302]

2003: Several private corporate scrips compete to establish their brands in cyberspace.

2005: In the US 1.6 million businesses engage in barter transactions totaling $31 billion.[303]

2006: A 'chaordic' alliance among international corporations uses a standardized Global Reference Currency called the Terra which includes a demurrage feature.

2007: 20% of all US retail trade has been displaced towards the Net, other cyber-active countries are following the same trend (similar to but much faster than the postwar spread of US-style supermarkets and mall distribution systems around the world).

2015: Global Reference Currency becomes an optional legal accounting standard for multinational corporations.

2020: The cyber economy has become the largest economy in the world. Private business scrip (including Terra) is involved in 50% of all international trade.

2   Three multinational currencies

After the euro replaced the national currencies in eleven European countries in 1999, the British and other European holdouts joined the system a few years later. This built up an irresistible pressure to create an Asian Yuan Currency zone, and finally a NAFTA dollar. It has indeed become obvious that regional economic integration can reach maturity only when a single currency levels the playing field for all economic participants. A single currency is the only way structurally to guarantee a unified information field.

What follows is the history of the creation of the three major multinational currency systems by the year 2020. Note that all these multinational currencies are conventional bank-debt currencies, their only distinction from the previous national currencies is their use over a wider geographical area than one single country.

Emergence of multinational integration currencies (1958-2020)

1958: Treaty of Rome starts the European 'Common Market' unification process, creating a free trade zone for six countries (Germany, France, Italy, Belgium, The Netherlands and Luxembourg).

1960: Stockholm Convention starts the European Free Trade Association (EFTA), spearheaded by the United Kingdom and including Austria, Denmark, Norway, Portugal, Sweden and Switzerland.

1967: Bangkok Declaration regroups five ASEAN countries (Indonesia, Malaysia, Philippines, Singapore and Thailand).

1973: The UK and several other EFTA countries join the six initial Treaty of Rome countries.

1978: Announcement by German Chancellor Schmidt and President Giscard d'Estaing of France of the need for a 'zone of monetary stability' in Europe.

1979: Creation of the European Currency Unit (ECU) as a monetary convergence and integration tool, and as an intra-European accounting and payment unit. Twelve countries are involved.

1984: Brunei joins ASEAN.

1992: 'Maastricht Treaty' commits Europe to a single currency by the turn of the century in what has now become the 'European Union' (EU).

1995: Vietnam joins ASEAN.

1996: Formation of the North American Free Trade Association (NAFTA), a free trade zone regrouping the US, Canada and Mexico.

1997: Laos and Myanmar join ASEAN. Japan proposes a $100 billion Asian Monetary Fund, separate from the IMF; this proposal is blocked by the US and the UK.

1999: The ECU is replaced formally by the euro, a single European currency with a core group of eleven countries. Mercosur (Brazil, Argentina, Uruguay and Paraguay) starts NAFTA negotiations.

2001: Chile joins NAFTA. Several additional European countries join the euro-zone.

2003: ASEAN formally announces the intent to create a single Asean Yuan currency zone. Japan and China become associate members of the Yuan currency project.

2004: Post-Castro Cuba and several other Latin American countries join NAFTA.

2005: The last European holdout, Britain, joins the euro after a hotly debated referendum.

2007: Taiwan peacefully joins China under a 'one country, one currency, several systems' principle.

2010: Single Yuan currency zone operational. Several additional Asian countries join the initial core group.

2012: Formation of the NAFTA dollar zone.

2020: Tripartite Treaty of economic cooperation between the three major free trade zones. (European Union, ASEAN and NAFTA).

3 Some national currencies

In many countries, national currencies will still be used for a long time. They continue to play an important role within any country that has not joined a formal multinational currency integration system. Most exchanges continue to involve national currencies at least in partial payments, if for no other reason than that they remain the official 'legal tender' with which national taxes are paid.

The main difference from the past is that national currencies do not maintain their totally monopolistic role as means of payment. Many payments are mixed – involving both national currencies, corporate scrips or Internet currencies in a single transaction.

The only places where the national currencies have kept intact their old monopoly are a few underdeveloped countries, such as Albania and a few other backward dictatorships, where the priority given to political control over the Net has kept the cyber economy completely out.

4 Local complementary currencies

This last level, the local one, has been the topic of Chapters 5 and 6. In reaction to economic globalization and running parallel to it, self-organization at the local level has become very popular. The Information Revolution also meant a systematic reduction of production and service-related 'jobs'. As jobs grew scarcer, communities created their own currencies to facilitate local exchanges among their members.[304] Once critical mass was attained, complementary currency clearing houses on the Net made it possible for members of these communities to participate in the cyber economy as well.

The following table projects its future growth beyond 1999.

Emergence of complementary currencies (1936-2020)

1936: Creation of the oldest currently still surviving complementary currency system: 'WIR' in Switzerland. (By 1997 its membership reaches 80,000 and annual trade volume $2 billion, demonstrating the potential scale of mature complementary currency systems.)

1982: Implementation of first postwar LETS (Local Exchange Trading System) in high unemployment areas in Canada.

1987: Creation of Time Dollars by Edgar Cahn in Florida, Chicago and Washington DC.

1990: IRS gives tax-free status to Time Dollar exchanges.

1992: Creation of Ithaca HOURS, first postwar 'fiat' complementary currency. Total number of local currency systems of all types reaches 200 worldwide.

1990s: Age of corporate downsizing begins, rapid expansion of number of complementary currency systems particularly in New Zealand, Australia, UK, Germany, France. The New Zealand central bank discovers that complementary currencies help to reduce inflation pressures on the national currency.

1993: Missouri first US state to use Time Dollars to fund its welfare system.

1995: Complementary currency systems top 1,000 worldwide.

1996: The US Federal welfare programmes are decentralized to state level.

1997: Thirty different US states start over 200 Time Dollar systems to foster 'self-help welfare'. Also, by private initiative, another 40 different Ithaca HOUR systems operational in the US.

1998: Minneapolis, Minnesota, experiments with the first dual-currency smart-card payment system (dollar and a local complementary currency).

1999: Experiments with a decentralized smart-card complementary currency system in Vancouver, Canada. More than 2,000 systems operational in a dozen developed countries.

2000: Complementary Currency Clearing House (CCCH) operational on the Net.

2003: European welfare reform, officially incorporating complementary currencies as a community development tool.

2008: Complementary currency systems top 10,000 for the first time worldwide.

2020: Complementary currencies represent 20% of total domestic trade in the most advanced countries.

There are of course countries around the world which have forcefully maintained the monopoly of national currencies, and turned their back to the new possibilities offered by the Money Wave and the cyber economy. The results of this are similar to what happened to countries – like China – that chose to block the development of railways during the early Industrial Revolution. They delayed the Industrial Revolution by almost a century, but at great cost to their population and their influence in the world. They became the 'Less Developed Countries' (LDCs) of the 20th century. Today, people are similarly choosing who will become the 'Information Deprived Countries' (IDCs) of the 21st century.

Knowing the monetary system which would best support Sustainable Abundance, we can now fully understand what was underlying the vignettes of 'The Four Seasons of 2020' (Chapter 1), as well as the four scenarios (Chapter 4). Both will now be briefly revisited.

■ The Four Seasons of 2020 revisited

This book started with a description of a Time-Compacting Machine and four vignettes which captured the possibilities offered by Sustainable Abundance in people's lives by the year 2020. They were synthesized as in Figure 9.10.

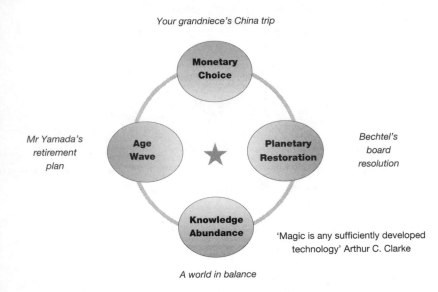

Your grandniece's China trip

Monetary Choice

Mr Yamada's retirement plan

Age Wave

Planetary Restoration

Bechtel's board resolution

Knowledge Abundance

'Magic is any sufficiently developed technology' Arthur C. Clarke

A world in balance

Figure 9.10 The four vignettes of Sustainable Abundance in 2020

At that time, I acknowledged that some of these stories may have appeared as 'magic', unreal fairy tales for adults. By now, the monetary technologies which underlie each one of these 'magic' stories have been demystified.

Both 'Mr Yamada's Retirement Plan' and 'A World in Balance' are the result of the sufficient availability of stable, Yin currencies.

The 'Bechtel Board Resolution' is the result of the use of a demurrage-charged Global Reference Currency as a standard accounting and planning tool by major global corporations.

Finally, 'Your Grandniece's China Trip' describes a world in which the Integral Economy, involving both Yin and Yang type currencies in appropriate balance, is taken for granted.

An Integral Economy would see these various currencies operate in ways complementary for each other. It would improve the quality of life even for those who choose to keep strictly to traditional industrial age 'jobs'. It would encourage the attitudes that Robert D. Haas, the CEO of Levi Strauss, forecasts: 'The most visible differences between the corporation of the future and its present-day counterpart will not be the products they make or the equipment they use, but who will be working, why they will be working, and what work will mean to them.'

The image that comes to mind is that during the Industrial Age we have become accustomed to a monetary toolbox with one single tool: a screwdriver. Now, screwdrivers are great, even the only way to go, if and only if you are dealing with screws. However, for those of us who want to paint, the screwdriver becomes a rather clumsy tool. It may be possible to paint with a screwdriver, but the results are not going to be too convincing. When we see, for example, non-profit organizations – each trying to bring good things to society – tearing each other apart to get scarce competitive money, they are really trying to paint with a screwdriver. The same image applies when we try to develop social capital such as taking care of children and the elderly exclusively with Yang type currency.

■ The four scenarios revisited

'The business of the future is to be dangerous.'

ALFRED WHITEHEAD

In Chapter 4, four different scenarios were summarized in the figure 9.11

Figure 9.11 The four scenarios of Chapter 4

We can now better understand how Sustainable Abundance relates to the other three scenarios. The Corporate Millennium is the result of what the Taoists would call an 'excess Yang' deviation from Sustainable Abundance, where Yang-driven businesses and currencies take over all other aspects of society as the old order dissolves. It would tend to occur if the benefits of information and money waves were monopolized by the corporate sector. This is most likely to happen if monetary and political authorities were to suppress the small-scale local currencies, while remaining unable or unwilling to tackle the corporate-issued currencies. In contrast, Careful Communities is an 'excess Yin' deviation where concerns about community cohesion have taken over when a monetary meltdown triggers widespread socio-economic disarray. Finally, Hell on Earth occurs when no faction in society fills in the power vacuum left after a monetary crash.

Alvin Toffler claimed: 'What appears to be emerging is neither a corporate dominated future nor a global government, but a far more complex system ... We are moving toward a world system composed of units densely interrelated like the neurons in a brain rather than organized like the departments of a bureaucracy.'

If Toffler is right, and if a monetary system compatible with this view is allowed to manifest, then Sustainable Abundance is our future.

■ Conclusion

We are not dealing with a traditional economic, financial or monetary crisis. We are living through a major mutation of the socio-economic fabric of our global civilization. This mutation can lead to several outcomes, and it is not preordained which one we will finally experience. The quicker we realize that the traditional solutions will not be appropriate for our current situation, the faster we can create the emotional, political and intellectual framework where appropriate solutions may emerge.

A post-Industrial mutation is upon us in any case, and I believe that the best way for us deal with it is by consciously uncentralizing and empowering human creativity at all levels. The three waves to Sustainable Abundance would enable this to happen.

As Sir Eric Tilgner put it: 'Destiny is not a matter of chance. It is a matter of choice.'

Just remember that *we* are doing the choosing for your children, for your children's children, and for a significant part of the biosphere as well.

Epilogue

■ *'The great challenge of the Modern Age is not to remake our world,*
but to remake ourselves.
Be the change you wish to see for the world.'

MAHATMA GANDHI

■ *'A problem cannot be solved*
with the same type of thinking that created it.'

ALBERT EINSTEIN

■ *'We don't see things as they are.*
We see them as we are.'

ANAIS NIN

Humanity and Planet Earth are at a cross-roads.

The next 20 years will either see an irretrievable loss of biodiversity and a deterioration of the quality of life for vast numbers of people, or we will have moved up the next evolutionary step. Given the remarkable motivation power of money, by changing the money system we can gently but surely tilt the direction towards which we are moving without having to completely re-educate or regulate the behaviour of billions of people. This book sketches a road map of how this could be achieved. It deals with money in the world *outside* us, describing money systems and their social effects.

However, there is still one other dimension to the money issue. To discover it, we need to journey into the imaginal world of money, the one residing *inside* our own heads. This other road map will provide a grasp of the collective emotions that operate around money. It integrates the 'right brain' symbols and myths active in our unconscious, where the unrelenting power of attraction of money finds its ultimate source.

It is unusual to connect these 'outside' and 'inside' world-views on any topic. To my knowledge, it is the first time that this is attempted for the topic of money. But closing the circle between the outside world and our inner worlds is nevertheless the richest route to our goal. This is the purpose of the book entitled *The Mystery of Money: Beyond Greed and Scarcity*.

This book delves into our collective psychology by addressing questions such as:

- What explains in our societies the social taboo around money issues? How are the three main taboos of our society of sex, death and money related to each other? Why is the money you have and where it comes from, an even bigger taboo than your sex life?
- Where did our contemporary obsession with money originate?
- Why did the conventional bank-debt national currencies become so exclusively dominant during the Industrial Age, spreading worldwide, independent of cultural or political context?
- Why are specific emotions – greed and fear of scarcity – built into our money system?
- Why is fundamental change in our money system transpiring now, after centuries of unthinking acceptance of the conventional national currencies?

The ongoing parallel mutations alluded to in the Value-Change Wave and the Money Wave (Chapter 9) offer today a historically unprecedented opportunity to *consciously* create Sustainable Abundance. Seizing this opportunity may be our most decisive challenge. To face this challenge, Wayne Dyer's comment may be relevant:

'*No one knows enough to be a pessimist.*'[305]

A Primer on How Money Works

'**T**he only people who claim that money is not an issue are those who have sufficient money that they are relieved of the ugly burden of thinking about it.' So thought the American writer Joyce Carol Oates. This Primer will explain why now even those fortunate few should think about it.

Have you ever wondered where your money comes from? How the value of your money is determined? Who is *really* in charge of your savings?

To start answering these questions, we need to understand the rules of the global money game, know who the players are and why they act the way they do. In this Primer, you will meet the key actors in our money system, and learn the essentials of the current system. Never before have monetary issues had such an influence on public policy worldwide, so this is a good time to educate ourselves about what is at stake. All of this will dramatically affect your money and your own future as surely as a radical climate change would affect the flowers in your garden.

The starting point is to become aware that 'your' money really represents a partnership between you and your country's banking system. You will learn how banking originated and how any form of storing value (properly, stocks, bonds and currencies) can be transformed into additional new money by banks.

The cause of the recent series of currency crises (Mexico, Asia, Eastern Europe) will be traced to unprecedented ongoing changes in the global currency markets. Because banks have proved historically to be very fragile institutions, specialized emergency 'firemen' or intervention organizations have been created: a central bank in each country, and on a global level the International Monetary Fund (IMF) and the Bank of International Settlements (BIS). Their role in managing the growing instability of the global money system will be assessed. We will then return to the initial questions on how all this affects your own money and future.

■ 'Your' money

'When I was young, I thought that money was important; now that I am old I know that it is,' was Oscar Wilde's view. Perhaps you have come to the same conclusion. Whatever you want to do with your life, you will invariably require *some* money to achieve it. Money is a most convenient medium of exchange, certainly more convenient than its barter alternative, as the story of Mlle Zélie illustrates (see sidebar). However, your money is never really 'yours' in the same sense that you own your eyes, your hands or your car or home, once all the payments have been made. 'Your' money is more like 'your' marriage: another party – your husband or wife – is intrinsically involved in the arrangement. *Modern money is also a bipartisan agreement. It is an asset to you only because it is someone else's liability.* And the modern banking system has been the necessary counterpart of such 'credit-money'.

Mlle Zélie's[306]

Mlle Zélie, a French opera singer on a world tour during the 19th century, gave a recital in the Society Islands. It was a great success, and for her fee she received one-third of the proceeds. By the way, some things do *not* change: this is still what Placido Domingo takes home from a performance.

But Mlle Zélie's share consisted of three pigs, twenty-three turkeys, forty-four chickens, five thousand coconuts and considerable quantities of bananas, lemons and oranges. Unfortunately the opera singer could only consume a small part of the total and (instead of declaring a public feast as would be local custom) found it necessary to feed the pigs and poultry with the fruit. A handsome fee ended up going to waste.

■ How does banking work?

The first party to whom you need to be introduced is therefore your bank, *not* because that is where you keep your money, but because that is where your *money is created*.

■ How did banking and 'modern' money start?

During the late Middle Ages, gold coins were the highest denominated currency. Goldsmiths were considered the best qualified to check the purity of these coins. Even more important, they owned strongboxes for keeping the gold safe from thieves. So it became a prudent practice to give gold to the goldsmith for safekeeping. The goldsmith would give a receipt for the coins and charge a small fee for the service. When the owner needed to make a payment, he or she would cash in the receipt and the goldsmith would pay out the coins. After a while, it became more convenient and safer to make payments by just using the receipts. If the goldsmith was known by everybody to be a trustworthy fellow, why take the risk of moving the physical gold? The goldsmith receipts soon became *tokens of a promise to pay*. So that whenever someone accepted the token as payment, they were implicitly entering into a loan agreement with the goldsmith. Thus we gradually shifted from money based on commodities, in this case gold, to money based on credit or a bank loan. This arrangement still exists today.

Non-Western money innovations

This Primer focuses on Western money and practices, not because they were historically the most advanced or important, but because the current world system is a direct evolution of these Western institutions. But the West was really quite a latecomer in this area.

For instance, the earliest samples of writing date from 3200 BC in the Sumerian city of Uruk and describe deposit banking, 'foreign exchange' transactions, secured and unsecured lending both locally and with neighbouring city-states. The first official banking laws were part of the Code of Hammurabi (around 1750 BC). The oldest private bank whose full name has been preserved is the 'Grandsons of Egibi' incorporated in Babylon in the 7th century BC. These Babylonian banks, 'by the detailed organization, by the number of branches and employees, by the daily records and accounts kept of the capital invested in them, may well be compared with the greatest banks of the nineteenth and twentieth centuries AD'.[307]

The first 'modern' style paper currency was issued in China during the reign of Hien Tsung (806-821 AD) as a temporary substitute for the traditional bronze coins.[308] Paper money was quite commonly in use in China by 900 AD, and in 1020 that country had also attained the dubious honour of living through the first hyperinflation in paper currency, as excessive paper money had been issued for a total of 2,830,000 ounces of silver in nominal value. 'A perfumed mixture of silk and paper was even resorted to, to give the money wider appeal, but to no avail; inflation and depreciation followed to an extent rivalling conditions in Germany and Russia after the first World War.'[309]

The first time the West heard about paper currency – with total disbelief – was from Marco Polo who was in China from 1275 to 1292. 'In this city of Kanbalu is the mint of the grand khan, who may truly be said to possess the secret of the alchemists, as he has the art of producing paper money . . . All his majesty's armies are paid with this currency, which is to them the same as if it were gold or silver. Upon these grounds, it may certainly be affirmed that the grand khan has a more extensive command of treasure than any other sovereign in the universe.'[310] Kublai Khan's paper currency also became one of the first world currencies as it was accepted at its maximum extent from mainland China to the Baltics, almost 500 years before the practice became widespread in Europe.

Soon the most successful goldsmiths noticed that the bulk of the coins stayed in their strongboxes most of the time. One enterprising goldsmith observed that he could issue receipts in excess of the gold coins he stocked, because the depositors would never retrieve all their coins at the same time.

In this way, he could increase his income without having to increase his gold reserves. So it was that European paper currency and 'modern' banking were born simultaneously on the goldsmiths' benches of 13th-century Italy; and why the word bank derives from *banco*, the Italian bench where those early transactions took place.[311] All the key ingredients were already there: paper money as a counterparty's liability, the importance of a good reputation for that counterparty and, what is now called 'fractional reserve system'. The latter's intimidating label belies the simple process it represents of enabling the banking system to create more money than the deposits it holds.

■ The secret of 'modern' money

The secret of creating money is being able to persuade people to accept one's IOU (a promise to pay in the future) as a medium of exchange. Whoever manages that trick can derive an income flow from the process (e.g., the medieval goldsmiths' fees, or, today, the interest on the loan that creates the money). Such income is called 'seigniorage', a word derived from the right of the Lord of the Manor (*Seignior* in Old French) to impose the use of his currency on his vassals.

As the nation-states became the powers-that-be, a deal was struck between the governments and the banking system. The banking system obtained the right to create money as 'legal tender'[166] in exchange for a commitment always to provide whatever funds the government needed. The longest surviving agreement of this kind can be traced back to 1668 with the licence of the 'Bank of the Estates of the Realm' in Sweden (whose name was changed in 1867 to *Riksbank* as the Swedish central bank is still known). The model was copied in Britain, a generation later at the founding of the Bank of England (1694)[313] from where it spread around the world. The Old Lady of Threadneedle Street, as the central bank is referred to in the City of London, 'is in all respects to money as St Peter's is to the Faith. And the reputation is deserved, for most of the art as well as much of the mystery associated with the management of money originated there.'[314]

A central bank accepts any government bond that the public does not buy, against which it issues a cheque for the corresponding amount. This cheque pays for the government's expenses, and in turn the recipient deposits it in his own bank account.

That is when the magical 'fractional reserves' come into play. For every deposit that any bank receives, it is entitled to create new money, specifically, in the form of a loan to a customer of up to 90% of the value of the deposit.[315] That new loan – for example, a mortgage that will enable you to buy a house – will result in the seller of the house making a new deposit somewhere else in the banking system. In turn the bank receiving that deposit is entitled to create another loan for 90% of that new deposit; and so the cascade continues from deposit to loan down through the banking system. What started as a $100 million cheque issued by the central bank (called 'high powered money'), by the time it works its way through the commercial banking system, has enabled banks to create up to $900 million of new money in the form of loans (see sidebar). If you understand this 'money alchemy' you have understood the most arcane secret of our money system.

Money alchemy

Modern money alchemy (officially called 'fractional reserve multiplier') starts with the injection of say 100 million 'high powered money' into the banking system, for instance, by having the Bank of England pay government bills for that amount. These funds end up being deposited somewhere in the banking system by the recipients, which enables the bank that received the deposit to provide a loan for 90 million to someone (the other 10 million becoming 'sterile reserves'). The 90 million loan will in turn lead to a deposit for that amount, enabling that next bank to provide another loan for 81 million, etc.

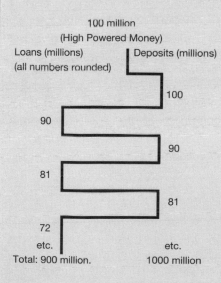

```
                    100 million
                 (High Powered Money)
Loans (millions)        |  Deposits (millions)
(all numbers rounded)   |

                                100

        90

                                90

        81

                                81

        72
        etc.                    etc.
Total: 900 million.        1000 million
```

This is how what started as 100 million Bank of England 'high powered money' theoretically can create up to 900 million in 'credit money' as it trickles down the banking system.

This is the convoluted mechanism by which the deal struck between governments and the banking system is implemented, and why 'your' money ultimately involves the entire banking system of your country. Money and debt are therefore literally the two sides of the same coin. If we all were to repay all our debts, money would disappear from our world, because the entire process of money creation illustrated in the 'money alchemy' would reverse itself. Reimbursing all the loans (the left side of the graph in the sidebar) would indeed automatically use up all the deposits (on the right side). Even the central bank's high powered money would evaporate if the government were able to repay its debts.

■ 'Old' and 'New' banking

In his classic book, *The Bankers*,[316] Martin Mayer recounts the following true story. A man was honoured for 50 years of loyal service to a Virginia bank. At the party celebrating his long service, he was asked what he thought had been 'the most important change that he had seen in banking in this half century of service?'. The man paused for a few minutes, then went to the microphone and said 'air conditioning'. In the sequel *The Bankers: the New Generation*, Mayer notes: 'Twenty years later, this story is prehistoric. It's still funny, but it's incomprehensible. In these twenty years, banking has changed beyond recognition . . . Almost nobody who has a job in a bank today works as his predecessors worked as recently as twenty years ago.'[317]

Banking has indeed changed more in the past 20 years than it has in hundreds of years. The 1970 US bank holding company law still defined a bank as an institution which 'agglomerates the transaction balances of a community to lend it at interest to its commercial enterprises', a definition quite consistent with Adam Smith's two centuries earlier. It is also, at its core, the same 'banking' business that the Babylonians and the Italian goldsmiths had started on their benches when they too gathered local savings and lent them out to businesses for a fee.

Today there are few such banks. Most surviving banks are involved in different businesses. In 1996, almost 85% of the banking industry's resources came from sources other than insured deposits. Instead of loans to businesses, credit card loans to consumers are the lifeblood of the largest banks (Citicorp makes more than $2 billion per year in this business – more than half its profits). In short, banks take their money where they can find it and use it for whatever activity the law allows that looks profitable. They have abandoned traditional banking and entered the 'financial services' business. The deeper reason for this unprecedented shift is the impact of the Information Age. It has fundamentally transformed competitive factors in the credit markets.

■ Credit markets

Mayer notes that in the 'olden days' of 20 years ago, 'banks used to fancy themselves as advisors to their clients'. In fact they simply took advantage of the monopoly they had over financial market information. When computers suddenly made it possible for *anybody* to have direct access to financial market quotes, the ground shifted under their feet. Many corporations used this access to issue their own commercial paper, bypassing the commercial banks in the process.

Traditional banks did not cope well with this massive change. Since 1980, over one-third of US banks have merged or disappeared in the turmoil that ensued. Even those that remain have reduced their staff dramatically. 'Banking hours' are now history. The proliferation of Automatic Teller Machines (ATMs) has taken care of that and eliminated some 179,000 human teller jobs (37% of US banks' workforce) over just one decade (1983-1993). This adaptation is still going – Deloitte, Touche in a 1996 study estimates that another 50% of present bank employees will be history within five years. Even all of this does not fully take into account the impact of the second wave of computerization which has just begun – the Internet revolution – the creation of a new cyber economy and a whole new world of open finance (described in Chapter 3).

■ Credit cards

Credit cards started as a convenience for the purchase of gasoline, frequent oil changes and repairs needed in the early automobiles in America. They were issued by oil companies to encourage brand loyalty – exactly as the airline industry is doing today with frequent-flyer miles.[318] In 1949, Diners Club created the first modern 'charge card' on the back of which it proudly listed *all 27* restaurants 'the finest in the country' where the card was accepted. As in Bellamy's time trip, they were made of cardboard (see sidebar). In 1955, Diners Club switched to plastic.[319] By 1958, the Bank of

America and the American Express Company, which had already established itself as 'the traveler's check company', each launched its own plastic credit cards. BankAmericard was relaunched as the VISA card alliance after a major reorganization in 1971. By 1999, VISA involves no less than 20,000 financial institutions all over the world, 400 million card members and an impressive $1.2 trillion in annual turnover. Although it is the biggest, this is only one of the thousands of credit card systems that have proliferated around the globe. Most significantly, a whole new way of lending money came into existence.

Magic money

A man fell asleep on May 30, 1887 and woke up on September 30, 2000. Among the most amazing things he discovered was that Americans still counted in dollars and cents, but paid for everything in large mall-sized warehouses with 'pasteboard credit cards'. This is the starting plot of a novel published in 1888 by Edward Bellamy entitled *Looking Backward: 2000-1887*. Novelists will invent the craziest things . . .

Interest rates applicable to credit card loans are much higher – often a multiple – of what banks would be able to obtain from normal business or consumer loans. This is what made this form of creating money irresistible to the issuers.

This is how – in less than one generation – banks came to abandon their centuries-old practice of providing credit to businesses, and replaced it with consumer credit cards.

■ Your savings: storing value

Now that you have obtained your hard-earned money, how can you preserve it for the proverbial rainy day? This is important not only for you personally. Whatever form the storage of value takes, it also becomes potential collateral for any additional bank-debt money that can be created, as described above in how the banking system works.

Contrary to what some people believe, money itself is *not* a good store of value. At best it is 'a temporary abode of purchasing power',[320] a way to keep value in the short term between the moment you receive income and when you spend it. If you stuff money under your mattress as savings, or even leave it in a bank account, the following inflation scorecard should warn you.

■ A scorecard

The clearest way to see what has happened to the value of your money is to look at what it purchases on a day-to-day basis. In recent years, most major currencies have kept enough of their value so that some people even claim that currency depreciation ('inflation' in the jargon) is now dead for ever. However, before accepting such a conclusion, it is worth examining this issue over a longer time period, say twenty-five years.

Let us look at the scorecard. For example, consider the performance over two decades of the Deutschemark, the world's most 'stable' currency since the World War II. If you had kept 100 Deutschemark under your mattress since 1971, the following table shows its purchasing power would have shrunk to 42.28 DM by end of 1996.[321] In other words, even the best-performing currency in the world lost more than half of its value in that period.

If you live in this country	The 1996 value of your currency is (1971 =100)	Ranking out of 108 major world currencies
Germany (Deutschemark)	42.28	1
Switzerland (Swiss franc)	39.79	3
Japan (Japanese yen)	33.24	11
United States (dollar)	24.72	17
Canada (Canadian dollar)	22.26	23
France (French franc)	19.48	31
Australia (Australian dollar)	**15.11**	**46**
United Kingdom (pound sterling)	**12.57**	**55**
Italy (lira)	8.65	68
Spain (peseta)	7.77	69
Mexico (peso)	0.066	101
Brazil (cruzeiro-cruzado-real)	0.000	108

Table P.1: What is your money worth?

Similarly, in 1996, 100 Swiss francs would be worth only 39.79 SF from 20 years earlier. The purchasing power of US$100 is just over US$24.72; and £100, £12.57, and so on.

Sometimes inflation can get really out of hand, with devastating consequences for the societies which experience them (see sidebar).

Money troubles end empires

Money can go wrong in different ways, the worst one being hyperinflation, the extreme form of inflation when currencies become practically valueless. Social disorder, even collapses of empires have been the outcome whenever the cost or prestige of an empire made it issue too much money, thereby provoking hyperinflation in its currency.

Sumer, the oldest city empire historically well documented, collapsed when continuous warfare with its neighbours provoked hyperinflation in 2020 BC. After Alexander the Great's death, as vast treasure looted from Persia was brought back home, hyperinflation resulted and destroyed the once-mighty Greek empire. The same thing happened 2000 years later, with the Spanish empire, when the gold and silver looted from the New World was imported back to Spain.

Hyperinflation is still a scourge in many countries. Among the more extreme examples during this century: Germany in the 1920s, Latin America in the 1970s and 1980s, Yugoslavia in 1989-91 and Russia in 1991-92 and again in 1998. In all these cases, hyperinflation provoked serious social and political disruptions.

Managing savings intelligently therefore boils down to allocating cash between the three classical major asset classes: real estate, bonds, and stocks. Over the past decade, another major asset class has appeared that is of particular interest to us: currencies. A few words about the changing role of each asset class over time puts this development into perspective.

■ Real estate

From the beginning of the Agricultural Revolution until last century, real estate, particularly land, was the dominant form of savings available in the world. The wealth of individuals could usually be evaluated by the quality and the size of the real estate they had accumulated. This all changed with the Industrial Age when stocks and bonds in commercial enterprises became a favourite investment vehicle. Today, most people's real estate holdings are limited to their house, and typically even that is mortgaged.

■ Stocks

A stock is a fraction of ownership in a business. Contrary to most people's perception, it is a very old investment instrument (see sidebar). During this past decade, all stock exchanges around the world have become much more intimately interlinked. There used to be a theory that by diversifying geographically it was possible to decrease stock investment risks. This theory was exploded in the simultaneous global stock market panic of 1987 which demonstrated that it has become harder to reduce risks through global diversification. Even if you only invest in domestic stocks, today the message is: think globally *and* act globally, for everything is impacted by global events.

What stock is new under the sun?

The earliest stock offerings date back to seafarer and caravan voyages lost in the mist of time. They were already practised among the Phoenicians in antiquity, and became openly tradable among the general public in Venice and Genoa by the 13th century. 'Men and women from all ranks of life owned shares . . . They were regarded as particularly good security for one of the favorite forms of investment across the sea, the sea loan . . . which was repaid only if the ship arrived safely.'[322] The oldest public stock exchange still functioning, dealing in all kinds of corporate stocks, is the one in Amsterdam, dating from the 17th century.

■ Bonds

A bond is a loan to the organization on whose behalf it was issued. It is a promise to pay the loan back at maturity. By purchasing a bond, one gives up liquid cash in exchange for that promise. The key feature that justifies doing so is the payment of interest on a periodic basis. 'Usury', or charging interest, has been frowned upon since their founding by all three religions (Judaism, Christianity and Islam) that have followed the books of their beliefs as revealed by God. Only Islam has remained true to the tradition of non-usury to this day. Henry VIII, after his break with Rome, legalized interest in Britain for the first time in 1545. But it was not until the 18th and 19th centuries that this investment option displaced real estate in people's portfolios. This was true even in Protestant countries. The Catholic church 'forgot' about the sin of usury only towards the end of the 19th century, thereafter including bonds or any other form of interest-bearing loans even in ecclesiastical portfolios.

In bonds we trust

Bonds presuppose a public trust in the long-term future of the value of the currency in which they are denominated. Therefore the length to maturity of a bond gives some idea about the level of confidence people have in the future of that currency. The 'champions' of such long-term trust are the Dutch 'dyke-building-bonds' which have no expiration date, and on which interest has been paid faithfully since the 16th century. In 1903, the British government could afford to issue 300 year 'gilts' at 2.5% interest. Compare that with today's 'long' bonds of 30 years maximum and 5% interest.

■ Currencies

Historically, for some specialists, such as money changers and banks operating internationally, currency has always been a significant type of asset. Any modern global portfolio has also, by definition, a currency component (e.g. holding a Japanese bond or stock means automatically having a position in Japanese yen). So holding positions in currencies by themselves has become a logical extension. It has now become a significant factor in most professional investors' portfolios.

Something extraordinary has been happening over the past decade: the currency market has become the biggest single market in the world. Foreign exchange transactions (purchases and sales of currencies) today dwarf the trading volume of all other asset classes, even of the entire global economy. As a result, currency markets are becoming vitally important to almost everyone for the first time in recorded history – although it is probable that the majority of people are still quite unaware of this.

■ Foreign exchange markets

If you have travelled anywhere abroad, you have dealt in the foreign exchange market. You went to a bank or money exchange office and exchanged your little bits of paper against more exotic-looking local bits of paper. The day after someone invented money, his neighbour must have started a money exchange. So what could be new in foreign exchange markets? Actually, quite a lot.

The first sign that something different is afoot is the sheer volume of currency transactions. Back in the prehistoric days of the 1970s, the typical daily volume of foreign exchange transactions, worldwide, fluctuated between $10-$20 billion. By 1983, that had risen to $60 billion. By 1998, that daily volume had reached a staggering $1.5 trillion[323] and the estimate for a 'normal' day in 2000 is about $2 trillion.

Mere mortals like us lose a sense of proportion when confronted with such numbers (see quiz question in sidebar). Let us put this into perspective. Such volume amounts to over 150 times the total daily international trade of all commodities, all manufactures and all services worldwide. It is in the order of 100 times the daily trading of all equities in all the stock markets around the world. It is even 50 times greater than all the goods and services produced per day (GDP) by all the industrialized countries. Furthermore, the volume of foreign exchange transactions continues to grow at a breakneck rate of 20-25% per year, compared to an average 5% annual growth for global trade. It is fair to conclude that something *very* unusual is going on in the global foreign exchange markets, something that we have never experienced before.

Quiz question

Assume that you have a printing press in your garage that produces dollar bills at the rate of one per second. When would this printing press have to be started for it to produce the two trillion dollars' worth of a typical foreign exchange market day? During World War I, the American Revolution, at the birth of Jesus Christ, the Neolithic, or Cro-Magnon? Answer: see footnote.[324]

~ William
Branhall

■ The global casino

What happened is that 'speculative' trading (i.e. trading whose sole purpose is to make a profit from the changes in the value of the currencies themselves) has all but taken over the foreign exchange markets. In contrast, the 'real' economy (i.e. transactions relating to the purchase and sale of real goods and services abroad, including portfolio investments) has now been relegated to a mere side-show of the global casino of the speculative monetary exchange game.

The Figure P.2 illustrates this complete reversal in importance between the 'real' and the speculative transactions. At this point, 98% of all foreign exchange transactions are speculative, and only 2% relate to the real economy.[325]

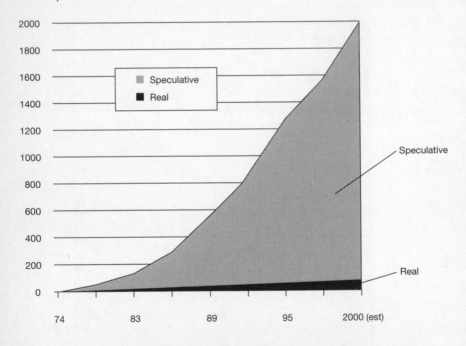

Figure P.2 Daily total foreign exchange transactions as reported by the Bank of International Settlements (BIS) versus foreign exchange transactions based on 'real' economic exchanges

Speculation can play a positive role in any market: theory and practice show that it can improve market efficiency by increasing liquidity and depth[326] in the market. But current speculative levels are clearly out of balance. 'Speculators may do no harm as bubbles on a steady stream of enterprise. But the position is serious when enterprise becomes the bubble on a whirlpool of speculation. When the capital development of a country becomes a by-product of the activities of a casino, the job is likely to be ill-done.'[327] Although over half a century old, John Maynard Keynes's opinion has never been as appropriate as it is today. Furthermore, currencies have now become the ideal speculation tool (see sidebar).

Currencies: an ideal speculation tool?

As a tool for speculation, today's foreign exchange markets offer some very useful features compared to any other asset class:

- A 24-hour very liquid market: this is the most liquid of all asset classes (more liquid than bonds or stocks whose trading is limited to local market hours, and more liquid than real estate).
- Very low transaction costs: buying or selling a currency in volume is far cheaper than buying stocks, bonds or real estate. The only cost is a small spread between buy and sell in foreign exchange, which locks in the bank's profits.
- Depth of the foreign exchange market: when professional investment managers have a large amount of money to place, buying a stock will drive up the price of the stock. Similarly, when they will sell this stock, again their own trade will make the market move against them. No such problems in foreign exchange: the depth of the currency markets is such that even billions of dollars won't make a blip.

The bulk of the speculative volume is due to banks' own currency trading departments. However, it is predictable that the hedge funds – mutual funds specializing in currency speculation – will be the ones that will bear the brunt of the public relations backlash if a global meltdown occurs, as they are the 'last kid on the block'. In all financial crisis – from the Dutch tulips in 1637 to the US stock market crash of 1987 – it is invariably the most recent financial innovation which bears the brunt of the blame.[328]

Figure P.3 provides a synthetic overview of the currency flows which triggered three crises between 1983 and 1998. A monetary crisis can be seen as the result of a sudden ebb of the global cash flow out of the target country, brutally reversing an earlier inflow.

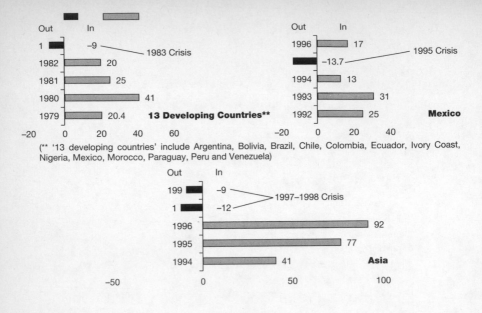

Figure P.3 Money's tides and ebbs and the resulting monetary crises (1983-1998) (billions of US$)[329]

Notice that the scale of the swings between monetary high and low tides keeps growing – they mirror the increase of speculative flows in Figure P.2. It took 13 countries in 1983 to produce a swing of around $30 billion between the last inflow and the outflow. Mexico was hit by a similar swing in 1995. Barely three years later, the Asian crisis saw a swing of well over $100 billion between 1996 and 1997. These swings are the consequence of massive speculative activity.

■ Why does speculation on currencies happen?

This extraordinary build-up of speculative activity can be explained by three cumulative changes over the past decades:

1 A Structural shift: On August 15, 1971, President Nixon disconnected the dollar from gold, inaugurating an era of currencies whose values would be determined predominantly by market forces. This gave rise to a systemic change in which currency values could fluctuate significantly at any point in time. This was the beginning of the 'floating exchanges' and a market that would prove highly profitable for those who know how to navigate it.

2 1980s financial deregulation: The governments of Margaret Thatcher in the UK and Ronald Reagan in the US embarked simultaneously on massive financial deregulation programmes. The Baker Plan (a reform package named after the then US Secretary to the Treasury, Mr Baker), imposed a similar deregulation in 16 key developing countries in the wake of the developing countries' debt crisis. These deregulations enabled a much larger array of people and institutions to become involved in currency trading than would have previously been possible.

3 Technological shift: In parallel to the above, the computerization of foreign exchange trading created the first ever 24-hour fully integrated global market. This shift raised to a whole new level the speed and scale with which currencies could be moved around the world.

During his survey of 5,000 years of money's history, Glyn Davies identified electronic money as one of only two exceptionally important technological innovations in money. 'There have been two major changes, the first at the end of the Middle Ages when the printing of paper began to supplement the minting of coins, and the second in our own time when electronic money transfer was invented.'[330] We know in retrospect that the first change enabled banks to take away from ruling sovereigns the lead role in money creation, but what will the second change create?

A titanic struggle has begun in relation to the control of emerging forms of money. Banks are now acting mostly like computerized telecommunications companies. But companies involved in telecommunications, computer hardware and software, credit card processing, Internet shopping, even cable television, have also discovered that they can perform many of the services of the banks. Whoever wins control over the new electronic money systems will ultimately be endowed with the power to issue money. As the banker Sholom Rosen claimed: 'It's definitely new, it's revolutionary – and we should be scared as hell.'[331] If well-informed bankers get scared of the scale and speed of money changes, what should the rest of us do?

■ Derivatives

Besides revolutionizing banking and accelerating the movement of currencies, computers have also played another role in the foreign exchange markets: they made possible the explosive development of a whole new wave of financial products, generically called derivatives.[332] Derivatives make it possible to unbundle each piece of financial risk, and trade each one separately. Charles Sanford, ex-chairman of Bankers Trust and one of the pioneers of the business, described derivatives as building a 'particle theory of finance'.

For example, a Japanese yen bond can be unbundled in at least three pieces of risk: a currency risk (the risk that the yen drops in value against your own currency), an interest rate risk (the risk that Japanese interest rates go up after you purchase your bond), and an issuer risk (the risk that the company issuing the bond defaults on the bond). Derivatives enable investors to select exactly which component of those risks they want to include or exclude from their portfolios.

Imagine that instead of buying a ticket to a concert or opera, you suddenly have the capacity to select and combine for yourself your favourite soprano, your favourite tenor, your favourite violinist, conductor, and so on, all interpreting your favourite compositions. If you know what you are doing, the result of this new freedom could be quite extraordinary and superior to what you can get in a normal 'pre-packaged' performance. However, if your knowledge is limited, your personal creation also could turn out quite catastrophic. Derivatives provide that kind of freedom for financial portfolios, but similarly require a lot more knowledge than average investors possess. Shifting risks from one place to another is fine as long as the party that ends up with the risk is both knowledgeable and strong enough to bear it. However, Martin Mayer made a law of the fact that 'Risk-shifting instruments ultimately shift the risk onto those less able to deal with them'.[333] Although I think this is too sweeping a generalization, there are many institutions that have been badly burned without understanding what it was that hit them. Barings, a top name in the City of London for 233 years, became one of the most spectacular victims of this process (see sidebar).

Barings

The Duc de Richelieu said in 1818 that there were six great powers in Europe – France, England, Prussia, Austria, Russia and Baring Brothers. This reputation did not help in February 1995 when one single young trader lost $1.5 billion – two times the bank's capital – in a few days on the Singapore derivatives market. The surprise must have been greatest inside the bank itself as Ron Baker, the head of the Financial Products Group of Barings Bank had made an enthusiastic assessment of the activities of Nick Leeson: 'Nick had an amazing day on SIMEX . . . Baring Singapore was the market . . . Nick just sees opportunities that are phenomenal, and he just takes them.'[334]

Derivatives are nevertheless here to stay, primarily because, when used correctly, they can be both useful to society and profitable to the financier. So we should get used to the idea that they may also provide us with some startling surprises, just like some of the amateur orchestral combinations in our earlier musical metaphor. As Dr Jekyll turned into Mr Hyde, so the blip on a computer screen can change the nature of a derivative position at the drop of a hat.

Capitalism's central nervous system

It is insufficient to look at currencies as just another asset class. A country's currency is indeed also much more. It plays the role of the central nervous system that commands the values of all asset classes in that country. This becomes clearer when we look at how all the other three traditional asset classes are affected directly by what happens to money. We have seen already that bonds are an attractive investment only to the extent that the currency in which they are denominated keeps its value (i.e. when inflation is low or falling). It is also well known that stock prices fall when interest rates rise, and interest rates tend to shoot up when a currency gets into trouble. The last asset class, real estate, presents a more complex situation. On the one side, real estate is the best protection available against inflation. On the other side it is also very illiquid (i.e. difficult to sell in a hurry); so when serious financial problems arise, people who cannot meet their mortgage payments may have to liquidate their real estate at undervalued prices. This makes real estate investing a double-edged sword.

Finally, the interconnection of the different financial markets makes monetary rot a contagious disease. Figure P.5 shows the spread of what was initially a Thai currency crisis through the stock markets of ten different countries.

%

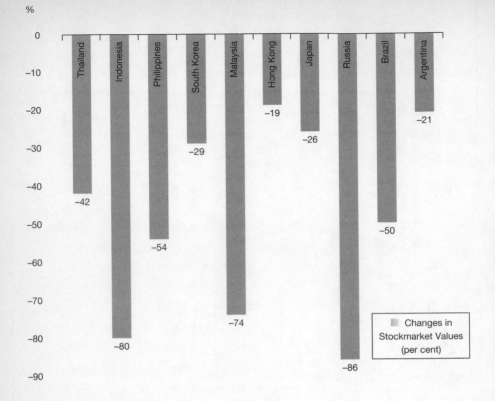

Figure P.5 Changes in stock market values in 10 countries (%) (June 1997-December 1998)[335]

When we discover that all our eggs end up in one money basket, I suggest keeping a close eye on that basket. Some well-qualified people are paid to do exactly that. Let me introduce you to them, and thereby complete the picture of the world's key money players.

Why are banks so fragile?

Banks have always been accident-prone. Only counting the most recent bank crises, in the US major banks got into trouble, in Latin America in the 1980s and the largest bail-out in history occurred with the Savings and Loans debacle in the 1990s. The Scandinavian banks needed rescuing in the early 1990s. Japanese banks got into trouble three times in a row: first the Less Developed Countries crisis in the 1980s, a real estate crunch in the 1990s, and the 1997 South-east Asian meltdown. The trickiest situations are those involving banks that are active globally, such as the BCCI débâcle of 1991, which is still being cleaned up in courts around the world.

Why have banks remained so fragile?

This is a dilemma that nobody has really solved so far. By the nature of banking, banks take low-risk assets (deposits) and invest them in higher-risk assets. When the risks pay off, these investments pay off and the bank's owners reap all the rewards. When the risk does not pay off and the bank fails, the losses are spread between the bank's owners and the depositors (or the governmental insurance safety net, which now protects the depositors). There is therefore a built-in temptation for banks to take high-risk/high-return

---

gambles. This is called a 'moral hazard' in central bank jargon.

The dilemma is therefore: if banks are not allowed to take any risks, there is no banking; but if a major bank takes excessive risks, should it be allowed to fail? Big bank failures can destabilize the entire financial system. Worse still, when loans to thousands of businesses are withdrawn the rot can spread quickly to all kinds of economic activities. Suddenly millions of jobs and livelihoods of real people can be at stake.

Banking is different from any other business for one more reason: bank troubles tend to become everybody's problems . . .

According to figures cited by the World Bank no fewer than 69 countries have endured serious banking crises since the late 1970s. and 87 nations have seen runs on their currency since 1975.[336]

■ Central banks and other firemen

The financial sector has always been 'special'. Even today the finance industry is not treated as just another service industry. There are positive and negative reasons for this:

- On the positive side, financial institutions – even the private ones – are really performing the vital public function of providing, hopefully, a stable currency for use by the participants in the economy.
- On the negative side, financial institutions have often proved the most fragile component of any society (see sidebar). And it has been demonstrated time and again – from Sumer to Yugoslavia – that whenever money gets into trouble, whole societies can crumble.

■ National level

Fires are rare, but when they occur they can be devastating. Entire cities have burned down because one single person has been careless, hence the invention of fire brigades and fire inspections. So it is with money: because financial institutions have proved so accident-prone, central banks were invented.

■ Whence central banks?

In the 19th century, the name 'central bank' referred to a bank, headquartered in a nation's capital, that enjoyed the monopoly of issuing paper notes in the national currency. Once in a while, these banks would provide some simple mutual support to each other. Such was the case in 1825, when the French helped the Bank of England by swapping a shipment of gold for silver when there was a run on gold in London; a favour which the English returned in 1860, when the Banque de France was in dire straits. But such cases of mutual help were rare, little publicized and certainly would not have been considered part of the official duties of a central bank. All this changed with the Bretton Woods Agreement, which set up the framework for the post-World War II global environment (see sidebar). Central banks now play much more complex roles.

Bretton Woods Agreement

In July 1944, 45 countries signed the first written global monetary constitution at the hotel Mount Washington in Bretton Woods, New Hampshire. According to that agreement, all countries had to fix their currencies to the US dollar, and the US committed in counterpart to keep its dollar convertible into gold upon request from any central bank at the fixed rate of $35 per ounce of gold. This system put the US$ in a *de facto* commanding role as linchpin of the global system. A new institution – the International Monetary Fund (IMF) – was created to police the system. Any change in the value of a currency required a preliminary approval from the IMF. The system worked well for over two decades until President Johnson introduced his 'guns and butter' strategy during the Vietnam War, putting welfare with warfare at the top of the political agenda. This triggered an unprecedented dollar outflow from the US. Some years later, it was these substantial dollar holdings in the hands of foreign central banks that were to force President Nixon in 1971 to renege on the convertibility promise of dollars into gold, thus officially ending the Bretton Woods Agreement.

However, the dollar's role as official linchpin of the world's money system remained intact. This further increased the influence of the US in global monetary matters, and the dependence of the world on the dollar, its linchpin currency.

Note that this remains true even with the euro, whose international value remains linked to the dollar.

- They serve as 'emergency firemen' whenever a bank or the whole system gets into trouble. This is called respectively 'lender of last resort' and 'systemic risk management' in the jargon.
- They carry the ultimate responsibility for controlling inflation in the country. Over the past decades, this task has been the one most closely identified by the general public as a central bank function.
- They achieve inflation control through various mechanisms that influence the quantity of money that the banking system can create. They do not give direct orders to achieve this, but only provide 'signals' such as changes in key interest rates, or purchases and sales of government bonds (called 'open market' transactions) and currencies in the foreign exchange markets (called 'interventions').
- Central banks are also banks, although they don't have retail customers:

their customers are the banks of their country, for which they settle payments.

■ 'Money's family portrait'

Figure P.6 shows a 'family tree' of how all the main monetary players relate to each other. It forms a kind of inverted pyramid, with thousands of commercial banks on top, a layer of 170 central banks in the middle (regrouped here in three types according to who owns them), and two supra-national organizations at the bottom.

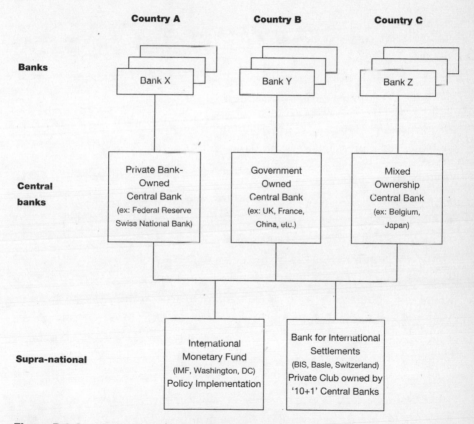

Figure P.6 Organization chart of today's global monetary system

I have placed banks in each individual country on top of the chart, as they are the front-line issuers of credit-money. The central banks were initially only their backstop, their fire extinguishers, in case of trouble. Until 1936, almost all central banks were directly owned by the main private banks in each country. To this day, nine of the central banks are still private corporations owned by private banks, including the US Federal Reserve, the Swiss National Bank, the Bank of Italy and the South African Reserve Bank.

By the 1950s, there were 56 countries with central banks. Now there are 170, with most of the newcomers being government controlled. But there are also central banks whose ownership situations involve both government and banks (e.g., Belgium or Japan). Contrary to expectations, there has been no evidence that the various ownership arrangements have made any significant difference to either central banks' actions or effectiveness. Some of the most prestigious and effective central banks can be found in all three types of ownership, as can some at the bottom of the league.

■ The supra-national level

Finally, there are two important family members who represent the main supra-national coordinating tools among central banks:

■ One is a policeman – the International Monetary Fund (IMF).
■ The other a private club – the Bank of International Settlements (BIS).

Created in 1945 as the enforcer of the rules of Bretton Woods, the IMF is the auditor of central banks around the world, and is the official political arm of the global money system. As of 1997, 182 countries are members. A 24-member Executive Board supervises a staff of about 2,300 professionals, mostly economists. The IMF is the 'lender of last resort' from whom member countries can obtain loans in case of emergencies from a pool of $210 billion obtained as 'quotas' from all member countries. Typically, such loans are conditional upon strict economic austerity measures, hence its reputation as a global economic policeman. The US has a dominant influence at the IMF. Not only does the US have veto power on decisions, but it also happens to be physically 'close at hand' in Washington DC.

The BIS has a more peculiar history. It was created in 1930 ostensibly to deal with German war reparation payments. It was to become a private club owned and operated by the key '10+1' central banks. The '10+1' are so called because there are 10 founding central banks on one side, plus Switzerland as host country on the other side (as a result of its 'active neutrality' strategy, Switzerland is often 'in' and 'out' at the same time; it still does not 'officially' belong to the IMF or the UN, for instance). The mission of the BIS was to address any important issues that would best be handled with efficient discretion. No politicians, no Treasury officials, no Ministers of Finance, not even Presidents or Prime Ministers are welcome.

One almost forgets that the BIS is also a bank, although its only customers are central banks. Hence its nickname as 'central bank of central banks'. It even has a substantial currency-dealing room recently installed to enable it to monitor the global money system in real time, and to provide wholesale market transactions for its member central banks. It remains a modest institution for the influence it wields: even today it has only 450 staff members including a research team of about 50 economists, who publish, among other things, a well-respected annual report on the state of the world financial system. The BIS has made its name in fire-extinguishing operations in the past; it will undoubtedly be part of any future fire brigades as well.

We have seen a snapshot of the key players in this piece. However, any notion that this money game is a static one is dispelled as soon as we put all the pieces of the money puzzle together.

■ Money as a system

The monetary game is indeed mutating in front of our very eyes. The changes that are occurring involve unprecedented speed, scale and complexity. Two different perspectives illustrate that point: the one of the 'firemen', and the one for the rest of us.

The firemen's viewpoint

From the perspective of the central banks, the world is definitely becoming tougher and more complex year after year. The explosive developments in the currency markets in particular have a series of implications that I divide under three headings:

– Power shift
– Increased volatility
– Stable or unstable, that is the question

Power shift

A major power shift in the world system has already occurred. Every government in the world, including the most powerful ones, such as the US, is actually being policed by the global foreign exchange markets. If a government anywhere in the world dares to challenge these financial diktats, capital flight will almost instantaneously force it back into orthodoxy. President Mitterrand in France in the 1980s; John Major in Britain and the Scandinavians in 1992; the Mexicans in 1994; the Thai, Malay, Indonesian, or South Korean governments in 1997; the Russian in 1998 – all paid the hefty price that is extracted under such circumstances.

Even *Business Week* concludes: 'In this new market . . . billions can flow in or out of an economy, in seconds. So powerful has this force of money become that some observers now see the "hot-money" (funds that move around quickly from one country to another) becoming a sort of shadow world government – one that is irretrievably eroding the concept of the sovereign powers of a nation state.'[337] The trickiest times occur when power shifts. They are by definition times of uncertainty. The form of uncertainty that central banks and other guardians of monetary order fear most is currency volatility.

Increased currency volatility

Currency volatility is a measure of change in the value of one currency against all the others. Central banks predictably do not like volatility in their currency, and volatility happens to be one of the unexpected consequences of the massive increase in speculative activities. Back in the 1960s, the proponents of freely floating currency exchanges used to argue that currency volatility would drop as soon as a free market was established. Foreign exchange markets are certainly now much more open and free than they were in the 1960s, when the Bretton Woods fixed-exchange-rate system was operational.

However, an OECD (the Organization of Economic Cooperation and Development based in Paris) statistical study came to some sobering conclusions, directly contradicting the theoretical forecast.[338] The past 25 years of floating exchanges have revealed an average foreign exchange volatility four times higher than under the Bretton Woods fixed-exchange system.

It does not require a statistical rocket scientist to understand why the volatility increases with the speculative volume of the trades. Simple common sense explains it just as well. Let us assume that your currency is under pressure, and that a modest 5% of the major currency traders 'take a negative view about that currency'. This means in practice that those who own your currency will sell it, and those who don't own it sell short.[339] In 1986, when total daily volume was around 60 billion dollars, such a move by 5% of the market volume would have represented a $3 billion move against the currency in question, certainly a challenge to a central bank, but a manageable one. Today, with volumes of $2 trillion per day, the same proportional move would generate an overwhelming $100 billion transfer against your currency, which no central bank would be able to withstand.

Stable or unstable, that is the question

From the above, we can surmise that central bankers are becoming increasingly uncomfortable. Not only are they dealing with a world of increasing uncertainty and currency volatility, but they themselves are being out-gunned in the currency markets as well. The 'official reserves' of central banks are exactly the equivalent of water reserves in a fireman's job: they consist of the foreign currency reserves that central banks can use to intervene in the foreign exchange markets. Typically, if a currency comes under pressure, and the corresponding central bank wants to stabilize the exchange rate it can prop up the currency by buying it in the marketplace.

'The most dramatic use of reserves were in the summer of 1992 and 1993 when the currencies of the European Union came under massive attack in the foreign exchange markets. Some DM400 billion (over US$225 billion) were mobilized in 1992 and a smaller amount in 1993 – amounts dwarfing those spent in any previous period. But despite all the money spent, the Central Banks lost, and the markets won.'[340]

Today, all the combined reserves of all the central banks together (about US$1.3 trillion, including about $340 billion in central bank gold, valued at current market prices) would be gobbled up in less than one day of normal trading. Compare this with the situation as recently as 1983 (see Figure P.7), when the reserves still provided a pretty safe cushion.

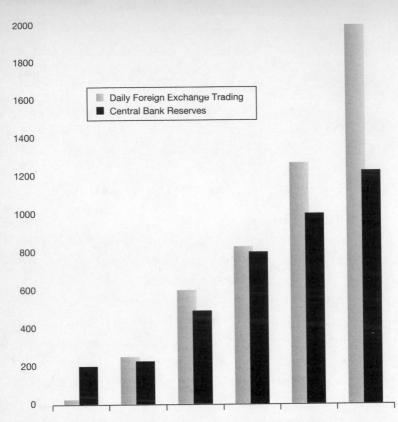

Figure P.7 Industrial nations central bank reserves compared to daily foreign exchange trading (Sources: BIS, IMF, *The Economist*. 1998 estimated)

Even people who profit from explosive speculative activity are becoming seriously worried. For instance George Soros, widely considered one of the biggest players in this game, states: 'Freely floating exchange rates are inherently unstable; moreover, the instability is cumulative so that the eventual breakdown of a freely floating exchange rate system is virtually assured.'[341] Joel Kurtzman, business editor of *The New York Times*, is even more damning. He titles his latest book *The Death of Money: How the Electronic Economy has Destabilized the World's Markets*.[342]

A master of understatement like Paul Volcker, ex-governor of the Federal Reserve, goes on record to express his concern about the growth of 'a constituency in favor of instability', i.e. financial interests whose profits depend on increased volatility.[343] Just to illustrate this last point, a typical comment by a foreign exchange trader quoted in the *Washington Post* reveals how a period of relative stability is perceived: 'You can't make any money like this. The dollar ... movement is too narrow. Anyone speculating or trading in the dollar or any other currency can't make any money or lose money. You can't do anything. It's been a horror.'[344]

The net effect of the actions of these 'constituencies for instability' are the monetary crises that regularly make front-page headlines (see an extract from *The New York Times* in sidebar, where all the key actors to which you have now been introduced play out a real-life drama). The question nobody dares to ask is: Who is next? Latin America? Western Europe? China? When will the US, the largest debtor country in the world, become a target? What would that mean?

This is not the only challenge that the money system is facing. We will see later that banks and financial services are just starting to change again, this time under the pressures of the cyber economy. We will discover that market innovations, such as Open Finance, will make it harder than ever for regulators to define what a bank is, or what money is theirs to manage.

Tide of Money Is Seen as Continuing Threat

If there is one clear lesson from the turmoil that has so badly jolted Asia, it is that the financial systems in many fast-growing countries were no match to the huge, skittish pools of money they attracted.

. . . National systems intended to supervise banks in their home country have proven unable to keep pace with the rapid development of a global financial market place that pays little attention to borders. There is no international body able to play the role of global regulator, and an inability by the United States and other powers to impose changes on the often-reluctant governments and banks in nations at risk. A result is that to a remarkable extent, individual nations and even the worldwide economy are suddenly more at risk because of the ineffectiveness of obscure banking regulations in far-off countries.

. . . With the International Monetary Fund taking the lead, multinational organizations and national governments have pledged more than $100 billion to bail out countries in Asia, the largest international rescue in history. Yet, paradoxically, there is no global body with the ability or the mandate to manage the problem.

'. . . In the last few years we've come to realize – and you may say it's late – that banking stability is more important for a wider range of countries,' said Andrew Crockett, the general manager of the Bank for International Settlements. 'It's the public sector, whose money is on the line, that prevents a financial meltdown, so the public sector has to have a voice.' Mr. Crockett said, 'How can we get these countries to adopt these standards. The answer is we can't.'

'. . . National supervision of complex global firms and global markets is inadequate to meet the requirements of the times,' said John G. Helmann, the chairman of global financial institutions at Merrill Lynch.

. . . The United States, acting at the behest of American banks, pressed South Korea to open its financial markets a few years ago, but Washington 'didn't help the Korean Government prepare for these things – it went too fast' said Yoon Dae Euh, a professor of international finance at the Korea University and former member of Seoul's Monetary Board.

. . . However the problem gets addressed, no one thinks it will be a quick, easy task.

(Extract from *The New York Times* 12/22/1997)[345]

■ Back full circle to you

We started this Primer with the questions: How is the value of your money determined? Who is really in charge of your savings? We can now answer these questions:

1 The value of your money is ultimately determined in an increasingly volatile global casino where 98% of the transactions are based on speculation.

2 Whether your nest egg is your house, some investment portfolio, or even the cash in your wallet, your savings are all highly interconnected within the money system. Therefore, whatever form you will give them, the future of your savings will depend significantly on what happens to your currency.

3 Even if you believe that you don't have anything to do with 'global finance', because you haven't invested yourself in the international money game, this is usually an illusion because your pension fund or your bank is directly or indirectly involved in such activities (see sidebar).

Of world markets, none an island[346]

The New York Times traced the money of the Paoni couple, a typical Midwestern family, through their local A.G. Edwards Money Market Fund to Bangkok Land, a Thai real estate development company which went bust in the baht meltdown; and to J.P. Morgan, one of the most active sellers of derivatives during the Asian crash. Through their Illinois State Pension Fund, part of their savings ended up in Gum, the prestigious supermarket in Moscow which went bankrupt after the rouble collapsed; and in Peregrine Investments, a Hong Kong investment bank which rose from nowhere to $25 billion in revenues in 1996, only to collapse in 1998 with more than 2,000 creditors owed more than $4 billion. Both these investments are now essentially worthless.

The globalization of the financial markets means that, even if you don't know it, now you are likely to be part of the global money game, and subject to the consequences of its instabilities.

---

4 Even if you have no investments or savings of any kind, your life will be touched because your country as a whole will be affected when money gets into serious trouble somewhere in the world. Figure P.8 shows the purchases of foreign stocks as a percentage of Gross Domestic Product for three countries. For instance, Germany has now invested the equivalent of two and a half times its total annual production in stocks abroad.

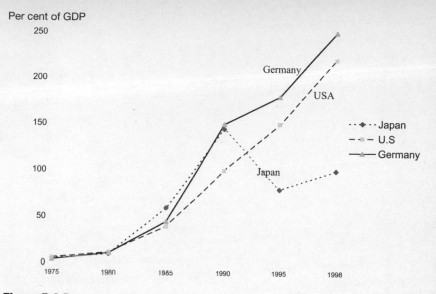

Per cent of GDP

Figure P.8 Purchases of foreign stocks as a percentage of Gross Domestic Product (1975-1998)[347]

The stakes are enormous. Ultimately money is trust, which lives and dies only in human hearts and minds. Money systems, including our current one, are mechanisms and symbols that aim at keeping that trust alive. Historically, entire civilizations have been built on trust, because it is at the core of the self-confidence required for a civilization to grow or even survive. On the negative side, when a society loses confidence in its money, it loses confidence in itself.

'The debate about the future of money is not about inflation or deflation, fixed or flexible exchange rates, gold or paper standards; it is about the kind of society in which money is to operate.'[348]

Other functions of money

The functions of today's money system – other than as a medium of exchange or payment – are recalled here to complete the descriptions of the Primer and Chapter 2.

National currencies today fulfil functions in addition to the one of medium of exchange. The most important of these other functions are a standard of measure, a store of value, an instrument for speculation, and in some cases a tool of empire.

Standard of Measure: The value of the proverbial apples and oranges can be compared by expressing each of them in the same standard, typically dollars for Americans, euros for Europeans, etc. Historically, many cultures have had standards of measure different from the medium of exchange. For instance, one important unit of measure in ancient Europe used to be cattle – Homer (8th century BC) would invariably express values in oxen for example. However, payments were often made in a more practical medium of exchange such as bronze artefacts, gold or silver bars and later coins.

Store of Value: Currency was not the preferred store of value in most civilizations. For example, the word *capital* derives from the Latin *capus, capitis,* which means head. This referred to heads of cattle just as in Homer, and still happens today in Texas or among the Watutsi in Africa – 'He is worth one thousand head'. In the Western world, from Egyptian times through the Middle Ages and until the late 18th century, wealth was stored mainly in land and its improvements (irrigations, plantations, etc.).

Instrument of Speculation: Most economic textbooks will not mention instrument of speculation as a function of today's money. But this has now clearly become one of its contemporary functions, as 98% of all foreign exchange trading has become speculative.

A Tool of Empire: Currency is a powerful way to create a homogeneous economic and information space. During the period when nation states were trying to establish their legitimacy, national currencies became an important symbolic tool (with the national flag, the national anthem, etc.). Aristotle considered the power to impose one's currency as a prerogative of empire.

Glossary

Bank for International Settlements (BIS): Private organization located in Basle, Switzerland, owned by the eleven key central banks in the world. Initially designed as a clearing house for transactions among central banks, it has evolved into a meeting ground for central bankers and a research centre about issues of interest to the monetary system as a whole. Website: http://www.bis.org/

Barter: The direct exchange of goods or services un-mediated by any type of currency.

Bond: Financial instrument sold by a borrower against periodic payment of interest and of the principal at maturity.

Bretton Woods: Township in New Hampshire where the Bretton Woods Agreement was finalized in 1945 after negotiations mainly between the British and the US. The system agreed upon has also been called the dollar-gold equivalence standard, because it gave the status of official global reserve currency to the US$, on condition that the US guaranteed the convertibility of dollars into gold on demand of other central banks, at a fixed rate of $35 per ounce. In August 1971, President Nixon unilaterally reneged on that latter clause by 'closing the gold window' when France and the UK requested such redemptions. This also inaugurated the era of floating exchanges in which the values of each currency and of gold would be left free to be determined by market forces.

Capital: In its narrow financial meaning, a sum of money from which an income can be derived. The two most traditional means for such income is interest (in case of loans) and dividends (in case of stocks). By extension, a resource that enhances life. The following types of capital can be distinguished in this extended meaning: financial capital, physical capital (plant and equipment), intellectual capital (patents, copyrights), social capital (relationships within communities) and natural capital ('Mother Nature').

Central Bank: Organization which is officially in charge of managing a national currency. Some central banks are owned by private banks (e.g. the US Federal Reserve Bank, or the Swiss, Italian or South African central banks); some owned by the government (e.g. Banque de France, and the UK's Bank of England since its nationalization in 1946); some are mixed (e.g. the Belgian central bank). All central banks are responsible for the internal stability (i.e. inflation-fighting) and external stability (i.e. value of the currency compared to other national currencies). They have a variety of means at their disposal to achieve these aims, including intervention (buying or selling the national currency in the market in exchange for other national currencies); changes in key interest rates; or fixing reserve requirements for the private banks. All these techniques really boil down to changing the maximum quantity of 'fiat' currency that the private banks will be able to issue and at what cost.

Commodity-Backed Currency: A currency whose value is guaranteed by the physical availability of the commodity which backs the currency. The owner of a backed currency can normally ask for delivery of the physical good or service in exchange for the currency. Backed currency is typically issued by whoever owns the product or service accepted as backing. (E.g. 19th-century gold standard backed by gold; Time Dollars backed by hours of community service.)

Currency: Synonymous with money, but emphasizing the medium of exchange function of money.

Currency Board: A monetary mechanism by which one national currency is issued backed one-to-one by a reserve currency. In other words, it is similar to a commodity-backed currency, but the backing is someone else's national currency. Argentina, Hong Kong and other countries have resorted to currency boards, where the backing is the US dollar.

Demurrage charge: A time-related charge on outstanding balances of a currency. Acts similarly to a negative interest rate, and was designed as a disincentive to hoard the currency. Savings would then occur in forms other than accumulation of the medium of exchange. Silvio Gesell developed the theory that money is like a public service (e.g. public transport), and therefore a charge is justified. Both John Maynard Keynes and Irving Fisher provided theoretical foundation for this approach, and it was last implemented in the form of 'stamp scrip' in the 1930s.

Derivatives: A financial instrument which enables the segmentation of different types of risks. The main types of derivatives are futures (when contracted in a regulated exchange), forwards (when contracted in the unregulated Over the Counter market) and options. Exotic derivatives are complex combinations of the simpler derivatives such as forwards and options.

Devaluation: Synonymous with depreciation. Reduction in value of one currency in terms of other currencies.

Discounted Cash Flow: Calculates the value of a future cash flow in terms of an equivalent value today. For instance $100 a year from now is the same as $90.909 today if one uses a discount rate of 10%, because $90.909 dollars invested for one year at a risk-free rate of 10% will yield $100.

Euro: Single European currency replacing the national currencies of 11 European countries as of January 1, 1999. Bills in euros will be circulating from 2002 onwards. The transition mechanism from the previous national currencies towards the euro was the ECU, a currency unit which was defined in 1979 as a basket of European currencies.

'Fiat' currency: A currency created out of nothing by the power of an authority. All national currencies are fiat currencies.

Fixed Exchange Rate: Rate fixed by an authority at which one currency can be exchanged against another. This was the rule in the Bretton Woods Agreement from 1945 to 1971, and the IMF was the authority which had to approve any changes in exchange rates. The rule of fixed exchange rates was replaced by floating exchange rates after 1972 for most national currencies.

Floating Exchange Rate: Rate at which one currency can be exchanged for another as determined by the free bidding and asking in the foreign exchange market. Has been the regime for most national currencies since 1972.

Fractional Reserve: When a currency is issued with only a fraction backed by whatever supports it. The practice of fractional reserves initiated in mediaeval goldsmiths' practices when they issued paper currency which was backed by the deposits in gold made by clients. It still is an important feature of today's modern banking system, because a bank can issue fiat currency while only having a small fraction of national currency or government bonds in deposit (this fraction varies with the kind of deposit – long or short term for instance – and is one of the variables that central banks can use to change money supply).

Gift Economy: Economy in which the exchange of gifts plays the key social role. Anthropological research has shown a direct relationship between gift exchanges and community building. The word 'community' itself shows this connection: cum = *together, among each other*; and munere = *to give*; hence community – to give among each other.

Global Reference Currency (GRC): A currency which would be a stable international reference for contractual and payment purposes worldwide, specifically designed for international trade. One example of a Global Reference Currency is the Terra which consists of a currency backed by a specific basket of a dozen commodities and services critical in international trade. The cost of storage of the commodities involved would be passed along to the bearer, and function therefore as a built-in demurrage charge. This feature reverses the tendency to discount the future, and therefore realigns the corporate financial interests with long-term sustainability.

Gross National Product (GNP): The value of all goods and services produced and exchanged in a particular country. The largest component of GNP is the **Gross Domestic Product (GDP)** which is the value of all goods and services consumed in a country. Foreign Trade makes up the difference between GNP and GDP.

Inflation: Depreciation over time of the value of a currency in terms of goods and services. An excess of money supply will tend to create inflation.

Interest: Time-related income for the lender of a currency, or time-related cost for the borrower of a currency. Charging interest was prohibited by all three major religions, Judaism, Christianism and Islam. Today, only Islam enforces this rule (hence 'Islamic banking' which is banking where interest charges are replaced with other types of fees). Interest is one of the key ingredients in the Discounted Cash Flow, which provokes discounting of the future.

International Monetary Fund (IMF): International organization based in Washington DC, initially created to administer the Bretton Woods Agreement. The US is the only country with veto power in it. Website: http://www.imf.org/

Investment: Spending money with the objective to improve or augment the productive capacity of a company or project. In economic language, is opposed to consumption.

'Legal tender for all debts public and private' means that if A owes a debt to B and offers to pay B with this currency, if B refuses the currency A can declare the debt void and have the courts support him or her (is particularly important in tax payments, and in all other legal settlements).

LETS: Acronym for Local Exchange Trading System. The most popular form of local currency mutual credit system in the world.

Market: Physical or virtual space in which demand and offer of a given product or service interact to create a price. Market economies presuppose price variability, for instance prices dropping automatically to clear what is on offer. Theory shows that true market economies require large numbers of small suppliers and consumers, and low barriers to entry. These perfect conditions are rarely prevailing in today's economy. The opposite of a market price is a price fixed by some authority – individual, government or corporate.

Micro-credit: Refers to loans in conventional national currency for small amounts to small-scale entrepreneurs. The Grameen Bank in Bangladesh has been a model of success in such activities.

Monetarism: Economic theory which posits that only the quantity of money determines prices, and therefore that it is counterproductive to use monetary adjustment tools for purposes other than inflation control. Monetarism also assumes that money is 'neutral', in the sense that neither production nor distribution are affected by money. It concludes that markets will invariably know more than individuals, including central bankers. Keynes challenged classical Monetarism, but Milton Friedman put it back on the agenda.

Money: Synonymous with currency. Our working definition is: an agreement within a community to use something as a medium of exchange, or more normally of a means of payment.

Mutual Credit: Process of creating money by a simultaneous debit and credit between participants in the transaction. Examples of Mutual Credit Systems include LETS, Time Dollars, Tlaloc and ROCS. For instance, in Time Dollars if Julia renders a service of one hour to James, she gets a credit for one HOUR, and James a debit for one HOUR. They have therefore created the Time Dollars necessary for their transaction by agreeing on the transaction itself. The main advantage of mutual credit systems is that they self-regulate to have always currency available in sufficiency.

Negotiated exchange rate: In contrast with 'fixed exchange rates', when the exchange rate is negotiated as part of the transaction itself. Currently under floating exchange rates, all national currencies have negotiated exchange rates among each other. Similarly, with ROCS the value of one hourly service is negotiated at the moment of a transaction: a dentist may charge five ROCS for each hour of work for example.

OECD: The Organization of Economic Cooperation and Development, based in Paris, and grouping the 'developed' countries in the world. Website http://www.oecd.org

Payment system: Procedure and infrastructure by which the transfer of a currency is executed from one person to another.

ROCS: Acronym for Robust Currency System. Incorporates all the most robust features of various monetary innovations. The unit of account is the hour, the currency is created by mutual credit, and a small demurrage charge is applied to it.

Scarce: In insufficient quantities. For instance, in all our national currencies 'bank debt money keeps value only by its scarcity compared to its usefulness'. For our purposes, the polarity of scarcity is *not* over-abundance, but sufficiency. For instance, in a mutual credit system there is always sufficiency of money (as participants create it among themselves as a debit and credit at the moment of a transaction).

Scrip: Private currency usually initially issued in the form of a paper IOU (I Owe You) by a corporation or an individual. For instance, frequent-flyer miles are evolving as a corporate scrip issued by airlines.

Stock: A fraction of ownership in a business. Stock markets are the regulated exchanges for stocks of companies listed in a particular exchange.

Structural Adjustment: A set of economic policies imposed by the IMF in exchange for new loans. Its main purpose is to improve the capacity of a country to pay for the interest and reimbursement of its external debt.

Sufficient: The polarity of scarcity. See scarce.

Time Dollar: A mutual credit system with as unit of account the hour of service, created by Edgar Cahn in the early 1990s. The US tax authority has given transactions in Time Dollars a tax-free status.

Value: Exchange value means the amount of currency that a particular good or service can obtain in the market. Use Value is the qualitative concept of the satisfaction or 'utility' that a user can derive from the product. Classical economists (including in this case Marxists) also defined a Work Value as the accumulation of human labour incorporated in a product.

Valued Currency: A currency is said to be valued by a commodity if its value is tied directly to the value of that commodity. For instance, under the gold bullion standard, the value of each currency was expressed in terms of the value of a fixed quantity of gold. There are only three ways of designing a currency system: 'fiat' (i.e. without reference to anything else); 'valued' by a commodity when its exchange value is expressed in terms of the value of that commodity; and 'backed' by a commodity when the currency is in fact a claim to a given quantity of that commodity (which requires to have a stock of that commodity on hand to meet such requests).

World Bank: Sister organization to the International Monetary Fund (IMF), also located in Washington DC. Initially, besides the IMF, two other organizations were created at Bretton Woods: the Bank of International Reconstruction and Development (BIRD) and the Agency for International Development (AID). The World Bank arose from combining these latter two international organizations. Its main activity is to finance large-scale development projects in the Third World. Website http://worldbank.org/

World Trade Organization (WTO): Organization succeeding to the General Agreement of Tariffs and Trade (GATT) which is in charge of negotiating and settling international trade issues. Website http://www.wto.org/

Notes

Part One: What *Is* Money?

1   Lapham, Lewis: *Money and Class in America: Notes and Observations on Our Civil Religion* (New York: Weidenfeld and Nicolson, 1988).

2   Trilling, Lionel: *The Liberal Imagination* (New York: Viking, 1950).

3   Drucker, Peter: *The Post-Capitalist Society* (Harper Business, 1993) p. 1.

Chapter 1: Money – The Root of All Possibilities

4   Mesarovic, Mihaljo and Pesterl, E.: *Mankind Turning Point: The second report to the Club of Rome* (New York: New American Library, 1974).

5   All the preceding data about ageing trends come from a conference in January 1999 in the San Francisco Bay Area by Ken Dytchwald, founder of Age Wave Inc., and author of a/o. *Age Wave*, and *Wellness and Health Promotion for the Elderly*.

6   The Organization for Economic Cooperation and Development (OECD), based in Paris, is the association of the most developed countries of the world.

7   Petersen, Peter G.: 'Gray Dawn: The Global Aging Crisis' in *Foreign Affairs* (January-February 1999) p. 43.

8   All data in this sidebar from Petersen, Peter G.: ibid. pp. 44-45.

9   Data in this paragraph from Petersen, Peter G.: ibid. p. 46.

10   Killinger, Barbara: *Workaholics: The Respectable Addict* (Toronto: Key Porter Books, 1991) p. 7.

11   'Job Stress Characterized as "Global Phenomenon"', *Oakland Tribune*, March 23, 1993, D-11.

12   Greider, William: *One World: Ready or Not* (New York: Simon and Schuster, 1997); juxtaposition quoted in *Success Digest*, March 1997.

13   William Bridges, author of *Understanding Today's Job/Shift* at a conference in San Francisco, 1995.

14   This period has been labelled by historians 'Europe's First Renaissance' and 'Europe's Common People Renaissance' because of the unusually high standard of living of the common people.

15   Quoted by Rifkin, Jeremy in 'After Work', *Utne Reader*, May-June 1995, p. 54. Several of the examples provided above are also quoted in that article.

16   Report of the Associated Press, filed by Donna Abu-Nasr on November 27, 1998.

17   Davidson, Keay: 'Ice of Antarctica May be Melting', *San Francisco Examiner*, August 2, 1998, p. A4.

18   *The Economist* (January 1, 1999) p. 32.

19   Caffrey, Andy: 'Antarctica's "Deep Impact" Threat', *Earth Island Journal* (Summer 1998) p. 26.

20   *Warning to Humanity*.

21   *Adbusters: Journal of the Mental Environment* (Winter 1997) p. 41.

22   As receiver of the John Bates Clark Medal, a prize given to the best economist under the age of forty.

23   Krugman, Paul: 'The Return of Depression Economics', *Foreign Affairs* (January–February 1999) pp. 42-74.

24   Russell, Peter: *The White Hole in Time* (New York: Aquarian/Thompson, 1992) p. 198.

25   Dee Hock, Founder and Chairman Emeritus VISA International.

26   Meadows, Donella, et al.: *Beyond the Limits* (Post Mills, Vermont: Chelsea Green Publishing, 1992) p. 191 (*italics in original*).

27   Oates, J.: *Babylon* (London, 1979) p. 25.

28   Sustainability as a process as opposed to a passive state has been identified earlier in the *Brundlandt Report* prepared for the World Commission on Environment and Development (WCED) entitled *Our Common Future* (Oxford: Oxford University Press, 1987) and in Meadows, Donella, et al. op.cit.

29   In a personal interview of Mr Hotta conducted by the author on February 20, 1999.

30   *US News and World Report,* December 30, 1996, p. 72.

31   Beck, Ulrich: 'Goodbye to all that Wage Slavery', *New Statesman* (March 5, 1999).

32   There are more than a thousand temples in Bali. Each temple has its *odalan* festival every 210 days, which last up to three days each. In addition there are cyclical festivals at every full moon, every four years, every ten years, every 100 years. There are also home-based ceremonies, and five or six major ceremonies in each person's life, the most important of which is the cremation which can take more than a month to prepare. All in all, Hindu Balinese men spend 30%, and women up to 40% of their time preparing for or performing in 'temple time'.

33   GEN includes a series of eco-villages around the world, including the Findhorn Community (Scotland), The Farm (Tennessee, USA), Lebensgarten (Steyerberg, Germany), Crystal Waters (Australia), Ecoville (St Petersbrugh, Russia), Gyûrûfû (Hungary), The Ladakh Project (India), the Manitou Institute (Colorado, USA) and the Danish Eco-Village Association. They have regional headquarters in Australia, Germany, the USA and Denmark.

34   The Russian 'Golden Crown' payment system is one of three case studies in Krüger, M. and Godschalk H.: *Herausforderung des bestehenden Geldsystems im Zuge seiner Digitalisierung – Chancen für Innovationen* (Karlsruhe: Institut für Technikfolgenabschätzung und Systemanalyse, November 1998).

Chapter 2: Today's Money

35   Galbraith, J.K.: *Money: Whence it came, Where it went* (Boston: Houghton Mifflin Co., 1975) p. 5.

36   Needleman, Jacob: *Money and the Meaning of Life* (New York: Doubleday Currency, 1994) p. 239.

37   Skidelsky, Robert: *John Maynard Keynes: The Economist as a Savior,* Vol. II (New York: Penguin, 1994) p. 312. Also quoted by Lawrence S. Ritter ed.: *Money and Economic Activity* (Boston: Houghton Mifflin, 1967) p. 33.

38   John Maynard Keynes: *A Treatise on Money* (London, 1930) chap. 1, p. 13.

39   *Mysterium Geld: Emotionale Bedeutung und Wirkungweise eines Tabus* (München: Riemann Verlag, March 2000).

40   Congressman Bill Dannemeyer, from southern California, wrote to his constituency that 'It is not an accident that the American experiment with a paper dollar standard, a variable standard, has been going on at the same time that our culture has been questioning whether American civilization is based on the Judeo-Christian ethic, or Secular Humanism. The former

involves formal rules from God through the vehicle of the Bible. The latter involves variable rules adopted by man and adjusted as deemed appropriate.' Quoted in William Greider: *The Secrets of the Temple* (New York: Touchstone Books, 1987) p. 230.

41 Ferguson, Sarah: 'Star Trek: The Next Currency', *Worldbusiness*, Spring 1995, p. 14.

42 Greider, William op.cit., p. 240.

43 Davies, Glyn: *A History of Money from ancient times to the present day* (Cardiff: University of Wales Press, 1994) p. 27.

44 Williams, Jonathan: Money: A History (New York: St Martin's Press, 1997) pp. 207–209.

45 These are explained in more detail in Appendix A.

46 Proust, Marcel: *Le Temps Retrouvé*.

47 Buchan, James: *Frozen Desire: The Meaning of Money* (New York: Farrar Strauss Giroux, 1997) pp. 19–20.

48 Zeitgeist would translate literally as 'Spirit of the Age', but the English translation does not really do justice to the original German. *Zeitgeist* also captures the mood, fashionable ideas, and the art forms through which this mood and ideas are expressed. It is interesting that the concept of *Zeitgeist*, and its accompanying constructs of *Weltanschauung* (literally, 'way of looking at the world') were developed in parallel with the concept of the nation-state by the German philosopher Hegel (1770-1831).

49 The German philosopher Georg Wilhelm Frederick Hegel developed the theoretical concept of a nation-state owned by the people who inhabit it, as opposed to private or oligarchical fief-doms which were the historical norm for kingdoms or empires.

50 Handy, Charles: *The Empty Raincoat* (London: Arrow Business Books, 1995) p. 108.

51 Committee on the Working of the Monetary System, Report (London: Her Majesty's Stationery Office, 1959) paragraph 345, p. 117.

52 These technical aspects are explained in Appendix A.

53 Jackson & McConnell: *Economics* (Sydney: McGraw Hill, 1988).

54 Please note that I use the word 'sufficiency' and not 'over-abundance'. Economists will – correctly – point out that if there is an over-abundance of anything (including money), it becomes treated as valueless. This is not true with sufficiency. Mutual credit systems – discussed in later chapters – create currency in sufficiency (for example service-time) which is not scarce, but is not over-abundant either.

55 The story of the Eleventh Round is a simplified illustration for non-economists, isolating the impact of interest on money on the system. To isolate that one variable, I have made the assumption of a zero growth society: no population increase, no production or money increases. In practice, of course, all three of these variables grow over time, further obscuring the impact of interest. The point of the 'Eleventh Round' is simply that – *all other things being equal* – competition to obtain the money necessary to pay the interest, which is never created, is structurally embedded in the current system.

56 Thuillier, P.: 'Darwin chez les Samourai' in *La Recherche* No. 181 (Paris, 1986) p. 1276-1280.

57 Sahtouris, Elisabet: *Earth Dance: Living Systems in Evolution* (Alameda, CA: Metalog Books, 1996).

58 Kennedy, Margrit: *Geld Ohne Zinsen und Inflation: Ein Tauschmittel das Jedem Dient* (Goldman Verlag, 1988) pp. 22 and 38. The value of gold in this calculation is fixed at the price of 18,500 DM per kg of gold, the value it had in January 1990, and the weight of the earth in kg. at .5,973 followed by 24 zeros. Calculations by Heinrich Haussmann: *Die Josefpfennig* (Furth, 1990).

59 Kennedy, Margrit: *Interest and Inflation Free Money* (Okemos, Michigan: Sava International, 1995) p. 26. Also German edition.

60   Source: Project Responsible Wealth, 37 Temple Place, Boston MA 02111.

61   Meadows, Donella: 'Wealthy stand up for greater equality', *Bennington Banner* (November 1997).

62   Korten, David: 'Money versus Wealth', *YES! A journal of Positive Futures* (#2 Spring 1997) p. 14.
       This number is based on a study performed by Sarah Anderson and John Cavanagh for the
       Institute for Policy Studies (1996).

63   Gates, Jeff: *The Ownership Solution* (Boulder: Perseus Books, 1998).

Chapter 3: Cybersphere – The New Money Frontier

64   Quoted by Mayer, Martin: *The Bankers: The Next Generation* (New York: Truman Talley
       Books/Dutton, 1997, p. 129.

65   *The Economist* (September 28, 1969): Survey of the World Economy, pp. 3-4.

66   Estimate by John Gage, Chief Scientist at Sun Microsystems at a conference in Berkeley in 1998.

67   von Tunzelman, G.N.: *Steam Power and British Industrialization to 1860* (Oxford: Clarendon Press,
       1978).

68   *The Economist* (September 28, 1969): Survey of the World Economy, p. 10.

69   Goldman Sachs Investment Research: The race to build the Broadband Kingdom (August 12,
       1998).

70   Cleveland, Harlan: 'Fairness and the Information Revolution', *World Business Academy* (Vol. 11,
       No. 2, 1997).

71   Cleveland, Harlan: *Leadership and the Information Revolution* (Minneapolis: World Academy of Art
       and Science, 1997); and *The Knowledge Executive: Leadership in an Information Society* (New York:
       Truman Talley Books/E.P. Dutton, 1985).

72   Rheingold, Howard: *Virtual Reality and Virtual Community* (New York: HarperPerennial, 1993).

73   Cleveland, Harlan: *Leadership and the Information Revolution*, op.cit.; and *The Knowledge Executive*,
       op.cit.

74   Rheingold, Howard: op.cit.

75   Remarks by Ted Hall, Director of Mc Kinsey and Co., at the State of the World Forum, San
       Francisco, November 1997.

76   Ibid.

77   This law dates back to agricultural economics. It points out that whenever one applies an addi-
       tional input such as fertilizer or labour to a given plot of land, each additional ton of fertilizer
       or worker-hour will produce less benefit than the previous one. At a certain point, too much
       fertilizer or labour will actually reduce the output.

78   Arthur, Brian: 'Increasing Returns and the Two Worlds of Business' *Harvard Business Review*
       (July 1996).

79   Gross Domestic Product.

80   Cleveland, Harlan: 'Fairness and the Information Revolution' in *Perspectives on Business and
       Global Change* (Vol. 11, No. 2, World Business Academy) (*all italics in original*).

81   Frank, Robert and Cook, Philip: *The Winner-Takes-All Society* (Free Press), see also the seminal
       1981 article by Rosen, Sherwin: 'The Economics of Superstars'.

82   Wired (November 1997) p. 202.

83   Hilzenrat, David S.: 'Change is Good, they Bet' and 'Fewer Middlemen, Bigger Margin' in
       Washington Post (October 21, 1997) p. 13.

84   Platt, Charles: 'Digital Ink' in *Wired* (May 1997) pp. 162-165.

85   These POD presses are currently owned by Ingram Book Company, the largest book whole-
       saler in the US. Their first application is to produce copies of out-of-print books, several
       hundred of which were already available in the summer of 1998. Optimists see this as a way to

keep books from going out of print. Pessimists see the risk of having many books never produced in 'the normal way'.

86   Boyle, David: *E-Money* (Financial Times Management Report, December 1999).

87   Gosling, Paul: *Changing Money: How the digital age is transforming financial services* (London: Bowerdean, 1999).

88   *Smart-card News*, February 1999.

89   At a meeting in Washington sponsored by the Treasury Department, quoted by Mayer, Martin: *The Bankers: The Next Generation* (New York: Truman Talley Books/Dutton, 1997) p. 34.

90   *The Forrester Report: Money and Technology – Open Finance* (Vol. 2, No. 4, December 1996) p. 3.

91   Boyle, David: 'The scandal of the tax havens', *New Statesman*, November 13, 1998.

92   Cendant is the largest on-line merchandiser with a sales volume on the Net of some $1.5 billion in 1997, also the topic of a case study in Chapter 4.

93   Wired (September 1997) p. 223.

94   The Eliot quotation is from *The Rock* and Cleveland's from *The Knowledge Executive: Leadership in an Information Society* (New York: Truman Talley Books/E.P. Dutton, 1985) p. 22.

95   Hayek was more sweeping with his comment that 'practically all governments of history have used their exclusive power to issue money in order to defraud and plunder people'. (Hayek: 'Choice in Currency: a Way to Stop Inflation', *IEA Occasional Paper 48* (1976).

Chapter 4: Five Scenarios for the Future

96   Valery, Paul: Historical Fact (1932).

97   Schwartz, Peter: *The Art of the Long View* (New York: Doubleday Currency, 1996) p. 43.

98   Botkin, J., Elmandjira M. & Malitza, M.: *No Limits to Learning: Bridging the Human Gap* (New York: Pergamon Press, 1979).

99   Schwartz, Peter: 'Foresee the Futures: The Art of the Long View' *Soundview Executive Book Summaries*, Vol. 13, No. 8 part 2, August 1991 pp. 1-3.

100 Sunter, Clem: *The World and South Africa in the 1990s*, and *The High Road: Where are we Now?* (Capetown: Tafelberg, Human and Rousseau, 1996).

101 Schwartz, Peter: *The Art of the Long View*, op.cit.

102 'Smart cards' look like plastic credit cards, but they contain a computer chip instead of the magnetic strip to store data. This makes possible not only the storage of a lot more information, but also local processing of such data for identification and encryption purposes.

103 The 'Plaza Agreement' was the accord reached among the G-5, the five most important central banks (the US, Japan, Germany, the UK and France), at the Plaza Hotel in New York in 1985 for a coordinated effort to gradually lower the value of the dollar in the world markets. It marked the end of the non-interventionist policy by the US in currency markets.

104 Named after the Dutch town where the European Union countries agreed to implement the next phase of the European integration process including a single currency, the euro, introduced in 1999.

105 This scenario terminology and methodology is borrowed from Schwartz, Peter: *The Art of the Long View*, op.cit., p. 19.

106 Havelock, Eric: 'The Muses Learn to Write: Reflections on Orality and Literacy' from *Antiquity to the Present* (Stanford, CN: Yale University Press, 1988).

107 Shlain, Leonard: *The Alphabet versus the Goddess: The Conflict between Word and Image* (New York: Viking, 1998).

108 McLuhan, Marshall: *The Gutenberg Galaxy: The Making of Typographical Man* (Toronto: University of Toronto Press, 1962).

109   See among others McLuhan, Marshall: *The Medium is the Message: an Inventory of Effects* (Hardwired, 1996).

110   The style of this scenario and part of its contents are inspired by two articles: 'Altered States' by Paul Rogers and 'The Wild Frontier' by Peter Popham, both in 'The Sunday Review' (Sunday Supplement of the *Independent*: October 13, 1996) pp. 10-14. While some ideas come from these articles, there are also substantial additions and differences to which the original authors may not subscribe, so I take full responsibility for these changes.

111   Handy, Charles: *The Empty Raincoat* (London: Arrow Business Books, 1992).

112   Greenspan, Alan: 'Fostering Financial Innovations: the Role of Government' in *The Future of Money in the Information Age* (Washington, DC: The Cato Institute, 1997) pp. 49-50.

113   *Wired* (February 1999) p. 149.

114   The information in this sidebar is summarized from *Wired*, July 1998, p. 86.

115   OECD is the Organization for Economic Cooperation and Development, based in Paris. It covers the 24 most 'developed' countries in the world.

116   *The Economist* (March 22, 1997, p. 143 and March 21, 1998, p. 135).

117   Sarah Anderson and John Cavanagh in a study carried out for the Institute for Policy Studies (1996).

118   Hawken, Paul quoted by Korten, David: *The Post-Corporate World: Life after Capitalism* (San Francisco: Berret Koehler, 1999) Chapter 2, p. 8.

119   Cited in *A Matter of Fact*, Vol. 25, July-December 1996.

120   Hacker, Andrew: *Money. Who has how much and why* (New York: Scribner, 1997) Chapter 8 (pp. 105-122).

121   Bureau of Census: Government Finances Series GF, No. 5 various years. See also Bartlett, Donald and Steele, James: *America: Who Really Pays Taxes?*

122   Hamelink, Cees J.: 'The Right to Communicate', *IDOC Internazionale* (January-June 1999).

123   Most of the examples provided were documented in *Adbusters: Journal of the Mental Environment* (Winter 1997). Exceptions are the examples of the beach advertising and Metro Cinevision that were reported on Public Radio International (PRI).

124   Stuart, Elliott: 'Digital Image Magic: Going where no Ads Have Gone Before', *International Herald Tribune* (October 2-3, 1999 pp. 9-10).

125   Swimme, Brian: 'The hidden heart of the cosmos' conference presented at the State of the World Forum, San Francisco, November 1997.

126   De Long, Bradford and Froomkin, Michael: 'The Next Economy' in Hurley, Deborah, Kahin, Brian and Varian, Hal: *Internet Publishing and Beyond: the Economics of Digital Information and Intellectual Property* (Cambridge: MIT Press, 1998). (*Italics added.*)

127   Kaplan, Robert in 'Was democracy just a moment?' *Atlantic Monthly* (December 1997) p. 73.

128   *Ibid*, p. 71.

129   Quoted by Kaplan, Robert in 'Was democracy just a moment?', Ibid., p. 73.

130   Lempinen Edward: 'Journalists Probe Their Own Credibility Gap', *San Francisco Chronicle*, Saturday, August 2, 1998, p. A7.

131   Keohane, Robert & Nye, Joseph: 'States and the Information Revolution', *Foreign Affairs* (September-October 1998, Vol. 77 No. 5) p. 90.

132   Lempinen, Edward: 'Journalists Probe Their Own Credibility Gap', op.cit., p. A1.

133   Baker, Russ: 'The Big Squeeze', *Columbia Journalism Review* (October 1997).

134   Barlett, Donald L. and Steele, James B.: 'What corporate welfare costs', *Time* (November 6, 1998).

135   All data in this sidebar from Barlett & Steele: Ibid.

136   Korten, David: *When Corporations Rule the World* (San Francisco: Beret Koehler Publishers, 1997) p. 74.

137   Abbreviated and adapted from the Scenario prepared by the Global Business Network about Generation X, *Netview* Vol. 7, No. 1 (Winter 1996) pp. 5-7.

138   See Mark Ludwig: *Milleniumb : Gateway to a Cashless Society* (American Eagle Publish., 1997)

139   Variations on such a crash have been forecast by Joel Kurzman, or George Soros (see both references in Preface) or Shelton Judy: Money *Meltdown: Restoring Order to the Global Currency System* (New York: The Free Press, 1994).

140   The last exception was the Swiss Franc, which was still backed by gold until 1999.

141   A dollar meltdown would be worse than the 1929 crash, not only because it would be more global, but also because it would affect almost all financial instruments. In 1929, for instance, only the main stock markets collapsed. One could have escaped the crash by simply putting one's savings in US government bonds, for instance. Most bond markets and the gold-based monetary exchange system came under a lot of pressure in the 1930s, but roughly held. It took the war to kill, finally and permanently, the old gold-based monetary order. In the case of a dollar problem, the monetary system would be the weaker link and would give in first. A panic in the bond and stock markets would be a predictable and direct effect of the money crisis.

142   Homease: *10 Points* (San Francisco, Spring 1989) p. 4.

143   *The Progressive Review* No. 105.7 (AFL-CIO website).

144   AFDC-HAP stands for 'Aid to Families with Dependent Children – Homeless Assistance Programs'.

145   Center for Common Concern: A Homebase Report (San Francisco, annual reports 1989, 1993, 1994, 1996).

146   City and Council of San Francisco: 'Comprehensive Housing Affordability Strategies for Siting Housing and Services for Homeless People': *Annual Plan for 1994.* (November 5, 1993).

147   Data from 'Report to Congress: Education for Homeless Children and Youth Program' (Stewart B. McKinney Homeless Assistance Act Title VII, Subtitle B) July 1995. This data captures only children who are reported as having special difficulties enrolling in school because they are homeless.

148   Waxman and Hinderliter: A Status Report on Hunger and Homelessness in America's Cities: 1996 (US Conference of Mayors, 1520 Eye St. NW, Suite 400, Washington DC 20006-4005).

149   'Affordable Housing' is defined technically as absorbing up to 30% of pre-tax earnings. 'Fair market price' is the cost of non-subsidized housing in the area.

150   Kaufman, Tracy: *Housing America's Future: Children at Risk* (Wahsington DC Low Income Housing Coalition, 1996).

151   Waxman and Hinderliter, Ibid. (1996).

152   Homes for the Homeless, Inc.: *The New Poverty: A generation of Homeless Families* (New York, 1992).

153   Children's Defense Fund (CDF) and the National Coalition for the Homeless: *Welfare to What? Early Findings on Family Hardship and Well-Being* (http://childrendefense.org/fairstart_welfare2what.html) December 1998.

154   *Quotable Women* (London: Running Press, 1991).

Part Two: Choosing Your Future of Money

155   Needleman, Jacob: *Money and the Meaning of Life* (New York: Doubleday Currency, 1991) p. 177.

156   Timberlake, Richard H.: 'Private Production of Scrip-Money in the Isolated Community', *Journal of Money, Credit, and Banking* Vol. 19 No. 4 (November 1987) pp. 437-447.

Chapter 5: Work-Enabling Currencies

157 Naisbitt, John: *Megatrends* (New York: Warner Books, 1982) p. 183.

158 *Chicken Soup for the Soul* (Deerfield Beach, Florida: Health Communications, Inc., 1993) p. 149.

159 First and second meanings of the word 'job' in the *Oxford English Dictionary*.

160 The original text is ' That weore waes begunnen onzean Godes willan' *Aelfric Homilies* (11th century).

161 Premier's Council on Health Strategy: *Nurturing Health: A Framework on the Determinants of Health* (Toronto, 1991) p. 7.

162 One of the better surveys of this problem is from Rifkin, Jeremy: *The End of Work: The Decline of the Global Labor Force and the Dawn of the Post-Market Era* (New York: Putnam, 1995). Several of the subsequent examples are extracted from this work.

163 Both the *Fortune* and *Wall Street Journal* references as quoted in *Netview* (Global Business Network News) Vol. 7, No. 1 (Winter 1996) respectively p. 16 and p. 9.

164 Data from *The Economist* (September 28, 1996) p. 13.

165 The book that got it all rolling was Hammer, Michael & Champy, James: *Reengineering the Corporation: A Manifesto for Business Revolution* (New York: Harperbusiness, 1994).

166 Quoted in *The New Leaders* (San Francisco: Sterling and Stone, Co.) May-June 1996, p. 6.

167 Bridges, William: Ibid.

168 Bassett, Philip: 'Decline of full-time work to continue, says forecast' in *The Times* (London: October 29, 1996).

169 Reported by Melania Brian in *Independent* (October 15, 1996).

170 Bridges, William: *Understanding Today's Job/Shift*, Conference in San Francisco, April 1995. Many of the US corporate examples provided in this section come from his research.

171 Krugman, Paul: *The Accidental Theorist and other Dispatches from the Dismal Science* (New York, London: W.W. Norton & Co., 1998) particularly Part I 'Jobs, Jobs, Jobs').

172 Greider, William: *One World, Ready or Not*; Reich, Robert: *Inside the Cabinet*.

173 Krugman, Paul: *ibid*. p. 31.

174 Keynes, John Maynard: *Essay on Persuasion* (1930).

175 Wiener, Norbert: *The Human Use of Human Beings* (New York: Houghton Mifflin, 1950) p. 162.

176 Machiavelli, Niccolo in the anthology by Bouthout, Gaston: *L'Art de la Politique* (Paris: Editions Seghers, 1969) p. 146.

177 Case material assembled by Jeremy Rifkin for an article 'African Americans and Automation', *Utne Reader*, No. 69 (May-June 1995) p. 68.

178 Nicholas Leman quoted by Rifkin, ibid.

179 Rifkin, Jeremy *The End of Work: The Decline of the Global Labor Force and the Dawn of the Post-Market Era* (New York: Putnam, 1995).

180 Cradall, B.C.: *Nanotechnology: Molecular Speculations on Global Abundance* (Cambridge: The MIT Press, 1996) p. 52.

181 Michael, Don: *Automation: the Silent Conquest*; Michael, Don: *The Unprepared Society*; Toffler, Alvin: *Future Shock*.

182 The philosopher Pogo Possum.

183 Cahn, Edgar: quoted in *YES! A Journal of Positive Futures* special issue on Money: Print your Own (#2 Spring 1997) p. 12.

184 There is a remarkable catalogue of over 300 pages which makes an inventory of several thousand examples of which sample currencies have been kept. See Mitchell, Ralph A. and Shafer, Neil: *Standard Catalog of Depression Scrip of the United States in the 1930's including Canada and Mexico* (Iola, Wisconsin 54990: Krause Publications, 1984).

The Chase Manhattan Bank Museum of Money of the World also has an extensive collection of these items.

185 Part of the Smithsonian Institution collection in Washington DC.

186 Among others, Prof. Joachim Starbatty (Tübingen), Prof. Oswald Hahn (Nürnberg), Prof. Hans C. Binswanger (St Gallen), Prof. Dietrich Suhr (Augsburg). Gesell's work in German includes 18 volumes *Gesammte Werke* (ed. Werner Onken). Only his main book was published in English under the title *Natural Economic Order*, but dates from 1958 (translated by Philip Pye). Among the noteworthy exceptions of the unfamiliarity with Gesell's work outside Germany, one could mention T. Cowen, R. Krosner, William Darrity and Mario Seccareccia all authors of recent publications about Gesell's work.

187 See Chapter 8.

188 Johnson, Paul: *Modern Times: The World from the Twenties to the Eighties* (New York: Harper and Row, 1983) pp. 134-135.

189 Detailed numbers are available in Whale, P.B.: *Joint-Stock Banking in Germany* (London, 1930, 1968) p. 210.

190 The election of November 6, 1932 has deliberately been left out of this graph because after the election of July 1932, Hitler had refused to become vice-chancellor under von Papen, forcing a new election only a few months later. As a consequence of this 'All or Nothing' attitude, the National-Socialists lost 2 million votes in November 1932, but this backlash clearly had to do with Hitler's intransigence and not with unemployment fluctuations.

191 Sources: Wörgl's 'Heimat Museum' and Schwartz, Fritz: *Das Experiment von Wöergl* (Bern: Genossenschaft Verlag Freiwirtschaftlicher Schriften, 1951).

192 Untergguggenberger's Program January 8, 1934 (Wörgl Heimat Museum).

193 Fisher, Irwing: *Stamp Scrip* (New York: Adelphi Co., 1933).

194 Mitchell, Ralph A. and Shafer, Neil: *Standard Catalog of Depression Scrip of the United States in the 1930's including Canada and Mexico*, op.cit.

195 Schwartz, Fritz: op.cit. p.14.

196 Sources come mostly from Internet websites, particularly http://transacton.net/money/community. This site surveys data from a variety of other sites including a/o: Landsman Community Services, Canada; Letslink, UK; *Grains de Sel*, France [http://altern.com/sel/letsww.htm]; Time Dollar Institute, Washington DC. Germanic countries http://www.talent.ch/adr/letslist.htm]. Ithaca Hours {http:www.publiccom.com/web/ithacahours/.

197 Linton, Michael and Greco, Thomas: The Local Employment and Trading System in *Whole Earth Review* No. 55, Summer 1987. Also for one of the best technical overviews on LETS and other alternative systems see Greco, Thomas *New Money for Healthy Communities* (Thomas Greco, Publisher, POBox 42663, Tucson AR 85733).

198 Adapted from Greco, Thomas: ibid. p. 92.

199 UK Department of the Environment: *Rural England* (HMSO, 1996); Social Exclusion Unit: *Bringing Britain Together* (HMSO, 1998).

200 Barnes, Helen, North, Peter and Walker, Perry: *LETS on Low Income* (London: New Economics Foundation, 1996); Croall, Jonathan: *LETS Act Locally* (London: Gulbenkian Foundation, 1997).

201 Blair, Tony: speech to national council for Voluntary Organizations (January 1999).

202 Mowat, Iain: *The growing trend towards Local Exchange Trading Systems within Industrialised Nations* (Honours Dissertation at the Department of Economics of the University of Strathclyde, 1997-98) p. 3-4.

203 New Economics Foundation: *Community Works* cited in *New Economics Magazine*, No. 41, Spring 1997.

204   Jackson, Mark: *Helping Ourselves: New Zealand's Green Dollar Exchanges* (Bendigo: La Trobe
       University, POBox 199, Bendigo 3550, Victoria, Australia, 1996). It is interesting that this the-
       sis was a result of the ANZAC Fellowship Programme, a reciprocal arrangement between
       Australia and New Zealand for people who have shown distinction in their fields and could
       benefit from research in the other country. Mark Jackson can also be contacted via e-mail on
       240102@basil.bendigo.latrobe.edu.au

205   Australian Social Security Office Press Release, December 8, 1993.

206   Suffrin, Claire and Marc-Heber: *Appel aux Intelligences.* The testimonies to the use of the system
       come from Maison de l'Amitié, Allée du Nondeux, 5570 Beauraing, Belgium.

207   Sources: *50 ans de Cercle Economique WIR* (publication in honor of the 50th anniversary of WIR)
       October 1984.
       Une entreprise de services et une banque pour le developpement economique des PME publication by WIR.
       Also E. Simon: *Enstehung und Entwicklung des Schweizerischen Wirtschaftringes* (Formation and
       Development of the Swiss Business Circle); and P. Enz: *Wie und warum der WIR entstand* (why
       and how the WIR was formed).

208   *WIR-Nachrichten* (WIR News) No. 1, November 1934.

209   Speech by Werner Zimmerman, Fall Conference of 1954.

210   Douthwaite, Richard: *Short CircuitL Strenghtening Local Economies for Security in an Unstable World*
       (Dublin: A Resurgence Book, 1996).

211   Based on personal discussions with Kato-san in Tokyo in September 1999, and on extracts
       from several documents including Kato, Toshiharu: *Silicon Valley Model* (NTT Books, in
       Japanese); and the website http:/kingfisher.kuis.kyoto-
       u.ac.jp/ecomoney/reports/topicsinJapan.html.

212   Kato, Toshiharu: 'Silicon Valley Wave: Toward the Creation of the Next Generation
       Information Society' (*italics added*).

213   Kato, Toshiharu: 'Eco-Money: Its Significance and Possibilities in the 21st Century'

214   See *Washington Post*, Monday, May 20, 1991, p. A1. Also *The Berkshire Record*, April 26, 1991, p.
       B1.
       All four experiments and several others are also analysed in Greco, Thomas: op.cit.

215   Worthington, Steve & Halsworth, Alan: 'Leominster card boosts town fortune' *Retail Week*, June
       28, 1996.

216   *Marketing*, May 9, 1996.

217   Boyle, David: *E-Money* (*Financial Times* Special Report, December 1999).

218   This field survey was performed on the BREAD system, a very young local currency system
       operating in Berkeley, California. It should be emphasized that the sample of 40 people inter-
       viewed was too small to be statistically significant, but 22 reported they had started the specific
       services they supplied to the network as a direct result of the creation of BREAD. See
       Kobayashi, Kazunori: *Community Currency* (Unpublished Senior Thesis, May 9, 1999). Berkeley
       Bread Case Study. More hard data on the social and micro-economic impact of complemen-
       tary currencies would clearly be useful.

Chapter 6: Community Currencies

219   Desmonde, William H.: *Magic, Myth and Money* (New York: The Free Press, 1962) p. 25.

220   Bruce, Judith: *Families in Focus* (New York: Population Council Publications, 1995) also
       reviewed in an article by Tamar Lewin: 'The decay of families is global, study says' *The New
       York Times* (May 31, 1995, p. A5).

221   Source: 'The family: home sweet home', *The Economist*, September 9, 1995, p. 6.

222   Bennet, William: *Index of Leading Cultural Indicators* (New York: Touchstone, 1994).

223   Schaef, Anne Wilson: *Native Wisdom for White Minds: Daily Reflections Inspired by the Native Peoples of the World* (New York: One World Balantine Books, 1995) January 6 reflection. (*Italics in orginal text*).

224   The anthropological literature on communities and the 'gift economies' that underlies them is vast. The best works on the topic of gift economies are the classic by Mauss, Marcel: 'Essai sur le Don: Forme et raison de l'échange dans les sociétés archaiques' in *L'Année Sociologique I* (1923-24) pp. 30-186; and in English Hyde, Lewis: *The Gift: Imagination and the Erotic Life of Property*. (New York: Vintage Books 1983, 3d edition). See also Levi-Strauss, Claude: *The Elementary structures of Kinship*, translated by James Bell et al. (Boston: Beacon Press, 1969).

225   'Venerable Beads' in *Discover: The World of Science* (October 1998) pp. 26-28.

226   Bhikku, Thanissaro: 'The Economy of Gifts: An American monk looks at the traditional Buddhist economy' *Tricycle: The Buddhist Review* (Winter 1996) p. 56. (*Italics added.*)

227   Marshall, Lorna: 'Sharing, Talking, and Giving: Relief of Social Tensions Among the !Kung Bushmen' in *Africa* (Journal of the International African Institute) 31, No. 3 (July 1961) p. 231-249.

228   Raymond Firth needed a complex whole-page diagram to explain this twenty-four step process in his 'Marriage Gifts among the Tikopia' in *Primitive Polynesian Economy* (London, 1939).

229   Malinowski, Bronislaw: *Argonauts of the Western Pacific* (London: George Routledge & Sons, 1922).

230   Barnett, H. G.: 'The nature of Potlatch' in *American Anthropologist* Vol. 40, No. 3 (July-September 1938): pp. 349-358.

231   Hagstrom, Warren O.: *The Scientific Community* (New York: Basic Books, 1965) p. 22.

232   Wilber, Ken: *Sex, Ecology, Spirituality: The Spirit of Evolution* (Boston & London: Shambala, 1995).

233   Interview with Prof. Kind published in the *Boston Globe*, November 3, 1980, p. 19.

234   Survey performed in 1995 by Paul Ray of American Lives Inc., the main survey of value changes in America.

235   *The Multinational Monitor* April '89.

236   Boyle, David: 'Time Brokers', *Guardian* (December 16, 1998).

237   Watford Council: *Choice, Independence and Influence: Better Government for Older People: The Watford Project* (Watford, March 1998).

238   *US News and World Report*, December 30, 1996 p. 72.

239   Ideas suggested by David Boyle in his chapter of 'Volunteer Currencies' (*Financial Times*, Management Report, December 1999).

240   Article by Lina Fina in *Washington Post* (Thursday, February 1, 1996),

241   Various sources, including a dozen first-hand interviews with local officials during a field trip to Curitiba in 1996-97. Some information about Curitiba's development strategy has also been published in English; see Rabinovitch, Jonas: 'Curitiba: Toward sustainable urban development' in *Environment and Urbanization*, Vol. 4, No. 2, pp. 62-73, October 1992; and Rabinovitch, Jonas and Leitman Josef 'Urban Planning in Curitiba' in *Scientific American* March 1996, pp. 46-53.

242   Over the more recent years a good part of the token distribution has been taken over by the private sector; 50 tokens are given per month by the corporations to their employees. In parallel, the component of fresh fruits and vegetables in exchange for garbage has increased. Also for the holiday seasons, panetone and other festive ethnic foods are supplied in exchange for 'garbage money'.

243   The respective *per capita* growth rates between 1980 and 1995 are 277% for Curitiba, 190% for Paraná and 192% for Brazil. Statistics from *Informaciones Socioeconomicas*, issued by the *Prefeitura*

da Cidade Curitiba (1996), compared with the Brazilian databases of SACEN, IPARDES and SICT/ICPI.

244   Source: *A l'écoute du Japon* (Brussels: Information bulletin of the Japanese Mission to the European Union) July 3, 1995, pp. 7-8.

245   Sources include personal conversations; the *Commonweal, Inc. Business Plan* (July 18, 1998); Hodroff, Joel: *Creating Jobs in a Decade of Downsizing: Introducing the Commonweal Currency Exchange Network* (March 17,1995); Morris, David: *Institute for Self Reliance: Memorandum on C$D* (Washington, DC, 1995); Commonweal, Inc. (PO Box 16299, Minneapolis MN55416) *Building Positive Futures for Youth and Communities* (Minneapolis, Spring 1998).

246   Rheingold, Howard: *Virtual Communities: Homesteading on the Electronic Frontier* (New York: Harper Perennial, 1993); also see Jones, Steve ed.: *Cybersociety* (Thousand Oaks, CA: Sage Publishers, 1995) and Jones, Steve ed.: *Virtual Culture Cybersociety* (Thousand Oaks, CA: Sage Publishers, 1997).

247   *Business Week*: (May 5, 1997, p. 80).

Chapter 7: Some Practical Issues

248   Issing, Otmar at the Annual Hayek Memorial Lecture, hosted by the Institute of Economic Affairs in London, May 27, 1999.

249   *European Central Bank Annual Report*, 1998 p. 106.

250   Lucas, Robert E. Jr.: 'Nobel Lecture: Monetary Neutrality', *Journal of Political Economy*, Vol. 104 #4, 1996.

251   Schrage, Michael: 'Frequent-Purchaser Programs Emerging as the Currency of the 90's' *Washington Post*, Friday, July 10, 1992.

252   European Commission: *Green Paper on Social Policy*, Brussels, 1993.

253   Boisonnat, F.: 'Combating unemployment, restructuring work', *International Labor Review* Vol. 135, No. 1, 1996.

254   Carlino, Gerald & Defina, Robert: 'Monetary Policy and the US States and Regions: Some Implications for European Monetary Union', *Federal Reserve of Philadelphia Working Paper No. 98-17 (1998)*.

255   One of the best summaries of that argument was provided by Prof. Otmar Issing, in his criticism of Hayek's proposal of multiple private currencies: 'In the absence of a single numeraire, financial communication would degenerate. This would probably result in a very poor coordination in the economy, with the efficiency of the decentralized decision making of firms and households which is the hallmark of capitalist economies, being jeopardized and the productive potential of the economy being gravely endangered.' Issing, Otmar: 'Hayek – Currency Competition and European Monetary Union', *Deutsche Bundesbank. Auszüge aus Pressartikeln* (May 27, 1999) p. 11.

256   Robert Wood Johnson Foundation: Service Credit Banking Project Site Summaries (University of Maryland Centre of Aging, 1990).

Chapter 8: A Global Reference Currency – Making Money Sustainable

257   Title of Introduction of Rueff, Jacques: *The Age of Inflation*, translation by A.H. Meeus and F.G. Clarke (Chicago: Henry Regnery Co., 1964).

258   Estimates by Edouard Parker, presented in Sunter, Clem: *The High Road: Where are we Now?* (Cape Town: Tafelberg, Human and Rousseau, 1996).

259 McKibben, Bill: 'A Special Moment in History' *Atlantic Monthly* (May 1998).

260 BBC World Report, August 24, 1998.

261 Klaus Toepfer, head of the the UN Environmental Program in the Report presentation in Nairobi.

262 The exact mathematical factor for discounting a cash flow with a discount rate d on year N is 1/(1+ d) at the Nth power. Most textbooks on finance have an appendix with the pre-calculated tables for these factors.

263 Korten, David: *When Corporations Rule the World* (San Francisco: Berret-Koehler Press, 1995) p. 208.

264 Estimate of the cost of a 27 global commodity reference currency by Albert Hart of Columbia University, Nicholas Kaldor of King's College in Cambridge, UK and Jan Tinbergen of the Netherlands School of Economics: *The Case for an International Reserve Currency* (Geneva: presented on 2/17/1964 – (Document UNCTAD 64-03482).

265 See for example: Harmon, Elmer: *Commodity Reserve Currency* (New York: Columbia University Press, 1959); Graham, Benjamin: *World Commodities and World Currency* (New York: McGraw Hill, 1944) and *Storage and Stability* (New York: McGraw Hill, 1937); Albert Hart of Columbia University, Nicholas Kaldor of King's College in Cambridge, UK and Jan Tinbergen of the Netherlands School of Economics: St Clare: Grondona, *Economic Stability is Attainable* (London: Hutchison Benham Ltd, 1975); Gondriaan Ian: *How to Stop Deflation* (London, 1932); Jevons W.S.: *Money and the Mechanism of Exchange* (1875).

266 Keynes, John Maynard:, *The General Theory of Employment, Interest and Money*, (London: Macmillan, 1936), p. 234.

267 Keynes: op.cit., Chapter 32, p, 355.

268 Details in http://www.rich.frb.org/monetarypol/marvin.htm and synthesis in http://www.wired.com/news/politics/0,1283,32121,00.html

269 Suhr, Dieter: *Capitalism at Its Best: The Equalisation of Money's Marginal Costs and Benefits* (Augsburg, Germany: Universität Augsburg, 1989).

270 The remarkable story of the Egyptian monetary system and its effects will be discussed at length in *The Mystery of Money*. The best source on the Egyptian monetary system is Preisigke, Friedrich: *Girowesen im Griechischen Ägypten enthaltend Korngiro, Geldgiro, Girobanknotariat mit Einschluß des Archivwesens*, (Strassburg: Verlag von Schlesier & Schweikhardt, 1910); reprinted: by Hildesheim (New York: Georg Olms, 1971).

271 See *The Mystery of Money: Beyond Greed and Scarcity* in which the connection will be shown between demurrage-charged currencies and the unusual prosperity during the Central Middle Ages (10th to 13th century, sometimes called 'The First European Renaissance' and the 'Age of the Cathedrals'), and during the classical Egyptian period.

272 Dolde, Walter: 'The Use of Foreign Exchange and Interest Rate Risk Management in Large Firms', *University of Connecticut School of Business Administration Working Paper 93-042* (Storra, Conn., 1993) pp. 18-19. Specifically, there was also consensus that interest rate risks were an order of magnitude less important than foreign exchange risks.

273 Dolde, Walter: Ibid. The 85% of the firms that routinely have to hedge have a capital averaging at $8 billion, compared to $2.5 billion for the 15% which never hedged (see exhibit 1, pp. 23-24).

274 Boyle, David C.: 'Barter Currencies', *Financial Times* Management Report (Special Report to be released December 1999).

275 Krugman, Paul: 'The Return to Depression Economics' *Foreign Affairs* (January - February 1999) pp. 42-74.

276   Tibbs, Hardin: 'Sustainability', *Deeper News* (Global Business Network: January 1999) p. 29.

Chapter 9: Sustainable Abundance

277   The first seven of the total nine mentioned here were already identified by Howard Gardner in Project Zero at Harvard and documented in his *Frames of Mind: The Theory of Multiple Intelligences* (Tufts Univ. Press, 1993). Another version of the same thesis is Armstrong's *Seven kinds of Smarts: Identifying and Developing your Multiple Intelligences* (Plume Books, 1999).

278   Tibbs, Hardin: Report for the Global Business Network 'Sustainability', *Deeper News* (Vol. 3, No. 1, January 1999) p. 5.

279   World Commission on the Environment and Development: *Our Common Future* (Oxford University Press, 1989) p. 200.

280   Daly, Herman E. and Cobb, John B.: *For the Common Good* (Boston: Beacon Press, 1989).

281   Ehrlich P. R. et al.: *Ecoscience: Population, Resources, Environment* (San Francisco: W.H. Freeman, 1977).

282   Quoted in Flemons, Douglas G.: *Completing Distinctions* (Boston and London: Shambhala, 1991) p. 112.

283   Flemons, Douglas G.: ibid , p. 32.

284   A rigorous treatment of this idea, expressed in the language of Western systems theory, has been made available by Yongming Tang. Tang, Yongming: 'Fostering Transformation through Differences: the Synergic Inquiry (SI) framework', *Revision* Special issue on Transformative Learning (Vol. 20, No. 1, Summer 1997) pp. 15-19.

285   Tarnas, Richard: *The Passion of the Western Mind* (New York: Balantine Books, 1993) p. 445.

286   Meadows, Donella, et al.: *Beyond the Limits* (Post Mills, Vermont: Chelsea Green Publishing, 1992).

287   Tibbs, Hardin: op.cit.

288   Tibbs, Hardin: ibid., p.39 (*Italics in original text.*)

289   See Ray, Paul and Anderson, Sherry Ruth: *The Cultural Creatives* (New York: Harmony Books, 1999). Also, *The Integral Culture Survey: A Study of the Emergence of Transformational Value in America* (Research Monograph sponsored by the Fetzer Institute and the Institute of Noetic Sciences, 1996).

290   Elgin, Duane and LeDrew, Coleen: *Global Paradigm Change: Is a Shift Underway?* (San Francisco, CA State of the world Forum, October 2-6, 1996) p. 20.

291   Eisenberg, David MD et al.: 'Unconventional Medicine in the United States', *New England Journal of Medicine* 328: 246-252 (January 28, 1993).

292   Langone, John: 'Alternative therapies challenging the mainstream', *Time* Special Issue, Fall 1996, p. 40.

293   Furness , William Henry III: *The Island of Stone Money* (1910) pp. 93, 96-100.

294   Friedman, Milton: *Money Mischief: Episodes in Monetary History* (New York, A Harvet book: Harcourt Brace and Co., 1992) pp. 6-7.

295   International Monetary Fund (IMF): *International Financial Statistics* Vol. 47/7 (Washington, DC, July 1994) p. 8.

296   Cassidy, John: 'The New World Disorder', *The New Yorker* (October 26 & November 2, 1998) pp. 199-200.

297   Title of a book by John Kenneth Galbraith about the new society we have moved into.

298   Waldrop, Mitchell: 'The trillion-Dollar vision of Dee Hock', *Fast Company* (October, November 1996).

299   Durrance, Bonnie: 'The Evolutionary Vision of Dee Hock: from Chaos to Chaords', *Training and Development* (April 1997) p. 26.

300   Huddle, Norie: *Butterfly: A tiny tale of great transformation* (New York: Huddle Books, 1990).

301   Greenspan, Alan: 'Fostering Financial Innovation: The role of government' in *The Future of Money in the Information Age* (Washington: Cato Institute, 1997) p. 48.

302   Source: *Forrester Research* based on interviews with numerous business executives.

303   Estimates by the International Reciprocal Trade Association (IRTA).

304   Chapters 5 and 6 provide many examples of this process already operational at the end of the 20th century.

Epilogue

305   Interview at New Dimension Radio.

306   Jevons, William Stanley: *Money and the Mechanism of Exchange* (London, 1875).

307   Heichelheim, F.M.: *An Ancient Economic History* (Leiden, 1958) Vol. III, p. 122.

308   Davies, Glyn: *A History of Money from Ancient Times to the Present Day* (Cardiff: University of Wales Press, 1994) p. 180.

309   Goodrich, L.C: *A Short History of the Chinese People* (London, 1957) p. 152.

310   Dent, J.M.: *The Travels of Marco Polo* (London, 1908) chapter XVIII of original text, pp. 202-205 in translation.

311   Durban, Charles F.: 'The Bank of Venice', *Quarterly Journal of Economics*, Vol. 6 No. 3, April 1892.

312   'This note is legal tender for all debts public and private' is written on every US$ bill. What this means in practice is the following: if you owe someone money and she refuses your offer to pay with US$ bills, you can walk away and simply declare the debt void. If needed, the courts will back you in such a declaration.

313   The charter giving *monopoly of emission of paper money* was assigned by King William of Orange to the Bank of England in 1694, when he urgently needed an additional £1.2 million for a war against the French. In the case of Sweden, the power of emission had similarly been transferred to the Bank of the Estates of the Realm when the crown needed urgent money to fund a war against Denmark. While the introduction of paper money made the transfer of the power of emission of money from sovereigns to banks possible, the proximate cause of that process was war.

314   Galbraith, John Kenneth: *Money: Whence it Came, Where it Went* (London: André Deutsch, 1975).

315   Because the regulations specify that only 10% of a deposit need be kept as 'reserves' in case the customer withdraws the funds. Therefore up to 90% is available to make new loans. Changing that percentage is one of the techniques whereby a central bank controls the quantities of credit money the banks will be able to create. In reality, the exact percentages vary with the kind of deposit made: the longer the term of the deposit, the lower the percentage of 'reserves' required. The 90% rule of this example, enabling a 'multiplier' of about 9 to 1 is only an illustrative average.

316   Mayer, Martin: *The Bankers* (New York: Weybright and Talley, 1974) p. 16.

317   Mayer, Martin: *The Bankers: the New Generation* (New York: Truman Talley Books/Dutton, 1997) pp. 16 and 19.

318   I will show that frequent-flyer miles are gradually becoming a private currency ('corporate scrip' in the jargon). Are frequent flyers one of the currencies of the future?

319   Moore, Carl H. and Russell, Alvin E.: *Money: Its Origin, Development and Modern Use* (Jefferson NC: McFarland, 1987) p. 74.

320 Friedman, Milton: 'Quantity Theory of Money' in *Money* (New York, London: W.W. Norton 'The New Pelgrave', 1989) p. 15.

321 Source of data from 1970 to 1990 from Table P.1 Deane, Marjorie and Pringle, Robert: *The Central Banks* (New York: Viking, 1995) pp. 352-354, plus International Labor Office *Monthly Bulletin of Statistics* from 1990 to 1996.

322 Byrne, E.H.: *Genovese Shipping in the 12th and 13th Century* (Cambridge, Mass: Mediaeval Academy of America, 1930) p. 14.

323 Bank for International Settlements (BIS) Triennial Central Bank Survey of Foreign Exchange and Derivatives Market Activity (September 1998).

324 Answer: None of the above. Two trillion seconds bring us back to a time older than Cro-Magnon (40000 BC).Your printing press would have had to be started by some Neanderthal. To be precise, two trillion seconds are equivalent to slightly more than 63,418 years!

325 These statistics are derived from the total daily foreign exchange transactions as reported every three years by the BIS, and compared to Global Annual Trade divided by the number of days. Some of the foreign exchange transactions are double counted, because a bank may not want to keep on its books particularly large client currency positions, and therefore offset them in the market. So that one single original speculative transaction can generate others. I know of no reliable statistic about the exact extent to which this occurs. But even if all speculative foreign exchange transactions were double counted, bringing the total volume of original speculative transactions down to one trillion, the percentages would change to 96% speculative and 4% 'real' instead of 98% versus 2%. My argument would still remain valid. Furthermore, the volume of speculative activity doubles now every three years, so that eliminating double counting just moves the time line up a few years.

326 'Liquidity' and 'Depth' of a financial market refers to the possibility of moving large volumes of money without significantly affecting prices. In a deep market, a lot of people are buying and selling. By contrast, in a thin market, because fewer people are trading, even one single large transaction could significantly affect prices.

327 Keynes, John Maynard: *The General Theory of Employment, Interest and Money*, op.cit., p. 159.

328 In the Dutch tulipmania of 1637 the existence of future contracts was blamed. In 1929 the Trusts, in 1987 computer-programmed trading. What is common to all these cases is that these were simply the latest financial innovations of the time. A deeper explanation, applicable to all major financial crashes of the past 350 years, will be provided in *The Mystery of Money: Beyond Greed and Scarcity*.

329 Source: Eisworth, Peter in The New York Times (February 16, 1999) p. A1A. Extracted from article by Kristoff, Nicholas D. & Sanger, David E.: 'How US Wooed Asia to Let Cash Flow in'.

330 Davies, Glyn, op.cit., p. 646.

331 Quoted by Weatherford, Jack: *The History of Money* (New York: Crown Publishers Inc.) p. 264.

332 The main types of currency derivatives are futures, forwards and options, whose technical definitions are:

   • Futures: A currency futures contract is an agreement to buy or sell a currency at a specified time and place (a commodity exchange) in the future at a specific price agreed to today.

   • Forwards: Similar to Futures, except that the price is today's price and the contract is not traded on an exchange but directly with one specific financial institution ('Over the Counter').

   • Options: A currency option is the right, but not an obligation to buy ('call') or sell ('put') a currency at a specific price. The development of the options market is credited to the theoretical breakthroughs by Professors Robert Melton and Myron Scholes in option pricing, for which they were awarded by a Nobel Prize in June 1997.

   These instruments are the building blocks whose combinations enable the transfer of many risks. Some of these combinations ('exotics') can become quite complex. All these instruments also exist for commodities other than currencies, but the volume of currency derivatives particularly of 'Over the Counter' trade, now dwarfs those of all other commodities.

333 Mayer, Martin: op. cit., p. 324. His argument: 'The obvious illustration is the S&P 500 futures pit at the Chicago Mercantile Exchange, where a couple of hundred ex-taxi drivers working as "locals" were expected to carry the dynamic hedging of "portfolio insurance" when the stock market broke on October 19, 1987.'

334 Telephone conversation from New York to London, a few weeks before the disaster, as reported by *Financial Times* (September 20, 1996, p. 10) excerpted from the book by Gapper, John and Denton, Nicholas: *All that Glitters* (London: Hamish Hamilton, 1996).

335 Data extracted from Peter Elsworth. C. T.: 'The Path of Crisis', *The New York Times* (February 17, 1999) p. A8.

336 Cassidy, John: 'The New World Disorder', *The New Yorker* (October 26 & November 2, 1998) pp. 199-200.

337 *Business Week*: 'Hot Money' (March 20, 1995) p. 46.

338 Edey, Malcolm and Ketil, Hviding: *An assessment of Financial Reform in OECD countries* (OECD working paper No. 154) 1995.

339 In foreign exchange, all positions are always simultaneously long one currency and short another. In our example, people could buy Deutschemark or dollars (go 'long' in the jargon), while selling French francs (go 'short' French francs).

340 Deane, Marjorie and Pringle, Robert: *The Central Banks* (New York: Viking, 1995) p. 178.

341 Soros, George: *The Alchemy of Finance: Reading the Mind of the Market* (London: Weidenfeld and Nicolson, 1988) p. 69.

342 Kurtzman, Joel: *The Death of Money: How the Electronic Economy has destabilized the World's Markets and created Financial Chaos* (New York: Simon and Schuster, 1993).

343 Volcker, Paul and Gyohten, Toyoo: *Changing Fortunes: The World's Money and the Threat to American Leadership* (New York: Times Books, 1992).

344 Carmine Rotondo, foreign exchange trader with Security Pacific Bank, quoted in Rowen, Hobart: 'Wielding Jawbone to Protect the dollar' *Washington Post* (March 15, 1987, p. H-1).

345 Gerth, Jeff and Stevenson, Richard W.: 'Poor Oversight Said to Imperil World Banking: Tide of Money is Seen as Continous Threat', *The New York Times* (December 22, 1997) p. 1.

346 Title and the data in the sidebar are from the last of the four double-page articles co-authored by Kristof, Nicholas D. with various other journalists (*The New York Times* February 16, 17, 18 and 19, 1999). Together, the four articles provide a survey of the world's monetary turmoils and its consequences for ordinary people, unprecedented in its scope in the US Press.

347 Source: *The New York Times* (Februrary 17, 1999) p. A10.

348 Georg Simmel: *Philosophy of Money* (original German edition 1900) (second English edition: London & New York: Routledge, 1990).

Acknowledgements

This book has been the result of five years of countless conversations with many people to which I owe the best ideas included here. I gladly acknowledge intellectual, editorial and/or emotional debts particularly to Art Warmoth, James Hillman, Julio Olalla, Mario Kamenetzki, Paul Ray and Sherry Anderson, Lisa Spiro, Barbara Schultz, Boudewijn Wegerif, Leonard Joy, Dean Ellias, John Levy, Philip and Manuela Dunn, Nancy Bord, Jacqui Dunne, Deborah Miller, Joyce Long, Anna Godfrey and Elizabeth Hennessy. I also gladly acknowledge the financial support of the Schweisfurth Foundation, Margrit Kennedy and Reinhart Hubner. Many more deserve to be mentioned, and I hope they'll forgive me for not making this list endless. My work was also inspired by the courage of the thousands of dedicated people who pioneered complementary currencies around the world.

The author gratefully acknowledges the following for permission to reproduce images and text:

Page 17 Cartoon 'Remaining locked in the prevailing interpretation of money . . .'. © Cardon.

Page 35 Alabaster Vase (Mesopotamia between 3100 and 2900 B.C.), showing the goddess Inanna. Photo 624.3014 of Hirmer Verlag. © Hirmer Fotoarchiv München.

Page 39 Photo (Yap Islanders) © The British Museum, London.

Page 49 Photo (Kreuzgang am Dom, Brixen Südtirol) © S. Wessel.

Page 65 Victoria Roberts, 'Can I call you back . . .'. © The New Yorker Collection 1997, Victoria Roberts from cartoonbank.com. All Rights Reserved.

Page 87 Peanuts 'Who are all these people . . .' by Charles Schulz © United Features Syndicate, Inc. Reproduced by permission.

Page 91 Cartoon (Corporate Buddhism) © Andy Singer.

Page 120 Cartoon (Remaining struck within the conventional interpretation of money) © 1990 by S. Gross.

Page 131 Cartoon (Cost Cutting Inc.) © Oswald Huber.

Page 135 Cartoon (Career Consultant) © Oswald Huber.

Page 190 The Far Side 'Einstein discovers that time is actually money' by Gary Larson © 1985 Universal Press Syndicate.

Page 236 Frank & Ernest 'Survival of the Planet . . .' by Bob Thaves © Thaves/Distributed by NEA, Inc. Reproduced by permission.

Page 277 Cartoon (Yin/Yang) © Roland Spinola.

Page 313 Cartoon (Stop. Halt. Border) © William Branhall.

The author and publishers have made all reasonable efforts to contact copyright holders for permission, and apologize for any omissions or errors in the form of credit given. Corrections may be made in future printings.

Index